THE INSIDERS' ® → GUIDE ←
TO
Savannah

THE INSIDERS' GUIDE TO

Savannah

by
Rich Wittish
and
Betty Darby

Insiders' Publishing Inc.

Published by:
Insiders' Publishing Inc.
105 Budleigh St.
P.O. Box 2057
Manteo, NC 27954
(919) 473-6100
www.insiders.com

Sales and Marketing:
Falcon Publishing Co. Inc.
P.O. Box 1718
Helena, MT 59624
(800) 582-2665
www.falconguide.com

•

1ST EDITION
1st printing

•

Copyright ©1998
by Insiders' Publishing Inc.

•

Printed in the United States
of America

•

Publications from The Insiders' Guide®
series are available at special discounts
for bulk purchases for sales promotions,
premiums or fundraisings. Special
editions, including personalized covers,
can be created in large quantities for
special needs. For more information,
please write to Insiders' Publishing Inc.,
P.O. Box 2057, Manteo, NC 27954 or
call (919) 473-6100 x 241.

ISBN 1-57380-039-2

Insiders' Publishing Inc.

Publisher/Editor-in-Chief
Beth P. Storie

President/General Manager
Michael McOwen

Creative Services Director
Giles MacMillan

Director of New Product
Development
David Haynes

Managing Editor
Dave McCarter

Fulfillment Director
Gina Twiford

Regional Sales Representative
Greg Swanson

Local Sales Representative
Penny Furst

Project Editor
Dave McCarter

Project Artist
Jason Cope

Preface

We're having a wonderful time in Savannah, and we're glad that you are coming to join us. That's not just a postcard cliche. Savannah calls herself the Hostess City, and a traditionally welcoming attitude toward visitors is part of that legacy.

Long before tourism was considered an industry, hospitality was regarded around Savannah as something akin to religion. If you aren't gracious to guests, you "don't know how to act" and are "an embarrassment to your mother" — two of the deadliest faults possible in the South's social self-portrait. So relax: You are about to tour a city composed of people who, by and large, do know how to act and who have very proud mothers.

With this book, we hope to give you the flavor of a city we have come to love, along with all the facts and figures you need to get yourself housed, entertained, fed and properly toured. No, we're not native Savannahians — that's a multi-generational thing — but between the two of us, we've logged more than 40 years in our adopted city. Job commitments brought us here with no real avowed intention of remaining, but over the years we forgot to leave.

Savannah is that kind of place. You could build a case that Savannah is a living laboratory for demonstrating the relativity of time. Time does seem to move at a different clip here. Change takes place slowly and is accepted even more slowly. Maybe "languidly" is a better term than "slowly," because it emphasizes that there is something deliberate and intentional about this pacing. Pick the right hour at one of the downtown squares, when the traffic is still, look around at the massive oaks and stately townhomes, and you could easily erase 100, even 150 years off the calendar. Pick a marsh view at sunset, and you could erase a few thousand.

But don't get the impression we're a moldy, moss-draped museum, either. The corporate bigwigs and entertainment moguls of the day jet through the skies on corporate aircraft built here. The Port of Savannah is one of the nation's busiest, taking in goods from throughout the world. Baryshnikov danced here; Blues Traveler rocked here; our symphony puts on 300 performances in a season (we're fudging a little — that includes ensemble sessions, but you get the point). There's diversity in our universities and colleges. In short, Savannah has a place in the world's appointment books of today, not just the history books of the past.

Now, on to business. We've shared lots of things to do in these pages, based on years of entertaining visiting friends and relatives (and ourselves, too). We'll tell you how to chow down on some of the most delectable food imaginable and how to hole up in some of the most charming bed and breakfasts in the country. Parasailing, meeting alligators, retracing history, buying antiques, beach bumming, taking yourself out to the ol' ball game — we tell you where and how (and how much it costs) to tap into these activities.

Additionally, if you've fallen in love with Savannah long distance thanks to a certain bestselling book or any one of several popular movies, we've included some tips on how to arrange your own personal brush with *Midnight in the Garden of Good and Evil* (the chapter is called The Book) or Savannah's film docket.

This is Savannah's first entry into the family of Insiders' Guide® publications. Revision and updating remains an ongoing process, to make sure that what you find within the pages of the guide you picked up last week accurately depicts the city you will find on your visit next week. You are invited to be part of this process. Comments, critiques and suggestions are welcome, and they can be shared easily with us and our publishers, either online or on paper. See How to Use This Book for details.

Savannah gives herself lots of names, and

others have added to the list — the Hostess City, the Coastal Empire, the Garden of Good and Evil, the Sovereign State of Chatham (Chatham County, that is) and so on. We firmly believe that, after your visit, you'll name her one of your favorite vacation destinations. We wager you'll be back. Like us, you may even forget to leave.

About the Authors

Rich Wittish

When Rich Wittish took a job with the daily newspaper in Savannah in 1974, he intended to stay for a short while, then move on to a larger media market. The charm and leisurely lifestyle of the region won him over, and more than 20 years later, he continues to enjoy the city and its surrounding areas. He and his wife, Linda, often spend parts of their weekends rediscovering the pleasures of meandering through the squares of Savannah's Historic Downtown or strolling on the beach at nearby Tybee Island.

Rich feels that one of Savannah's most attractive qualities is its size — it's large enough to be interesting and small enough to make you feel at home. That atmosphere reminds him of the city where he grew up, Jacksonville, Florida, and the way it was in the late 1950s and '60s before it boomed and became the "Bold New City of the South."

Although Rich was born in New Jersey, he considers himself a Southerner: He spent his boyhood in north Florida, attended college at Auburn University in Alabama, was stationed in rural North Carolina during much of his time in military service and is married to a lady who's a Georgia country girl at heart. Rich came to Savannah after serving four years and nine months in the U.S. Air Force, a stint he began immediately after graduating from Auburn with a degree in journalism. He was a navigator and attained the rank of captain while employed by Uncle Sam.

After fulfilling his military obligation, Rich left the Air Force to see if he could put into practice what he had learned in college. He got plenty of opportunities at the *Savannah Morning News* while covering a variety of beats as a reporter — including police, politics and business — and serving as an editor on the city desk and in the state news department. During his last seven years at the *Morning News*, Rich headed up the company's community newspapers department.

After working at the paper for 22 years, Rich decided in May 1996 to go in a somewhat different direction and try his hand at freelance writing. Since then, he's co-authored a book on the aviation history of Savannah, done some public relations work and written several articles for *Savannah Magazine* and *Georgia AnchorAge*, a publication of the Georgia Ports Authority.

On some Saturdays when they're not nosing around Savannah or working around their house on Wilmington Island, Rich and Linda head west to Macon, Georgia, to visit their daughter, Erica, an A student and former all-city basketball player who is attending Mercer University. They also keep busy with activities at their church, First Presbyterian, where they are involved with the congregation's community-outreach ministries.

Betty Darby

Betty Darby is a journalist who has made Savannah her home since 1980.

She is a 1977 graduate of the University of Georgia, where she majored in journalism and minored in political science. She even studied Russian, with some vague idea of covering the 1980 Olympics in the Soviet Union. The subsequent American decision not to partici-

viii • ABOUT THE AUTHORS

pate in those games was a bit of a relief, since she hadn't mastered much of the language.

Betty got her first newspaper assignment in the summer following her freshman year at college, working for the *Rome* (Ga.) *News-Tribune* in her hometown. She returned to the paper for summer and holiday breaks throughout her college years, then joined the reporting staff full-time. She later took a reporting position with the *Savannah Morning News*, where she covered various hard news beats along with writing movie reviews and serving a stint as a copy editor. Over the course of her newspaper years, Betty covered politics, crime and education, wrote features and interviewed subjects ranging from John Wayne on his final movie promotion junket to George Bush in his vice-presidential years.

After nine years with the Savannah newspapers, she moved into public relations and marketing work with public schools for several years. Later, she wrote and edited a quarterly magazine for a Savannah hospital. Betty currently works with Porter Communications Inc., a Savannah marketing firm. She continues to write for magazines and other outlets and occasionally dusts off a half-finished novel manuscript she's working on.

While in Savannah, Betty has ranged wide over the city's residential real estate. She has lived on some of the grandest squares in the Historic Downtown (albeit in some of the humbler apartments) and in the suburban enclaves of the Islands area. She has now settled in the city's Midtown section in a circa 1930s bungalow.

Photo: Kyle Cason

The look of downtown Savannah is a mixture of old and new.

Acknowledgments

Rich Wittish

Writing a book of this scope involves obtaining a lot of help from a lot of people. With that in mind, I offer special thanks to the following: John Burke and Michael Richter, who provided valuable information and insights for the fishing and boating sections of the Parks and Recreation chapter; Becky Bowden, who helped me get started in the right direction when I began writing the Hilton Head chapter; Ron Perry, a Hilton Head Realtor who aided me in gathering data on the island's planned communities; journalist Richard Fogaley, who gave us much-needed advice concerning Savannah's restaurants; Phyl Gatlin, who provided photographs for the Close-up in the Restaurants chapter; Preston Russell and Barbara Hines, authors of a splendid history of Savannah who graciously checked this book's History chapter for accuracy and content; Martha Giddens Nesbit, who allowed us to use a recipe from her *Savannah Collection* cookbook; and Cheryl Lauer, who lent her photographic skills to this endeavor along with encouraging words when they were needed.

Thanks also to many other folks who took time out of their busy schedules to talk with me or otherwise assist me. Among them are a horde of public relations and marketing specialists and other people who served as spokespersons for their respective businesses, agencies and organizations. Those who were especially helpful were, from Savannah, Jenny Stacy of the Savannah Area Chamber of Commerce, John Howell of the Metropolitan Planning Commission, Eileen Baker of the City of Savannah's Cultural Affairs Department, Ed Poenicke of the Chatham County Extension Service, Rick Lott of the Savannah Waterfront Association, Sue Cole of Oatland Island Education Center, Dan Sams of Historic Savannah Foundation, Elizabeth Stewart of Savannah Onstage, Henry Lewandoski of Chatham

County Mosquito Control, Scott Smith of the Coastal Heritage Society, Dr. Carol Brown of the Dr. Martin Luther King Jr. Observance Day Association, Velma McKenzie of the Ralph Mark Gilbert Civil Rights Museum, Mike Beytagh of the St. Patrick's Day Parade Committee, Margie Richter of Discover Montessori School, Janice Lewis of Maggie's Morning School, Carol Collie of Lutheran Ministries of Georgia, Bonnie Eminger of the Child Care Licensing Section of the Georgia Department of Human Resources, Richard Shinhoster of Savannah Technical Institute, Earl Etheridge of the City of Savannah's Department of Recreation Services, Vicki Blumberg and Anthony Russell of Chatham County's Department of Parks, Recreation and Cultural Affairs, Danny McConnell of the YMCA of Coastal Georgia, Pat Metz of the U.S. Fish and Wildlife Service, Don Gardner of the Park and Tree Commission, Chica Arndt of Wormsloe Historic Site and Duane Harris, Stuart Stevens and Terry West of the Coastal Resources Division of the Georgia Department of Natural Resources.

Special thanks also to Hilton Head islanders Angela Herndon of the Hilton Head Chamber of Commerce, Mary Trostle of Sea Pines, Manny Peralta of the Spanish Wells Property Owners Association and Ed Drane and Nan Johnson of the Town of Hilton Head Island. Many thanks to my editor, Dave McCarter, who was ever upbeat in his dealings with me and ever vigilant in perusing my copy.

And thanks most of all to my wife, Linda, and daughter, Erica, for the love and support they gave me, particularly when the light at the end of the Insiders' Guide® tunnel seemed somewhat dim.

Betty Darby

A massive project such as this can be daunting at best, and when you join it when it is well advanced, as I did, it can feel a bit overwhelming. Thanks to the help of dedicated professionals in the information field and ordinary Savannahians who were eager to share the good parts of our city, however, I managed to play catch up and even enjoy myself along the way.

Much of the information that goes into such a project comes by way of professional "question-answerers." Any well-run organization of any size has at least one individual or department, variously known as the public relations department, public affairs office, media contact, official spokesperson and so on, whose job it is to field questions. While it's their job to pass on information, they are to be commended for their cheerful attitude, enthusiasm about their mission and attention to detail. One hesitates to start naming names in this category for fear of leaving someone out, so I'm intentionally keeping my list short here. Andrew Recinos, associate director for development and marketing at the Savannah Symphony, was a big help on this major cultural resource. Mark Keller of the Savannah Police Department provided a solid briefing on alcohol regulations and their enforcement. Jay Self from the city's film office spared me time during a hectic premiere week. Everyone at Senior Citizens Inc. made a special effort to help me understand their many missions.

Writers take shameless advantage of their friends and family when working on such projects. My friends, acquaintances and even co-workers at Porter Communications no doubt tired of me constantly asking things like, "Yeah, but where else do you take visitors?" and "Where do you go at night when you don't go home?" I also leaned heavily on the expertise of friends. Cheryl Lauer took my photo and allowed herself be recruited as photo liaison for the entire project. Suzanne Aikens was a big help on musical questions, for example, and Midge Schildkraut filled me in on Savannah's Jewish community. My mother, Rosalyn Darby, let me drag her along on tours to get an outsider's viewpoint (although that didn't work too well, since she's been a regular visitor to the city for years). She even accompanied the small group I put together for my research mission to the drag show, and she says she had a nice time.

I shouldn't forget to give thanks to those who gave us something worth writing about. Savannah was planned, built and preserved by visionaries, known and unknown, and populated in both the past and present by people interesting and hospitable enough to make it worth visiting (and living in.) With that in mind, special thanks to anyone who preserved a building or defended a tree that a developer thought was inconveniently placed.

A closing word of thanks goes to Coleman Prophett, B.C. Akins and Tommy Toles, the leaders of my first newsroom who recognized the importance of teaching the trade to wet-behind-the-ears journalism students.

Special thanks . . .

Insiders' Publishing Inc. would also like to recognize Cheryl Lauer for gathering the photographs used throughout this guide and for writing the corresponding captions. In a very short period of time, she provided us with a wealth of images that perfectly portrayed the city — from the antebellum homes in the Historic District to the antics of St. Patrick's Day. Thanks, Cheryl.

CHUTZPAH & PANACHE

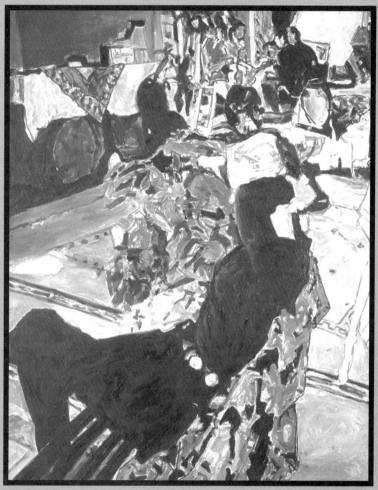

Nestled in one of Savannah's most impressive townhouses, this sophisticated mix of extraordinary original clothing, jewelry, accessories and gifts for the home is combined with a fabulous Southern Bistro. A must when visiting Savannah.

Monday-Saturday 10:00-5:30
Bull at Liberty

Table of Contents

Directory of Maps

Greater Savannah Area Map

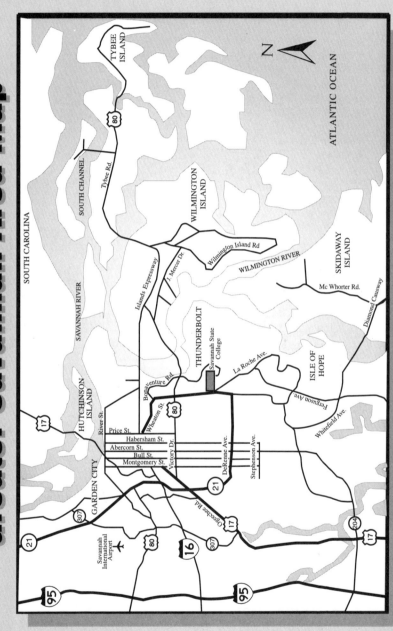

Highway Access
to Savannah

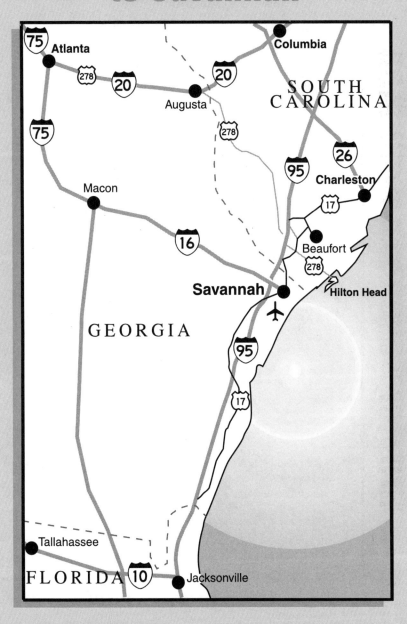

Downtown Savannah

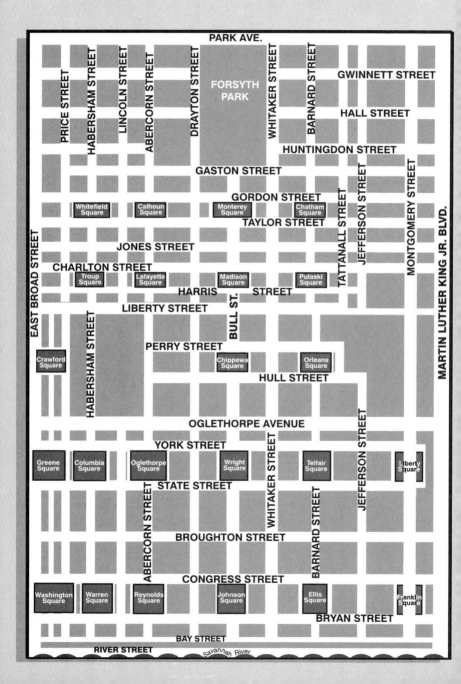

Hilton Head Island

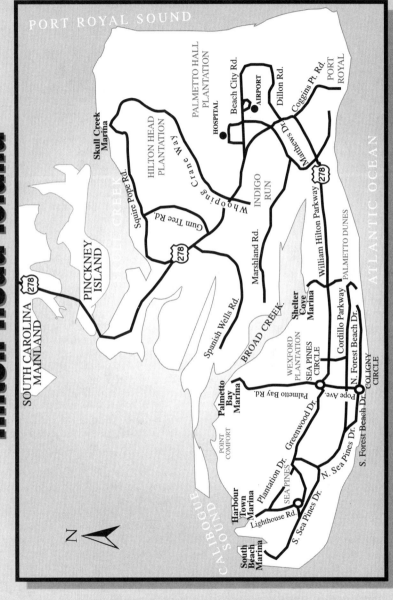

PORT ROYAL SOUND

ATLANTIC OCEAN

CALIBOGUE SOUND

SOUTH CAROLINA MAINLAND

PINCKNEY ISLAND

SKULL CREEK

Skull Creek Marina

Squire Pope Rd.

HILTON HEAD PLANTATION

Gum Tree Rd.

Whooping Crane Way

INDIGO RUN

Marshland Rd.

PALMETTO HALL PLANTATION

Beach City Rd.

AIRPORT

HOSPITAL

Dillon Rd.

Coggins Pt. Rd.

PORT ROYAL

Matthews Dr.

278

Spanish Wells Rd.

BROAD CREEK

Shelter Cove Marina

WEXFORD PLANTATION

SEA PINES CIRCLE

Cordillo Parkway

William Hilton Parkway

PALMETTO DUNES

N. Forest Beach Dr.

COLIGNY CIRCLE

Palmetto Bay Rd.

Pope Ave.

S. Forest Beach Dr.

Palmetto Bay Marina

POINT COMFORT

Greenwood Dr.

N. Sea Pines Dr.

Plantation Dr.

SEA PINES

Harbour Town Marina

Lighthouse Rd.

S. Sea Pines Dr.

South Beach Marina

278

N

How to Use This Book

We hope you'll treat this book as you would a valued traveling companion, taking it with you wherever you go during your time in Savannah, Tybee Island and Hilton Head and consulting it whenever you need help, advice or answers to questions. Don't leave it home alone or in your hotel room; stick it in your travel bag, briefcase or backpack so you'll have it handy when you need info on where to eat, shop or spend the night.

We've organized this book so you can flip to whatever subjects interest you while bypassing those that don't. Of course, it's our hope that eventually you'll take a look at every chapter, because each contains valuable information and tips. Even if you're not a history buff, for instance, it's probably a good idea to read the History chapter early in the game so that you can have an understanding of Savannah's past — a past that plays a vital role in its present and comes alive when you walk the city's streets.

For the most part, we've arranged the content of chapters geographically, then alphabetically within geographic sections. This was done in an effort to make restaurants, accommodations, attractions and other points of interest as easy as possible to find. We've divided the local area into four sections; you'll find an explanation of the territory the sections cover in the Area Overview chapter, and you can see where they are by referring to the maps at the front of the book. Another good way to find specific topics of interest is by looking in the extensive index in the back of the book. You'll note that the area code for almost every phone number listed is 912. We

provide small FYI boxes throughout the guide to remind you of this fact.

In addition to giving you a full rundown on the many topics you might expect to find in a guidebook, we've included a couple of chapters regarding subjects unique to Savannah. One chapter is entitled The Book and involves the phenomenon that is *Midnight in the Garden of Good and Evil*, the bestseller that has made the city a mecca for its readers. The other special chapter concerns Savannah's celebration of St. Patrick's Day, the city's favorite holiday.

We know that plenty of folks who make it to Savannah also have Hilton Head, South Carolina, on their travel itinerary. With this in mind, we have included a thorough chapter on Hilton Head, providing information on its history, accommodations, popular planned residential communities, restaurants and nightlife and, of course, golf. In turn, we have also devoted an entire chapter to another nearby destination that you may not be so familiar with — fun and quirky little Tybee Island.

We've done our darnedest to make this book as comprehensive and accurate as possible and to include the best that our area has to offer, and we've covered a lot of territory. Naturally, when you take on a project that's as massive and challenging as this one, you realize that omissions are inevitable and that most everyone has different tastes and opinions. If you discover a favorite restaurant, nightspot, shop or other business that we've missed or something that's in error, please let us know so it can be added or corrected in future editions.

We'll be updating, improving and expanding our guide every year. Contact us with comments or suggestions online via our website at www.insiders.com, or write us at:

The Insiders' Guide® to Savannah
Insiders' Publishing Inc.
P.O. Box 2057
Manteo, North Carolina 27954

James Edward Oglethorpe supervised the first phase of the building of Savannah, and he nurtured the city during its infancy as a town.

History

Perhaps no other city owes as much to one man as Savannah owes to James Edward Oglethorpe, the English soldier and politician who founded Georgia. Oglethorpe was the mastermind and driving force behind the development of the colony of Georgia, whose first city was Savannah. He selected the site of the city and christened it, giving it the same name as the river that flowed beside it. Oglethorpe supervised the first phase of the building of Savannah, and he nurtured the city during its infancy as a town. He defended it in its early years, militarily and financially.

More than that, Oglethorpe bestowed on Savannah a gift that has flourished throughout the decades and centuries since his passing. He designed and laid out the town and, in so doing, created the atmosphere that makes Savannah unique among cities. He left a legacy that has been admired and enjoyed by countless residents and visitors — a treasure that will be the pride of the city for as long as it stands.

Oglethorpe and His Idea

Oglethorpe was born into a family that had a long history of service to England. After serving in the British army and fighting the Turks as the aide-de-camp of an Austrian prince, Oglethorpe was elected to the lower house of Parliament in 1722 at the age of 25. He developed an interest in the misfortunes of the poor, in particular the plight of debtors who had been thrown into prison by creditors hoping the debtors' friends would secure their release by paying the debts. He worked for prison reform and attempted to find solutions to England's unemployment problems.

Together with John Perceval, another member of Parliament, Oglethorpe hatched the idea of giving people who were out of work

a fresh start by transporting them to a new colony in America that would be located between the English colony of South Carolina and Spanish Florida. Oglethorpe and Perceval petitioned King George II for a charter, which the king signed on April 21, 1732. The deal was not one-sided: The crown was motivated by the prospect of having colonists raise produce and raw materials to ship to England while serving as a market for English goods. The idea of having the new colony act as a buffer between the Spanish and thriving South Carolina was not lost on the royals either. To top it all off, the colony was to be named Georgia in honor of the king.

The colony would be managed by Oglethorpe, Perceval and 19 other trustees, who would receive no pay and no land for their involvement. There were also rules for the colony: Slavery, lawyers and "brandies and distilled liquors" (in particular rum) were prohibited, as were Catholics. In time, all would be allowed. Those who took advantage of the free passage to Georgia offered by the trustees agreed to remain in the colony for three years, and each received a town lot for a house and 50 acres to farm. A colonist would not own the acreage and could occupy it only as long as he farmed it properly. Grants of 500 acres were available to people who paid their way to the colony.

The trustees adopted as their motto the Latin phrase "Non Sibi Sed Allis" — "Not for themselves but others." It appears on Georgia's original seal, which also bears a rendering of a silkworm crawling across a mulberry leaf; it was hoped that the colony would produce silk in abundance.

A Whole New World

The trustees recruited 114 colonists comprising 35 families for the first voyage to Georgia and the task of starting a settlement there.

Accompanying them was Oglethorpe, the only trustee to make the trip. They left Gravesend, England, on November 17, 1732, aboard a 200-ton vessel named the *Anne* and arrived in what is now Charleston, South Carolina, on January 13, 1733. The settlers then made their way south down the South Carolina coast and, after transferring to smaller boats, landed in the new colony on February 1. That was the date of Georgia's founding according to the Julian calendar. When that calendar was abandoned in favor of the Gregorian calendar 19 years later, the date became February 12 — the day now celebrated as Georgia Day.

Oglethorpe had gone ahead of the colonists several days before their landing and chose a site for the town of Savannah on a 40-foot-high bluff overlooking the Savannah River — Yamacraw Bluff. In a letter to the trustees explaining his choice of the site for a city, he stated that he "thought it healthy" and wrote, "The last and fullest consideration of the Healthfulness of the place was that an Indian nation, who knew the Nature of the Country, chose it for their Habitation."

The Indians were the 100-odd members of the Yamacraw tribe of the Lower Creek nation, led by an 80-year-old chief named Tomochi-chi. The Yamacraws would prove friendly and helpful to the colonists. Other new neighbors were Mary and John Musgrove — a half-white, half-Indian couple who ran a nearby trading post. They would serve as interpreters for the Europeans and the Native Americans.

The colonists spent their first night in their new home camped out in an area that is now the site of a small park at Bay and Whitaker streets. In the following days and weeks, Oglethorpe and Col. William Bull of South Carolina laid out the new city, and the settlers set about clearing the pine woods on the bluff with the help of black slaves from the neighboring colony. They also began cultivating a 10-acre plot that would be known as Trustees Garden. On this parcel, at the present Bay and East Broad streets, were planted fruit trees and the mulberry trees that were envisioned as the basis of Georgia's silk industry.

Things went well at the outset. By fall 1734, according to a letter from a South Carolina merchant who had visited the town, there were 80 houses and 40 more being built. During Georgia's first decade, the trustees sent more than 2,000 settlers. Other new arrivals brought diversity to the colony. Among them was a boatload of Jews from Portugal who established a Jewish congregation, Mickve Israel. It was the third founded in America and continues today as the South's oldest. Another was a group of Germans, the Salzburgers, who settled 21 miles upriver from Savannah in what is now Effingham County. Their community of New Ebenezer prospered, and the house of worship they built in 1769 is the oldest standing church in Georgia.

Oglethorpe remained involved with the colony during its first 10 years, and in July 1742, he led a contingent of soldiers and Indian allies in a battle that forever wrested control of the region from the Spanish in Florida. In the Battle of Bloody Marsh, his band of defenders surprised and defeated a numerically superior Spanish invasion force about 70 miles south of Savannah at St. Simons Island. The Spanish never attempted another invasion, and a peace treaty between Spain and England was signed in 1748.

Oglethorpe left Georgia on July 22, 1743, never to return. Even before his departure, Savannah began to decline as the population dwindled due to the hardships of bringing civilization to a wilderness — insects, alligators, extremes in the weather, difficulties in growing crops. The colony remained a trusteeship

INSIDERS' TIP

Among Savannah's tributes to founder James Edward Oglethorpe is a large bronze statue of the Englishman in Chippewa Square. The monument is the work of Daniel Chester French, sculptor of the Minuteman statue of Concord, Massachusetts. You'll notice that Oglethorpe faces toward Florida, still guarding his beloved Savannah against an invasion from the south.

until 1752, when the trustees, burdened by financial problems and turnover in their ranks, relinquished their charter to the crown a year before it was to expire. As Preston Russell and Barbara Hines wrote in their lyrical *Savannah: A History of Her People Since 1733*: "Non Sibi Sed Allis had fallen on its nose. The dream was long since dead, but Savannah was here to stay."

A Royal Comeback

Under control of the crown, Georgia's government changed from the benevolent dictatorship of the trustees to a more traditional setup headed by a governor and having an assembly of elected representatives. Under this arrangement, Georgia was upgraded from colony to province, with Savannah serving as the seat of government.

The first Royal Assembly met in Savannah in January 1755, and one of its first acts was to adopt a law allowing slavery. The first of Georgia's three royal governors, John Reynolds, began a two-and-a-half-year tenure in October 1754; he was succeeded by Henry Ellis, who gave way to James Wright in 1760. Wright, who ruled as governor until January 1776, was a godsend for Savannah's struggling economy. "In mere months, Wright led the youngest colony through stages of development that had required years in other colonies," states Edward Chan Sieg in his book *Eden on the Marsh: An Illustrated History of Savannah*. "Wright's administration was geared to accommodate the 'men of substance' who began to pour into Georgia from other colonies and from the plantations of the Indies. Aided by liberal credit policies and cheap labor, they transformed the coastal plains into the great plantations of legend. Wharf facili-

ties and warehouses appeared on the bluff as shipping demands increased almost daily."

The major export was rice, the growing of which had been made possible by the repeal of the ban on slavery. The idea of making Savannah a silk-production center had flopped, apparently due to a combination of mismanagement and the silk worms' problems with the climate. By 1766, Wright was estimating that the province of Georgia was inhabited by as many as 10,000 whites and 7,800 black slaves — up from a total of 3,000 people nine years earlier — and that exports of rice had tripled over a six-year span.

The Great Rebellion

In the mid-1760s, many residents of England's American colonies reacted with outrage to what they deemed unfair taxation of imported items by the mother country. As the following decade unfolded, their dissatisfaction grew to the point that they sought independence from England.

The fervor for freedom took hold somewhat slowly in Savannah, but by mid-1774, it began to show itself in the actions of a group of dissidents called the Liberty Boys. Despite Governor Wright's efforts to stop them, they met several times to protest England's closing of the Boston Harbor as punishment for the Boston Tea Party. In January 1775, Noble Wimberly Jones, a Liberty Boy who had been speaker of the Royal Assembly, convened a meeting of Georgia's First Provincial Congress. Wright dissolved the body, but on July 4, a meeting of a second provincial congress was held, with the 102 delegates electing representatives to the colonies' Second Continental Congress.

In the interim, members of the Liberty Boys

INSIDERS' TIP

If you stop by Faber's Gyro and Pizza Pub on the northwest corner of Broughton and Whitaker streets, you will be standing on the site of Tondee's Tavern, which was a favorite meeting place of the freedom-seeking Liberty Boys during the days leading up to the American Revolution. When Savannahians celebrated the signing of the Declaration of Independence, the tavern was one of four places in town where the document was read aloud in public.

in May celebrated the opening shot of the American revolution by breaking into the city's munitions room, stealing 600 pounds of powder and shipping it to Boston to be used in the fight against the British. The powder really hit the fan on January 18, 1776, when three British warships showed up off the coast of Savannah. The provincial government placed Wright under house arrest, putting an end to British rule in Savannah for the time being. The governor later slipped away and escaped on an English vessel.

On August 10, Savannahians aching for freedom celebrated the signing of the Declaration of Independence, a document endorsed by three Georgians — George Walton of Savannah and Lyman Hall and Button Gwinnett of St. John's Parish. The new state of Georgia elected Archibald Bulloch as governor and completed a constitution in February 1777. Bulloch died during his first year in office and was replaced by Gwinnett.

Savannah, being in an exposed position on the far southeastern reaches of the new United States, paid for its location on December 29, 1778, when 3,000 British troops commanded by Col. Archibald Campbell routed the city's 700 defenders. The enemy had landed below Savannah two days before and slipped behind American Gen. Robert Howe and his forces. The British sacked the city, and James Wright returned to take control of Savannah. He and a small redcoat garrison found themselves under siege in September 1779 by a force of Frenchmen, Irishmen and volunteers from Haiti. They were joined by a contingent of American troops from South Carolina, and on October 9, the overall commander of the allied forces, French Count Charles Henri d'Estaing, ordered an attack on a defensive position southwest of the city in an area near the existing Savannah Visitors Center. The assault on this position, the Spring Hill redoubt, was, in the words of authors Russell and Hines, "a disaster, the bloodiest single hour in the entire Revolution."

"Through three valiant advances and the staggering retreat," they wrote, "French and Americans were slaughtered by land and naval artillery from Spring Hill redoubt and from . . . ships in the river . . . ." The defenders lost 55 men; the attackers suffered more than 1,000 casualties, including the deaths of two men later immortalized in monuments in Savannah's squares — Casimir Pulaski, a Polish count who had brought a group of lancers to the fray, and Sgt. William Jasper, who fell while attempting to save the flag of his South Carolina regiment. Savannah remained in possession of the British until after the climactic Battle of Yorktown. Wright and his compatriots evacuated the city several months after that American victory in Virginia, and American forces took control of the city on July 11, 1782.

The Antebellum Era

The Revolutionary War left Savannah a shambles, but the city recovered and prospered in the years between the end of that fight for freedom and an even grimmer struggle in the 1860s. Much of Savannah's prosperity in the years after the Revolution and before the American Civil War was due to a machine invented in 1793 on a plantation west of the city. While serving as a tutor at Mulberry Grove — a plantation owned by the widow of Revolutionary War Gen. Nathanael Greene — a Connecticut school teacher named Eli Whitney perfected the cotton gin, a device for removing the seeds from cotton bolls. The machine helped revolutionize the cotton-producing industry and, in so doing, reinforced the value of slavery in the agrarian South — a circumstance that would bring disaster to the region and Savannah.

The Square Deal:
Savannah's Municipal Idiom

The squares of Savannah lend the town a beauty and charm that's unique among American cities. But it's likely that James Edward Oglethorpe had defense as much as aesthetics in mind when he included the little parks in his plan for the city.

According to *Historic Savannah*, a survey of the city's buildings published by the Historic Savannah Foundation in 1979, "military considerations certainly played a major role" in the plan. The smallness of the squares and lots surrounding them "made the town more compact and easier to defend." The squares were also places where colonists living in the outposts that formed a sort of early warning system for the city could bring their families and livestock if attacked by Spaniards or Indians.

As conceived by Oglethorpe, the squares were at the center of the town's wards. Each ward had four "tythings," with each tything containing 10 lots for houses. In a ward, the tythings were on the northern and southern sides of the square, with the eastern and western sides of the square set aside as trust lots for public buildings. Oglethorpe laid out six wards and their squares. Four of these squares — now named Johnson, Wright, Ellis and Telfair — were laid out in 1733, with Johnson being the first. Later, Oglethorpe laid out Reynolds and Oglethorpe squares.

A total of 24 squares eventually were created. Two of them, Elbert and Liberty, have been "lost" to progress — bisected by Montgomery Street, they now exist as half-squares, with one half still park-like and the other half covered by public buildings. A third square, Ellis, is completely covered by a public parking garage.

No one knows for sure what inspired Oglethorpe to design Savannah as he did. "Perhaps his interest in town planning grew out of his friendship with an English

— continued on next page

Photo: Savannah Area Chamber of Commerce

The memorial to Sgt. William Jasper graces Madison Square, one of 21 "little parks" that make Savannah such a unique city.

architect, Robert Castell . . ." surmises *Historic Savannah.* "Perhaps, because of his previous military service under Prince Eugene of Savoy, Oglethorpe followed the traditions of old Roman military camps. And perhaps he may have seen and utilized a plan of Peking, originally printed in 1688 and reproduced years later. . ."

Castell, who died in debtors' prison, a circumstance that might have prompted Oglethorpe's interest in prison reform, had published a book named *The Villas of the Ancients*, and Oglethorpe owned two copies. According to historian William Harden, the book was "richly illustrated, and containing matter certainly of interest, and very probably of utility to one who might have in view the founding of a town or planning the laying out of pleasure grounds." Whatever Oglethorpe's inspiration, it lives happily on in the form of Savannah's priceless jewels, her squares.

But in the early 1800s, cotton brought wealth to the city's port. Wrote Russell and Hines of the city's transformation: "In 1790 cotton exports were one thousand bales; by 1820 they were ninety thousand bales a year. In 1794 Savannah's population was two thousand with export revenues under $500,000. By 1819 she was America's sixteenth largest city with exports exceeding $14,000,000." As Savannah prospered, its residents built elegant homes and other imposing structures. Probably the most famed of the designers of these buildings was architect William Jay, who came to the city from England in 1818, stayed for seven years and is responsible for existing masterpieces such as the Richardson-Owens-Thomas House, the Scarbrough House and the Telfair Academy of Arts and Sciences.

Savannahians experienced some giddy high points during the years between the wars. Among the highest was the transatlantic voyage of the S.S. *Savannah*, a vessel that was bankrolled by local merchants and propelled by steam and sail. The ship left Savannah on May 22, 1819, and arrived in Liverpool, England, a record-breaking 29 days and 11 hours later. On the return trip, the *Savannah* shattered that record by four days. A much more lasting achievement involving transportation occurred in 1847 when the Central of Georgia Railroad was completed, with Savannah as its eastern terminus. At that time, "Savannah reached its antebellum zenith," stated author Edward Chan Sieg.

"Now profits really soared and Savannah enjoyed a period of unprecedented growth. In addition to cotton, other sources of income were tobacco, rice, corn, lumber and naval stores. . . . The population tripled, the city limits were extended, gas lighting made its appearance. Hospitals, churches and orphanages grew in number for blacks and whites as excess wealth permitted the emergence of the charity traditions which were Savannah's birthright."

Other highly memorable moments occurred when two heroes of the Revolution visited the city. In May 1791, none other than George Washington, then serving as the first president of the United States, came to town for four days and attended numerous get-togethers. One of these was a ball at which, according to William Harden's *A History of Savannah and South Georgia*, the Father of Our Country was "introduced to ninety-six elegantly dressed ladies." In appreciation of his stay, Washington presented the militiamen of the Chatham Artillery with two brass cannon used at Yorktown; they now occupy a spot on Bay Street just east of City Hall. The other visitor was Washington's French ally, the Marquis de Lafayette. He stopped over in March 1825 and was honored with a parade and many toasts.

Unfortunately, there were also some low points, including fires that destroyed large parts of the city in 1796 and 1820, deadly outbreaks of yellow fever in 1820 and 1854 (the epidemic of the former year killed 666), and a storm in 1804 that caused the drowning of more than 100 slaves, submerged Hutchinson Island and greatly damaged many of the area's plantations. But as bad as those occurrences were, they were almost insignificant when compared to a disaster that was yet to come.

The Bethesda Home for Boys is the oldest orphanage in the United States.

The Worst Kind of War

Disputes between Northern and Southern states over slavery and states' rights boiled over in the mid-1800s with cataclysmic results: the secession of Georgia and her Southern neighbors from the Union, the South's forming of a Confederacy and the fighting of a war of the worst kind — a civil war. Although the war started in Charleston on April 16, 1861, when Confederate forces fired on and captured Fort Sumter, it was Savannah that, in the words of writers Russell and Hines, committed "the first belligerent act of the rebellious South."

Three months before Sumter, members of three militia outfits traveled by steamer from Savannah to Cockspur Island and seized Fort Pulaski, a large masonry edifice guarding the mouth of the Savannah River. Wrote Col. Charles H. Olmstead, who commanded the Confederates: "In due time Fort Pulaski was reached; its garrison, one elderly United States sergeant, made no defense, and the three

companies of the First Volunteer Regiment marched in with drums beating and colors flying, and so for them a soldier's life began." Olmstead and others thought Fort Pulaski impregnable. But 15 months after its bloodless seizure, shells from rifled Federal cannon emplaced on Tybee Island left the thick walls of the fort looking like Swiss cheese (see our Tybee Island chapter). After 30 hours of bombardment, Olmstead realized that holding the fort was impossible and surrendered it and its 385 defenders.

Following Pulaski's fall, the new occupants of the fort and their comrades in the Union navy began a blockade of Savannah. The city's exports of cotton and other goods were thus bottled up, and the residents spent most of the war enduring the hardships of the siege by sea and mourning the loss of relatives and loved ones who fell on faraway fields of fire. Among those who died were brothers Joseph C. and William N. Habersham, killed in fighting near Atlanta on the same day in July 1864.

Later that year came Union Gen. William

T. Sherman's devastating March to the Sea across Georgia. The prize at the end of the trek was Savannah. Sherman took it on December 21, but not before a battle at Fort McAllister south of Savannah near Richmond Hill and a skirmish at what would become the town of Pooler. And not before the Union commander allowed a force of 10,000 badly outnumbered Confederate defenders to slip out of the city and into South Carolina. In an oft-quoted telegram to President Abraham Lincoln that the commander-in-chief received on Christmas Eve, Sherman wrote: "I beg to present you as a Christmas Gift, the City of Savannah with 150 heavy guns and plenty of ammunition; and also about 25,000 bales of Cotton."

Savannah was out of the war and its citizens settled in to cope with the city's occupation by Union troops. For the most part, it was a benign affair. "The occupation was a model of order, even occasional pleasantry, with both sides generally behaving like ladies and gentlemen," wrote Russell and Hines. This, even though some of the women of the town refused to walk beneath the American flag.

Bouncing Back Again

Unlike some Southern cities, Savannah survived the Civil War without being decimated by shell fire or burned to the ground, although a fire that broke out a month after the city's surrender destroyed 100 buildings. But the war took its toll, leaving the city bankrupt and its people in need of food. However, within a year of the end of hostilities, said Sieg in *Eden on the Marsh*, "Savannah was rolling again," a beneficiary of the rapid rebuilding of the South's railroads and a resurgence in cotton production. In Savannah, "Exports for 1867 exceeded fifty million dollars," wrote Sieg. "The predictors of doom following the loss of slave labor were proved wrong as a rising market pushed cotton production to levels never realized" under slavery.

After the war, Savannah and the rest of the South entered into an 11-year period of Reconstruction during which radical Northern politicians hoped to build a power base of former slaves. Ultimately they failed, and slavery was replaced by a caste system and the creation of a "separate but equal" society. In Savannah, "blacks entered a long period of assimilation," said Sieg. "As a result, they developed their own culture, built their own institutions, formed their own business associations, created their own art, music, and literature — and in the process, developed a black elite that led the march into the twentieth century." Among the institutions founded was the Georgia State Industrial College, which is now Savannah State University (see our Education and Child Care chapter).

Economically, the last quarter of the 19th century saw the rice plantations around Savannah go out of business; turpentine and rosin from Georgia's pine forests rival cotton as the city's chief export; and the port enhanced by the dredging of the Savannah River shipping channel to a depth of 26 feet from 14 feet at the end of the war. There was also a spate of disasters during the last 25 years of the 1800s: Yellow fever killed more than 1,000 people in 1876, and the city was damaged by five significant fires, a tornado, two hurricanes and an earthquake.

Racing Into the 20th Century

Savannah focused international attention on itself early in the 20th century by hosting Grand Prix and Vanderbilt Cup automobile racing in 1908, 1910 and 1911. During the first decade of the new century, the city expanded in other ways; a new City Hall was built, and much of the present-day skyline took shape. In the years that followed, Savannah began stretching southward from downtown with the creation of the city's first residential subdivi-

INSIDERS' TIP

Abercorn Street, the city's main drag to the Southside, was named for the Earl of Abercorn, who, as historian William Harden put it, "was a generous benefactor" of the colony of Georgia.

An avenue of live oaks leads to Wormsloe Historic Site.

sion, Ardsley Park, after World War I. In the black community, residents formed the Negro Civic Improvement League to clean up over-crowded neighborhoods and started their own businesses, including the Wage Earners Savings Bank, which by 1915 covered a downtown block.

Not all was rosy, however. By the early 1920s cotton production in the South had fizzled out as laborers moved to the industrialized North and the boll weevil decimated Georgia's fields. Late in the decade came the Great Depression, and with it financial stagnation. During the '30s, Savannah received an economic boost when the Union Bag and Paper Company set up shop just west of the city, bringing with it nearly 600 jobs and a payroll of $1 million. The coming of Union Bag, which is now known as Union Camp and is still one of the city's largest employers, helped end Savannah's hard times, as did another, more far-reaching event — World War II.

On the Home Front

Savannah contributed mightily to America's war effort. At the Southeastern Shipyard, some 15,000 workers built Liberty Ships. The city's little airport, Hunter Field, was appropriated by the military and turned into a huge air base. In 1943, it became a staging area for bomber aircraft and crews headed for duty in Europe; some 9,000 planes and 70,000 men were processed out of Hunter during the war. With their airport gone, city officials began building another one in western Chatham County. It, too, was taken over by the government and became a training base for the crews of heavy bombers. Called Chatham Field, the base eventually became the site of Savannah International Airport. Hunter continues to be used by the military and is now known as Hunter Army Airfield.

"The war turned Savannah from a sleepy,

Photo: Kyle Cason

Photo: Kyle Cason

Colonial Cemetery is the final resting place for many early settlers.

traditional, backward-looking town on a muddy river into a full-fledged, twentieth-century American city," wrote Edward Chan Sieg. "Savannahians gave what they had to the war effort, burying another generation of their youth and generously entertaining the youth of other cities." Savannah boomed, what with the influx of workers who came from the countryside to build ships, and because of the city's popularity with military personnel from nearby bases, including the Marine Corps basic training complex at Parris Island, South Carolina.

The boom ended when the war did. The shipyard closed and most of the troops went home. "What remained was a partially deserted, once-fashionable Historic District," said Sieg. "Savannah had moved south to low-roofed suburbs, abandoning hundreds of high-ceilinged townhouses to the dereliction of uncaring tenants, little or no maintenance, and, worst of all, unprofitable values. No wonder that the postwar business leaders reached the conclusion that if Savannah were to survive and flourish, the old city must make way for progress. But the preservationist attitude found its way into the lives of a handful of influential residents who became dedicated to the principal that demolition was not the only answer to decay."

Preserving the Past and Making Progress

Savannahians reacted with shame in 1946 when Great Britain's Lady Astor called the city "a beautiful lady with a dirty face." They were moved to action when the town's City Market on Ellis Square was demolished in 1954 and replaced with a parking garage. The following year, a group of seven women led by Anna C. Hunter chartered the Historic Savannah Foundation for the purpose of saving noteworthy structures from destruction. By the time of the foundation's first general membership meeting in November 1955, the organization had 700 members.

Its first project was saving the Isaiah Davenport House, and it was successfully followed by many others. Wrote Russell and Hines of the group's efforts: "The foundation determined to reawaken interest in Savannah's heritage, to convince the public of the economic benefits of restoration, and to promote tourism. . . . During the next decade the foundation would deluge the city with a massive public relations campaign, arrange for a professional inventory of historic buildings, establish a revolving fund, and help establish a tourism and convention bureau within the Chamber of Commerce."

The group formulated a preservation plan that became a national model and the basis of the city's Historic Zoning Ordinance. By 1970, the foundation had saved more than 150 structures that were resold to individuals for restoration; the organization continues its efforts today from offices on Broughton Street.

In recent years, the Savannah College of Art and Design (SCAD) (see our Education and Child Care chapter) has stepped forward as a leader in historic preservation. Among the many buildings the college has restored to house classrooms and offices are former public school buildings, the old Chatham County Jail and portions of what was once the Central of Georgia Railroad complex. In the 1970s, the city government beautified River Street by creating Rousakis Plaza along the waterfront and started a revitalization of the Broughton Street shopping district that is a work in progress.

Since then, Savannahians have witnessed other progressive developments, including the construction of a new airport terminal, the replacement of the aging Talmadge Memorial Bridge and improvements and growth at the city's port facilities. In 1996 Savannah found itself back on the international stage it had trod during the time of the great auto races; this time, the city was hosting the yachting events of Atlanta's 1996 Summer Olympic Games. The opening and closing ceremonies of the games in Savannah were held at the eastern end of Bay Street, very close to where Oglethorpe and his little band of colonists landed 263 years before.

Because of its history, diversity and charms, Savannah is a melting pot.

Area Overview

Head south to Savannah from South Carolina on U.S. Highway 17, and you find yourself on a two-lane road winding through marshland and passing by a few fireworks stands and video poker parlors. You're in the far reaches of the Lowcountry, and if you didn't know better, you'd swear you were in a desert . . . a desert where marsh grass stands in for sand. You're becoming convinced that you've driven all the way to Nowhere — that you've exiled yourself by automobile to the end of the world.

Then you round a bend of the highway, and suddenly you're staring at civilization in the form of the graceful towers of the Eugene Talmadge Memorial Bridge. Travel a bit farther, and you see the horizon to the left of the bridge filling with the low skyline of a city. In a few minutes, you leave South Carolina and the marsh behind and begin crossing the Savannah River into Georgia. Cresting the crown of the bridge, you're 196 feet above the water and looking down and ahead toward your destination, the city of Savannah.

Glancing to your left, you see the golden dome of City Hall and a riverfront of brick cotton warehouses that have been converted into shops and restaurants. Beyond the waterfront a canopy of trees stretches to the south, punctuated here and there by the spires of churches and the upper floors of a hotel, a few office buildings and an apartment complex or two. Off to your right, the river is bordered by manufacturing plants and the docks, warehouses and towering cranes of the Georgia Ports Authority. Straight ahead is a network of roadways, with some of the thoroughfares leading to the Southside, where many Savannahians live and many more do their shopping.

This seagull's-eye view of the area gives you a pretty good idea of the lay of the land, and your tires haven't even settled on Georgia ground yet. Read deeper into this chapter, and we'll give you a more complete picture of the region, including brief looks at some places you can't readily see from the bridge — Savannah's inshore islands.

As you learned in our How to Use This Book section, we've arranged many of the chapters in this guide by geographic sections. The boundaries and makeup of those sections are discussed here. Before we get into that, however, let us toss your way some nice-to-know, getting-grounded information about the Savannah area.

Vital Statistics

Savannah is the seat of government of Chatham County, one of the most populous counties in the largest state (in terms of area) east of the Mississippi River. Some 233,500 people live in Chatham, with about 143,100 residing within Savannah's city limits. About a quarter of the county's 443 square miles are unincorporated, and there are also seven other municipalities within Chatham's borders: Bloomingdale, Garden City, Port Wentworth, Pooler, Thunderbolt, Vernonburg and the city of Tybee Island.

The people who live here have a broad variety of backgrounds, jobs and interests, which is what you might expect from a place that dates back to 1733 and serves as a port, a center of higher education, a tourist destination, a site for industrial plants, a home to the military and a mecca for artists and historic preservationists. Because of its history, diver-

Photo: Kyle Cason

This downtown fountain honors Savannah's German heritage.

sity and charms, Savannah is a melting pot: Grab a morning cup of coffee at the Express Cafe & Bakery on Barnard Street, and you could be standing in line with a college student who just blew in from the North or a society matron whose ancestors walked up the Savannah River bluff with Georgia's founder, James Edward Oglethorpe.

Chatham County's population is about 59 percent white, 38 percent African American, 1 percent Asian and 1 percent Hispanic. The growth rate from 1990 through '96 was 6.1 percent, and projections indicate the county will continue to grow until the year 2015 at an annual rate of from 0.9 percent to 1.5 percent, depending on which study you look at. Savannah's population is also getting older, with the percentage of people 25 and younger declining and the percentage of folks 65 and older increasing. The experts say this situation is the result of several factors including a lower birth rate, the aging of the baby boomers, increased longevity due to medical advancements and healthier lifestyles, and the county's growing popularity as a retirement community.

In 1995 nearly a third of Chatham's work force was involved in the service sector, 20 percent was engaged in retail trade and 13 percent worked in manufacturing. Chatham's major employers are Memorial Medical Center, St. Joseph's and Candler hospitals, the Kroger supermarket chain, Gulfstream Aerospace Corporation, Union Camp Corporation, Great Dane Trailers, Hunter Army Airfield, the Savannah-Chatham County Board of Educa-

INSIDERS' TIP

The average sale price of a residence in Chatham County in 1995 was $103,503. According to Coldwell Banker, a 2,200-square-foot, 10-year-old home with four bedrooms and two-and-a-half baths would have cost a Savannahian $147,000 in the autumn of 1995 — more than comparable homes in Charleston ($140,975) and Jacksonville ($144,000), but less than in Atlanta ($160,100) and Miami ($169,500) and much less than in Stamford, Connecticut ($323,187) and Chicago-Lincoln Park, Illinois ($425,535).

tion and the governments of Georgia, Savannah and the county. Per capita income in 1994 was $20,579, and Chatham was the ninth highest-ranked of Georgia's 159 counties in this economic category.

The Savannah area is blessed with a climate classified as semi-tropical. Average seasonal temperatures are 51 in winter, 66 in spring, 80 in summer and 66 in autumn. From these figures, you can see that the best times to visit (as far as most folks are concerned) are the spring and fall. The days can get mighty hot and sticky during the summer — according to the Savannah Area Chamber of Commerce, the city on average experiences 67 days each year when the mercury climbs higher than 90.

Winters are fairly mild, with the temperature dipping below freezing an average of (ironically) 32 days a year. We seldom see snow, and the descent of even a few flakes is cause for excitement. The average annual rainfall is 49.7 inches, and Mother Nature delivers some frog-choking downpours now and then, particularly during the summer in the afternoons. Because Savannah is in a low-lying area and much of the city's sewer system is antiquated, streets are prone to flooding when tides are high — be careful if you're driving around and get caught in a sudden storm.

Being on the southeastern coast, Savannah often finds itself threatened by hurricanes. In recent years, the city has been spared the destruction caused by major storms. Savannah had close calls from Hurricane Hugo in 1989 and Bertha in 1996, but the last hurricane to hit here was David in 1979, when winds as strong as 90 mph caused widespread power outages that lasted for several days.

That gives you the big picture. Now let's look more closely at the four areas into which we've divided the county.

Here's Looking at You, Savannah

Historic Downtown

Our downtown area is bordered by the Savannah River on the north, East Broad Street on the east, Park Avenue on the south and Martin Luther King Jr. Boulevard on the west. This is the section of Savannah most visitors come to see. It's the oldest part of the city — Oglethorpe landed here when he arrived to found Georgia more than 260 years ago. The city squares he laid out — those green jewels in Savannah's crown — are here.

This is the site of the Historic District, 2.5 square miles of beautifully restored homes and historic churches. It's an area that's been designated by the U.S. Department of the Interior as a National Historic Landmark. It's a place of monuments, shady sidewalks and a cemetery that's a park. It's where SCAD students sit on curbs while sketching old buildings, where the Irish and others put themselves on parade on St. Patrick's Day, and where tourists look for places mentioned in *Midnight in the Garden of Good and Evil*.

The downtown is also a place for fun, good eating and shopping. River Street and City Market are here, with their stores and restaurants, and so is Broughton Street, which was once the city's main shopping district and is making a comeback after losing customers to the malls of the Southside (see our Shopping chapter). Downtown also hosts festivals, with many of Savannah's major annual events being held along the river, in City Market and at Forsyth Park, a lush green playground on Bull Street (see our Annual Events and Festivals chapter).

INSIDERS' TIP

The wispy, gray vegetation hanging from the trees is Spanish moss, a plant that takes its moisture and nutrients from the air. This member of the pineapple family is not a parasite, but it can harm a tree if it covers too much foliage and blocks out the sunlight needed for photosynthesis. Don't lie in a bed of Spanish moss or drape it from your body; it is the home of mite-like creatures called red bugs that can cause skin irritations.

The downtown is the home of the city's financial district, Johnson Square, which is ringed by the main offices of several banks. There are also numerous museums and the Savannah College of Art and Design. SCAD is the largest school of its kind in the nation, and its 3,000-plus students bring much vitality and creativity to the area (see our Education and Arts and Culture chapters).

Interestingly enough, Savannah's downtown is not really "down," geographically speaking. If you look at a map of the city, you'll see it's in the northern part of town. That's because Savannah got its start on a bluff on the south bank of the river, causing the heart of the city to be north of everything else. When you're in downtown Savannah, you can't go much farther north and still be in Georgia. Savannah has not grown to the north, across the channel of the Savannah River known as the Back River, because what's over there is mostly marshland, and it's also South Carolina.

Having said that, we must mention that when you're downtown on River Street gazing across the Savannah River, you're looking at Hutchinson Island, a part of Georgia that's in the process of being developed. An automobile racetrack opened there in the spring of 1997, and plans for the island call for the creation of a $92 million resort complex and the $70.5 million Savannah International Trade and Convention Center by the turn of the century.

Because Savannah hasn't been able to expand to the north, most early growth was southward, and much recent growth has been to the east and west.

Islands

The growth eastward has occurred principally on Chatham County's inshore islands, referred to as such because they're not on the Atlantic Ocean. They're separated from the mainland and neighboring islands by salt marsh, rivers and tidal creeks. The islands in our Islands area are those immediately east of

Savannah — Oatland, Talahi, Whitemarsh and Wilmington — and those southeast of the city — Dutch, Skidaway and Isle of Hope. Because of its unique qualities and status as a destination for tourists, we have devoted a separate chapter to Tybee Island, which is also east of Savannah.

The development of the eastside islands took off in the late '80s, and Whitemarsh Island (pronounced "WHIT-marsh") was the fastest-growing part of the county in 1996, with Wilmington Island not far behind. Most of the building has been residential, although a large shopping center and three schools have been constructed on Whitemarsh in recent years.

Despite the buildup, the eastside islands retain a natural beauty and laid-back quality. You can still take an evening stroll on an island street, look up at a sky brilliant with stars and listen to the plaintive calls of mourning doves and the chuck-will's-widow. The eastside islands remain quiet havens where folks sit on their docks and watch the marsh turn from gold to green as the seasons change; where oaks festooned with Spanish moss bend over roadways to create cool, verdant tunnels; where you can hop in your car, drive around the corner and enjoy a meal of fresh seafood.

Farther to the south you'll find the gated residential enclave of Dutch Island; Skidaway Island, site of The Landings, a private community of upscale homes; and Isle of Hope, with its dignified old houses adorning secluded narrow streets. The Landings covers much of Skidaway Island with 2,800 beautifully landscaped dwellings, two marinas, six private 18-hole golf courses and two tennis complexes. Isle of Hope is entirely residential except for the marina on Bluff Drive (see our Neighborhoods and Real Estate chapter). Bluff Drive is a lovely lane running alongside the Skidaway River, and it's our choice as the Savannah area's most picturesque street. The Isle is also the location of Wormsloe Historic Site, the place where one of Georgia's first settlers con-

A Gnasty Welcome to Savannah

"What just bit me?"

"What's that smell?"

Visitors to Savannah sometimes ask those questions even before inquiring about where to eat, what to visit and how to find the Garden of Good and Evil.

Close-up

The smell can hit you out on Interstate 16, miles before you get to town, and the biting can begin as soon as you leave the safety of your car. You might think those unseen forces making lunch of your bare forearm are a figment of your imagination, but they're not. They're sand flies. Savannahians call them sand gnats and sometimes refer to them as "no-see-ums."

A sand gnat feeds on a human by slashing skin with its teeth and drinking the pool of blood that forms. Sounds gross, but you can't see this carnage taking place because your average sand gnat is about a millimeter long — so tiny it can fly through standard window screen without grazing its wing tips. What you might see, particularly if you are prone to allergies, are small welts appearing where gnats have feasted. Try not to scratch; if you leave the bumps alone, they will disappear in about an hour.

Incidentally, the gnats biting you are females. They need the protein in blood for laying eggs. Sand gnats breed in the mud of salt marshes and are most prevalent in the spring and fall, but a few days of temperatures in the 60s can bring them out at other times. Although some folks recommend dousing yourself with a certain brand-name skin softener as a defense against sand gnats, entomologists say you can best fight these bugs by applying insect repellent containing the chemical compound DEET and by wearing long clothing and hats.

Savannahians have a love-hate relationship with sand gnats. They detest the gnat as an insect but adore it as the mascot of the city's minor-league baseball team. The management and fans of the Savannah ball club chose the Sand Gnat nickname when the team became an affiliate of the Los Angeles Dodgers organization in 1996. (They've since become affiliated with the Texas Rangers.) Sand Gnat merchandise is so popular, it's a bestseller among fans of minor-league teams.

Not nearly as lovable as the baseball team's bug-eyed mascot is the rotten-egg, cabbage-being-cooked smell that periodically wafts over Savannah. The odor emanates from the industries lining the banks of the Savannah River. The dominant component of the smell is sulfur dioxide, a pungent gas released during the manufacture of paper. Industry officials say they have spent big bucks attempting to eliminate the smell, and they assure us they have lessened it. The smell persists, however, as do the sand gnats. Savannahians have learned to live with both, and you can too.

Photo: Kyle Cason

Azaleas are a hallmark of Savannah's springtime.

structed a Colonial estate (see our Attractions chapter).

Southside/Midtown

Southside/Midtown is the vast area south of Historic Downtown. Note that the locals refer to the northern portion of this area as Midtown. Midtown starts in the vicinity of the southern end of Forsyth Park and runs south to DeRenne Avenue, although some folks might tell you that it extends all the way to Oglethorpe Mall. Most of Savannah's Victorian District and all of the South Victorian District are in Midtown. The districts are filled with Victorian-style frame houses and are on the National Register of Historic Places.

That distinction also applies to Ardsley Park and Chatham Crescent, two other areas in Midtown. Among the streets of Ardsley Park is one of Savannah's prettiest — oak- and azalea-lined Washington Avenue. At the eastern end of the avenue is Daffin Park, site of a lake and public tennis courts and athletic fields used by recreation league teams playing baseball, softball, football and soccer. Daffin is also the stomping ground of professional athletes — the members of the city's minor-league baseball team, the Savannah Sand Gnats (see our Spectator Sports chapter). The Gnats play their home games at Grayson Stadium, which stands among the tall pines in the eastern portion of the park.

You'll find several shopping centers in Midtown, the main library (which is undergoing extensive renovations expected to be completed by 1999) and much of Savannah's healthcare community. Clustered just north of DeRenne Avenue, between Reynolds Street and the Truman Parkway, are numerous doctors' offices, pharmacies, medical laboratories and two of the city's hospitals, Memorial Medical Center and Candler Hospital (see our Healthcare chapter).

Once south of DeRenne, you are in the part of town most locals call the Southside. It's an area of subdivisions, churches, recreational facilities and commercial development. Savannah's main drag, Abercorn Street, turns into the area's primary retail strip here. We think of Abercorn south of DeRenne as the Land of a Thousand Curb Cuts. That's an exaggeration, but not much of one. The six-lane thoroughfare is nicked by a myriad of entrances and exits to and from restaurants, motels, office complexes, convenience marts, both of Savannah's malls, auto dealerships, used-car lots, strip shopping centers and megastores selling building materials, pet supplies, party goods, books, liquor and office equipment. Interrupting this cascade of commercialism on Abercorn are St. Joseph's Hospital and the doctors' offices that have sprung up around it (see our Healthcare chapter), and the campus of Armstrong Atlantic State University. The area we've designated as the Southside is also home to several other institutions of higher education, including Savannah State College, Savannah Technical Institute and South College (see our Education chapter).

Outdoor activities abound in the Southside. Just east and southeast of Oglethorpe Mall is a city- and county-owned recreational complex consisting of softball diamonds, soccer fields, tennis courts, a public golf course, a stadium where high school football teams play and a lake surrounded by a walking/jogging track. The Southside past Oglethorpe Mall is where suburbia evolved in the 1950s and '60s, mainly in the sprawling subdivision of Windsor Forest. Residential growth has continued in recent years farther out Abercorn Street at Georgetown, the second-fastest growing area in Chatham County (see our Neighborhoods and Real Estate chapter).

To the west of the residential and commercial development of the Southside is Hunter Army Airfield, a 5,400-acre military post and site of the Army's longest runway. More than 4,100 soldiers and 700 civilians work at Hunter, the home of a Ranger battalion and units of the Third Infantry Division (Mechanized). The bulk of the division is based an hour away at Fort Stewart, the largest Army installation east of the Mississippi River. With its 11,000-foot runway, Hunter serves as a location from which troops and equipment of the Third can be deployed throughout the world.

Two of Chatham's other municipalities are in Southside/Midtown — Thunderbolt, a quaint fishing village of 2,900 people living alongside the Wilmington River, and Vernonburg, a settlement of 143 souls who reside on a handful of streets leading to the banks of the Vernon River. South of Vernonburg are the rustic residential communities of Beaulieu and Coffee Bluff.

West Chatham

West Chatham is where folks roll up their sleeves and get to work. It's where much of the area's industry flexes its muscles. This is the home of the county's largest manufacturers, Gulfstream Aerospace Corporation, which employs 3,700 people and produces corporate jet aircraft, and Union Camp Cor-

Savannah's City Hall sports a real gold dome.

poration, whose 2,600 workers are involved in making kraft paper (the strong brown paper used for bags and wrapping). West Chatham is the site of the headquarters of the Georgia Ports Authority, which operates two deep-water terminals on the Savannah River. Most of the cargo handled on Savannah's docks is shipped in containers, and the city is one of the busiest container ports in the United States.

Many of the people who work at the port and the industries west of Savannah live in West Chatham's four municipalities. Of these, Garden City is the largest in terms of population — 7,680 people call it home. Port Wentworth, the town closest to the river, has a population of 3,890, and Bloomingdale has 2,380 residents. Pooler, a town of 5,980, is the West Chatham municipality covering the most area, and it's one of the fastest-developing parts of the region. Another rapidly growing section of West Chatham is Southbridge, an upscale residential community just off Interstate 16 and south of Pooler. About 350 homes were built at Southbridge as of spring 1997, and the development was expected to top out at 950 to 1,000 residences (see our Neighborhoods and Real Estate chapter).

West Chatham is also the location of Savannah International Airport, where a $68.5 million terminal was opened in 1994 (see our Getting Here, Getting Around chapter).

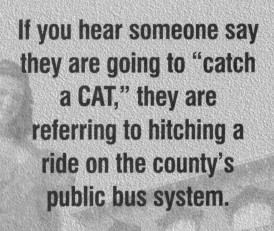

If you hear someone say
they are going to "catch
a CAT," they are
referring to hitching a
ride on the county's
public bus system.

Getting Here, Getting Around

Georgia's first city is in the southeastern corner of the state about 17 miles inland from the Atlantic Ocean. Head north, and within a few miles you will be in South Carolina. Travel in the other direction, and about two hours later your car crosses into Florida.

Some of the first people to get to Savannah arrived in sailing vessels. Gen. James Edward Oglethorpe, Georgia's founder, came in 1733 to settle the colony and establish, among other things, a thriving port. Today, people still arrive along Savannah's shore. The majority, however, come in gigantic container ships with millions of dollars worth of cargo. Savannah is the 10th-largest container port in the United States, with about 2,000 ships making their way into the narrow Savannah River every year to load or unload their goods. On a very rare occasion, you'll see a cruise ship that has docked in Savannah.

Most people coming to visit arrive one of the standard ways — in planes, trains and automobiles. To help facilitate these visitors, Savannah opened a new $68.5 million airport terminal in 1994. If you've ever navigated your way through big-city airports like those in Chicago or Atlanta, Savannah International Airport will be a nice change. Like that of its namesake city, the pace is a little slower and friendlier at our airport, and there are no football-field-length corridors to run through in order to make your connections. For rail and bus riders, Amtrak and Greyhound make stops every day in Savannah. And, of course, you can always just jump in your car and head for Interstate 95 or Interstate 16, both of which pass right by.

Once you get here, there are several options to get you around. One of the newest are "pedicabs" — big tricycles powered by very in-shape tour guides who can pedal and talk at the same time. Overall, you should find Savannah to be a pretty friendly and easy place for traveling. You won't find elaborate freeway systems with HOV lanes or throngs of harried commuters rushing to catch their 5 o'clock train. Sorry, Savannah just isn't big enough for that stuff.

What we do have is a network of parkways that will take you around certain sections of the city. There are two-lane roads passing through beautiful marshes, and one-way streets designed to get you quickly from one place to another. And, of course, there are the squares — the very construction of which forces you to slow down . . . take your time . . . enjoy the scenery. This isn't to say we don't have congested streets and other roadways that seem more like speedways, especially in the commercial sections of the city. But big traffic jams are usually big news and might even make the morning paper the next day.

You may notice people also tend to move slower here — especially during the very hot and humid summer months. If you sit at a green light for a few seconds trying to figure out where you are, chances are good that the person behind you is not going to lay on the horn or gesture in an unfriendly way. And if you are lost, ask a local. More likely than not, they will be happy to get you headed in the right direction. Having said all this, remember that Savannah is still a city. It may feel, particularly in the Historic Downtown, like a small town, but it isn't. Always use the same precautions you would in any city: Be aware of your surroundings, don't venture out alone at night and keep your wallet or purse secure.

We have broken this chapter into two sections. Getting Here is just what you would expect — a look at the various modes of transportation to get you to Savannah. Getting Around helps you navigate once you've arrived. It includes a look at parking, public transportation, local roadways and more.

Getting Here

By Air

Savannah International Airport
400 Airways Ave. • 964-0514

The Savannah International Airport is about 10 miles north of Savannah at Exit 18-A off I-95. There are 25 daily departures, with nonstop or direct flights to a variety of U.S. cities including Atlanta; Myrtle Beach, South Carolina; Hartford, Connecticut; and Newark, New Jersey. **Delta**, (800) 221-1212, and **USAir**, (800) 428-4322, are the largest carriers and also have been with the airport the longest. Together, they account for 16 daily departures. The other airlines are smaller, discount carriers including **AirTran**, (800) 825-8538, **Midway Corporate Express**, (800) 446-4392 and **Continental Express**, (800) 525-0280. During the last few years, there have been a number of changes with the airline roster, and airline officials say this trend should continue. Although Savannah International doesn't have any international flights, it is equipped to handle them should an airline ever make such an offer.

While the airline getting you here may change, one constant will be where you will arrive. In May 1994, Savannah opened a $68.5 million terminal with eight gates, restaurants, gift shops, ATM machines, a postal center and even a hair salon. When passengers depart they walk through Savannah Square, a relaxing seating area patterned after Savannah's famous downtown squares. There are snacks, shops and restaurants to enjoy in this area.

Private Plane Service

Signature Flight Support
1006 Bob Harmon Rd., Savannah International Airport • 964-1557

Signature Flight Support is open 24 hours a day seven days a week. It offers tie-down service for single- and twin-engine planes, along with parking for jets. Fees depend on the aircraft, but if you purchase fuel, there is no charge. Repair service is available.

Savannah Aviation
Hangar Rd. • 964-1022

Savannah Aviation is open Monday through Friday from 6 AM to 10 PM and from 7 AM to 9 PM on the weekends. Tie-down service is available. Fees vary depending on the aircraft and whether you get fuel. Repairs can be made to small planes.

Rental Cars

Passengers have a choice of several rental

INSIDERS' TIP

Lost in Historic Downtown? Can't remember where you parked your car or which way back to your hotel? Look for somebody doling out parking tickets. Under the "Ask Me" program, parking enforcement attendants — the ones buzzing around in those little blue and white carts writing parking tickets — are trained to assist tourists in need. They can give directions, help point out the nearest bathroom, even use their radios to track down misplaced cars.

car agencies on the premises. Servicing Savannah International are **Alamo**, 964-7364; **Avis**, 964-1781; **Budget**, 964-4600; **Payless**, 966-5696; **National**, 964-1771; **Thrifty**, 966-2277; and **Hertz**, 964-9595.

Taxi Service

The airport distributes a rate brochure (available either outside near all the cabs or inside near the baggage claim) giving passengers an idea what it will cost to take a taxi to local bed and breakfasts, hotels, motels and inns. Typically, it costs around $18 to get to the Historic Downtown, $26 to reach Southside/Midtown, $6.50 to $10 to get to West Chatham and about $40 for a ride to Tybee Island. These rates are regulated by the Airport Commission and, of course, are subject to change. Taxi service can be procured by calling the taxi stand at 964-8016, or by simply hailing a cab. **Low Country Adventures**, (800) 845-5582, provides airport shuttle service to and from Hilton Head for $24 one way (see our Hilton Head chapter).

There is no scheduled provider of limousine service to and from the airport. However, there are several private limousine services in the city, and these are listed subsequently in this chapter. If you are interested in a ride from the airport, always inquire when calling as to whether the company has a permit to pick up at the airport.

By Train

Amtrak
2611 Seaboard Coastline Dr. • 234-2611

The *Silver Meteor*, *Silver Star* and *Silver Palm* take turns coming into Savannah as part of their treks along the Eastern Seaboard. Savannah is in the New York-Miami Amtrak corridor, and travelers have a choice of six depar-

ture times each day. Northbound trains: leave at 5:17 AM to arrive in New York at 11:10 PM; depart at 6:48 PM to arrive in New York at 9:45 AM the next morning; and leave at 10:25 PM to arrive in New York at 4 PM the following afternoon. Trains heading south: depart at 11:08 PM to arrive in Miami at 11:50 AM; leave at 5:14 AM to get to Miami at 4:45 PM; and depart at 9:51 AM and arrive in Miami at 9:35 PM.

The Amtrak station is about 4 miles from the Historic Downtown. Heading west on I-16, take the Chatham Parkway exit. At the stop sign turn left, then take your first right. The station is open every day from 4:30 AM to noon and from 4:30 PM to midnight. Taxicabs are at the station when each train pulls in. Rental cars are not available at the station.

By Bus

Greyhound Bus Lines
610 W. Oglethorpe Ave. • 232-2135

Savannah is on Greyhound Bus Lines' busiest eastern corridor — the stretch between New York City and Miami. Buses depart the city 23 times a day, seven days a week, with the most frequent departures, as would be expected, headed north toward New York and south to Miami. There are also westbound options. If you are coming to Savannah on Greyhound, you will disembark at the terminal on the far western reaches of Oglethorpe Avenue, one of the Historic Downtown's main thoroughfares. Head out the front door of the station and walk to your left along Oglethorpe — within a few blocks you will be in the heart of the Historic Downtown. If you arrive at night, use caution when walking, as you would in any city. (If you make a right turn, you will have to cross a very tall bridge into South Carolina.) Taxi service is available at the bus terminal.

INSIDERS' TIP

While you won't find massive traffic jams in Savannah, it does get pretty congested, particularly in the Southside/Midtown area during rush hour. If you can, avoid traveling DeRenne Avenue and Abercorn Street early in the morning and during late afternoon.

By Car

Savannah is reachable by car via two major interstates — I-95 from the north and south and I-16 running east and west. I-95 is the main artery along the eastern seaboard, stretching from Maine to the tip of Florida. It is especially busy in the Savannah area during spring, when snowbirds and spring-breakers are heading south for some winter relief. I-16 cuts an east-west path across middle Georgia before merging with Interstate 75, which takes you into Atlanta. Following is a helpful rundown on how to get to the main geographical sections of the city from either interstates.

To Historic Downtown

The best option to get to the Historic Downtown is to use I-16 heading east. The interstate dead-ends near the west boundary of the Historic Downtown — the corner of Liberty and Montgomery streets. Take a left onto Montgomery Street, then your next right on Martin Luther King Jr. Boulevard. On your left you will see the Savannah Visitors Center. For those traveling north or south on I-95, Exit 17, which is about 10 miles outside the city limits, puts you onto I-16. From there, use the previous directions.

To Islands

There are a couple of options to get you to Tybee or the eastern islands of Oatland, Talahi, Whitemarsh and Wilmington. Take I-16 into the Historic Downtown area and get on any northbound street until you reach Bay Street. Continue east on Bay Street, which in less than a mile merges with President Street, then the President Street Extension. Follow the President Street Extension until it becomes Islands Expressway. In about 3 miles it will merge with U.S. Highway 80, which is the main route to Tybee and the eastern islands.

A second option to get you to Tybee, along with the eastern and southeastern islands (Dutch, Skidaway and Isle of Hope), involves leaving I-16 at Exit 35 (37th Street). Take 37th Street to Abercorn Street, take a right, then proceed to Victory Drive, where you will turn left (east). To reach the southeastern islands, look for Skidaway Road off Victory Drive and take a right. This will get you to Dutch Island and Isle of Hope. If you continue east on Victory, it will become U.S. 80, which will take you to the eastern islands and Tybee.

To Southside/Midtown

If you are staying near the Southside, you might want to consider exiting I-95 at Exit 16, which puts you on Ga. Highway 204 in the southern reaches of the county, about 20 miles south of the Historic Downtown. Ga. 204 is also Abercorn Street, the main north-south thoroughfare running throughout the entire city. After exiting, head north. After about 5 miles you will enter the Southside — the city's main commercial district, with strip shopping centers, hotels, car dealerships and Savannah's two malls.

Another option to get to the Southside or Midtown area: Take Exit 34 off I-16, which will put you on William F. Lynes Memorial Parkway. After about 4 miles it turns into DeRenne Avenue, a main east-west thoroughfare. Take a right onto Abercorn Street off DeRenne, and you are at the edge of the Southside. If you go left onto Abercorn, you will be heading to Midtown.

To West Chatham

Exit 31 off I-16 will take you to Bloomingdale via Bloomingdale Cross Road, and I-95 Exit 18 will take you through the heart of Pooler on Louisville Road. From I-95 you can also take the Pooler Parkway, which will connect you to U.S. 80 and take you through Bloomingdale, Pooler and Garden City.

Getting Around

Once you have made it to Savannah, there are several ways you can navigate within the city — from public transportation to a comfortable pair of shoes. Following are some ideas for getting around and a few things to watch out for while traversing the town.

Hitting the Road

Historic Downtown

If it wasn't for the squares, Savannah's Historic Downtown would follow a fairly simple grid pattern. There are 13 main north-south

Photo: Kyle Cason

The Talmadge Bridge spans the Savannah River, linking Georgia and South Carolina.

streets in the Historic Downtown, stretching from the northernmost point of the city — the Savannah River — south to Forsyth Park. These streets include (listed east to west) East Broad, Houston, Price, Habersham, Lincoln, Abercorn, Drayton, Bull, Whitaker, Barnard, Jefferson, Montgomery and Martin Luther King Jr. Likewise, there are 23 main east-west streets, starting (for our purposes) at East Broad and ending at Martin Luther King (which was formerly known as West Broad). These main east-west roadways include River, Bay, Bryan, Congress, Broughton, State, York, Oglethorpe, Hull, Perry, Liberty, Harris, Charlton, Jones, Taylor, Gordon, Gaston, Huntingdon, Hall, Gwinnett, Bolton, Waldburg and Park.

If our streets resemble a series of necklaces, then some of them are lucky enough to have pearls in the form of squares. In fact, six of the north-south streets — **Montgomery, Barnard, Bull, Abercorn, Habersham** and **Houston** — have these jewels, placing them among the most beautiful streets in the Historic Downtown. Everything, however, emanates from famous Bull Street. Located in the center of the Historic Downtown and easy to spot because it begins at golden-domed City Hall, Bull Street offers some of the most notable squares in the city — including the one

INSIDERS' TIP

Whenever entering a square, always yield to traffic already moving within the square. Once traffic has cleared, enter the square driving straight ahead or always to your right.

where Forrest Gump spent his time and where the main plot unfolds in *Midnight in the Garden of Good and Evil*.

It is crucial that you understand how to navigate around the squares while traveling in the Historic Downtown. Imagine heading north or south on one of the six streets with squares. Every couple of blocks you are going to run into one. Although there are stories about people driving through the squares (don't try it . . . it's illegal), it is much preferred that you go around.

No, these aren't your standard traffic circles. There is only one lane, and traffic moves in a counterclockwise direction around a beautiful park filled with trees, benches and, in some instances, a monument or fountain. The traffic moves very slowly, so you have ample time to figure out where you would like to exit. You can exit onto a north and southbound street, or an east-west-running street (unless it is one way). You have your choice. When entering a square, always yield to any car making its way around the square — they have the right of way. Once the coast is clear, enter the square driving to your right.

If you don't want to hit any squares, you can take a straight southbound route through the Historic Downtown on either **Price Street** or **Whitaker Street**. Both are one-way. **Drayton Street**, a one-way northern thoroughfare, will get you all the way to the Savannah River without being interrupted by squares. Note that you also will run into squares when traveling east to west in the Historic Downtown. The majority of the east-west routes pass by to the north or south of the squares, but a few intersect them. Again, when approaching a square from the east or west, you must yield to any traffic that is already making its way around the square. Once traffic has cleared you enter the square by traveling to your right or going straight ahead. **Liberty** and **Oglethorpe** are the main east-west streets without squares. Others include Jones, Gaston, Broughton and Bay.

Islands

The eastern islands, including Whitemarsh, Talahi, Oatland and Wilmington, are directly off **U.S. 80**, which is also the only route to Tybee Island. It is a fairly wide, four-lane highway taking you through scenic marshlands before narrowing into a two-lane road as you near Tybee. **Skidaway Road** leads to Dutch Island and the Isle of Hope. Waters Avenue is the direct route to Skidaway Island. This well-marked, two-lane road is very busy and congested most times of the day. While driving on Skidaway, keep your eyes open for people turning on and off the road. (Please see our Tybee Island chapter for more information on getting around there.)

Southside/Midtown

Abercorn Street is the main artery running through Savannah's Southside. It begins at the Savannah River in the Historic Downtown and continues south some 20 miles to I-95. All the motels, hotels, shopping centers, car dealerships and other businesses in the Southside are either right on Abercorn or on a street just off this main drag. The six-lane street is heavily traveled and usually very busy. Try to avoid Abercorn during morning and afternoon rush hours — typically 7:30 to 9 AM and 4 to 6 PM.

DeRenne Avenue, which becomes I-516, is the main Southside east-west route. You will find two of the city's hospitals off DeRenne, along with gas stations, shopping centers, banks and several medical offices. This road also is heavily traveled and should be avoided during morning and afternoon rush hours. **Victory Drive** is Midtown's main drag. It travels through residential neighborhoods and by shopping centers and Grayson Stadium, home of Savannah's minor-league baseball team — the Sand Gnats (see our Spectator Sports chapter). When traveling east, Victory Drive is U.S. 80, the main route to Tybee and the eastern Islands. **Eisenhower Drive** is another major east-west road that accesses Hunter Army Airfield to the west and Skidaway Road to the east. It parallels DeRenne and Victory.

West Chatham

Bay Street, which runs right in front of City Hall in the Historic Downtown, continues to West Chatham, eventually taking you to Garden City and Port Wentworth. **George Washington Highway**, which turns into Augusta Road, is also another main thoroughfare for this part of town. U.S. 80 runs through the area as well, running through Bloomingdale, Pooler and Garden City.

Parking

There is good news and bad news when it comes to parking in Savannah. Most of the time, you shouldn't have too much trouble finding a spot (that's the good news), but if you are in the Historic Downtown, it is going to cost you. We focus our parking information section on that part of town for a couple of reasons: It's the place most tourists want to roam, and it's the main area in the city where you have to pay to park. Venture outside the Historic Downtown to Southside/Midtown, Islands or West Chatham, and you shouldn't have any trouble finding ample free parking.

Despite the high volume of vehicles jostling for places in the Historic Downtown every day, a metered spot or one in a garage or parking lot usually is available. You might not find a place right next to the square or shop you want to visit, but chances are good you will find one within comfortable walking distance. Be advised that it gets more crowded as you get closer to River Street — a main tourist hub overlooking the Savannah River. And remember that no matter how good the parking situation may be the rest of the year, it is going to be tough, if not altogether impossible, to get a spot near downtown on St. Patrick's Day. (See our St. Patrick's Day chapter for more information on the perils of parking during the city's big fest.)

Parking for the majority of the Historic Downtown area (and a little farther south) is metered, costing 15¢ to 50¢ an hour to park.

As we mention in other chapters, the downtown area is patrolled by vigilant parking enforcers who are out in force from 8 AM to 5 PM, Monday through Friday. Leave your meter expired for even 15 minutes, and chances are pretty good you are going to get a ticket. The damage will cost you anywhere from $8 for an expired meter to $50 for expired or missing state vehicle license tags. The majority of the tickets range between $8 and $15, and you have seven days to pay up. After that, an additional $8 is tacked on. . . . Wait 30 days to pay and your $8 ticket suddenly costs you an additional $18.

You won't find meters along Broughton Street, the main shopping district in the Historic Downtown that is experiencing a resurgence with new businesses, shops and restaurants after years of decline. To help bring people into the area, the city allows free two-hour parking along Broughton Street (with a few spaces that allow only 30 minutes of parking). You also can find free parking on three of the ramps taking you down to River Street. These free three-hour parking spaces can be reached by taking the Barnard, Abercorn, Lincoln and East Broad street ramps off Bay Street. You also will find free one-hour parking at the Visitor's Center at 301 Martin Luther King Jr. Boulevard. After the first free hour, the second hour is $1, and subsequent hours are 50¢.

City Parking Garages

The city has three public garages, where parking costs $1 for the first hour and 50¢ for each subsequent hour. At the **State Street Parking Garage** (at State and Abercorn streets) and the **Robinson Parking Garage** (at Montgomery and York streets), you can park all day for $4. Both are open weekdays from 6 AM to 9 PM. Hourly rates are the same

---

INSIDERS' TIP

Savannah is prone, especially in the late spring and summer months, to sudden, violent thunderstorms. The local television stations do a very good job at tracking these storms and will issue alerts. Typically, the storms roll out as quickly as they roll in. But always take cover. It should only derail your plans for about 20 minutes or so. In the meantime, enjoy the light show from somewhere safe.

Photo: Kyle Cason

Chatham Area Transit buses cover much of the county.

at the **Bryan Street Parking Garage** (Bryan and Abercorn streets), but it costs $5 to park all day. The Bryan Street garage is open and manned 24 hours a day, seven days a week.

City Parking Lots

The city operates a few public parking lots as well. Two are on **River Street** and cost $1 for the first hour, 50¢ per additional hour or $5 for the day. For easy access to the lots, from Bay Street take the Abercorn, Lincoln or Barnard street ramps to River Street. From the Lincoln ramp, turn left to reach the lots. From the Abercorn or Barnard ramps, turn either way on River Street to reach a city lot.

The city also operates the **Liberty Street** lot at the corner of Liberty and Montgomery streets on the western edge of the Historic Downtown. It's $2 per day to park there. And there is limited parking in the parking lot at the city's **Civic Center**, which is on Montgomery Street between Liberty and Oglethorpe streets. If there isn't an event going on, it will only cost you $1 to park at the center for the entire day.

There are a handful of private parking garages and lots in town. Most cater strictly to local businesses and have lengthy waiting lists to get in.

Visitor Parking Day Passes

Here's a real bargain. To take the hassle out of feeding meters, the city offers a Visitor Parking Day Pass. The pass, which costs $5, is valid for 48 hours and allows visitors to park at any meter in the Historic Downtown, at time-controlled lots and parking spaces, in the three city parking garages or at the city parking lot. The pass, which must be displayed on the driver's-side dash, is not valid in all the areas you would expect — private parking lots, hotel parking garages, sweeping zones, freight zones, bagged meters (meters that are covered to tell you that parking is not allowed), etc. You can purchase a day pass or find out more information on parking at the Visitor's Center or at the offices of City of Savannah Parking Services, 100 E. Bryan Street, 651-6470.

Public Transportation

Chatham Area Transit
900 E. Gwinnett St. • 233-5767 (TDD)

If you hear someone say they are going to "catch a CAT," they are referring to hitching a ride on the county's public bus system.

Chatham Area Transit (CAT) has a fleet of 63 buses (easy to spot with the outstretched cats on their sides) traveling on 22 routes throughout the county. Are the buses busy? In 1996, ridership was 3.5 million people.

You can get just about anywhere you want by catching a CAT, including the city's two malls, the Historic Downtown area and the Islands (except Tybee). CAT buses do not, however, go to West Chatham. It costs 75¢ every time you board a bus, and there are no transfers. Children shorter than 40 inches tall — the height of the fare box — get to ride free (limit two free children's fares per adult), and the fare for riders 65 and older and persons with disabilities is 37¢ each way. If you plan on doing a lot of traveling around Savannah on CAT, there is a weekly Flash Pass — good for unlimited rides — available for $12.

CAT buses run each day from 6 AM to midnight. Bus stops are marked with bright orange signs throughout the city. There is no service on Thanksgiving, Christmas or New Year's Day. CAT produces a comprehensive bus booklet, explaining everything from how to enter the bus to what routes will get you to different historic sites. The bus book, which also contains all the system's routes, can be found in area grocery stores, libraries and malls, among other places.

CAT also operates a paratransit van system for Americans with Disabilities Act (ADA) eligible riders. ADA-eligible visitors are welcome to use the TELERIDE service. In order to use the door-to-door service, visitors must present an ID card from their hometown transit system that proves their eligibility. TELERIDE costs $1.20 each way. For more information, call 354-6900. If you are in the Historic Downtown and want to purchase tokens, passes or talk to someone about a route, stop in at CAT Central, 124 Bull Street, in the city's historic courthouse.

CAT Shuttle

Chatham Area Transit, 900 E. Gwinnett St.
• **233-5767 (TDD)**

Although the CAT shuttle is another service of the county's public transportation system, it rates a separate entry because it caters in large part to the thousands of tourists exploring Savannah's Historic Downtown. The shuttle — which includes in its fleet smaller, electric-powered buses — makes a continuous, wide loop through Historic Downtown, stopping along the way at the Visitor's Center, several hotels, City Market, River Street and many historic points of interest. The shuttle stops are clearly marked with signs that have a map of the route and timetable. It costs 75¢ for a one-way ride on the shuttle, but there is a $2 pass that's good for unlimited trips for an entire day. You can pick one up at CAT Central or from a shuttle driver. All shuttles are wheelchair-accessible. More information on the shuttle can be found by calling CAT or stopping by CAT Central, 124 Bull Street.

Taxis and Limousines

While you will see cabs motoring around town, the best thing to do if you want taxi service in Savannah is to call the cab company directly. There are several companies in town, typically charging $1.20 to $1.30 per mile. In Historic Downtown, you will find many cabs lining up at major hotels and motels.

Limousine service also is available from a variety of local companies. Limos typically cost around $45 to $65 per hour, and some of the companies require a two-hour minimum. Advanced reservations are required to ensure prompt service.

Taxi services include **Adam Cab Inc.**, 927-7466; **Airport Taxi Service**, 269-5586; **All American Cab**, 961-7433; **Savannah Cab Company**, 236-2424; and **Yellow Cab**, 236-1133.

INSIDERS' TIP

You don't have to worry about feeding parking meters if you want to do some browsing on Broughton Street in Savannah's Historic Downtown. To encourage shoppers to come to the area, the city allows free two-hour parking along this busy thoroughfare.

For limousines, try **A & E Luxury Limousine Service**, 354-2982; **Low Country Adventures**, 966-2112, (800) 845-5582; and **Sherrie's Diamond's**, 355-8449.

Pedicab Savannah

Pedicabs are one of the newest ways to get around Savannah. These are the big, human-powered tricycles you see roaming around town. Usually there are a couple of tourists occupying the small red passenger seat in the back. Pedicab Savannah, 232-7900, has cabs available seven days a week from 11 AM to midnight. It costs $20 for a half-hour ride and $35 for an hour. In between peddling, your driver also will fill you in on historic sights as you pass by. If you want to take a shorter trip — like from your hotel to dinner — the pedicabs are available for short jaunts as well. Typically it costs between $5 and $10 for shorter excursions. Reservations are welcome.

Bicycles

At present, Savannah is not exactly a bike-friendly city. In fact, because of its age, layout and other considerations, there are only a few bike paths in town. However, relief may soon be in sight. In 1997, voters passed a measure that would allow several million dollars to be used to construct a series of bike paths throughout the county. As of this writing, it isn't known when construction of the bike paths is supposed to start.

Until then, if you see people in the historic area on bikes, they are usually the nice, comfortable kind with a basket on the front for carrying groceries. This is not to say you can't get around on a bike in Historic Downtown or a few other places — some people do. It is just not the preferred (or the safest) mode of transportation. In fact, there is one Historic Downtown road, Bay Street, that we recommend completely avoiding on your bike. Bay Street is a very narrow, heavily traveled road

where bikers will find themselves competing for space with 18-wheelers.

The designated bike paths in the city include:

West to East Corridor — 52nd Street to Ward Street to LaRoche Avenue to the entrance of Savannah State College.

North to South Corridor — Habersham Street to Stephenson Avenue to Hodgson Memorial Drive to Edgewater Drive to Hillyer Drive to Dyches Drive to Lorwood Drive to Tibet Avenue to Largo Drive to Windsor Road to Science Drive.

McQueens Island Trail — 6 miles for hiking and biking between Bull River and Fort Pulaski along U.S. 80.

McCorkle Trail — Wilmington Island at Charlie C. Brooks Park, 7001 Johnny Mercer Boulevard.

If you're in the Historic Downtown and are interested in renting a bike, try Wheelman Bicycle Shop, 103 W. Congress St., 234-0695.

Walking

The best way to enjoy Savannah's Historic Downtown is with a comfortable pair of shoes. In fact, *Walking Magazine* dubbed Savannah one of the Top 10 walking cities in the United States. To help find your way around on foot, we have included a walking tour in the Attractions chapter — that's a good place to start. Before you set out, however, here are a few tips, along with some rules of the walking road to make your trip a little easier.

Enjoy the Squares, Carefully

Historic Downtown is only about 2.5 square miles, so it is fairly easy to see the entire area on foot. Savannah's famed squares make the trip even easier because they are perfect for strolling. Besides spacious walkways, there are also many benches in case you need to take a rest between jaunts. Unlike some cities, pedestrians do not have the right of way in Savannah, so always yield to any traffic. Be particularly cautious when entering or exiting the squares. It is tempting to just keep on strolling, but it isn't always easy for drivers to see what is ahead as they make their way around.

Crossing Bay Street

Although the Historic Downtown is generally very pedestrian-friendly, one area that isn't is Bay Street. This is the main street running east to west in front of City Hall. Many tourists encounter Bay Street, as it must be crossed to reach River Street, the tourist haven running along the Savannah River. As mentioned in our Bicycles section, Bay Street is a very busy, narrow four-lane road that serves as the main throughway for 18-wheeler traffic trying to make it to other areas in the city. Many visitors think they can beat the traffic on Bay Street, get halfway across and find themselves stuck in the middle, dangerously close to traffic and unable to safely pass to the other side. To alleviate this problem, the city is in the process of constructing pedestrian-safe zones. These islands in the center of the street will give visitors a place to stand when crossing and are expected to be completed by the summer of 1998. However, the best way to safely cross Bay Street is to always use the signaled crosswalks. There are several to choose from along the street, and the familiar lighted "Walk" sign will always help usher you to the other side.

Getting to River Street

There are a couple of other pedestrian pitfalls you might encounter while trying to get to River Street. One option to get to River Street on foot involves walking down a flight of stairs. There is a hodgepodge of choices available — from the very steep and narrow to the very wide but close together. All are old, and many aren't particularly easy to navigate. Be extremely careful, and if you want, walk down the ramps that cars use to get to the river.

While you can avoid the tricky stairs this way, you won't avoid the cobblestone roads, another potential pedestrian pitfall. Although very beautiful and not as steep as the stairs, beware walking on cobblestone with any type of heeled shoe. These roads and ramps are uneven and difficult to walk on, even for people with the flattest feet. To help make the trip down to River Street easier, the city is install-

ing an elevator behind City Hall on Bay Street. The elevator will whisk riders down to River Street, avoiding the stairs and the cobblestone streets on its way. Like the pedestrian islands, the elevator project is expected to be finished by summer of 1998.

Quick Trips

Here are a few suggested routes that may save you some time and frustration when getting from a few popular point A's to point B's. Note that all these jaunts are in the 15-to-20-minute range.

Historic Downtown to Oglethorpe Mall — Option One: Take Whitaker Street south about 2 miles to Victory Drive. Turn left on Victory Drive, then right at the second light onto Abercorn Street. The mall is about 4 miles down Abercorn Street. Turn left into Oglethorpe on Mall Boulevard.

Option Two: Take Bay Street east. In less than 1 mile it runs into Presidents Street Extension. From President Street Extension, take Truman Parkway. After about a mile, exit to the right on DeRenne Avenue, then turn left onto Abercorn and look for Mall Boulevard after about 0.5 mile.

Historic Downtown to Savannah Mall — Take I-16 4 miles west to the Lynes Memorial Parkway exit and go south. After 2.5 miles on the Lynes Parkway, exit at the Southwest Bypass (also known as the Veterans Parkway) and continue 7.5 miles until it ends at Ga. 204. Turn left onto Ga. 204, which becomes Abercorn Street, and the mall will be some 3 miles ahead on your left.

Historic Downtown to Grayson Stadium — Take Bay Street east to President Street Extension, then take Truman Parkway to Victory Drive. Head west on Victory after exiting, and the stadium will be your left after about 1 mile.

Historic Downtown to Savannah International Airport — Take I-16 west to I-95 north. The airport is 14 miles away at Exit 18-A off I-95.

Historic Downtown to Amtrak Station — Go west on Liberty Street, which turns into Louisville Road after less than a mile. Take a left on Telfair Road, then a right on Seaboard Coastline Drive.

One innkeeper told us
she wanted her guests
to feel like they had just
visited one of their best
Southern friends.

Bed and Breakfast Inns

Savannah is perfect for romance. Scattered around the Historic Downtown are the city's "other" accommodations — bed and breakfasts, guest houses and inns. From a single suite in a privately owned 19th-century home to magnificently restored mansions, the city offers it all. Stay here and just outside your window you are apt to see horse-drawn carriages, magnolia trees in bloom and parks perfect for strolling. Many times you'll also spy a bride and groom coming up the stairs to enjoy their honeymoon — for the first or second time.

There are about 40 of these establishments to choose from, exclusively in Historic Downtown, and the list continues to grow. According to local innkeepers, one of the latest trends in this niche of the hospitality industry is the upsurge of smaller establishments with fewer than five bedrooms. These take many forms, but generally it's a case where homeowners have decided to convert a portion of their home into a bed and breakfast inn. There are more than 25 of these smaller establishments (more are coming), and they provide an interesting mix to the already established lot of bed and breakfast inns. Stay at one of these small newcomers, and you might have an entire ground floor of a house to yourself or share a historic townhouse with another couple.

No matter which one you choose, there is one constant: Each is as unique as its owner.

There are lavish, sophisticated inns where sit-down breakfasts are served every morning promptly between 8 and 10 AM in a meticulously restored parlor, and there are relaxed and comfortable places — so much so you feel compelled to take off your shoes and prop your feet up on the slightly worn couch.

The decor can be just as diverse. Maybe you will find a beautiful courtyard with fountains and wrought-iron furniture just right for quiet conversations . . . perhaps there will be marble fireplaces, whirlpool tubs and 18th-century antiques. Many bed and breakfast inns boast "Savannah Colors," a group of 56 historically accurate colors discovered by a local artist who went around scraping the newer paint off historic buildings and crawling through attics to uncover the hues Savannahians used to color their lives in earlier times. In these places the restorations are so exacting you may feel transported back to another era. Some hosts won't be happy until you are dripping with Southern hospitality. One innkeeper told us she wanted her guests to feel like they had just visited one of their best Southern friends. But if privacy is what you are looking for, that can be found too. Check into a few bed and breakfasts in town, and you might not see the owners for the entire visit.

Another great reason to choose these accommodations is that no matter where you

INSIDERS' TIP

Need a prescription filled in the wee hours of the morning? The Revco in Medical Arts Shopping Center across from Memorial Medical Center is open 24 hours.

stay, one of the most beautifully preserved historic areas in the entire country awaits just outside your doorstep. All of Savannah's 40 or so bed and breakfasts, guest houses and inns put you within comfortable walking distance of museum houses, squares, historic churches, monuments, art galleries, coffee shops and restaurants. If you choose, you can park your car and not see it for your entire stay.

Although owners may call their establishment a bed and breakfast, an inn or a guest house, in many cases the terms are interchangeable. In fact, the most popular term to describe an establishment of any of these types in Savannah seems to be "inn." However, you may find a one-room inn or a 32-room inn.

Whatever the title, guests can expect to find the amenities expected in finer accommodations including air conditioning and private baths. Most accept major credit cards, and a few allow pets. Because of the age and historic value of the properties, many of these lodging options, especially guest houses and smaller bed and breakfasts, no longer allow smoking inside. A few have limited or no wheelchair access, and some don't allow young children. Unless otherwise noted, assume that the listed establishments accept major credit cards, are wheelchair-accessible and do not allow pets. Our listings will point out which accommodations do not allow children. Still, we suggest calling ahead to check on these details if they are important to you.

And one note on parking. Parking is at a premium in the Historic Downtown. Most of the area, including residential neighborhoods, has metered parking that is patrolled by very vigilant enforcers. Leave your meter expired for even 15 minutes, and you are going to be ticketed. Do not make the mistake of thinking that because you have out-of-town license plates you will get a courtesy reminder — that doesn't happen here. It is important to inquire about the parking situation when you call to find out about your accommodations.

Finally, because of the limited number of rooms available and the popularity of Savannah, innkeepers suggest making reservations

FYI

Unless otherwise noted, the area code for all phone numbers listed in this guide is 912.

at least one month in advance. At some places, you may find six weeks is needed. To help with your reservations, there are several private reservation services in town, each having access to a portion of the market. Remember, these services only have a set number of bed and breakfast inns as clients. When making reservations, you may want to check with more than one reservation service to get a good idea of what is available. Two of these services are RSVP Bed and Breakfast Reservation Service of Savannah, 232-7787, (800) 729-7787, and Savannah Historic Inns & Guest Houses Reservation Service, 233-7666, (800) 262-4667. The Savannah Area Convention & Visitors Bureau also offers its own reservation service at (800) 444-CHARM.

Pricing Key

Our price code is designed to make it easier for you to gauge the cost of staying at one of the city's bed and breakfast accommodations. The dollar signs match up with a price range that indicates the average cost for a one-night stay for two adults, not including taxes, gratuities or add-on amenities. Most of the establishments charge anywhere from $10 to $25 extra for additional guests. Please inquire about the additional fee when you call for your reservation.

$	$99 and lower
$$	$100 to $150
$$$	$151 to $200
$$$$	$201 to $250
$$$$$	more than $251

Remember, this code indicates the average cost of an inn's options. Due to the wide variety of room options at some bed and breakfasts, it is not uncommon for one inn to offer both very modest, lower-priced accommodations and luxurious, upscale suites. Be specific when calling for details.

Historic Inns
of Savannah

Bed & Breakfast Inn 117 W. Gordon Street	800-238-0518
East Bay Inn 225 E. Bay Street	800-500-1225
Eliza Thompson House 5 W. Jones Street	800-348-9378
Foley House 14 W. Hull Street	800-647-3708
Jesse Mount House 209 W. Jones Street	800-347-1774
Joan's On Jones 17 W. Jones Street	800-407-3863
Lion's Head Inn 120 E. Gaston Street	800-355-5466
Magnolia Place Inn 503 Whitaker Street	800-238-7674
Manor House 201 W. Liberty Street	800-462-3595
Olde Harbor Inn 508 E. Presidents Street	800-553-6533
Planters Inn 29 Abercorn Street	800-554-1187
President's Quarters 225 E. Presidents Street	800-233-1776
River Street Inn 115 E. River Street	800-253-4229
The Gastonian 220 E. Gaston Street	800-322-6603
17Hundred90 Inn 307 E. President Street	800-487-1790

Integral to Savannah are its historic inns. They represent the core of the historic district and offer a glimpse of life in Old Savannah. Not only will you encounter Southern Hospitality at its best, you will also discover the singular flavor of what life in the past was like. Each is unique but each retains the elegance of this historic city. Each historic inn has its own personality. Some are elegant mansions that offer full service; some are beautiful suites in private homes. They range from colonial English architecture to Italianate. Most have enclosed private courtyards, ornate fireplaces, heart-pine floors, exposed Savannah grey brick walls, and all have wonderful antique and period furnishings. Each is located conveniently to all the sights you'll want to see in Savannah.

WWW.BBONLINE.COM

Following are our bed and breakfast listings. They are arranged in alphabetical order. Our entries are not meant to offer an all-inclusive list of city inns. Instead, we hope to give a good sampling of the variety of special bed and breakfast inns doing business in Savannah.

Azalea Inn

$$ • 217 E. Huntingdon St. • 236-2707, (800) 582-3823

There is something definitely different about the Azalea Inn. The furniture in the pale blue Victorian home is a little worn. The coffee table in the living room is just waiting for you to put your feet on it. The dishes aren't always picked up immediately from the table — just in case you want to stay and chat a few minutes longer. And you might, if you're lucky, find homemade beer bread on your continental breakfast menu. Innkeepers Maria and Tom Burns wouldn't want it any other way. "We are more casual, more homey and relaxed," Marie Burns says of the establishment. The Burnses treat their guests like family and friends who have come to visit their own home, because they have. They live in the seven-room inn on the outer reaches of the Historic Downtown.

The Azalea is decorated in an array of flowery Victorian colors and textures. There are velvet sitting chairs in the parlor, which has a light pink ceiling and lace curtains in the window. In the guest rooms you are apt to find four-poster beds, armoires and fireplaces, again surrounded by flowers blanketing the walls. You would almost feel like you are at your grandmother's house if it wasn't for the mural. Filling the walls in the dining room is an elaborate mural the Burns call "historical and hysterical." It depicts famous scenes and people from history. But look closely, and you might find both the innkeepers' faces among the legendary figures. Look even closer, and you may discover that instead of shoes the

generals or their ladies are wearing bunny slippers or are holding a baseball.

The Azalea Inn accepts pets with a $25 non-refundable fee. The inn is not wheelchair accessible.

The Ballastone

$$$-$$$$ • 14 E. Oglethorpe Ave. • 236-1484, (800) 822-4553

The Ballastone is a magnificently restored, four-story 1838 mansion just off Bull Street, one of the historic area's main thoroughfares. Arriving guests will notice the beautiful Queen Anne staircase in the entryway and the warm, lavishly decorated parlor off to the right. Ceiling fans, rice poster and canopy beds, marble-topped tables and fireplaces are some of the things you might find in one of the 18 individually decorated rooms. All are lavishly appointed and meticulously kept.

The Victoria Room, decorated in rich yellows, reds and greens has a massive king bed and whirlpool tub, while the Gazebo Room has deep greens and two queen beds. Besides the wonderful surroundings, guests enjoy afternoon Victorian tea along with evening hors d'oeurves. There is a terry-cloth robe waiting in the bathroom and nightly turndown service with chocolates and cordials. On weekday mornings, you can choose to have continental breakfast in your room, the parlor or outside in the courtyard. On Saturday and Sundays, guests are treated to a full breakfast at their choice of location. Children 12 years of age and older are welcome at The Ballastone. The inn has been recommended by *Brides*, *Glamour*, *Gourmet* and *Condé Nast Traveler*.

Broughton Street Bed & Breakfast

$$ • 511 E. Broughton St. • 232-6633

Staying at the Broughton Street Bed & Breakfast is like having your own private townhouse in the heart of Savannah's Historic Downtown. Because you do. There are just

---

INSIDERS' TIP

A great way to visit many of the bed and breakfast inns in town is to come to one of the annual tours of homes (see our Annual Events and Festivals chapter) that are held in the city. Many inns open their doors to allow people to come through and have a look.

two bedrooms in this small inn, located at a quiet end of Broughton Street, one of the area's main commercial thoroughfares, which is in the midst of a resurgence after years of decline. Innkeepers Tonya Snow-Saleeby and her husband, J.P. Saleeby, a local physician, purchased the 1883 townhouse in 1993. The couple lived there for two years, completing major cosmetic changes in preparation for converting it to a bed and breakfast inn. The master bedroom includes a four-poster bed, working fireplace, spacious bay window overlooking the street and a small whirlpool bath and shower combination. The other bedroom has a queen sleigh bed and bay window with a view of a small courtyard in the rear. There is no television in this second bedroom.

Besides their private quarters, guests get the run of the remainder of the home, which includes a library with a huge, inviting leather couch and fireplace. There is a main parlor and dining room perfect for relaxing. In the kitchen you will find a warm brick fireplace and a refrigerator stocked with wine, juices and other goodies. All the rooms are nicely decorated in antiques, like the beautiful pie safe in the kitchen. Original artwork, which is for sale, covers the walls throughout the home. Guests can expect a "continental-plus" breakfast, which includes things like fresh quiches and other delicacies. Wine and hors d'oeurves are served during the evening, and there is nightly turndown service featuring brandy and sweets. The inn is not wheelchair accessible. Children 12 and older are welcome.

Colonial Park Inn
$$ • 220 E. Liberty St. • 232-3622, (800) 799-3622

Spend some time with innkeepers Alice and Bob Clark, and you get the idea they like what they do. Since 1995 the Clarks have been inviting people into their Liberty Street home inn to stay in their two guest suites. They have gotten to know some of their guests so well they keep in contact with them, and the Clarks

have even received gifts — including a cherub that graces the courtyard — from satisfied customers. "It feels like we are getting paid for having friends come and stay," says Alice.

The Colonial Park Inn is a no-frills, comfortable, private alternative to some of the more formal inns in town. When asked what makes their establishment different from others, Bob says, "We don't have a Jacuzzi . . . this is not the Poconos." There are two complete, private entrance suites including a ground-floor apartment and carriage house. Decorated in soft colors such as lavenders and pinks, the rooms offer many of the things needed for a comfortable stay. The Garden Suite has two bedrooms: one with twin brass beds, the other with a queen. There is also a nicely decorated living room with fireplace, a cozy full kitchen and a washer and dryer. The suite looks out into the garden, which the Clarks were in the process of sprucing up when we visited. Behind the main house is the Carriage House Suite, a small, private accommodation with a king bed that can be converted to two twins. Decorated in soothing blues and pinks, it also has a small kitchen and a shower. Children 12 and older are welcome at Colonial Park Inn.

Columbia Square Inn
$$ • 125 Habersham St. • 236-0444

There are two things you notice when entering the Columbia Square Inn — the wonderful, wide heart pine floorboards and the white walls. While some innkeepers prefer lavish draperies and antiques to match, proprietor Barbara Wall's tastes are understated and elegant. There is no clutter here. The floors are nearly uncovered as are the windows, which reveal a view of the fountain in the center of Columbia Square and a magnificent magnolia tree reaching to the top of the home.

All rooms in the home, which the Walls restored several years ago (they occupy the ground floor), are spacious and decorated in the same manner. A leather settee or chair is neatly arranged in front of the fireplace along with a sofa to form a comfortable sitting area in each room. There are four-poster beds and armoires, and one of the rooms has an extra bedroom and a small veranda filled with gigantic ferns. Wall likes to give her guests their space, so everything they might need, from an ironing board to a cold drink, can be found in the rooms. There are small refrigerators, coffee makers and microwaves in each. She has found, however, that one of the most popular items she supplies are the Band-Aids — to take care of those blisters that come from all that exploring. Continental breakfast is served in the rooms, but guests are welcome to spend their time in the other parts of the inn including the parlor and dining room.

East Bay Inn

$-$$ • 225 E. Bay St. • 238-1225, (800) 500-1225

If you are looking for the charm and ambiance of a larger inn for a more moderate price, try the East Bay Inn. Located along bustling Bay Street, it features 28 rooms, each with 18th-century furnishings, hardwood floors, four-poster rice beds, high ceilings and large beautiful windows. Some of the rooms have exposed brick walls that add to the charm. All are very nicely done and meticulously kept. You will feel comfortable whether here on business or for a romantic getaway.

Although one of the larger accommodations in this category, East Bay Inn still has an intimate feeling. Continental breakfast is served every morning in a small cafe that was formerly a bar. It features pretty tables for two covered in white linen. Evening cordials are presented in the lobby decorated in deep greens and reds. Two rooms at the inn are set aside for pet owners; the $25 pet fee is non-refundable. The inn is not wheelchair accessible.

Another nice addition to the inn's offerings is Skyler's Restaurant. Located in the basement, with exposed brick walls and a huge, beautiful fireplace, Skyler's is a popular choice among locals, especially during the lunch hour. The menu is eclectic, offering items from fresh chow mein to chicken hoagies and crab cakes.

You can't beat the teriyaki chicken Caesar salad!

Foley House Inn

$$$ • 14 W. Hull St. • 232-6622, (800) 647-3708

When you first walk inside this 1896 brick home, you are struck by the rich burgundy and blue colors blanketing the walls and floors. The sumptuous design and detail extends throughout the parlor and all of the 19 individually styled rooms. Look out your window at Foley House Inn, and you will see beautiful Chippewa Square. There is historic First Baptist Church across the street and a statue of Gen. James Edward Oglethorpe, the founder of Georgia, in the center of the square.

FYI

Unless otherwise noted, the area code for all phone numbers listed in this guide is 912.

When asked what makes her inn distinctive, owner Inge Svensson Moore replies simply, "I am European." The influence is evident. As *National Geographic Traveler* put it, ". . . Moore has successfully fused continental with southern." In one suite decorated in deep pink, there is a canopied bed, two fireplaces and a lovely bay window. In another, the walls are painted rich yellow, and red draperies hang in the sitting area situated by the bay window. They also frame the bed. A large, ornate armoire with his-and-her mirrored closets fills one wall.

All the rooms include fireplaces, and many have whirlpool baths. Tea and hors d'oeuvres are served each afternoon in the parlor, and guests can choose to have their continental breakfast there, in the small courtyard or in their rooms. Evening cordials are also featured, as is concierge service for making all your dining and exploring reservations. Note that the inn is not wheelchair accessible.

The Gastonian

$$$ • 220 E. Gaston St. • 232-2869, (800) 322-6603

Everything about The Gastonian makes you want to come in and relax. From the magnificent verandas taking up one side of the house to the beautifully landscaped courtyard and warm rooms, innkeeper Anne Landers works hard to create an inviting atmosphere

---

Savannah's bed and breakfast inns welcome guests with warm Southern hospitality.

for her guests. And she succeeds. Little details sometimes make the biggest impressions, and that is what you notice at The Gastonian. Come back from dinner, and you will find pralines on your pillow, the fireplace going (when the weather's right) and soft music playing on the radio. There is a concierge who is friendly and ready to make all your reservations, from dinner to horse-drawn carriage tours. The inn is actually two historic, wonderfully preserved mansions next to each other along Gaston Street. It is in a residential neighborhood just a short walk from one of Savannah's most beautiful parks — Forsyth.

Georgian and Regency period antiques fill the main parlors, while all of the 18 rooms are styled individually. Each has a working fireplace, high ceilings, wooden floors, Persian rugs and is named for a noted Savannahian. In the Mary Hilyer room, you will find a beautiful antique quilt with green and red flowers covering one wall. There is a whirlpool bath with a basket of Cawell Massey soaps and lotions nearby and a wonderful stained glassed window. French doors take you out to the veranda, where a wicker lounge chair awaits. Newlyweds often come to The Gastonian to have their pictures taken in the beautiful courtyard. There is also a sundeck with a hot tub —

a perfect spot for enjoying continental breakfast. Children older than 12 are welcome at The Gastonian.

The Grande Toots Inn
$-$$ • 212 W. Hall St. • 236-2911

There was something about the dilapidated 1890 mansion that Dolores Ellis just couldn't ignore. That is, once she got past the plywood that boarded up the front door. "When I put my foot in the foyer, I saw all the beauty that had been beaten up . . . I said, 'Who let that grand ol' lady go down like that.'" What Dolores did know is that she had to have it. Thus began a long, arduous and sometimes painful restoration process that started in 1989 and ended September 20, 1996, with her grand opening. Today, the magnificent Grande Toots Inn is one of the newest and most unique additions to the city's bed and breakfast scene.

Dolores, who lived in several places including Washington, D.C., and California before settling in Savannah, brings a highly individual eye to her inn, which she completely decorated herself in rich colors and textures. A few blocks away from Forsyth Park, in a neighborhood being revitalized on the outer reaches of the Historic District, there is Italian marble on the floor, leaded-glass doors and handsome wallpapers. Look in one corner and you may find a piece of fine modern sculpture; another may have a beautiful antique cabinet with a glass door to show the white linens inside. One of the most striking things about the inn — something that separates it from many others — is that many of the wood surfaces were left unpainted, revealing wonderfully rich and warm browns throughout the house.

Besides the parlor, small dining room and large dining room (set up with intimate tables for two) where breakfast is served, guests have a choice of five different accommodations in a variety of styles and price ranges. Phyllis' Room is spacious, light and airy and includes a fireplace, Colonial queen bed with white antique coverlets and couch. The bath, which is full of windows and also very airy, has a whirlpool tub. If you want the experience of staying in a grand, restored inn but your budget is a little tight, you can choose from two smaller rooms. In Connie's Room there is a patchwork quilt on the bed and a fireplace. It shares a hall bath with the other smaller room. The Grande Toots Inn accepts small pets.

Habersham at York Inn
$$ • 130 Habersham St. • 234-2499, (800) 249-2899

Beautiful, richly detailed wrought-iron balconies extend along the front and side of Habersham at York Inn, greeting visitors to the 1884 Victorian residence. The same ironwork is found on the railings leading up to the handsomely restored home overlooking Columbia Square. Refinement and gentle manners are the hallmarks of this inn, owned by innkeeper Midge Rossini, who is careful not to intrude on her guests while giving them the personal attention they will appreciate and remember. One couple on their honeymoon arrived to find a gigantic white bow over their doorway . . . a young child once returned from dinner to discover Raggedy Ann sitting on her bed.

Two guest accommodations are available, both on the ground level and sharing a private

entrance. The rooms are finely appointed with period antiques. One, decorated in rich blue, has lace curtains, a chandelier, fireplace and sitting area. The massive, four-poster king bed was made from an iron fence, making for an interesting and striking presence. The second room has two sleeping quarters, one with a beautiful 1850 antique bed. The other has a twin. The entryway guests pass through to get to their rooms has been converted into two sitting rooms. This intimate and elegant space is where breakfast is served. It is also decorated with fine antiques and fresh flowers and is where a Christmas tree is placed each December for guests to enjoy. There is also a wet bar here, where a butler dressed in classic white, Mr. Wright, sees to his guests' needs.

Hospitality House
$$ • 409 E. Charlton St. • 236-6448

Behind a beautiful iron gate is the Hospitality House, a charming bed and breakfast on E. Charlton Street. This one-room suite takes up the entire bottom floor of Rita and Mike Spitler's house. Stay here and you will notice that the Spitler's have paid attention to detail. The suite, which includes a full kitchen, living room and bedroom, has many nice extras like a small entryway that is also a library, open-beam ceilings, a brick fireplace in the kitchen and a wonderful courtyard in the back with a mural painted on the gate. You will also find a pretty queen-size poster bed, microwave and even an ironing board.

Another nice amenity is Rita herself, who does all her own baking. Wake up and you may find made-from-scratch coffee cake, muffins or sticky buns on the menu. Fruit, bagels and many extras are also often a part of this deluxe continental breakfast that is served in your room.

Ivy Inne
$$ • 505 E. President St. • 236-1122

You will discover privacy, space, comfort and a very good value at the Ivy Inne. The inn consists of the entire ground floor of the innkeeper's home and includes a private entrance, living room, bedroom, kitchen and breakfast room. Staying here is like having your own apartment in Savannah's Historic Downtown. The living area is comfortably appointed with a sleigh bed, couch and brick fireplace. Just off the living room is the bedroom, where you will find another brick fireplace and a queen bed. Small, arched doorways bring you into the full kitchen. The little breakfast room is full of windows and overlooks the side yard. This light, airy and inviting space is the perfect spot to enjoy breakfast, which can include anything from Belgian waffles to seafood quiche and breakfast pizza. While some establishments discourage bringing small children or forbid them altogether, the Ivy Inne has a crib and high chair available. You will find other useful things such as an ironing board and umbrella in the hall closet. The inn is not wheelchair accessible.

Joan's on Jones
$$ • 17 W. Jones St. • 234-3863, (800) 407-3863

Joan's on Jones is one of the most established of the smaller bed and breakfast inns in Savannah. Innkeepers Joan and Gary Levy have been welcoming guests to their Jones Street home since 1990. The experience has taught them many things, Joan says, including the ability to sense who wants attention and who wants to be left alone. Whichever you need, the Joneses are ready to satisfy.

The inn features two suites, both with private entrances and ample room. It is another establishment where you'll feel as if you have your own apartment in the heart of the city. This particular apartment is in a restored 1883 Victorian townhouse on one of the city's most scenic streets. The Jones Street Suite is painted a rich terra cotta that Joan discovered in a local historic home and reproduced in her own. It is formally decorated and has pretty stained glass windows and two fireplaces. Over one fireplace is a collection of old letters

and other correspondence found behind the mantel during the restoration process. Reading lamps are over the bed for convenience, and there is a small kitchenette. The Garden Suite — just off the back courtyard that is perfect for relaxing with its lounge garden chairs — has a huge, brick cooking hearth, queen iron bed and exposed brick walls. There is also a full kitchen. This suite is less formal but more intimate and romantic.

When we visited, one of the producers from the movie *Midnight in the Garden of Good and Evil* was staying for an extended visit. When you arrive at Joan's on Jones, you will find a bottle of wine waiting for you. Well-behaved dogs are allowed in the back suite for a $50 non-refundable fee. Continental breakfast is served each morning, and if you are really hungry, one of the most popular Southern restaurants in the city, Mrs. Wilkes', is just down the brick-paved street (see our Restaurants chapter).

The Kehoe House
$$$ • 123 Habersham St. • 232-1020, (800) 820-1020

Listed on the National Register of Historic Places, the Kehoe House is a brick Victorian mansion overlooking the fountain in Columbia Square. Everything about this sophisticated, European-style inn — one of Consul Courts offerings — is grand and opulent, from the beautiful, leaded glass doors to the chandeliers dripping from the ceiling to the massive table that seats 10 in the double parlor.

Each of the 15 spacious rooms is furnished separately with armoires, decorative fireplaces and elegant antiques. Some of the rooms peer out into a nice side courtyard or have verandas for enjoying the cool breezes. English afternoon tea is served every day at 4 PM, and guests enjoy a full breakfast in the parlor. Children older than 12 are welcome at the Kehoe House.

INSIDERS' TIP

Don't forget about St. Patrick's Day. This is the busiest day of the entire year. If you are hoping to stay on or near the parade route, reservations should be made many months in advance. Some prime spots are booked a year ahead of time.

Lion's Head Inn
$-$$ • 120 E. Gordon St. • 232-4580, (800) 355-LION

A gold lion greets all visitors approaching the Lion's Head Inn, a 19th-century Federal-style mansion. Constructed by J.R. Hamlet, the inn is massive, formal and filled with period antiques found during the many travels of innkeepers John and Christy Dell'Orco. Several elegant pieces of furniture, including a beautiful yellow settee, fill the home's double parlor. There are also two identical marble fireplaces, French bronze and Italian marble statuary, a floor-to-ceiling mirror and several portraits. The library off the dining room has a wonderful day bed draped in red and gold satin. Oil lamps with crystals dripping from the sides date from the 1790s and rest near the brick fireplace. The room is opulent and soothing enough to sit down and relax. Off the parlor is the veranda, where you will find a white wicker swing overlooking the side garden and marble courtyard. There are several chairs — relax and enjoy the sound of the water in the small fountain.

The inn offers six guest rooms, two of which are suites. Like the rest of the house, the rooms are spacious, tall-ceilinged and formally appointed with Federal antiques. One room, decorated in rich, reddish-pink colors, has a beautiful portrait over the fireplace, an antique rocking chair and a matching sofa. Another room features more neutral colors and is light and airy with a four-poster bed. An afternoon wine and cheese reception is served in the double parlor. There is nightly turndown service, and continental breakfast is provided each morning in the dining room.

The Manor House
$$$ • 201 W. Liberty St. • 233-9597, (800) 462-3595

If you are looking for a little more space, The Manor House offers five lavishly decorated suites that feature a master bedroom and parlor. Some even have kitchens. Built as a private residence in the 1830s, it was formerly a part of The Ballastone, another one of Savannah's premier bed and breakfast inns (see previous listing). Some of the suites include huge whirlpool baths and lovely verandas perfect for relaxing with a book or pleasant conversation. Gigantic pocket doors that slip into the wall separate the master bedroom and parlor, providing privacy when needed.

The Twelve Oaks Suite, decorated in rich reds and greens, has two fireplaces, a queen sofa bed and a bench for two at the foot of the regular queen bed — the perfect spot for enjoying continental breakfast. Terry-cloth robes are provided, and this suite also features a huge whirlpool bath for soaking. Guests at The Manor House, which is across the street from the city Civic Center, will be treated to nightly turndown service featuring brandy and chocolates and a continental breakfast each morning in their room or the main parlor. It's so romantic and inviting, you may forget about the beautiful city just outside your doorstep. The Manor House is not wheelchair accessible. Children older than 12 are welcome.

McMillan Inn
$$-$$$ • 304 E. Huntingdon St. • 233-1447

The two-room McMillan Inn is another recent addition to the city's list of smaller bed and breakfast establishments. In February 1996, innkeepers Gray and Rose Hickman celebrated the grand opening of the inn, located in the couple's 1888 residence they affectionately refer to as Big Mac. While formal in some respects, it is completely lacking in pretension. Rather, the McMillan Inn is warm, inviting and romantic. The double parlor, which includes sitting and dining rooms, is decorated in a soft pink. There are lace curtains in the window and a lace tablecloth with pretty rose-colored place settings. A velvet settee takes up one corner of the dining room, while fanciful rococo chairs and a settee make up a nice seating area in the parlor.

INSIDERS' TIP

Because of new regulations passed by local government, all bed and breakfast inns now opening in Savannah must provide off-street parking for their guests.

When we visited there were two available accommodations and two more under consideration. The Lincoln Room features two queen beds, a gas fireplace with a pretty wooden mantel, an armoire with an oval mirror and a small secretary. The bath is very nice and open with a high ceiling, claw-foot bathtub and tall windows to let in the light. The Huntingdon Room is very spacious, with a four-poster bed and a nice seating area in a wonderful turret. Like the Lincoln, it is open and airy with a refrigerator, coffee and tea. Continental breakfast, featuring a bread tray, melons, other fruit and coffee cakes, is served in the dining room every morning from 8:30 to 9:30 AM. The inn is not wheelchair accessible. Children 12 and older are welcome.

The Jesse Mount House
$$$ • 209 W. Jones St. • 236-1774, (800) 347-1774

The Jesse Mount House is everything you might envision a grand Southern inn to be. From the massive entryway with its beautiful wooden staircase to the deep, red parlor and gigantic Oriental rugs, it is traditional with a hint of modern . . . extravagant, yet a little eccentric. Innkeepers Rob and Judy Cunningham purchased the inn after visiting Savannah on vacation and now preside over the 1854 Philadelphia-brick rowhouse on one of the city's prettiest blocks. There is, however, one Southern staple you won't find at the inn — Spanish moss. It was removed from the oak trees in front of the home several years earlier by the producers of the film *Glory*, who wanted — gasp! — to depict the street as a Northern village.

When entering the inn you immediately notice the large spaces, the colors and the rich decor. Look up in the parlor to the very high ceilings, and you will see a huge chandelier hanging from a gold-leaf medallion. There is also a modern, oversized, comfortable couch for relaxing. Walk through the parlor into the spacious, pretty dining room, which is decorated with huge red-flowered wallpaper, an oval table for eight and a gold mirror that takes up most of the wall over the fireplace. At the table, guests enjoy a sit-down gourmet breakfast, which includes such yummy things as poached pears and muffins.

When we visited there were six (soon to be seven) guest rooms ranging from the Garden Room — a bright, casually appointed carriage house complete with full kitchen, queen canopy bed, whirlpool bath and view of the courtyard — to the more traditional Jesse Mount Room, finely detailed in European linens with a rice canopy bed and softer, more muted colors. The Peter Tondee suite, on the street level with a separate entrance, is where actor Kenneth Branagh stayed recently while filming a movie in Savannah. Children older than 12 are welcome.

The Perry-Winkle Inn
$$$ • 119 W. Perry St. • 232-5816, (888) PERRY-WINKLE

The Perry-Winkle Inn is one of Savannah's newest bed and breakfast options. As they explain in their literature, innkeepers Karen Magrath and Stephen Perkins fell in love with the city when they would meet here and stay at local inns during their long-distance courtship. After they were married they decided to permanently live where they fell in love — an inn in Savannah. The couple spent a year renovating the ground floor of their Orleans Square home into a bed and breakfast suite. The results are fresh, light and inviting. It is also one of the few inns in town offering a suite with two complete bedrooms.

The inn is named for the flowers that grow in abundance in Karen's native Florida. Inside the suite, you will find beautiful antique brass beds, Battenburg lace and wooden floors taken from old barns and refinished to a high gloss. The living room has exposed beams and is painted white with a huge fireplace. On the walls there is artwork created by various members of the innkeepers' families — all pictures of periwinkles. The full kitchen is stocked and overflowing with everything from fresh fruit to soup. It also comes complete with dishes, glasses and everything else you might need during your stay. A huge whirlpool tub for two is in the freshly decorated bath. The couple is busily completing more rooms to add to their inn. By the time our guide reaches bookstores, at least two more rooms should be available. "Well-behaved" children are welcome. The Perry-Winkle is not wheelchair accessible.

Photo: Kyle Cason

The architecture of many Savannah bed and breakfasts recalls a bygone era.

912 Barnard
$ • 912 Barnard St. • 234-9121

One of the few bed and breakfast establishments in Savannah's Victorian District, 912 Barnard is on the fringe of the Historic Downtown area. This section of the city is filled with large, elaborate and beautiful Victorian homes and is one Savannah's most active areas of restoration. On some blocks you will find boarded-up homes in desperate need of rescuing, while others are well on their way to being revitalized.

There are two guest rooms at 912 Barnard, which is on a block where lots of restoration has taken place and is ongoing. This nice Victorian rowhouse is small, relaxed and laid back. The one formality hosts Kevin Clark and Don Musick impose is the sit-down breakfast every morning in the dining room, where you will find the table decorated with a lace tablecloth and pretty antique china. The adjoining parlor, also decorated in antiques, is light, airy and very relaxing with several beautiful windows to bring in the surrounding trees.

The Charleston Room, one of the guest accommodations, features a huge, wonderful bay window, a queen-size Charleston rice bed, sitting area and fireplace. In the less-sedate Miami room, you will find hubcaps from a '72 Cadillac Seville lining one wall. The art-deco inspired room also has a private balcony, and if you look closely you might find a pink flamingo or two. When we visited there were only two rooms available, but there are plans to open up two additional rooms in the near future.

Hotels and Motels

As you might have noticed while reading the Area Overview chapter, Savannah is a city of great diversity, and that characteristic holds true when it comes to the accommodations it offers its visitors. Savannah has several hotels that are large and contemporary, and others that are medium-size and quaint. It has motels that are moderately priced but comfortable, and others where, for a few dollars more, you'll be awash in amenities. Many of the hotels and motels offer suites in addition to rooms with the standard two double beds or one king-size bed, and a couple of establishments have nothing but suites.

For visitors seeking more of a personal touch, there are numerous bed and breakfast inns scattered throughout Historic Downtown; so many, in fact, we've devoted a separate chapter to them (see our Bed and Breakfast Inns chapter). Most of the hotels and motels described here are situated in one of two locations: on or very near Bay Street in Historic Downtown, or on or just off Abercorn Street near Oglethorpe Mall in the Southside/Midtown area. There are several motels in two other nearby locales — on or near the beach at Tybee Island, which is about 25 minutes from downtown Savannah, and out on Interstate 95, 10 or more miles from the heart of the city. The motels at the beach are discussed in the Tybee Island chapter of this book. The accommodations out on I-95 represent several major chains and should offer no surprises, but we recommend that, if your destination is Savannah and not the House of the Mouse or some other touristy spot in Florida, you stay closer to our city and soak up some of the atmosphere of our historic old town.

You can be in the midst of that atmosphere by taking a room at a hotel or motel in the downtown area. In most cases, you'll pay accordingly for the location, but you can find some values if you're not too picky about the view from your room and extras you receive. Another cost-saving option is to stay at lodgings in the Southside/Midtown area. You'll be out of the mainstream of tourism but not by much — many of the motels and inns in Southside-Midtown are only 5 miles from Bay Street, which equates to 12 to 15 minutes traveling time if you avoid rush-hour traffic. While most of these establishments are geared toward people on business trips, the innkeepers are more than happy to have tourists stay with them. Another reason to take a room in Southside/Midtown is that parking will be free. That's not necessarily the case if you stay in Historic Downtown, and we've indicated in our listings if and what you'll have to pay to park at a hotel or motel there.

Each of the hotels and motels described in this chapter accepts major credit cards and is accessible to the handicapped. Almost all have nonsmoking rooms, and most do not allow pets; if a hotel or motel does not have nonsmoking rooms or does accept pets, that information is included in our listing for the establishment. Also, expect that all accommodations will have color cable TV. If you're looking for premium channels, a phone call might be in order.

Price Code

Each entry includes a symbol denoting a price range for the average one-night stay, in-season, for two adults. Note that these prices do not include tax, gratuities and add-on amenities such as premium movie channels or room service. Here's the code:

$	$65 or lower
$$	$66 to $90
$$$	$91 to $125
$$$$	$126 or more

The in-season generally runs from mid-March through October. Some establishments decrease their rates during the hot summer months, and others jack them up on weekends, so you should call in advance to ascertain how much you'll have to spend. If you're planning to stay here on St. Patrick's Day weekend, expect to fork out considerably more than you would at any other time of year and make reservations months in advance. (See our St. Patrick's Day chapter for more information.)

Historic Downtown

Best Western Historic District
$$ • 412 W. Bay St. • 233-1011

Once you arrive at the Best Western Historic District, you can park your car and leave it for the rest of your stay, according to the folks who run the 142-room motel. The Best Western fronts on Bay Street, and the motel's rear building is on the western end of River Street, placing the three-story establishment about a block from the shops and restaurants along the river and in City Market (see our Attractions chapter). It's within walking distance of much of the Historic District. If you want to do your sightseeing while riding, hop on a tour bus or trolley at the motel's front door. The Bottleworks restaurant just off the lobby serves breakfast from 6 until 11 AM, and there's

a fenced-in pool for swimming and sunning on the River Street side of the property. Eighty-seven of the rooms have two full-size beds, and the rest have kings. Parking is free, and pets are allowed at this motel, which has been accommodating visitors to Savannah since the early 1970s.

Days Inn-Days Suites Historic Riverfront
$$$ • 201 W. Bay St. • 236-4440

When you stay at this Days Inn, you're a block from two of Savannah's meccas for tourists — River Street to the north and City Market to the south. This three-story brick motel is built right on the sidewalk of Bay Street, and if you take a suite, you'll be staying in a building that dates to 1851 and was once the home of the Bargain Corner, a grocery store that was a local landmark. The 57 suites have high-ceilinged bedrooms with queen-size beds, kitchens with full-size refrigerators and living-dining rooms with pull-out sleeper sofas. Including the suites, there are a total of 253 rooms, all of which are entered from interior hallways secured by a coded access system. There's an outdoor pool and the Daybreak restaurant, which serves breakfast, lunch and dinner. Parking is complimentary in a secured garage adjacent to the motel.

DeSoto Hilton Hotel
$$$$ • 15 E. Liberty St. • 232-9000, (800) 426-8483

A $6 million renovation completed in the summer of 1997 left the 245-room DeSoto Hilton looking like . . . well, 6 million bucks. The extensive makeover gives the hotel an aura that's both classical and rich: The lobby, hallways and rooms are adorned with white columns, dark wood paneling and burgundy and forest-green furnishings. The 15-story hotel stands in the midst of the Historic District, and the views from rooms on the upper floors, particularly those with balconies, are spectacular. The concierge floor — the 13th, numbered as such by hotel officials apparently unconcerned with superstition — offers what staff members call the "skyline view." You'll pay $30 extra to stay there, but you'll get the view, a room featuring deluxe amenities such as the Hilton's trademark terry cloth bathrobes and the use of a private lounge serving continental breakfasts in the morning and drinks and hors d'oeuvres in the evening. Step out on the balcony of the lounge and enjoy a panoramic look at the graceful Eugene Talmadge Memorial Bridge and Savannah's riverfront. If you really want to stay in style, request a "corner king" — a room with a king-size bed, balcony, two large corner windows and a bathroom equipped with a double vanity. You can dine on the premises at The Pavilion, a first-floor restaurant serving breakfast, lunch and dinner Southern-style, and you can unwind at the Lion's Den lounge, where the bar brings back memories of TV's *Cheers* and the library is stocked with real books.

The hotel pool is on a second-floor deck that can accommodate outdoor gatherings of as many as 150 people. The Hilton has 19,000 square feet of meeting space indoors in the form of executive board suites with seating for five to 30 people; the Harborview Room, whose 15th-floor location makes it the highest meeting room in the city; and a 5,408-square-foot ballroom with 18-foot ceilings and elaborate crystal chandeliers. Also available for get-togethers is a recently refurbished atrium on the hotel's ground floor. The Hilton was built in 1968 on the site of the DeSoto Hotel, which was constructed in 1890 and was a Savannah landmark for decades. A sitting room off the lobby of the Hilton affords guests a glimpse of the old hotel — the walls are covered with memorabilia, including framed banquet programs from visits by several U.S. presidents. Covered, secured parking is available for $7 a day, and valet service is $10. There is also a limousine shuttle service.

Hampton Inn Savannah Historic District
$$$ • 201 E. Bay St. • 231-9700, (800) HAMPTON

The Hampton Inn only opened in January 1997, but the eight-story hotel fits right in with the city's Historic District. The stucco, brick and ironwork of the exterior has the look of old Savannah. So does the lobby with its authentic gray bricks that were found on the site during construction, heart-pine floors from an old mill in central Georgia, antique and traditional furniture, Persian rugs and dark wood bar — from England, but purchased at a local antique store. The regal way to stay at this Hampton is in a king special — a corner room with windows on two walls, a king-size bed, a refrigerator and a microwave. The hotel has eight of these, each for $20 extra.

The Hampton is at Bay and Abercorn streets one block south of River Street. Check out the glorious view of the Savannah River, the Eugene Talmadge Memorial Bridge and Historic Downtown from the rooftop pool, but wear shades on a sunny day — it's bright up there. The hotel offers a complimentary, deluxe continental breakfast each day from 6 until 10 AM. There is 1,450 square feet of meeting space with limited food service for groups of 30 or less, and catering by outside sources is allowed. You can park in the hotel's underground garage for $2.50 a day, and if it's full, the fee will get you a spot at the city-owned garage across Abercorn or at metered spaces throughout the city.

Hyatt Regency Savannah
$$$$ • 2 W. Bay St. • 238-1234, (800) 233-1234

You can't sleep where James Edward Oglethorpe laid his head while founding Georgia in 1733, but you can get darn close by bedding down at the Hyatt Regency Savannah. The spot where Oglethorpe pitched his tent is in the small park on Bay Street in front of the 364-room hotel. But that's not the main attraction of the Hyatt Regency — the hotel's drawing card is its location overlooking River Street and the Savannah River. The hotel is

---

INSIDERS' TIP

The Old Town Trolley swings by motels near Oglethorpe Mall each morning around 9 AM to pick up people who want to take tours of Savannah's Historic District. The trolley makes a return trip at 3:30 PM. If your motel isn't a regular stop, ask the desk clerk to call Old Town and have them come by and get you. The tours are $15.

built over the brick street, creating a tunnel for autos and occasionally the *River Street Rambler*, a switch engine pulling a handful of railroad cars.

This location places guests in the midst of Savannah's waterfront shops and festivals and affords terrific views of the river and the ships plying it. You'll pay $25 extra for a room on the river, but where else can you get accommodations with a "Ships Passing Light" that's activated when a huge oceangoing vessel glides by your window? On the fourth of the hotel's seven floors, you're at eye level with the decks of freighters and other ships as they make their way in or out of port. There are also great views of River Street and/or the river from the Hyatt's second-floor sundeck, various meeting rooms, a glassed-in restaurant aptly called the Windows and an adjoining lounge named MD's. Speaking of glassed-in, that's a perfect description of the hotel's Harborside Center, an 11,000-square-foot gathering place on River Street offering floor-to-ceiling views. The Hyatt has a total of 28,000 square feet of meeting space, including an 8,000-square-foot ballroom and a banquet room.

The hotel lobby is an atrium with the aura of a rain forest. Palm trees and bird-of-paradise plants adorn the floor of this open space, which stretches seven floors to the ceiling, and bright green philodendrons cascade from the balconies of interior rooms. The atrium is also the headquarters of a concierge who can schedule tours of the city and help plan your stay, and you can board tour buses at the front door of the hotel. The Hyatt accommodates fitness buffs with an exercise room and a heated indoor pool. If you're arriving in style, there's a helicopter pad on the roof. Valet parking is $10 per day.

Planters Inn
$$$ • 29 Abercorn St. • 232-5678, (800) 554-1187

Built in 1912 as the John Wesley Hotel, the Planters Inn has been thoroughly remodeled but retains the elegance and charm of the early days of the 20th century. The hotel's high ceilings, four-poster beds, lavish draperies and

FYI

Unless otherwise noted, the area code for all phone numbers listed in this guide is 912.

antique furniture give you the feeling you've stepped back in time, but the friendly staff and the services they provide will make you aware you're very much in the present. Among the extras are nightly turn-down service and complimentary continental breakfast at nearby Eli's Delicatessen. Parking is available at a neighboring garage for $5.25 per day.

The seven-floor hotel is on the site of a three-story residence built in 1812 as one of two twin houses. The other house still stands next door to the hotel. The exquisite lobby of the Planters Inn is part of the original house, which mirrored the one built beside it. If you decide to stay at this hotel, ask about a room with a fireplace (there are two on the seventh floor), a balcony (there are four) or a view of Reynolds Square, the little park in front of Planters Inn. The centerpiece of the square is a statue of John Wesley, the founder of Methodism for whom the hotel was originally named.

Quality Inn Heart of Savannah
$$ • 300 W. Bay St. • 236-6321, (800) 228-5151

One of the operators of the Quality Inn Heart of Savannah likes to say that the tourist hot spots of River Street and City Market grew up around this motel on Bay Street. The Quality Inn opened in 1963, long before those two nearby areas became popular with visitors. The two-story, 53-room motel continues to provide guests with friendly service and well-maintained accommodations. Rooms with two double beds or queen beds are available. There's no pool, but a complimentary continental breakfast is available in the lobby from 7 until 10 AM each day, and pets are accepted free of charge. Tour buses stop at the front door, and the folks who man the front desk will help you make arrangements.

River Street Inn
$$$ • 115 E. Bay St. • 234-6400

If you're seeking accommodations with a historic atmosphere in the midst of the activity of River Street, this inn might be for you. The guest rooms of this 44-room hotel occupy the top three floors of a renovated five-story cotton warehouse on the Savannah River. The main entrance to the inn and its "parkside" rooms look out on Bay Street; the back side of the inn has rooms overlooking River Street and the river. Occupants of 11 of the riverside rooms can step out onto small French balconies for a grand view of the street and the waterway.

Each of the inn's rooms is different; there are various decors featuring a mixture of authentic period antiques and reproductions, including four-poster and canopy beds. Hardwood floors, area rugs and polished brass bathroom fixtures complete the elegant look of old-time Savannah. The lower floors of the structure housing the River Street Inn were built in 1817 to store cotton for export, and the top three floors were added in 1853. The inn was opened in 1987.

Full continental breakfasts and passes to an enclosed, seven-story parking garage about a block away are included in room charges. Guests also receive complimentary newspapers in the morning and homemade chocolates before retiring in the evening, and there's a wine reception in the afternoon. The inn can accommodate small meetings and conferences, with seating for 15 in its Board Room and for 40 in its Meeting Room. None of the rooms at the inn are designated as nonsmoking, and there's no swimming pool.

Savannah Marriott Riverfront
$$$$ • 100 General McIntosh Blvd.
• 233-7722, (800) 228-9290

When we think of the Savannah Marriott Riverfront, the word "spacious" leaps to mind. The atrium at the heart of the hotel has 7,000 square feet of carpeted space that can easily accommodate themed events and trade shows attended by as many as 500 people. A total of 140 rooms on the seven upper floors of the hotel open onto balconies with views of the atrium, the north side of which looks out on the Savannah River through expansive, floor-to-ceiling panes of glass. The hotel's 15,000-square-foot ballroom is the largest in the city, and there are an additional 9,000 square feet of meeting space in the form of conference rooms and boardrooms.

Among the hotel's 46 suites are 10 deluxe models, each containing 1,500 square feet of space. The Marriott's two restaurants — T.G.I. Friday's and River's Edge — seat 250 and 95, respectively. You get the picture — everywhere you look, there are scads of space. The real lure of the Marriott, though, is its location on the Savannah River and the riverwalk at the eastern end of River Street. A total of 119 of the hotel's 383 rooms face the water, and for $20 to $35 extra, you can be, as the Marriott folks say, "perched on the river" with a knockout view of passing ships. Special accommodations include rooms on the concierge floor and deluxe suites with walk-around wet bars, glass-topped dining tables and large bathrooms featuring double vanities. Guests staying on the private, keyed concierge floor (the eighth) enjoy complimentary continental breakfasts and hors d'oeuvres in late afternoon.

There are two pools — one outside and the other in the atrium — and fitness and whirlpool rooms just off the atrium. You can get breakfast and a great view of the river at the River's Edge, lunch and dinner at Friday's, room service from 6:30 AM until midnight and complimentary coffee in the atrium from 6 to 9 AM. If you'd like a tour of the city, you can make arrangements at the trolley desk in the lobby. Parking in one of the hotel's 627 spaces is $7 a day. The hotel, which opened in 1992 as a Radisson and was converted to a Marriott in 1994, hosted 750 athletes, trainers and coaches while serving as the Olympic village for yachting events in 1996.

INSIDERS' TIP

When you visit Savannah, you're staying in "the most beautiful city in North America," according to Le Monde, one of the leading newspapers of Paris, France. Condé Nast Traveler magazine reader polls named Savannah one of the Top 10 U.S. cities to visit in 1994, '95 and '96.

The Mulberry
$$$$ • 601 E. Bay St. • 238-1200, (800) HOLIDAY

The Mulberry aims for a classic Savannah look and hits the mark. Traditional furnishings, oil paintings, polished hardwood floors and chandeliers grace the lobby, and antique furniture is sprinkled throughout the hallways and sitting areas. Reproductions of antiques and burgundy and forest-green furnishings carry out the theme in the 122 rooms, 26 of which are suites. The two- and three-story establishment — a Holiday Inn historic hotel — surrounds a tree-shaded brick courtyard adorned with wrought-iron tables and chairs. Then there's the name of the inn, which refers to the mulberry trees planted by Georgia's colonists in an attempt to raise silkworms. The trees grew on a site that is now Trustee's Garden, across East Broad Street from the hotel.

Want more history? The Mulberry's got it. The two-story portion of the inn housing the lobby was built as a cotton warehouse and livery stable in the mid-1800s, then was converted to a Coca-Cola bottling plant in the early 1900s. The building was transformed into an inn and expanded in the 1980s. The front desk occupies the spot where the bottling machinery did its work, and there are photos on one of the walls of the lobby to prove it. The Mulberry's elegant Cafe Courtyard serves breakfast, lunch and dinner, and the inn presents a complimentary tea each afternoon from 4 until 6 PM — hot and iced tea, coffee and dessert treats are provided for guests. Other features of the inn are a secured outdoor pool, a rooftop hot tub and Sgt. Jasper's Tavern, a full-service lounge. The hotel has three meeting rooms, with the largest accommodating 200 people theater-style, and the inn offers full banquet and catering services. Parking at a garage across a side street is $5 per day.

Southside/Midtown

Best Western Central
$ • 45 Eisenhower Dr.
• 355-1000, (800) 528-1234

This motel at Eisenhower Drive and Abercorn Street, near one of the main entrances to Hunter Army Airfield, is part of the nationwide chain but has some distinctive touches that give it a local flavor. An arbor draped with star jasmine adorns the pool area, which is set in a large grassy strip crowned by a huge oak tree. The bar of The Edge lounge, above the motel lobby, is decorated with color photographs of patrons. On the last Wednesday of each month, complimentary hors d'oeuvres, beer and wine are served from 5:30 until 7:30 PM at a manager's reception. The two-story motel has 87 rooms with two double beds and 42 rooms with king-size beds. A complimentary continental breakfast is available from 6 to 10 AM each day in an area off the lobby that doubles as meeting room for as many as 50 people seated theater-style. There's also an upstairs meeting room that can accommodate 75. Small pets are allowed for a $10 fee.

Clubhouse Inn of Savannah
$$ • 6800 Abercorn St. • 356-1234, (800) 258-2466

The folks at the Clubhouse Inn strive to create a "home away from home" atmosphere at their spacious motel on Abercorn Street. They serve a complimentary buffet each morning that gives guests the opportunity to enjoy a full breakfast in a glassed-in dining room looking

---

INSIDERS' TIP

Savannah should have 403 more guest rooms in the spring of 1999. That's when the Westin Savannah Harbor Resort, a $98 million luxury hotel, is scheduled to be completed on Hutchinson Island. The 16-story structure will have 20 more rooms than the Savannah Marriott Riverfront, which will make the Westin the largest hotel in the city.

out on the pool and patio. In the evenings from 5 until 7 PM, the manager hosts a reception where each guest can have up to four complimentary mixed drinks. And once each month there's a cookout featuring steak dinners for $10 per person. The two-story inn, part of a small chain of motels scattered throughout the United States, has 138 interior rooms that include 16 suites. Each suite has a bedroom and a sitting area/kitchen with a wet bar.

Courtyard by Marriott
$$$ • 6703 Abercorn St. • 354-7878, (800) 321-2211

Savannah's Courtyard by Marriott stands between two of the city's busiest thoroughfares, Abercorn Street and White Bluff Road, but the three-story motel's beautifully landscaped grounds will give you a feeling of being away from the madding crowd. The centerpiece of the motel is the tree-filled courtyard with its quaint gazebo and swimming pool. Just off the pool is an enclosed whirlpool surrounded by lots of space for lounging, and there's a recently renovated fitness room near the lobby that sports all-new exercise equipment. The Courtyard's large dining area is open for breakfast, with a full meal priced at $6.95 and continental servings available. There are 144 interior rooms including 12 suites, and all have sleeper sofas. Rooms on the upper floors open onto balconies. There are two meeting rooms, each of which can accommodate 24 people seated at tables.

Days Inn Oglethorpe Mall
$ • 114 Mall Blvd. • 352-4455, (800) DAYS INN

This two-story motel is definitely near the action. It's within easy walking distance of Oglethorpe Mall, near about 30 restaurants and right next door to a miniature golf course. However, the 122 rooms and pool are set well back off busy Mall Boulevard. Seventeen of the rooms have queen beds, and the others

have two doubles. The Days Inn was built in 1973 and for years has been the site of Taylor's Restaurant, which serves breakfast, lunch and supper in a dining room off the motel lobby.

Days Inn Southside
$ • 11750 Abercorn St. • 927-7720, (800) DAYS INN

Days Inn Southside is a little farther out of the Historic Downtown than the other motels in this section, but it's an ideal place to stay if you want to be close to Armstrong Atlantic State University, St. Joseph's Hospital and Savannah Mall, all of which are just down the road. If you want to ride downtown to do a little sightseeing, you can be on Bay Street in about 20 minutes, providing you make the 8.5-mile trip at a time other than rush hour. All 114 rooms were thoroughly remodeled in 1996, and the "business rooms" designed for corporate travelers have small refrigerators with microwave ovens sitting atop them. The Hospitality Suite adjacent to the lobby offers complimentary, full continental breakfasts (including ham and sausage biscuits) from 7 until 10 AM each day. The nicely kept grounds are the site of a pool and — no kidding — a helicopter pad (the owner of the two-story motel, Savannahian Merritt Dixon, added the pad to accommodate his chopper).

Fairfield Inn by Marriott
$ • 2 Lee Blvd. • 353-7100, (800) 228-2800

The three-story Fairfield Inn, one of Marriott's economy motels, gives guests several options involving entry to rooms. The first floor has "drive-up" rooms accessible from the parking lot, the second floor has rooms with secured balconies, and the third floor has rooms entered from interior hallways. Guests use key cards to activate the elevator to the second and third floors. The inn has rooms with king-size beds, two double beds and full-size beds. The Fairfield, on Lee Boulevard between Abercorn Street and White Bluff Road,

INSIDERS' TIP
Savannah welcomed 5,142,000 visitors in 1996. Figures for 1997 weren't available, but a continued rise in tourism seemed likely, due to the effects of a certain piece of literature. Keep reading that book, y'all.

offers complimentary continental breakfast from 6 until 9 AM on weekdays and 7 to 10 AM on weekends, and there's free coffee in the lobby around the clock. If you're seeking some exercise, try the outdoor pool or drive the short distance to the Family Center YMCA on Habersham Street — your visit there is free when you show your Fairfield key card.

Hampton Inn Midtown
$ • 201 Stephenson Ave. • 355-4100, (800) 422-2671

This Hampton Inn is just off the beaten path of Abercorn Street and, like the motels nearby, is close to Oglethorpe Mall and the stores and offices that surround it. The Hampton is where Habersham Street dead-ends into Stephenson Avenue, which is about a block from the Family Center YMCA, where you can show your motel key card and gain access to the Y's extensive fitness facilities. If you'd like to do some swimming, take a dip in the motel's kidney-shaped pool at the rear of the property far from passing traffic.

The Hampton was built in the mid-1980s but underwent a $900,000 renovation in the summer of 1997 that refurbished the motel's 129 rooms (single king bed and two double bed options are available). The two-building, two-story motel offers complimentary continental breakfast for guests from 6 until 10 AM in a dining area off the lobby that seats about 80 people, and punch and cookies are set out for snacking from 10 AM until 6 PM. There are two meeting rooms, each capable of accommodating 20 people, that double as sleeping rooms.

Holiday Inn Midtown
$$ • 7100 Abercorn St. • 352-7100, (800) 255-8268

As its name implies, this 174-room Holiday Inn stands smack dab in the middle of town. The two two-story wings of the motel flank a courtyard that includes a spacious pool area set among oleanders and magnolias. Some rooms have king-size beds, others have two doubles. The Marketplace restaurant serves breakfast and dinner, and Mulligan's, the recently remodeled 110-seat lounge, contains an entertainment center featuring video games and a golf simulator. The Holiday Inn Midtown offers same-day dry cleaning service and a shuttle service to Savannah International Airport. Kids 12 and younger stay and eat free. The motel's several meeting rooms can accommodate up to 300 people.

Homewood Suites Hotel
$$$ • 5820 White Bluff Road • 353-8500

The largest all-suite establishment in Savannah offers guests free local telephone calls, an Executive Center for business travelers and free transportation within 5 miles, which will get you all the way to Savannah's River Street. The Executive Center sports a typewriter, com-

INSIDERS' TIP

As best we can determine, Savannah's first hotel was a place called the Mansion House on Bay Street. While poking around the Georgia Historical Society, we found an article from a *Savannah News-Press Magazine* of 1969 stating the city's "earliest inns were the Mansion House, City Hotel and the Screven (House), all of them operating about the middle of the last century." Englishman John Lambert, writing in his *Travels through Lower Canada and the United States*, published in 1810, said he stayed in March 1808 at "the hotel of Colonel Shelman," a house "fitted up with separate sleeping rooms." Lambert indicated the hotel was the only establishment of its kind in Savannah. A blurb in the *Patriot and Commercial Advertiser* newspaper of June 1, 1807, refers to the arrival of General Moreau at the Mansion House hotel, leading us to believe the places where the general and Lambert stayed were one and the same.

puter and printer, and you can arrange to send and receive faxes at the front desk.

The 106 suites are configured as either one-bedroom "Homewood" suites, the hotel's most popular offerings; as master suites, which have fireplaces; or as two bedroom, two-bath suites. Each suite features a fully equipped kitchen with two-burner stove, microwave and full-size refrigerator; a sleeper sofa; and telephone with voice mail. Leave a grocery list at the front desk, and your shopping will be done for you and charged to your room. In addition to the three-story building and two two-story buildings housing the suites, there is a spacious lodge that can accommodate 50 people for the hotel's complimentary, deluxe continental breakfasts and evening socials. The socials, held from 5 until 7 PM each day, offer guests beer, wine, soft drinks and hors d'oeuvres such as pizza and stuffed potatoes. A pool and whirlpool are situated just outside the lodge, and there is a court nearby where you can play basketball, tennis or volleyball. If you need to burn off more energy, try the fitness room off the lobby in the lodge. The hotel also has two meeting rooms — one for up to 50 people and the other for 10. Pets are welcome, but there is a non-refundable $70 charge for housing them.

Imperial Suites
$$ • 7110 Hodgson Memorial Dr.
• 354-8560, (800) 344-4378

Although Imperial Suites is near Oglethorpe Mall and nestled amid the shopping centers and office parks of the Southside, this three-story hotel looks and feels as if it belongs in downtown — downtown New Orleans, that is. The hotel is built around an atrium decorated with palm trees, exotic plants, a gurgling fountain and intricate black ironwork.

The French Quarter theme surfaces in the sitting rooms of the hotel's 52 suites with their wrought-iron tables and chairs. Each sitting room also contains a sofa, coffee table, easy chairs and a wet bar with a small refrigerator, microwave oven and coffee maker. Six luxury suites have larger sitting rooms, king-size beds and whirlpool bathtubs. All rooms are entered from the interior of the hotel. Guests can exercise in the outdoor pool at the rear of the hotel

or work out at the nearby Family Center YMCA on Habersham Street, where visits are free, compliments of Imperial Suites. Afterward, you can relax in the hotel's combination whirlpool bath-steam room. Many of the guests are business people, and there is a conference room seating 45.

La Quinta Inn
$ • 6805 Abercorn St.• 355-3004,
(800) 531-5900

The La Quinta opened in the late '70s and is one of the older motels on Savannah's main drag, Abercorn Street. The rooms, however, look brand-new because of a remodeling in the spring of 1996. With its red-tile roofs and stucco exterior, the motel has the distinctive Southwestern appearance of all La Quinta Inns and espouses the chain's credo of providing spacious, comfortable rooms and "100 percent guest satisfaction." The two-story motel has 154 rooms with kings and doubles housed in two buildings that ramble over nicely landscaped grounds between Abercorn and White Bluff Road. The outdoor pool is tucked in a secluded nook set way back off the street, and there is HBO on the tube. A complimentary continental breakfast is available from 6 until 10 AM each morning in an area off the lobby. La Quinta accepts pets weighing 20 pounds and less.

Residence Inn by Marriott
$$$ • 5710 White Bluff Rd. • 356-3266,
(800) 331-3131

This Residence Inn has 66 one- and two-bedroom and studio suites under one roof. All suites have kitchens, and each of the two-bedroom accommodations has two full bathrooms, three televisions and a wood-burning fireplace. Kitchens are equipped with ovens, stoves and dishwashers, and the staff of the inn will do your grocery shopping for you. Just leave your shopping list at the front desk, and the groceries will be charged to your bill and deposited in your room by 6 PM. Copies of *USA Today*, the *Savannah Morning News* and Sunday's *Atlanta Constitution* newspapers are free, as are deluxe continental breakfasts served in the Gatehouse sitting area. The Gatehouse is also the scene of social hours held from 5 to 7 PM Monday through Thurs-

Photo: Kyle Cason

Decorative ironwork distinguishes homes in the Historic Downtown.

day — complimentary appetizers, beer, wine and other beverages are served, and guests attending these gatherings snack on goodies such as hot chicken wings, nachos, lasagna and black beans and rice. For those seeking recreation, you can enjoy an indoor pool and whirlpool, an exercise room and an outdoor court for tennis, basketball or volleyball. Pets are welcome, but there is a $70 non-refundable cleaning fee.

Suburban Lodge

$ • 10614 Abercorn St. • 920-7700, (800) 951-7829

The Suburban Lodge, which opened in March 1996, offers accommodations geared to business people and travelers who are staying in town for a week or more. Although the Lodge will rent its neat, compact rooms for shorter periods of time, rates are structured for week-long stays — $169 a week for one person, $183 for two people and $227 for three. Each of the 130 rooms at the two-story motel has a kitchenette and television with HBO. There is a laundry room containing five washing machines and six dryers. There are no nonsmoking rooms and no pool, but pets weighing less than 20 pounds can be housed for a fee of $25 per week.

MICHAEL FABER'S

Clarys CAFE

Where Savannahians have
been enjoying
great food and lively
conversation since 1903.

SERVING

BREAKFAST • LUNCH • DINNER
HOMEMADE DAILY SPECIALS

OPEN 7 DAYS A WEEK

Located in the Heart of
Historic Savannah

Jones at Abercorn Street

912-233-0402

Restaurants

Your taste buds will be glad you came to Savannah — but your waistline might not. The city offers a quantity and variety of restaurants completely out of proportion to its size. The recipe just adds up: Take plenty of fresh shrimp, crab and fish from local waters, mix in the cultural contacts that go with more than 250 years as a seaport, consider the long growing season and the agricultural tradition of the South in general, then flavor with a generous helping of legendary Southern hospitality. The result is scores of restaurants serving just about every type of food imaginable.

The setting improves the flavor of food, as any good hostess will tell you. Savannah's restaurants serve their guests in unique settings that include the stone-walled halls of former cotton warehouses on the riverfront, balconies overlooking breathtaking marshes, historic mansions with antique furnishings and unpretentious little places nestled under towering oaks.

Remember the scene in the movie *Forrest Gump* in which the character Bubba launched into a list of ways to prepare shrimp — a list which clearly took him several hours to recite? Well, in Savannah you'll find at least that many ways of serving this local favorite. If your day takes you out to Tybee Island, you're likely to spot shrimp boats, often working surprisingly close to the beach. And if your meal involves shrimp, you are about to discover what an amazing difference real freshness — as opposed to being iced down and flown inland — can make in its flavor.

With a little pushing and shoving, you can put Savannah's restaurants into four main categories: seafood, soul food or regional cooking, ethnic and a sprinkling of haute cuisine. Some, of course, will defy labeling, and others will boast a menu that has a grip on one or more categories.

We make no claims to offer a complete and comprehensive restaurant listing here. Instead, we've singled out places we like to go, places our friends talk about, and places that have been fixtures for Savannah travelers for years. We've tried to make sure that we included something for every pocketbook, as well as something for every taste.

We've assigned price codes to help you anticipate in advance what you'll find in the price column of the menu. Remember, though, that these are guidelines only. Your selections could easily bump the meal up or down by at least a category. That said, however, we add that we find the cost of eating out in Savannah compares favorably with the cost of similar meals in other cities.

Price Code

Here is our price chart, based on dinner for two, minus beverages (alcoholic or otherwise), appetizer, dessert, tax and tip.

$	$15 and lower
$$	$15 to $20
$$$	$21 to $50
$$$$	$50 and higher

Since we've left many of the desirable parts of a special meal out of our calculations — things like the perfect wine to complement a complex seafood dish or a sherry-flavored Savannah trifle as dessert — you'll want to use these as general guidelines only.

You'll also note that we haven't included chain restaurants, except in a very few exceptions where location or other circumstances make them especially significant. Savannah boasts a wide range of such chains, with many fine examples among them, but we feel our readers will already know what to expect from these restaurants. You'll find these listed in the Yellow Pages of your telephone directory.

City ordinances require restaurants to provide nonsmoking sections, and you'll find some restaurants restrict smoking entirely. We've noted these and have pointed out some special provisions made for smokers.

Parking in the Historic Downtown is always an adventure, so give yourself plenty of time to find a space, particularly if you have dinner reservations. Restaurants outside the downtown area generally have plenty of nearby parking.

If your travels take you to nearby Tybee Island or Hilton Head, South Carolina, note that restaurants in those two locales (a smattering of eateries in Tybee, more than two dozen outstanding dining spots in Hilton Head) are discussed in the individual chapters that cover those two island destinations.

FYI

Unless otherwise noted, the area code for all phone numbers listed in this guide is 912.

featured on the lunch menu is the Southern pecan chicken salad.

The dinner menu offers specialties such as salmon Oscar, rib-eye steak flamed with Irish whiskey and Cuban chicken with black beans. There's room for 65 diners inside and 45 on the patio; you can smoke outside or in the bar but not in the main dining room. Maher, who opened the cafe in 1991, recommends making reservations for dinner on weekends during the spring and summer.

Chutzpah & Panache
$$ • 251 Bull St. • 234-5007

Ladies who lunch often lunch here. The trendy upscale clothing is in the front; the charming lunch spot is in the back. Lunch is the only meal served. Our favorites from the menu include grilled eggplant sandwiches and the crab salad. When picking a side dish, opt for the potato salad. The dessert selections tend toward the decadent, cheesecakey type of entry and change often. (See the Clothing section of our Shopping chapter for more information.)

Historic Downtown

The Cafe at City Market
$$$ • 224 W. St. Julian St. • 236-7133

Dine indoors at this restaurant in the eastern part of City Market, and you'll experience the atmosphere of a big-city bistro during the 1930s, '40s and '50s, with recorded music to match (Sinatra is a favorite in the evenings). Dine outdoors, and you'll be sitting under an awning on an open-air patio "watching the world go by," as owner and chef Matt Maher puts it. At either location, you choose from a menu that's somewhat international in content and contains an item or two you've probably never encountered before, such as these lunchtime sandwiches: grilled cheese with artichoke hearts, mushrooms and prosciutto ham; and Parmesan-crusted crab cake. Also

Clary's Cafe
$$$ • 404 Abercorn St. • 233-0402

Visitors to Savannah know Clary's as the place where characters from *Midnight in the Garden of Good and Evil* congregated, but this cafe at Jones and Abercorn streets was, as owner Michael Faber puts it, "famous before The Book." Clary's opened in 1903 and, as a pharmacy and soda fountain, has been a hangout of Savannahians throughout its existence. Faber bought it in February 1994, during the week that *Midnight* hit the bookstores, and he renovated the building and converted the pharmacy into dining space. He's made the most of the restaurant's connection to The Book, with touches such as a stained-glass window depicting the Bird Girl and the *Mid-*

night in the Garden T-shirts worn by employees. (For much more on the phenomenon du jour, see The Book chapter.)

As stated earlier, however, there's more to Clary's than it's association with the bestselling book. The restaurant has extensive menus for breakfast, lunch and dinner, each offering food that Faber says is made from scratch each day, including the four different soups. Among the breakfast specialties are the malted waffles and pancakes made with a special flour brought in from Michigan; for lunch, there are a variety of salads, burgers, sandwiches and those aforementioned soups; and in the evening, featured items are the seafood pot pie, the fillet of red snapper served on a seasoned oak plank, the old-fashioned pot roast and the Triple Peaks salad, which has scoops of tuna, chicken and shrimp salads on fresh greens and pasta salad. Leading the list of appetizers are the crab cakes and fried green tomatoes à la Clary's. Faber, who was in the restaurant business in Chicago for 35 years before moving to Savannah in 1988, also takes great pride in the cafe's desserts, milk shakes and malts. Clary's is open daily but closed on Wednesday nights.

Crystal Beer Parlor
$ • 301 W. Jones St. • 232-1153
$ • 6710 Waters Ave. • 691-1033

We go to the Crystal for the onion rings and the burgers, which are made from fresh sirloin ground in the beer parlor's kitchen, but there are many other selections on the menu — crab stew, shrimp salad sandwiches, chili dog platters, hot roast beef sandwiches and the baked stuffed flounder. The Crystal on Waters Avenue at Stephenson Avenue also serves prime rib, and the corn bread (homemade and served by the loaf) is a big seller at both locations.

The downtown Crystal at the corner of Jones and Jefferson streets is a local landmark, having been a favorite of Savannahians since it opened in 1933. Owner Conrad Thomson — the grandson of the Crystal's original proprietors, Blocko and Connie Manning — says some longtime customers have told him they've been dining at the restaurant ever since it's been in existence. The Crystal on Jones Street, with its high-back, padded booths and dark-wood paneling, retains the feel of the '30s. If you want to get an idea of what Savannah and its people were like 40 or 50 years ago, take a look around the old Crystal, where the walls bear enlarged photographs depicting those times.

If you dine in the evening at the downtown Crystal, you might have the pleasure of being served by the genial, gracious Monroe Whitlock, who began waiting tables there in the early 1950s. He still works a couple of nights a week and has been honored for his long service with a photograph on the restaurants' menus.

The new restaurant on Waters Avenue, which opened in January 1997, carries out the old-time theme in its decor. There is a full bar offering 10 draft beers (the bar at the original Crystal is in the main dining room, and six beers are on tap). Both eateries serve lunch and dinner. The Southside restaurant is open seven days a week; the original Crystal is closed on Sundays. Reservations aren't required, but they're taken and are recommended for groups of 10 or more.

Debi's Restaurant
Debi's After Dark
$$$ • 10 W. State St. • 236-3516

Professional people flock to Debi's at lunchtime for the salads and specials, which change daily and consist of a meat and two vegetables. In the evenings, the restaurant on State Street between Whitaker and Bull streets becomes Debi's After Dark, which offers fine dining featuring seafood and steaks — in particular, "Steaks on the Hot Rock." The rocks are lava rocks imported from Italy, and your steak continues to cook on one after it arrives at your table.

Debi's opened in 1992 in what had been a men's clothing store, but owner Debi Christiansen and members of her family have been in the restaurant business in Savannah for 25 years. (Her mom runs Mary's Seafood and Steakhouse on the Southside.) Debi's seats 130, has a full bar and also serves breakfast. A note for movie buffs: Debi's is the restaurant where Forrest Gump's girlfriend Jenny waitressed while living in Savannah.

The Exchange Tavern & Restaurant
$$$ • 201 E. River St. • 232-7088

The oldest restaurant on River Street, The Exchange serves lunch and dinner in what was once a cotton warehouse built in 1799. The Exchange opened in 1971 and for a time offered mainly sandwiches, but the restaurant later expanded into the dinner market. Among the standouts on the dinner menu are the shish-kebab dishes and the teriyaki tuna — yellowfin tuna marinated in soy sauce and fruit juices, chargrilled, basted with herb butter and then brushed with a brown sugar, sesame and ginger glaze. The folks at The Exchange haven't forgotten how to make outstanding sandwiches, in particular their reubens and our favorite, a chargrilled hamburger they call the Congress. With your sandwich, you get a choice of a side dish, and we recommend the zesty German potato salad.

The Exchange occupies two rooms — one's a full bar where you can eat and which is the only smoking area during lunch. At night, part of the dining room has tables for smokers. This eatery is owned by Eric Traub, the nephew of legendary Savannah restaurateur Herb Traub, who operated The Pirates' House for many years.

The Express Cafe
$$ • 39 Barnard St. • 233-4683

This popular breakfast and lunch spot has a European air. We've never had anything here that wasn't good, and we've worked our way through the menu over the years — quiche, stuffed croissants, soup in bread bowls, sandwiches loaded with fresh vegetables, fresh baguettes and so on. The desserts are special things as well. The Express opens at 7 AM weekdays and 8 AM weekends, closing at midafternoon. It's closed Monday and Tuesday.

Garibaldi's Cafe
$$$ • 315 W. Congress St. • 232-7118

A varied and sophisticated menu of continental dishes awaits at this small, attractive restaurant that is part of a small chain (there's another one in Charleston, South Carolina). Dinner is served nightly, and there's a full bar and extensive wine selections. Try the whole scored flounder in apricot sauce. Pasta dishes are staples, and there are always interesting seafood selections along with decadent desserts. Reservations are available, and dress is business attire on up.

Huey's
$$$ • 115 E. River St. • 234-7385
$$$ • 7804 Abercorn St. • 692-0022

Huey's brings the Big Easy to Savannah with its New Orleans-style cuisine. The River Street Huey's, with floor-to-ceiling windows right on the sidewalk, also offers a great view of the Savannah River, a circumstance that makes a breakfast of cafe au lait and beignets something special. For those unfamiliar with "N'awlins," as Huey's owner Bill Hall refers to his Louisiana hometown, beignets (pronounced ben-yeas) are delectable French doughnuts. Huey's also has some specialties for breakfast eaters with heartier appetites, in-

INSIDERS' TIP

If you're looking for a lunch or an afternoon snack that's healthful and fast, stop by the Brighter Day natural foods and organic produce store at the corner of Bull Street and Park Avenue. Brighter Day's juice bar deli caters to folks with a vegetarian outlook by offering a variety of salads, soups, sandwiches and smoothies — beverages made with fruit, fruit juices, yogurt and other stuff that's good for you and tastes good too. You can carry out your food or eat inside or outside at small tables facing the south end of Forsyth Park. We recommend the baked cheddar sandwich — a meatless alternative to the BLT — and the Strawberry Yummie Yogurt Smoothie — a frothy concoction made with frozen strawberries, bananas, yogurt and apple juice. The deli is open daily from late morning until late afternoon.

Photo: Kyle Cason

This historic mansion now houses a restaurant.

cluding eggs Benedict and eggs sardou, the latter consisting of a bed of creamed spinach with artichoke hearts on a toasted English muffin with two poached eggs topped with hollandaise sauce.

For lunch and dinner, there are dishes such as red beans and rice served with andouille sausage, and muffuletta, a sandwich made with freshly baked bread, Genoa salami, cappicola ham, provolone cheese and an olive dressing. The food is zesty but moderately spiced; if you want more zip, there's Tabasco sauce on your table.

Huey's has seating for 70 in its streetside dining room and for 20 in the adjacent patio bar. Smoking is allowed in the bar but not the dining room. The restaurant has been in business on River Street since 1987; Savannah's second Huey's opened in fall 1997 in Oglethorpe Mall. The menu and size of the new restaurant are the same as those of the downtown Huey's, but, alas, there's no view of the river.

Il Pasticcio
$$$ • 2 E. Broughton St. • 231-8888

You'd never guess this large, upscale bastion of fine Italian cuisine once was a low-end department store. They're proud of their wines, and the dinner-only menu is creative and extensive, with ambiance to spare. Consider this one on the dressy side, with reservations recommended.

The Lady and Sons
$$ • 311 W. Congress St. • 233-2600

There's a menu at this Southern specialty restaurant, but unless you're going to be here long enough to return repeatedly, skip it and go directly to the buffet. This is the slow-

If you decide to get a take-out meal along River Street (or anywhere else near the water), resist the urge to share it with that single begging seagull that will invariably show up. Otherwise, hordes of its friends will arrive, and you will have no peace.

cooked, perfectly seasoned stuff that Southerners consider real home cooking. Fried chicken, squash casserole, seasoned greens, "hoecakes" (ask, if you don't know), cheese biscuits — you get the picture. Lunch is served daily, and dinner is available on Thursday, Friday and Saturday.

Morrison's Cafeteria
$ • 15 Bull St. • 232-5264

This landmark on Johnson Square has offered cafeteria-style dining to tourists and Savannahians working in the heart of the downtown area since 1960. You can get a relatively inexpensive lunch or dinner here quickly, so don't be discouraged when the line to the serving counter is long — it sometimes is at lunchtime, especially when a tour bus has pulled up. The menu changes daily, but you can bank on seeing old standby entrees such as turkey and dressing, roast beef, fried chicken, fried fish and liver and onions. Also prominently displayed on the serving line are numerous scrumptious-looking desserts; diet-conscious as we are, we always find it a challenge to pass by these sweets without succumbing to the temptation to stick one on our tray, particularly the sweet potato pie.

Mrs. Wilkes'
$$, no credit cards • 107 W. Jones St. • 232-5997

Lunch at Mrs. Wilkes' is served beginning at 11 AM, but the line of customers starts forming well before then on the shady sidewalk alongside Jones Street. The line usually moves at a fairly rapid clip, but Mrs. Wilkes says folks have told her of waiting for two hours to get in the door of her establishment, which is in the basement of a three-story house. "They said it was worth the wait," says Mrs. Wilkes, whose first name is Sema. It's worth the wait because

dining at Mrs. Wilkes' is about more than eating lunch; it's about having a unique experience.

At 11, after the first group of diners has filed in and taken their places around the seven 10-seat tables in the two low-ceilinged dining rooms, Mrs. Wilkes rings a little bell and says grace. Then members of her family and staff place heaping platters and bowls of Southern-style food on the tables, serving it country-style. Chatting with newly made acquaintances at your table, you dig in and pass around the platters and bowls (sometimes as many as 18 of them). After you've finished eating, you help clear your table, taking your dishes and silverware to the rear of the room. As you're leaving, a new group of 10 diners is admitted to take their seats at your table.

At our most recent visit to Mrs. Wilkes', the tables were loaded with fried chicken, barbecue chicken, beef stew, sausage, baked ham, collard greens, snap beans, black-eyed peas, squash, rice and gravy, okra and tomatoes, mashed potatoes, candied yams, pickled beets, apple salad and macaroni salad. The menu is changed on a daily basis, "because some people eat here every day," says Mrs. Wilkes. However, you'll always be served beef stew, baked ham and fried chicken, the latter being a specialty of the house. When asked about her fried chicken by Bryant Gumbel during an interview on NBC television's *Today* show, Mrs. Wilkes said, "If the Colonel's was as good, he'd be a general."

Mrs. Wilkes got started in the food service business in 1943 when her husband's job brought him to Savannah from the central Georgia town of Vidalia. L.H. Wilkes took a room at a boarding house in the building where Mrs. Wilkes' is now. Mrs. Wilkes would visit L.H. on weekends, got to know the owner of the boarding house and eventually began help-

---

INSIDERS' TIP

In a rush for lunch? Whip into Tanner's sandwich shop at 21 E. Broughton Street and grab a couple of chili dogs and the orangiest orange drink you'll ever taste or see — a mixture of fresh and frozen orange juices, water, a little salt and plenty of sugar. Tanner's, in business since 1942, is on the south side of Broughton near the corner of Drayton Street, and it's open in the morning and afternoon Monday through Saturday.

ing her out by cooking for the boarders. The Wilkeses eventually raised a family in Savannah and in 1965 bought the boarding house, which they restored and converted into apartments. Mrs. Wilkes also cooked and served meals, first for her neighbors, then for visitors; word of the quality of her food and her down-home hospitality spread, to the extent that *Condé Nast Traveler* magazine in 1990 named her place one of the 50 most distinguished restaurants in the United States.

Lunch at Mrs. Wilkes' is $10, and you can eat breakfast there for $5. The dining rooms are open Monday through Friday. Mrs. Wilkes doesn't take credit cards but says she will accept a check "if it's good." Smoking is prohibited.

Nita's Place
$$ • 140 Abercorn St. • 238-8233

Definitive soul food is what you will find at Nita's Place. This bastion of home cooking has acquired a reputation far bigger than its little hole-in-the-wall location in the heart of downtown would lead you to believe. Dig in to the slow-cooked, superbly seasoned vegetables and meats that distinguish classic African-American cooking. The menu varies daily, but look for favorites like squash casserole and macaroni and cheese.

The place is small, so you are likely to have to wait for a seat at one of the elbow-to-elbow tables. Pass the time reading the walls and the windows, which are festooned with national magazine clippings about Nita's, letters of praise from patrons local and foreign and snapshots of customers tackling their meals. Dress is casual. Nita's serves lunch only and is closed on Sunday.

The Olde Pink House Restaurant & Planters Tavern
$$$ • 23 Abercorn St. • 232-4286

Experience Savannah as it was in post-Colonial days by dining at the Georgian-style mansion that is The Olde Pink House. This is the only restaurant in Savannah — lodged in a historically significant house — a structure built in the late 1700s for wealthy merchant James Habersham Jr. and expanded in the early 1800s when it was the Planters' Bank, the first such establishment in Georgia. Known also

as the Habersham House, the building on the northwest corner of Abercorn and Bryan streets has a pink exterior because it was constructed of bricks made from red clay and covered with white stucco; the red bled through the stucco, coloring it pink, and the structure has been painted that hue ever since. A tea room was opened in the house in the 1930s, and it has been a restaurant for the past 50 years.

The Olde Pink House serves regional cuisine in seven elegant dining rooms occupying the upper two floors of the building, which has a basement housing the Planters Tavern. Examples of this type of cooking are the sautéed shrimp with country ham and grits, she-crab soup laced with sherry, Caesar salad with corn bread oysters, crispy scored flounder with apricot shallot sauce and grilled pork tenderloin crusted with almonds and molasses.

Before dining, you might want to walk downstairs to the tavern and relax with a drink while sitting in front one of the large brick fireplaces on either end of the room, which was originally the house's kitchen. Take a good look around and you'll notice a metal door that once was part of a bank vault; it now leads to the restaurant's wine cellar. Other points of interest within the house are the oil painting of residents of old Savannah and notable Americans such as George Washington, a display featuring Habersham's somewhat gaudy shoe and knee buckles, and the staircase winding from the first floor to the second.

The Olde Pink House is open for candlelight dinners seven days a week, and a jazz pianist performs in the tavern every evening except Mondays. The bar is also the only place where smoking is allowed. Reservations are definitely recommended; if you're interested in dining in the restaurant's most romantic spot, ask for a table by a window in the second-floor Office Room — it has a view of picturesque Reynolds Square.

Olympia Cafe
$$$ • 5 East River St. • 233-3131

This authentic Greek restaurant is a welcome respite from the glare and bustle of River Street. Brick walls and flooring, lots of plants and soft lighting add to the atmosphere, but that's all incidental to the food. Favorites here include Red Snapper Aegean, served with to-mato sauce, spices and feta cheese. Lamb chops marinated in olive oil and herbs before chargrilling are another favorite. Spanakopita is one of those dishes by which a Greek restaurant is measured, and you'll find this version of the flavored spinach pastry measures up well. On the lighter and less-expensive side of the menu, you can choose gyro sandwiches and chicken kabobs. Beverage selections include Greek coffee, and there is a full bar. Dress is generally nice and casual, but kick it up a notch for weekend dinners, when reservations are recommended. Don't be confused when you arrive — Olympia Cafe also operates a quick-and-casual takeout place to one side and a 35-flavor ice cream parlor to the other.

The Pirates' House Restaurant
$$$ • 20 East Broad St. • 233-5757

This restaurant is a local institution. Locals have been coming here, and steering tourists here, for decades. The restaurant wanders from room to room, all of which are atmospheric (haunted, in fact, by some accounts). These quarters are Savannah's link to Robert Lewis Stevenson's classic *Treasure Island*. When you have children in your party, it's hard to find a classy restaurant that accommodates younger patrons. The Pirates' House does this quite well, without damaging arrangements for adults out for a dress-up dinner. The menu is varied and includes lots of seafood. Locals head for the lunch buffet and always remember the fried chicken. The dessert menu is vast and intimidating: We suggest you consider dining here and skipping dessert, then making a return trip for dessert only before you leave Savannah. Nice casual will do for dress, but brush up a little bit for dinner. There's full bar service, and Hannah's, an attractive nightclub, is upstairs (see our Nightlife chapter). The restaurant also has a gift shop.

The Riverhouse Restaurant
$$$ • 125 W. River St. • 234-1900

The Riverhouse and its bakery occupy four bays of an old cotton warehouse near the west end of River Street, and the bricks and thick wooden beams of the building lend charm to the upscale but casual atmosphere. Operated by the Harris family, which established it in 1982, The Riverhouse specializes in fresh seafood. Featured dishes include the grouper Florentine, which is served atop angel-hair pasta, and salmon Anna Marie, in which the fish is encrusted in potato and onion and served with Pinot Noir and lemon-butter sauces. Among the appetizers are the seafood strudel — a light pastry filled with spinach, feta cheese, shrimp and scallops — and blackened shrimp served on cheddar cheese grits with a tasso gravy. The restaurant serves lunch and dinner, and breakfast is available in the bakery.

606 East Cafe
$$ • 319 W. Congress St. • 233-2887

Good American food in a fun and funky setting is what you can expect here. Among other aspects of the far-out, anything-goes decor, you might find a basket of wind-up toys on your table and lingerie hanging from a line overhead. Choose from various burgers (plain to boursin burger and back), lasagna, a dozen-plus sandwiches including meat loaf, and more. Lunch and dinner are served seven days a week. A full bar is available, and there's outdoor seating when weather permits (it usually does).

INSIDERS' TIP

Vegetarians won't find a dedicated vegetarian restaurant in Savannah, but they will find some accommodating selections on most menus. A word of warning is in order, however — Savannah cooks traditionally season vegetable dishes or soups with "side meat" such as salt pork or ham hocks. If a strictly vegetarian regimen is important to you, check with your server before casually assuming a restaurant's vegetable plate is entirely meat-free.

Six Pence Pub
$$ • 245 Bull St. • 233-3156

A restaurant serving lunch and dinner daily, the Six Pence takes on the more convivial atmosphere of a pub as the evening unfolds. What you'll find here is what you might expect from a pub in Great Britain in terms of food and cozy atmosphere. Six Pence offers specials each day, with patrons having a particular liking for the shepherd's pie, the meat loaf and mashed potatoes, the French onion and potato soups and a meat pie made with mushrooms and beef that's been marinated in beer.

Most of the memorabilia adorning the walls and bar is authentic — from the Toby mugs to the coronation collectibles dating to 1898 to the pub signs, some of which are more than 200 years old. Be sure to look for the ship's bell that's a replica of the one on the *Titanic* and was a souvenir gift from that ill-fated vessel's maiden voyage. Also search out the handwritten, handpainted proclamations presented to King George VI in 1937.

Stop by on Friday and Saturday evenings, and you'll hear live performances of jazz, blues or Irish folk music. The pub also has its own ghost, a fellow who reportedly hangs out in the basement and has a penchant for turning faucets and light fixtures on and off. Nicknamed "Larry" by Six Pence owner Wendy Snowden, this apparition has the appearance of a young man from the late 1800s.

Spanky's Pizza Gallery & Saloon
$$ • 317 E. River St. • 236-3009
$$ • 308 Mall Way • 355-3383
$$ • 200 Governor Treutlen Rd., Pooler
• 748-8188
$$ • 404 Butler Ave., Tybee Island
• 786-5520

Ansley Willilams, Alben Yarbrough and Dusty Yarbrough opened the first Spanky's on River Street in 1976, intending to bring pizza to the area. They also served burgers and chicken sandwiches at the restaurant, which is housed in what had been a cotton warehouse. According to Williams, the chicken breasts used for the sandwiches were too large for the buns on which they were served, so the restaurateurs sliced off the excess chicken and, not wanting to be wasteful, battered and fried the strips of meat and sold them as "chicken fingers." Their concoction was a hit with locals and has become a mainstay of eateries throughout southeast Georgia. The success of the River Street location led to the opening of Spanky's restaurants in other parts of the state and locally on the Southside near Oglethorpe Mall, in Pooler and on Tybee Island (that one's called Spanky's Beachside). Williams and the Yarbroughs eventually went their separate ways, with Williams retaining ownership of the Spanky's on River Street and the Yarbroughs remaining involved with the others.

Although the Spanky's restaurants have different owners, the menus are basically the same, with the chicken fingers, pizza and burgers still featured. Another favorite of veteran customers are Spanky's Spuds, which are circular-sliced potatoes that are battered and fried. The restaurants are open daily for lunch and dinner.

Vinnie Van GoGo
$$, no credit cards • 317 W. Bryan St.
• 233-6394

Vinnie's serves pizza with real character — thin crust with fresh ingredients, including options like spinach, artichoke and broccoli. Experiment with pesto instead of regular sauce. A regular 14-inch pie is $9 to start, plus $1.50 for each ingredient. Dine in the cramped interior or at outside tables overlooking City Market (semi-enclosed when it's cold). Pizza is available by the slice, and one of those with the excellent spinach salad is an ample meal. Beer is available. Get the wine list: Your options are cork and screw-top. Your most casual duds are probably too dressy for Vinnie's, but the food's tops.

Walls' Barbecue
$ • 515 E. York Ln. • 232-9754

Ninety-five percent of the barbecue pork, barbecue chicken, deviled crabs and other food sold at Walls' is taken out by customers. Walls' is essentially a building with a kitchen and counter on York Lane, which runs from Price to Houston streets between York Street and Oglethorpe Avenue. If you want to eat in, there are three tables where you can sit. Walls' also offers fried fish, fried chicken, spare ribs and vegetable plates, and all the dinners come with red rice, potato salad and a vegetable.

Margaret T. Weston, who has owned Walls' since 1979, says the business was started in the mid-1960s by her parents, Richard and Janie Walls, in a building in back of their cottage on York Street. "My daddy had a wood yard and he got tired of chopping wood, but he wanted security for my mother and me — he wanted us to be able to take care of ourselves." So Richard Walls started his barbecue business, choosing it, says Mrs. Weston with a smile, "because it was something he could get out of." Soon after the business opened, Walls began driving a taxicab, leaving Mrs. Walls and her daughter to do the cooking, and cook they have, much to the delight of Savannahians who love barbecue. Walls' is open for lunch and dinner Wednesday through Saturday.

Windows
$$$ • 2 W. Bay St. • 944-3620

Windows is aptly named. At this restaurant, four floors above River Street in the Hyatt Regency Hotel, the windows run from the floor practically to the ceiling, giving diners spectacular views of the Savannah River and the graceful Eugene Talmadge Bridge. Windows serves breakfast, lunch and dinner 365 days a year. It's a popular spot for weekday business lunches because of the "live" salad and pasta bars, where cooks prepare huge salads and pasta dishes to the specifications of customers. Also popular at lunchtime are dishes from the wok, either vegetarian or featuring chicken and scallops, shrimp and scallops, or Hunan pork and shrimp. The breakfast menu offers a full range of standard items, and the dinner menu changes seasonally. Drinks are available, made at the bar at adjacent M.D.'s lounge (see our Nightlife chapter). Reservations aren't required, but by making one, you'll enhance your chances of getting one of the 11 window tables.

Islands

Desposito's Seafood
$ • Macceo Dr., Thunderbolt • 897-9963

On evenings when the weather's nice, Desposito's owner David Boone and his mom, Walton, open the windows of the enclosed porch of this little cinder-block and wood eatery at Thunderbolt. You can sit out there at tables covered with newspaper and eat boiled shrimp, crab legs and steamed oysters as the breeze from the nearby Wilmington River wafts through the place.

Desposito's — which Walton Boone bought in late 1982 and David took over in December 1996 when she "retired" (she still works about 20 hours a week) — also serves deviled crab; homemade chili; pecan pie and potato salad; and the Lowcountry basket, which is filled with shrimp, corn on the cob, sausage and the aforementioned potato salad. In addition to the porch, there's a dining room, and a bar that serves beer and wine and has one of those old-fashioned bowling machines. Desposito's is open for lunch and dinner daily; MasterCard and Visa only are accepted. It's on the eastern side of the Wilmington River and north of U.S. Highway 80.

The Lightship Tavern
$ • 618 Wilmington Island Rd.
• 897-6142

This eating and drinking place at Sail Harbor marina on Wilmington Island affords patrons terrific views of Turner Creek and its marsh and of sunsets over the nearby Wilmington River. The tavern, with an exterior that resembles a lightship and an interior with a nautical look, features wall-to-wall windows, a full bar and an outside wooden deck beside the marsh. You can get lunch here on Saturday and Sunday and dinner seven days a week — mainly sandwiches and appetizers, including the Ultimate Nachos and a sampler consisting of nachos, potato skins and chicken fingers. On Friday and Saturday night, you can dance to live bands, and on Sundays you can relax to the sounds of a duo playing acoustic guitar. If you're coming by boat from downtown via the Wilmington River, you can tie up at the marina.

Williams Seafood Restaurant
$$$ • 8010 Tybee Rd. • 897-2219

Members of the Williams family have been providing Savannahians with seafood since 1936, when Tom Williams began selling the fish and crabs he caught while tending the bridge over the Bull River on the road to Tybee

Island. Tom's wife, Leila, developed a special recipe for deviled crab, and sales to motorists headed to and from the beach boomed; the Williamses opened a roadside stand and eventually a restaurant near the bridge. On the site of that original spot is the existing Williams Seafood Restaurant, and it's operated by a third generation of the Williams family.

The deviled crab is still on the menu. Other favorites of the families who have made Williams a regular part of their lives through the years are the shrimp and flounder. This large, unpretentious-looking restaurant seats upwards of 500 people and also serves steak, hamburger and chicken. Beer and wine are available, as are catering and banquet facilities. The restaurant is open for lunch and dinner.

Williams is just off U.S. 80 at the western end of the newest bridge over the Bull River. Remnants of the bridge Tom Williams once tended can be seen nearby.

Southside/Midtown

Barnes Restaurant
$$ • 5320 Waters Ave. • 354-8745
$$ • 4685 U.S. Hwy. 80 • 898-0220

The folks at the two Barnes restaurants pride themselves on the fact that everything from the barbecue sauce to the potato salad to the sweet iced tea is homemade. The sauce on Barnes' chopped pork and sliced beef barbecue is made according to a recipe developed by restaurant founder Nesbert Barnes and perfected over the years by his son, Hugh; it's spread on meat that's slow-cooked at low temperatures over oak and hickory wood. There's a step-by-step guide for making the tea, and an employee specifically designated to perform the task; if the tea maker is not present on a given day, the manager gets the job.

When Barnes opened in 1975 just south of where the existing building stands on Waters Avenue at 68th Street, it filled only takeout orders. A dining room was added three years later, and the existing restaurant opened in summer 1993. The island restaurant went into operation two years afterward.

Today families, business people and retirees flock to Barnes for the barbecue and the tea. Chicken fingers, ribs, shrimp salad and onion rings are other big sellers at both the Midtown location on Waters and the Whitemarsh Island site on U.S. 80. Barnes serves lunch and dinner, and you're likely to encounter a line of customers waiting at the Waters Avenue restaurant if you get there around noon. Don't be discouraged; the line moves fast and the Lowcountry/Southern-style food is worth waiting for. Each restaurant accommodates 220 people, with much of the seating in high-backed, well-padded booths. Reservations can be made by groups of 15 or more people, and there are banquet facilities seating up to 80 at each location.

Bella's Italian Cafe
$$$ • 4420 Habersham St. • 354-4005

Located on Habersham Street between 60th and 61st streets, Bella's is "where Savannah eats Italian," according to owner Joyce Shanks. She claims the manicotti at Bella's is the best south of Brooklyn, and she ought to know. She grew up in that New York borough, learning to cook manicotti and other Italian dishes in the kitchen of her grandmother, Bella. Joyce's manicotti is stuffed with a mixture of three cheeses, baked in marinara sauce and topped with bubbling cheese. Her chicken Parmesan — a double chicken breast deep-fried in bread crumbs and baked with marinara and melted cheeses — is another popular entree, but we could make a meal of just Bella's breadsticks — yeast dough that's deep-fried, tastes like doughnuts and is served with marinara and herb butter.

Bella's, which has been at its existing site in Habersham Village shopping center since 1993 after a four-year stint at Savannah Mall, can accommodate 60 diners in cozy, family-oriented surroundings. The restaurant serves dinner seven days a week and lunch on weekdays. Beer and wine are available. Bella's doesn't take reservations, and it's a good idea to arrive early if you're dining on a weekend. There are only a few parking spaces in front of the restaurant but plenty of spots in the lot at the corner of Habersham and 61st. Bella's accepts major credit cards with the exception of Discover.

Carey Hilliard's Restaurant

$ • 3316 Skidaway Rd. • 354-7240
$ • 8410 Waters Ave. • 355-2468
$ • 514 U.S. Hwy. 80, Garden City
• 964-5671
$ • 5350 Ga. Hwy. 21, Garden City
• 963-0060
$ • 11111 Abercorn St. • 925-3225

That there are five Carey Hilliard's in Savannah should tell you something about the popularity of these restaurants, which provide casual dining in an atmosphere geared toward families. Founder Carey Hilliard opened his first establishment in 1960 on Skidaway Road in what had been an A&W Root Beer stand. The drive-in, curb-service feature was retained, and all five restaurants offer it today. Order from your car, and you receive many of the amenities you would by dining inside, including china plates and silverware.

Barbecue has always been and still is a big seller at Carey Hilliard's, which serves lunch and dinner, but seafood dishes account for about half the orders these days. Among the favorites of customers are the fried shrimp, oysters and deviled crabs. Seating at the restaurants averages 250. Beer and wine are available.

The Delivery Room Cafe

$ • 4829 Waters Ave. • 691-0063

Since it's in Medical Arts Shopping Center and is across Waters Avenue from Memorial Medical Center, Savannah's largest hospital, you might think the name of this 85-seat restaurant is related to the healthcare field, but it's not. The moniker stems from the owners' idea of providing fast but healthy fare that patrons can carry out or have delivered. The only food that's fried at The Delivery Room are the french fries, and the cafe does a brisk business in grilled chicken salads, quiches, homemade soups and sandwiches featuring chicken. We darn near swoon over the potato cheese soup, a creamy concoction laced with chunks of potato and bacon.

If you're not grabbing takeout food or having the staff bring lunch to you, the restaurant presents a relaxed atmosphere where customers are encouraged to watch television and read newspapers. It opened in 1996 in a spot that once housed Leopold's, a longtime soda and sandwich shop. The Delivery Room serves lunch on weekdays and also offers breakfast on weekdays and Saturdays. Smoking is prohibited.

Eli's Delicatessen

$$ • 4430 Habersham St. • 355-3287
$$ • 28 Drayton St. • 233-3547

This classic delicatessen built its reputation on such standards as its corned beef sandwich and shrimp salad. Owner Eli Karatassos boasts that the deli makes all of its salads and other dishes and buys only ingredients, not prepared foods. They even make their own reuben dressing. The menu includes soups and a vegetable lasagna that is worth a try. Locals buy the various salads and side dishes to transfer into bowls at home and pass off to guests as homemade. There's a bakery on site that even wholesales to other restaurants. Breakfast, lunch and dinner are served at the original Habersham location. The Drayton Street location downtown, a more recent addition, closes in late afternoon. Both are closed on Sunday.

Elizabeth on Thirty-Seventh Street

$$$ • 105 E. 37th St. • 236-5547

This is where national food writers dine when they come to town. It's also where locals celebrate and entertain to impress. Chef/owner Elizabeth Terry is pretty much considered the queen of local haute cuisine, and she produces a Southern regional menu that is hard to characterize, but sophisticated and appealing. (In other words, don't look for the overcooked or fried, flat qualities some folks consider regional cooking.) It makes the best of local offerings, but that does not mean you are faced with seafood selections only. Dress up and dig in for dinner only. Reservations are strongly recommended.

Hirano's Restaurant

$$ • 4426 Habersham St. • 353-8337
$$ • 13015 Abercorn St. • 961-0770

Japanese cuisine became a major hit in Savannah with the opening of this small storefront restaurant on Habersham Street. Folks stand in line for a chance to order simple, fresh food from a limited menu. Large servings and reasonable prices are hallmarks here. The teriyaki chicken, served with rice and salad, runs less than $5, so if you pick your items carefully, this can be a budget meal as well as a real treat. Combination plates carry higher prices.

The food is prepared at open griddles behind the counter — this is not one of the showy knife-twirling restaurants. If you are eager to get started at the Habersham site, opt for a seat at the counter overlooking the cooking: Those seats come open more quickly than the small stock of tables. The Habersham store has a separate sushi bar, but call ahead if you are interested — it tends to keep shorter hours. Both sites serve a delicious California roll of avocado and cooked crab rolled in rice for those who are wary of traditional sushi.

Johnny Harris Restaurant
$$$ • 1651 E. Victory Dr. • 354-7810

Stepping into the main dining room at Johnny Harris is like fox-trotting back into the late 1930s and the '40s, when this establishment was an elegant supper club on the outskirts of Savannah. The bandstand that occupied the middle of the floor is gone, but the room retains the charm of that bygone era. Remaining from those good old days are the dark-wood paneling of the Old English decor and a 75-foot-high ceiling adorned for a starry, night-sky effect. You can also still slip into one of the booths lining the perimeter of the oval-shaped room and place an order by pushing a service button that illuminates a green light overhead.

The restaurant has been a favorite of Savannahians for decades, and many patrons bring their grandchildren and great-grandchildren so they can experience the atmosphere, service and food — in particular the barbecue, fried chicken, prime rib and crab meat au gratin: meat of the crab's claw folded in a cream sauce and baked with two cheeses. Johnny Harris is the oldest restaurant in Savannah and one of the oldest in Georgia, but you'll notice it's not in the Historic Downtown. It's in Midtown, on Victory Drive just east of Bee Road. That intersection is where the original restaurant was built in 1924 by a Southerner from out of town named Johnny Harris; the original wooden building was torn down, and the brick structure that houses the existing restaurant was built in 1936. Johnny Harris died in 1942, and the restaurant has been run by the Donaldson family of Savannah ever since.

Johnny Harris has seating under one roof for 275 people in the main room, the adjacent cafe area, a lounge with a full-service bar and a banquet room that can accommodate up to 60. Smoking is allowed in the cafe area and lounge but prohibited in the main room, where live dinner music is provided on Friday nights and dancing to tunes of the '40s, '50s and '60s is featured on Saturday nights. Hearkening back to the restaurant's earlier days, the management requires that male dancers wear coats. Johnny Harris serves lunch and dinner and takes but does not require reservations.

If you get the chance, stroll through the restaurant's back hallways and take a gander at the more than 60 framed menus hanging on the walls; they bear the autographs of well-known entertainers, politicians and sports figures who have eaten at Johnny Harris. The first to scribble his signature was the late comedian Red Skelton; among the most recent was actor and filmmaker Clint Eastwood. You might also consider purchasing some of the restaurant's barbecue sauce to take home with you. It's bottled hot and sold at Johnny Harris and other outlets in Georgia, South Carolina and Florida, and it is shipped worldwide via mail order.

INSIDERS' TIP

Soup's on at The Great Savannah Soup Company at 106 W. Congress Street in the Historic Downtown. This restaurant ladles up standby soups such as beef vegetable, 16-bean, Vidalia French onion and seafood gumbo and offers daily specials in addition to sandwiches and salads. The Soup Company is open for lunch and early-evening meals Monday through Thursday and for lunch and dinner on Friday and Saturday.

Larry's Restaurant
$ • 3000 Skidaway Rd. • 355-8272

Eat your vegetables at Larry's. You'll select three when you order an entree from the luncheon menu, which changes daily. Among the favorite choices are the sweet-potato soufflé, the squash casserole and the turnip greens, and they go just fine with the fried chicken, beef stew or chicken and dumplings. There's plenty more to choose from at this eatery, which has been serving breakfast and lunch since 1981 on Skidaway Road a couple of blocks south of Victory Drive.

Larry's is a hangout of locals — one of those places where the parking lot is usually filled with vehicles (many of them pickup trucks), and the waitresses call customers by name. The food and atmosphere aren't fancy, but the homestyle grub is good, plentiful and inexpensive, and the air hums with the conversation of folks talking with longtime cronies or renewing old acquaintants. Larry's, which seats 150, is closed on Sundays.

Mary's Seafood and Steakhouse
$$$ • 12308 Largo Dr. • 927-1300

Fried and broiled seafood platters, crab legs, stuffed flounder, filet mignon and the queen-size prime rib grab the spotlight at Mary's, which has three dining rooms and a bar, all decorated in the style of an English pub. The filet mignon and the New York strip steak are served on a hot lava stone that continues to cook the meat after it is brought to your table, and you can ask for other dishes to be served on the "hot rock." The Southside restaurant, owned by Mary Buckley since 1988, offers dinner seven days a week. Mary's is on Largo Drive, less than a block south of Abercorn Street Extension.

The Mill Brewery, Eatery and Bakery
$$$ • 7805 Abercorn Ext. • 355-1625

The Mill does a lot of different things and does them well. The menu is among the most varied in town, with pizza, pasta, seafood and sandwich offerings. Basil chicken and the Brewmaster Steak, a beer-marinaded steak, are among the more popular offerings, but we vote for hamburgers, which are uniformly good and come in a variety of styles (try the bleu

cheese one). The menu includes selections for those who are trying to eat healthy.

There's a full bar, but the major attraction for the thirsty crowd is the selection of microbrewed beers. The restaurant also sells supplies for home beer brewing. This is actually part of a small chain, but there is enough atmosphere and so many tasty original dishes, most of the local following are unaware of that fact. Dress is casual.

Scampi's
$$$ • 12426 White Bluff Rd. • 920-4562

Scampi's offers seafood and Italian cuisine in a relaxed but intimate atmosphere. Devoted customers keep coming back for the crab and eggplant and another speciality — the pescatore, which consists of shrimp, scallops and clams in red sauce served over linguine. Scampi's is on the Southside on White Bluff Road near the intersection with Windsor Road. Dinner is available Tuesday through Saturday, and reservations are recommended.

Semolina
$$ • Twelve Oaks Shopping Center, 5500 Abercorn St. • 353-9335

Semolina specializes in pasta, but it's not an Italian restaurant. The main dishes served at this eatery in Twelve Oaks Shopping Center on Abercorn Street just south of DeRenne Avenue are international in flavor, meaning they combine pasta with fare from several cultures. Two of the favorites of Semolina fans are chicken cordon bleu pasta and chicken enchilada pasta, in which rigatoni is adorned with chicken, onions, green peppers and black beans sautéed in a tortilla cheese sauce. Appetizers also have an international flair: There's baked feta cheese and marinara sauce, and shrimp Napoleon — shrimp, Gouda cheese and tasso layered between rounds of eggplant and smothered in a spicy cream sauce. The crowd-pleaser dessert is bread pudding made with apples and cinnamon and served hot; one order is big enough for two diners.

Semolina has seating for 102 in booths or tables in an upbeat atmosphere featuring sponge-painted walls and oversized strands of linguine (they're rubber) and huge vegetables (they're papier-mâché) hanging from

Regional Cuisine Offers a Taste of Savannah

When you're in Savannah, you might run across some cuisine you're not likely to find in other parts of the country. Two examples, the Lowcountry shrimp boil and the oyster roast, combine food with other elements you might have noticed being mentioned throughout this book: Savannahians' love of getting together and their fondness for being outdoors.

You can order Lowcountry boil in a restaurant, and the same goes for oysters, but perhaps the best way to experience them is by attending an outdoor party at which they are the featured components. Lowcountry boil—also known as Frogmore stew because it supposedly originated in Frogmore, South Carolina, which is about 90

minutes northeast of Savannah — consists of smoked sausage, corn on the cob and shrimp all boiled together in a large pot. Some cooks add other ingredients, with new potatoes seeming to be the most popular.

Oysters served at an oyster roast are roasted on a big piece of tin or steel that's supported by cinder blocks. A red-hot fire is built under the sheet of metal, and the oysters are placed on it and covered with wet cloth — burlap sacks do nicely. The oysters will steam open in about 20 minutes, and they're ready to eat. Special oyster knives are used to help dig the oysters out of their shells, and it's a good idea to wear gloves to prevent being cut by the oyster's tough exterior.

We think the best way to enjoy a Lowcountry boil or oyster roast is by standing around on a crisp day in autumn, chatting with friends and diving into a pile of oysters or a big heap of sausage, shrimp and corn that's been dumped on a table covered with newspaper. It doesn't hurt, by the way, if there's a keg of beer handy.

Among other foods associated with this area are Savannah red rice, a dessert called trifle and a cookie known as the benne wafer. The benne wafer has a taste all its own because it's made with benne seeds, which is what folks in the Lowcountry call sesame

— continued on next page

Photo: Phyl M. Gatlin

Cooks at an oyster roast pour a batch of oysters onto a table as a hungry guest waits to dig in.

seeds. Trifle, a gift of the English colonists to Savannah, consists of pound cake that's been sprinkled with sherry, layered with custard and topped with whipped cream. Savannah red rice goes great with fried chicken and seafood. The following is a recipe for this distinctly local dish provided by Martha Giddens Nesbit, who edited and wrote much of the food section of Savannah's daily newspaper for more than a decade and is the author of the *Savannah Collection* and *Savannah Entertains* cookbooks.

In her recipe, which serves four people, Martha uses four slices of bacon that have been fried crisp, crumbled and reserved, one chopped onion, one chopped celery stalk, a cup of raw rice, one 16-ounce can of tomatoes, three-quarters of a cup of water, a teaspoon of salt and a quarter-teaspoon of cayenne pepper.

Fry the chopped onion and celery in bacon fat, then remove some of the fat, if desired, and add the rice, tomatoes, water, salt and pepper. Combine the ingredients and transfer them to a one-and-a-half-quart baking dish. Bake at 350 degrees for 20 minutes or until the rice is soft but not dry. Stir in the reserved bacon and serve hot or at room temperature.

Something else you're likely to encounter during mealtimes in Savannah is sweetened iced tea, which we call just plain ol' "sweet tea." Savannahians drink it year round, and here's a good way to make a gallon-size pitcherful: Place three family-size tea bags in the basket of your automatic coffee maker and brew up a coffee potful of tea. Put about a cup of sugar in the pitcher, and pour the hot tea on top. Stir it up and add a coffee potful of water and stir again. When it cools, you've got sweet tea.

the ceiling. Beer and wine are available. Semolina — one of a chain of 15 restaurants in Georgia, Florida and Louisiana — serves lunch and dinner. Smoking is not allowed.

Tubby's Tank House
$$$ • 2909 River Dr., Thunderbolt • 354-9040

Tubby's specializes in fresh seafood, much of it caught by part-owner Stan "Tubby" Strickland, a sport fisherman with a knack for hauling in mahi mahi, grouper, tuna and wahoo. In fact, says fellow owner Ansley Williams, Tubby's is a seafood restaurant because of Strickland's ability as an angler. Williams says that in 1994 when he, Strickland and managing partner Ray Clark decided to start a new restaurant, they settled on opening a seafood place because Strickland "was catching so much fish we needed a place to distribute it." The result was Tubby's, a rustic-looking restaurant perched on the bluff at Thunderbolt.

In addition to the aforementioned sports fish, Tubby's serves shrimp, scallops, oysters and Tubby's Tank Out, a seafood platter that, according to Williams, "is more than one hu-

man can eat." Burgers, chicken fingers and a variety of salads are available for those not inclined toward eating fish.

Another feature of Tubby's is its splendid view of the Intracoastal Waterway, which in these parts is the Wilmington River. When the weather's nice, the best seats for a look at the water are outdoors on Tubby's wide porch or on the rooftop deck. Tubby's serves lunch and dinner seven days a week, hosts oyster roasts on Thursday nights during the winter and Thursday sunset parties in the summer, and offers dancing in the back room on Thursday, Friday and Saturday nights.

Wang's II Chinese Restaurant
$$ • 7601 Waters Ave. • 355-0321

Wang's II offers Hunan and Szechuan cuisine for lunch and dinner seven days a week. Some of the dishes on the extensive menu are spicier than others, but they're designated as such and can be cooked to suit your taste. All the food at this restaurant on Waters Avenue between Eisenhower Drive and Mall Boulevard is monosodium glutanate-free, according to manager Charles Lin. Among the more popular dishes are the crispy fish; sauteed string beans with chicken, beef, shrimp or roast pork; and General Tso's chicken, which consists of chunks of chicken in a spicy brown sauce.

Wang's II, which opened in 1991, has a full bar and seating for 150 in an elegant dining room featuring black lacquer chairs and glass-topped tables. The restaurant does not take Discover, and reservations are recommended on Friday and Saturday nights. In case you're wondering, there's no Wang's I.

West Chatham

Love's Seafood Restaurant
$$$ • 6817 Basin Rd. • 925-3616

Love's is in southwest Chatham County 14 miles from the Historic Downtown, but city dwellers are more than happy to make the ride to this restaurant on the banks of the serene Ogeechee River. A major reason for the pilgrimages is Love's fried catfish, 90 percent of it caught in the river and all of it battered with a fine cracker meal that makes it so light it seems to float off the plate. Besides, says Fulton Love, who runs the restaurant with his wife Donna, you can get there from downtown in 15 minutes if you take Interstate 16, Interstate 95 and Ga. Highway 204 to U.S. Highway 17 and the Chatham-Bryan county line.

The restaurant is where the U.S. 17 bridge crosses the river and has been there since 1949, when it was started as a fishing camp by Fulton's folks, O.F. and Thelma. If you've watched the movie *Forrest Gump* — and who hasn't? — you've seen the bridge and the restaurant in one of the scenes where Forrest and his girlfriend part company. You can see the beautiful Ogeechee from about 250 of the 304 seats at Love's, but the best views are from the porch, which seats 50 and is a non-smoking area.

Love's serves steak and chicken fingers in an atmosphere that's rustic but upscale; however, the main draws here are the catfish and seafood, in particular the fried shrimp, shrimp and red snapper stuffed with crab meat and the seafood fettucine. Beer, wine and mixed drinks are available.

Love's, which serves about 600 pounds of catfish a week and is probably the oldest catfish restaurant in Georgia, takes reservations for parties of 12 or more people. It's open Tuesday through Saturday for dinner and Sunday for lunch and dinner; it's closed on Mondays when the owners are, as they put it, "Gone fishing."

Lovezzola's Pizza Restaurant
$$ • 320 U.S. Hwy. 80 E., Pooler • 748-6414

Pizza fans, rejoice! There is real pizza, as opposed to the franchise mass-production type, south of the Mason-Dixon Line. Paul Lovezzola has been hand-throwing the dough for New York-style pizza at his restaurant for the past 19 years. This transplanted New Yorker hasn't lost his accent or his taste for slow-cooked sauces and individually prepared pizzas in those years.

Sit in his casual, family-style dining room at a table with red-and-white checked plastic tablecloths, and he'll point out his ancestral hometown on the map of Italy featured on the placemats. He serves up his pizza with the usual selection of toppings and offers pasta dishes, submarine sandwiches and a salad bar as well. His regulars include not only travelers along I-95 (he's just off Exit 18A) and expatriate Northerners, but also a solid group of Southern converts who have been won over to the concept of pizza as a real food.

Pooler is one of Chatham County's municipalities on its western side, easy to find because it is close by the interstate and worth the drive for a taste of what pizza was before it became fast food. Takeouts are available, as is delivery in a limited area that includes the motels clustered around the Pooler exit off I-95.

You'll probably get tired of locals gleefully telling you the favorite question posed to a newcomer is, "What do you drink?"

Nightlife

After a day spent beaching, boating, shopping, eating, fishing, touring, visiting museums, checking out aged graveyards and getting acclimated to the local heat and humidity, what do you do when the evening sun goes down? After an especially active tourist day, many folks would just opt to turn in early. Don't worry, though: You'll recover before your stay is over, and you'll want to sample Savannah's nightlife.

Savannah's traditional nightlife is an at-home thing. We have perfected the art of hospitality and party-giving here, and the night's best food, drink and entertainment is probably being served and going on in someone's back yard, on their dock or in their living room. If you have friends, family or savvy business acquaintances in town, chances are good you'll get a chance to see what we mean.

That doesn't mean you're out of luck if you don't have an invitation, however. Savannah has plenty of nightspots to entertain guests, and locals turn out too when they're tired of the homegrown party thing. The bar and entertainment scene falls into three general categories: You've got River Street, a restored area along the Savannah River that was refurbished with just this sort of thing in mind; City Market, a restored quadrant of the Historic Downtown that's heavy on clubs and bars as well as shops; and a variety of watering holes and entertainment sites scattered along routes to the south of the city (the Southside, in local parlance).

If you don't have something very specific in mind (say, stand-up comedy or a sports bar), our advice is to follow your ear, literally. Visitors will fare better on River Street and in City Market, where there are lots of nightspots clustered together. You can follow the music you hear spilling out the doors and wander conveniently from site to site. We're not scoffing at the Southside offerings: It's just that the nightspots there are more scattered, and it's harder to include a variety of options as a result.

Which brings us to the question of alcohol and the law. Savannah's folklore stresses the city's hard-drinking reputation, with tales that the town was never dry, even during Prohibition (which lingered long in Georgia, where some counties are still dry). You'll probably get tired of locals gleefully telling you the favorite question posed to a newcomer is, "What do you drink?" Believe all this if you want to, but don't base your actions on it. Local law enforcement aggressively pursues alcohol offenses. Drivers can face charges with a blood-alcohol level of .08 percent, and unless you have a medical lab in your back seat, don't try to guess how many drinks it takes an individual to reach that level. Remember that the law prohibits open containers with alcohol in vehicles.

The law provides "zero tolerance" for alcohol levels in those younger than the legal drinking age of 21. In addition to drunken driving laws that the Georgia General Assembly has tightened up in recent years, however, Savannah offers its own, city-specific reasons for designating a non-drinking driver, calling a cab or drinking near where you are staying. Most of our tourist nightspots are in an area of narrow, often one-way, streets. Also, streets throughout the city tend to be lined with trees — either unyielding live oaks of massive girth or palm trees that are easily uprooted or snapped by collisions.

Don't be surprised (or flattered) to find yourself carded in many drinking establishments. Savannah has a large college and military population, and many soldiers and students are not of legal drinking age. With their licenses at stake, bars and restaurants tend to be thorough on the question of age. While bars can stay open until 3 AM, many of them pack it in early on slow nights, especially through the week.

Also note that city ordinances prohibit open bottles or cans on the street, but if you want to wander out of a River Street watering hole or a City Market club, most places are glad to provide you with a plastic or foam cup. Based on what we know of elsewhere, Savannah is pretty unusual in letting you stroll and drink. (Remember, Tybee Island is a municipality unto itself, and alcohol is not allowed on the beach at all.)

We've spent a lot of space covering alcohol, but we don't mean to give you the impression that all nightlife has to do with booze. We've included coffeehouses, which are growing in popularity, as well as movies and other activities. Also, Savannah is home to an active Alcoholics Anonymous family: If you want to catch a meeting and talk firsthand about alcohol-free nightlife in Savannah, call 354-0993 for the extensive schedule.

FYI

Unless otherwise noted, the area code for all phone numbers listed in this guide is 912.

Bars

Coach's Corner
3016 E. Victory Dr. • 352-2933
550 Mall Blvd. • 355-4444

The sports bar has become an American institution. Coach's Corner, with two locations, is a good example. More televised sports than you thought the airwaves could provide are on the multiple TV sets here. There's a full bar, but beer's the main drink of choice. A limited food menu is available. Dress is casual, needless to say. Come by the Victory Drive site during October of a good season for the Atlanta Braves, and you can catch a giant motorized tomahawk chopping away, backed up by an occasional live chopper.

Hannah's East
20 East Broad St. • 233-2225

Ah, a bar for grownups! There's good mu-

sic and good drinks here in a bar that's upstairs at (and unaffiliated with) The Pirate's House Restaurant. Club owner Ben Tucker is an accomplished jazz musician himself, and you may catch him and his trio performing. Emma Kelly, dubbed the "Lady of 6,000 Songs" by Savannah lyricist Johnny Mercer, is a regular here. Whoever's on, expect a good caliber performance of standards and jazz.

Kevin Barry's Irish Pub
117 W. River St. • 233-9626

Savannah prides itself on its Irish heritage, not just during the elaborate St. Patrick's Day observance, but year round. Just check out this pub. The stone-walled setting is dark and atmospheric, brightened considerably by a constantly changing program of authentic Irish performers (Wednesday through Sunday nights). Count on acceptable food, standard drinks and an impressive collection of bottled and draft beers and ales. There's even a small gift shop for Irish goods. Brush up on your Irish history (and learn who the real Kevin Barry was) by reading the captions to the framed photos of figures who were either historic freedom fighters or long-dead terrorists, depending on your outlook.

Malone's Food and Spirits
27 Barnard St. • 234-3059

This large nightspot and restaurant anchors a corner of City Market. Inside, there's a little bit of everything over a lot of floor space: sports on TV, pool tables, food and drink. There are even outside tables, and live bands often perform outside on weekends. It's a mixture of a young night-out crowd and older after-work folks. Lunch and dinner are served.

M.D.'s Lounge
2 W. Bay St. • 238-1234

Before or after a nice dinner at one of the

Photo: Kyle Cason

When night falls Forsyth Fountain isn't the only spot to find after-hours activity.

classier River Street restaurants, you may not be in the mood to nightcap it at one of the street's singalong suds pubs. M.D.'s is a nice alternative — a dressier place for a drink. The decor is upscale and subtle, the drinks are fine, and there's usually an inoffensive and unobtrusive musical lounge act. The whole thing would fall into the "very nice but forgettable" category if not for the view. This bar is inside the Hyatt Regency Savannah (see our Hotels and Motels chapter) and has glass walls overlooking the Savannah River (literally — this portion of the hotel overhangs River Street). If you are lucky (or determined enough to stay put for a while), you'll get to see one of the giant container ships headed to or from the port upriver. Granted, you can see them from the street too, but from M.D.'s vantage point, you're more on eye level with the oceangoing giants.

Mulligan's
7100 Abercorn St. • 692-0072

This newly redesigned lounge inside the Holiday Inn Midtown (see our Hotels and Motels chapter) offers Savannah's best examples of virtual-reality games. (Actually, we think it offers the only examples of virtual-reality games, short of temporary promotional setups at the malls and such.) For $1 a shot and up, you can try your hand at navigating a life-size Jet Ski through a projected water course or climbing onto a ski machine that looks like something out of your gym and plunging down a computer-generated slope. There's a car race game that features a wired, interactive seat. The largest and most elaborate game is a golf simulator the size of a small room. You use real clubs to drive a real ball against a projected image on a padded screen, while a

INSIDERS' TIP

Sunday liquor sales are a strange issue in a Bible Belt town with a drinking heritage. Liquor and package stores are closed on Sunday, and grocery stores can't sell their beer and wine either. To sell drinks or beer on Sunday, an establishment must document it derives a large share of its profits from food sales. In other words, if it's a bar that admits it's a bar, it won't be open on Sunday. That's why most watering holes offer some kind of menu.

computer analysis of the velocity and trajectory determines where your ball lands. Players can choose from a variety of famous courses — say, Pebble Beach, or for those more interested in local venues, Hilton Head's Harbour Town.

Several smaller and less elaborate games of the interactive, computer-video type are available too. Don't expect anything overwhelming here (except perhaps the golf), but the effects were advanced enough to give us a mild case of motion sickness. For more traditional gamers, pool tables are available. The bar itself is modern, clean and nondescript, attracting a 30-something after-work and after-date crowd. Although the games no doubt would appeal to minors, only those 21 or older are admitted.

Oglethorpe Brewing Company
21 W. Bay St. • 232-0933

Savannah's first (and so far, only) brewpub makes and serves between six and eight different house brews per week. Watch the whole process, if you are lucky enough to show up during brew time: Glass windows overlook the tanks. This is also a restaurant serving lunch and dinner from an extensive menu (including several dishes whose ingredients include the aforementioned brews), but the main attraction is the beer. Dress is on the slightly upscale side of casual. There's occasional entertainment starting at 10 PM.

Pinkie Master's Lounge
318 Drayton St. • 238-0447

This modest neighborhood watering hole is legendary in Savannah as a political bar. Journalists once plied local sources with alcohol here; Jimmy Carter (yes, THAT Jimmy Carter) once gave a speech standing on the bar. What you'll find today is a small bar where regulars talk back to the television set. There's an eclectic jukebox and a few game machines, along with the beer and the booze.

Stogies Cigar Bar
112 W. Congress St. • 233-4277

Savannah has joined the national cigar craze in a major way, and Stogies is a good upscale example. The circa 1820s building is furnished with sofas and oversized chairs designed for long, comfortable conversations and long, comfortable smokes. There's a walk-in humidor and a pool table upstairs. The bar stocks liquor, cognacs, ports and wines. It caters to an older, more sophisticated crowd. Light, recorded background jazz doesn't drown out conversation. While you don't have to be dressed to the hilt, you'll feel more comfortable in your town-and-country casuals or business attire here.

Wet Willie's
101 E. River St. • 233-5650

This high-volume River Street bar caters to younger drinkers. The drinks are frozen concoctions with names like the infamous Spring Break potion, Sex on the Beach. Beware! Grain alcohol gives a single drink here the punch of at least two conventional alcoholic beverages. There's a light food menu, a small dance floor and lots of loud recorded music.

Billiards

B&B Billiards
411 W. Congress St. • 233-7116

On the fringe of City Market, this is a popular spot to shoot some pool and hang out with friends. Look for a mix of students, middle-aged locals and the occasional tourist. If you want to rack 'em up, the cost is $6 an hour.

Players' Place Billiards and Deli
1100 Eisenhower Dr. • 351-9026

Players' offers a slightly more suburban, upscale take on the pool parlor, complete with

---

INSIDERS' TIP

A walk on the beach can be a romantic conclusion to an evening out. Stroll out onto the Tybee Pier and Pavilion, lean against the rail and watch the moon rise out of the Atlantic Ocean.

Club One and Lady Chablis: Anything But a Drag

In a city as inherently conservative as Savannah, you wouldn't expect tourism and the gay nightlife scene to intersect. You would be wrong.

Close-up

Club One Jefferson has been the most prominent social setting, under various names, for Savannah's out-of-the-closet gay community since the 1980s. Its dance and performance scene had attracted the occasional bolder and curious straights, but for the most part, Club One was a world unto itself.

The Lady Chablis changed all that.

The flamboyant drag queen (is there any other kind?) caught the eye of author John Berendt when he was writing the book that would become the phenomenal best seller *Midnight in the Garden of Good and Evil*. The self-titled "Grand Empress of Savannah" is featured prominently therein. That alone was enough to make the performer famous, but then she went on to play herself in the movie version.

As the cult following for The Book grew, its readers flocked to Savannah. They wanted to gawk at The Book's houses, tour The Book's cemetery, and buy The Book trinkets. Most particularly, they wanted to get a look at The Lady Chablis.

And that presented the folks at Club One with a dilemma: How could they tap into that market without scaring the tourists back to Peoria, while at the same time keeping the flood of Book fanciers from displacing their regular clientele? Fortunately, they've come up with a smooth compromise. When Chablis is in town, they put on an earlier, somewhat tamer version of her show, reserving the stronger material for the later shows. It works well: Tourists get a sample of the strong stuff without a full dose, and the regular customers do not find their entertainment diluted, since the club's gay scene doesn't get moving until later anyway.

Don't misinterpret us here. Even though the early show (8:30 PM is early) is milder, it isn't mild. If you don't understand what a drag show is or are not at peace with the concept, don't go. Don't go if you can't take earthy language. Skip it if you feel too

Photo: Betty Darby

nervous, although we went to the early show with a group of friends (first-timers all) and didn't feel uncomfortable at all once we got there.

You can't take it for granted that you'll see Chablis. She no longer lives in Savannah, although she usually performs twice a month or so. Call the club at 232-0200 to find out who's on the schedule for the week. You'll usually get a recorded message, and the phone menu includes directions from various parts of town.

The show bar is upstairs, and it's perfectly adequate but not particularly luxurious. It's also small. There are small tables on the front and along the sides and several rows of seats. Don't fret if you don't get a front seat — the place is small enough for you to see from all angles. In fact, if you're male, don't sit

Club One Jefferson frequently features the Lady Chablis.

— continued on next page

down front at all, unless you're willing to be flirted with by the performers. You'll have to fetch your own drinks from the bar on the upstairs level. Check the speaker location before you sit down: The room is small, but the speakers are big.

A drag show consists of female impersonators in drop-dead glamorous gowns and jewelry, dancing and lip-synching to recorded music. The show we caught featured one performer who was convincing as a beautiful woman, one performer who was convincing as an attractive woman who was trying very hard, one performer who was convincing as a homely but brave woman and two others who were pretty unconvincing. The Lady Chablis emcees when she is there and performs several numbers. She also explains to the audience that they can come down front and tip performers if they wish. Bring folding money if you want to try that and don't worry: For the early show at least, it's a modest hand-to-hand exchange instead of the risque version you probably imagined (besides, the performers are wearing more clothes than the audience).

At the conclusion of the early show, Chablis comes back out to sign autographs, so bring your copy of The Book or Chablis' own book, *Hiding My Candy*.

Club One Jefferson has shows every Wednesday at midnight and Friday, Saturday and Sunday at 10:30 PM and 12:30 AM. They only stage the 8:30 PM show when Chablis performs. Other performers vary, but drag shows are staples, along with the occasional beauty pageant or striptease act. Normal cover is $5. Our Chablis tickets were $15 each, but that included cover for the rest of the club. Remember, this was shortly before the movie was released, so rates may go up. Again, check that surprisingly clear and helpful telephone message referenced above.

Elsewhere in Club One Jefferson, you'll find a video bar with what the management describes as the largest video wall in the Southeast, full restaurant service and a full bar. Dance music downstairs is Top 40, while the main level has techno and house music.

Pretty much anything goes by way of dress, but it's predominately casual. The club takes major credit cards and has an ATM on site. It's at 1 Jefferson Street, just off Bay Street at the edge of City Market.

---

a bar (beer and liquor) and restaurant. Dress is casual but nice. This is next door to the Eisenhower Cinemas, so there's a substantial pre- and post-date crowd. The cost to play is $2 per hour before 7 PM. After that it's $4 an hour to shoot solo, $6.40 for couples.

Coffeehouses

The coffeehouse movement has just hit Savannah, and new examples of the genre seem to be springing up overnight. Here are a few to get you going.

Gallery Espresso
6 E. Liberty St. • 233-5348

This is one of the city's first (and our personal favorite) on the coffeehouse scene. Coffee, both plain and in its multiple new forms, is augmented by a limited menu of baked goods. There's an occasional poetry reading or casual performance. The walls are home to dis-

plays by local artists, and there have been some really appealing exhibits shown here.

Joe Bean's Coffeehouse
21 W. York St. • 231-1600

Steer for the downtown branch of the post office and federal building (it's a Gothic-looking marble palace), and you'll be near Joe Bean's. You'll find coffee, some light food items and comfortable places for solo reading or quiet conversation.

Savannah Coffee House
102 W. Congress St. • 233-5311

This favorite hangout for Savannah College of Art and Design students proves a good place to take a break, even if you aren't an art student. In addition to the cappuccino, lattes and plain old coffee, you'll find baked goods and snacks. Oversized chairs and couches invite you to linger. Try your hand at the board and card games on hand.

Comedy

The Comedy House Theatre
711 Mall Blvd. • 356-1045

Chris Rock, along with some equally well-known comedians and others far less so, has been among the performers at the 350-seat Comedy House Theatre on the Southside. While stand-up comedy is the backbone of the six-night-a-week performance schedule, you also can catch the occasional hypnotist or psychic performance artist. The club serves a dinner menu and has a full bar. "Eighteen to laugh, 21 to drink" is a club slogan, meaning they will let you join the audience at age 18, but you can't buy alcoholic drinks. The crowd tends to be young and fun-loving, dressed casually but neatly (think date-night quality).

Cover charges depend on the artist of the week, but the minimum is $6 for weeknight shows and $9 for weekend shows. On Tuesdays through Thursdays, the single show is at 8:30 PM; Friday and Saturday shows are 8 and 10:30 PM; and Sunday's show is at 8 PM. Two of the week's shows — Wednesday night and Friday's first show — are designated as nonsmoking. Reservations are strongly recommended, and essential if the performer is well-known. They can be made by phone; credit cards and local checks are accepted. Banquet facilities are available, with or without show tickets.

Movies

Savannah has typical movie offerings for a city its size, nothing more and nothing less. The blockbusters and major releases open here the same weekends they open everywhere else, but you may have to wait longer (or even until video) to catch, say, the Sundance winners or other non-mainstream fare.

Savannah has 35 movie screens scattered among five multiplexes owned by three theater companies. If that sounds like a lot of screens, don't get excited: Duplication eats up a lot of them. For example, we counted the offerings for a holiday November weekend and found only 14 different movies. At the moment, Savannah is without alternative movie outlets such as mug houses or dollar houses. The daily newspaper has showtimes, but we've saved

ourselves disappointment more than once by calling the recorded message to double-check. You'll find those numbers by each listing below. Diversions, the entertainment section that appears in Friday's *Morning News* and is distributed free throughout the week at various restaurants and nightspots, contains a good little sketch map to help locate the theaters, all of which are outside the Historic Downtown.

Abercorn Cinemas
12056 Abercorn St. • 925-2383

You'll find six screens here and regular ticket prices of $6.25. Matinee, senior and children's tickets are $4.25.

Carmike Cinema 10
511 Stephenson Ave. • 353-8683

There are (you guessed it) 10 screens at Savannah's newest theater. Regular tickets are $6.25, with $4.25 matinee, senior and student tickets and $3 specials on the last matinee of the day. The smallest of these auditoriums is the most likely to house art or foreign films, though it's more often running a major release in its waning week of popularity.

Eisenhower Cinemas
1100 Eisenhower Dr. • 352-3533

This multiplex has six screens. Tickets are $6.25 for adults, with $4.25 tickets for seniors, children and matinees. The last matinee of the day can be viewed for $3.25.

Tara Cinemas
Largo Dr. • 925-2135

This four-screen multiplex is the oldest in Savannah and includes the largest auditorium and screen. Weekday matinees are only offered in summer. Prices are $6.25 for regular tickets and $4.25 for seniors, children and matinees. The day's last matinee shows for $3.25.

Victory Square Cinemas
3001 Skidaway Rd. • 355-0110

This nine-screen complex is harder to spot than the others. It's in the sprawling conglomeration of shopping centers that fill the southwest quadrant of the intersection of Victory Drive and Skidaway Road. Again, ticket prices are $6.25, with $4.25 student and matinee tickets.

Savannah is the regional shopping center for a large chunk of southeast Georgia.

Shopping

Someday an enterprising psychology student is going to conduct ground-breaking research and discover what we already know: When you are traveling for pleasure, your hold on your purse strings is looser. Admit it! You'd never consider buying goofy-shaped mugs or snide T-shirts at home, at least not at full price. Ah, but when vacationing, that's a different story.

First of all, there are all those obligatory gifts — something for the neighbor who is feeding the dog, something for the grandkids or the grandparents, some kind of group offering for the office crowd. More important, however, are the travel gifts you buy yourself. These are things you would love under any circumstances — an attractive print, an antique armoire, the perfect addition to a prized collection. These things take on added significance when they remind us of a special trip, and we're more likely to treat ourselves to something we really want when we're shopping with the laid-back attitude of the vacationer.

So, if shopping is part of your vacation behavior, Savannah is your kind of vacation destination. Savannah is the regional shopping center for a large chunk of southeast Georgia; many people (outside of Brunswick, that is) consider it the only real metropolitan area until you get to Jacksonville, Florida (two and a half hours down Interstate 95), or in-state Macon (three hours west on Interstate 16). In 1996, something like $3.7 billion in taxable sales took place in Chatham County (the sprawling county of which Savannah is the seat and predominant municipal entity). With that much money changing hands, you can rest assured that you'll be able to find just about any kind of item you are looking for here.

With all this retail territory to cover, it stands to reason we had to be selective about what we included in this chapter. Let's share with you the rhyme and reason of what we left in and what we left out. First of all, we figured travelers don't need a comprehensive list of grocery stores and shoe shops. No, we're not implying that you should travel hungry and barefoot, but since we know you are basically eating in restaurants and dragging your wardrobe around with you in a heavy suitcase, we left these and similar fundamental stuff out. We also skipped most of the chain stores: We don't mean to slight anybody, but our Wal-Marts probably look just like your Wal-Marts, and your hotel concierge or bed and breakfast host can point you in the right direction if you need one.

Instead, we've tried to concentrate on the needs of recreational shoppers while still steering the retail-impaired to the places where travelers are most likely to get the things they need. We concentrated on including shops that stock items of local or regional interest. Then we added places that struck us as unusual or interesting. Next, we included places where we like to browse and buy for ourselves. Chances are good, if you are a devoted shopper, that you will find a few memorable shopping places we didn't include: Share your finds with us via the Internet at www.insiders.com (where there is a comment page), or simply drop us a line at the address listed in How to Use This Book.

About Locations

Before launching into our own category-by-category rundown of stores, we thought we would review the major shopping locations with you and provide a few pointers along the way.

River Street

River Street is literally along the Savannah River. It is reached by street ramps that lead down from the bluff-level Bay Street. In between these two levels is Factors' Walk. River Street is a major part of Savannah's tourist scene, and you'll find it is a prominent player for restaurants, nightlife and annual events. But don't forget shopping! This restored waterfront strip features a steady progression of shops all along its length, beginning at the west end across from a small power plant (whose smokestacks make handy landmarks) and extending eastward many blocks until you reach the Waving Girl statue that is a local riverfront landmark. Factors' Walk, which parallels River Street halfway up the bluff, also features shops.

Parking is scarce. There are a few small private lots, where you pay as you enter. The city of Savannah maintains two small lots as well, where you must buy a timed permit from a vending machine on the lot and display it on your dashboard — a tedious process that's easy to overlook and can cost you a parking ticket. There's limited streetside parking on the various streets leading to River Street. Lots of motorists park illegally along River Street itself, but it's a bad idea — that railroad track that runs down the middle of the street is still active.

We always opt to park at the Bay Street level and hike down, avoiding driving on tricky cobblestones. If you follow our example, however, watch your step and wear appropriate footwear: The stairs (located in each block) are steep and irregular, and once you get to the cobblestones, you'll find them as hard to walk on as they are to drive on. The going is much smoother once you get to the River Street level.

Don't expect much in the way of bargains here: These shopkeepers saw you and your credit cards coming a mile away, and just as you will in any touristy area in any city, you'll find few discounts. Still, River Street offers a great variety, mingling local and regional goods, Savannah-themed merchandise imported from elsewhere and generic trinkets and gifts. Even if you don't buy, you'll enjoy looking at goods that range from the genuinely artistic to the genuinely tacky (such as doormats bedecked with Confederate flags and the slogan "Yankee Go Home," which a shopkeeper assured us sell well to Northern visitors).

City Market

This restored area in the commercial section of the Historic Downtown runs from Barnard Street to Montgomery Street, north of Broughton Street. The complex is made up of nightclubs, restaurants, art galleries and shops. The stores here tend to be more thematic — cat motif merchandise, New Age, outdoor furniture and gifts and so on — than their cousins a few blocks away on River Street.

FYI

Unless otherwise noted, the area code for all phone numbers listed in this guide is 912.

Broughton Street and Historic Downtown Areas

Broughton Street was where Savannah shopped before malls seized control of the retail world. It suffered the same fate as Main Streets all across America but has begun a comeback as a home to restaurants, college activities and trendy shopping, including a slew of antique dealers. Watch this space: Broughton Street is poised for takeoff, and we predict that interesting shopping opportunities will continue to expand there.

You'll find plenty of intriguing stores scattered throughout the Historic Downtown. One eye-catching congregation clusters at the intersection of Bull and Liberty streets around the DeSoto Hilton Hotel. The intersection of Jones and Whitaker streets forms the nucleus for another appealing set of shops that mostly specializes in arts and collectibles. You'll also find individual shops, especially antique shops, sprinkled throughout the Historic Downtown.

Malls and Shopping Centers

Savannah has two malls, both south of downtown in a heavily trafficked area of suburban and chain-store development. There are

various ways to get there, but the most direct route and the one hardest to get lost on (although it's also the most crowded and traffic-light plagued) is straight out Abercorn Street from town. About 6 miles from the Historic Downtown, you'll spot Oglethorpe Mall on your left (you really can't miss it). Another couple of miles south, and you'll spot Savannah Mall on the right.

As for that ubiquitous American retail staple, the strip shopping center, Savannah has it's share scattered mainly in the Southside/Midtown area. Since you know what to expect in most of these — a grocery store, major discount retailer, chain or local drug store, etc. — we have left them out as a rule. However, the Habersham Shopping Center, with its handful of very interesting shops, merits a special mention, which we have included here.

Oglethorpe Mall
7804 Abercorn St. • 354-7038

Oglethorpe Mall is the city's original mall, with Sears, JCPenney, Belk and Rich's (a Southern unit of the famous Atlanta department store) as its anchors. There are 140 specialty stores here, mostly on a single story although some of the anchors have a second level. There's ample parking, but the multi-level parking deck comes in handy around the holidays and when it rains. You'll find a predictable array of stores inside (The Gap, Victoria's Secret, CD and tape stores, etc.), along with a few restaurants and food-court outlets. There's also a B. Dalton Bookseller offering books, paperbacks and magazines, along with gift items. You'll find it in the newest part of Oglethorpe Mall, on the corridor leading to Rich's. Waldenbooks is represented

as well, with a stock that will be familiar to you from similar stores in your area.

If you are traveling with kids who are young (or look young), you need to be aware of mall policies requiring adult supervision of anyone age 16 or younger during most weekend business hours. From 4 to 9 PM on Fridays, 1 to 9 PM on Saturdays and noon to 6 PM on Sundays, those younger than 17 must be accompanied by a parent or guardian at least 21 years old. Anyone 21 or younger will be asked for ID, with mall management considering driver's licenses, official state ID cards, college student ID cards, passports or visas and mall employee IDs as acceptable identification.

Savannah Mall
14045 Abercorn St. • 927-7467

The city's newest mall, which opened in 1990, is anchored by Parisian, J.B. White, Montgomery Ward and Belk, and offers 120 specialty stores on two stories. Again, the collection of stores is fairly standard, including Abercrombie & Fitch, The Disney Store, Foot Locker, Champ's Sports, Victoria's Secret, Banana Republic, a Hallmark shop, etc. There's a Waldenbooks that is roomier than the one at Oglethorpe Mall. We've had good luck in getting clerks to check with the other location if one store doesn't have what we're looking for. There's a large food court, several full-service restaurants and a large carousel that periodically offers rides for tickets (prices vary with promotions) or in exchange for points earned by purchases.

Habersham Shopping Center
Habersham St. at 60th to 63rd Sts.

This small strip shopping center runs on

INSIDERS' TIP

Sales taxes in Georgia vary by county, ranging from a minimum of 4 percent (the state's share) to as much as 7 percent, depending on local voter willingness to up the ante. In Chatham County, it's 6 percent, but you won't always have to pay it. The state portion on some grocery items is being phased out. Also, state law exempts Bibles from sales tax, although you'll find many bookstore clerks are unaware of this.

Photo: Kyle Cason

Savannah's streets are full of interesting nooks and crannies to explore.

both sides of Habersham Street, from just after its intersection with 60th Street to 63rd Street. It appears modest at first glance — a small grocery story, an Eckerds, a dry cleaner and other businesses clearly set up to serve the surrounding established neighborhood — but look closer and you'll find some interesting specialty shops. They include Regina's Books and Cards; Punch and Judy, a children's store; and Merry Times, a card and gift shop.

Shopping Savannah

Anything south of, say, DeRenne Avenue is dubbed the Southside by Savannahians. It is here you'll find the strip malls, discount houses, shopping centers, megastores, etc. The Savannah Festival Factory Outlet Center, a typical example of this new kind of strip mall, is at the far southern edge of the city, where Abercorn is better known as Ga. Highway 204 and passes under Interstate 95. This outlet center includes a Springmaid/Wamsutta factory store, Bugle Boy and Bass Shoes.

East and west of Savannah, you'll find mainly grocery stores and other retail outlets in support of the suburban residential development there, with a few interesting shops thrown in and a large spate of beach-oriented shops at the end of the road on Tybee Island.

Now that we've roughly covered the general shopping areas, let's get more specific.

We've divided our featured stores into categories. Join us on a quick shopping trip.

Antiques

In this section, we cover a sampling of both high-end and low-end antique dealers. Serious collectors with serious budgets should seek out the upscale places; collectors and browsers will have better luck in the more mainstream, less expensive stores.

Abercorn Antique Market
201 E. 37th St. • 233-0064

This rambling yellow Victorian home houses collections from 50-plus dealers. Look for French country furniture, statuary, oil paintings, crystal, jewelry and so on. This is a good browsing location with a wide price range — stuff for the serious collector and less pricey offerings as well.

Alexandra's Antique Gallery
320 W. Broughton St. • 233-3999

This conglomeration of some 60 antique dealers in a single four-story building offers something for everyone, be it high-end furniture or browsers' plunder. Don't be put off by the humble exterior or intimidated by the size: There's an elevator to help you along. We stop by periodically, sometimes finding treasures and sometimes coming up empty.

On our most recent trip, we found the basement stocked with furniture and fixtures salvaged from an old shoe store. The first floor sported plenty of Victorian furniture, with cookbooks, other books, glassware, collectible toys, old panoramic photos, quilts and china spread out over the other floors. One section of the first floor contains new gift merchandise, and there are several Savannah-themed items in stock. The arrangement calls for leisurely browsing. This is one place you can bring a non-antiquing friend or spouse with you without feeling guilty or pressured; there's enough variety and sheer oddity among the displays to keep just about any adult entertained. Only the bravest would consider bringing a child into this environment, however.

FYI

Unless otherwise noted, the area code for all phone numbers listed in this guide is 912.

The Attic
224 W. Bay St. • 236-4879

Looking for antique fishing lures? Good examples can fetch $65 and up, and you'll find them among some of the other sports antiques here, along with fencing masks and old skis. It's an eclectic stock of mainly American antiques and collectibles — furniture, jewelry, glassware. It's not what you would call high-end, but it's fun. The location itself is of interest to fans of *Midnight in the Garden of Good and Evil*, since it was the location of the financially ill-fated Emma's, a piano bar that is featured in that bestseller.

Fran Campbell Antiques and Interiors Inc.
17 W. McDonough St. • 238-5400

This shop specializes in upscale 18th- and 19th-century English and American furniture, Chinese export porcelain, antique accessories and objets d'art. Design services are available. The storefront is discretely placed in the side basement of a circa 1852 mansion facing Chippewa Square, just past the point where W. McDonough and Bull streets intersect.

Capra Capra Antiques
319 Abercorn St. • 236-9004

Located directly across from the front door of the Cathedral of St. John the Baptist, this could well be the most elegant and beautiful antique shop you will ever visit. The 1888 building has been carefully restored, and it houses high-end antiques in room settings that show them to great advantage. Specialties include Biedermeier pieces and Russian art and antiques, including the occasional Faberge and Bolin piece. Other offerings are Neoclassical pieces, Chinese porcelain and bronzes from the 18th and 19th centuries, ivory from Japan and China during those same time periods, as many as 200 clocks and a limited number of modern sculptures and contemporary artworks to demonstrate how quality from different styles and periods can work together.

Cobb's Galleries Inc.
417 Whitaker St. • 234-1582

This crowded shop in the more residential part of the Historic Downtown focuses mainly on American collectors' items, neatly organized and really packed into the store's two stories. American art pottery is a major line, with some 2,000 pieces in stock. Upstairs there's a collection of more than 3,000 cookbooks dated from the 1920s through the present. The eclectic stock also includes smaller concentrations of coins, glassware, china, bric-a-brac, toys and huge baskets full of the plastic figurines given away by fast-food restaurants.

Savannah Galleries
30 E. Bryan St. • 232-1234

Here you'll find 10,000 square feet of high-end antique English, French and American furniture, silver, porcelain and Oriental rugs. Pieces range from elegant marquetry to rustic

INSIDERS' TIP

Combine shopping with the national pastime. The Savannah Sand Gnats organization, the local minor league farm team currently associated with the Texas Rangers, sells a variety of caps, shirts and so forth with the team's attractive (but pesky) logo.

painted pine pieces. Design services are available as are search services, and the staff will assist in building collections. Cleaning, repair and appraisal of antique and modern Oriental rugs are also available. The owners, native Savannahians, have restored many fine old homes and are familiar with the furnishings such projects require. This establishment has been in operation since the 1960s and is experienced in shipping its merchandise.

Southern Antiques and Interiors Inc.
28 Abercorn St. • 236-5080

This shop offers 12,000 square feet of high-end furniture, mostly English and Continental pieces from the 18th and 19th centuries. Reproductions are also available, usually made to order in the English workshops with which the firm has a relationship. Southern Antiques specializes in larger pieces and has both case goods and soft (upholstered) furniture. The store carries about $1 million in inventory and is experienced in shipping since the bulk of its business involves out-of-town customers. Custom constructions can be designed to fit specific spaces, and the time frame for custom work is less than that for placing special orders with commercial manufacturers.

Bookstores

The Book Lady
17 W. York St. • 233-3628

Used and rare books are what you will find at The Book Lady, a quaint bookstore across from the post office on York Street. Owner Anita Raskin has filled her store with hundreds of previously owned books — some on topics found in most bookstores, and some that aren't. Besides art, architecture, religion, fiction and the usual fare, you will also find sections called Pretty Books and Nice Old Books among the lot. There are also several local titles on Savannah and the area. For that hard-to-find book, Anita offers a search service.

Books A Million
8108 Abercorn St. • 925-8112

This national retail chain offers thousands of titles, with deep discounts on bestsellers. The selection of magazines is the most extensive in the city, along with the largest selection

INSIDERS' TIP

If you've got military privileges, you'll find a PX and commissary at Hunter Army Airfield in Savannah.

of out-of-town Sunday papers (several days delayed, however). The local and regional section includes an extensive collection of Southern titles. The store also offers children's books, gifts, cards and gift wrap. Grab one of the free book newsletters and settle in at the in-store coffee shop.

Ex Libris
228 Martin Luther King Jr. Blvd.
• 238-2427

Ex Libris is part coffeehouse, college bookstore and gift shop. Owned by the Savannah College of Art and Design, it is one of the recent additions to the campus. The shop is on the western edge of the Historic Downtown and may be a little out of your way, but it's worth the trip. After browsing through art books, posters, framed art and many other eclectic and fun items you most likely won't find anywhere else in Savannah, you can sit and relax on the gigantic leather sofa and simply enjoy the beautifully restored building. A magnificent stairway takes up the center of the building and is the focal point of the room, along with "pillars" made out of thousands of encyclopedias. The store is especially beautiful during the Christmas season, when the college opens its holiday shop and offers decorations and other festive items.

Media Play
11701 Abercorn St. • 925-9201

OK, OK, so this isn't exactly a bookstore. The national chain is about equally divided among books, tapes and CDs, videos and computer software. We're calling it a bookstore because books are what we buy here. There's a reasonably good magazine collection, deep discounts on bestsellers and a schedule of special events for readers.

The Reading Edge
202 E. Broughton St. • 236-1006

This small bookstore carries a large selection of titles including fiction, current events, women's issues and more. If you are in the Historic Downtown and want to read more about the area, this store carries several titles relating to Savannah and the Lowcountry. Magazines and newspapers are sold, along with hot and cold drinks. It's just the right mix for relaxing with a good book.

Regina's Books and Cards
4515 Habersham St. • 353-7447

This friendly, independent bookseller offers a wide range of hardcovers and paperbacks, including a substantial selection by Savannah and Georgia authors. Inventory also includes children's books, and the store offers special orders. There's also a stock of attractive and original cards and a handful of other gifts, mainly book-related. Regina's is a frequent host of book signings, and shop cat Sophie takes refuge in the window when things get too crowded.

E. Shaver Bookseller
326 Bull St. • 234-7257

Book lovers will delight in this independent bookstore, which occupies the ground floor of the Shaver's Historic District home. An impressive array of hardcover and paperback books are available, and the knowledgeable staff offers solid advice. Local titles are well represented. The shop also offers a selection of carefully chosen used books and provides an efficient book-search service for older titles. A whole room is devoted to children's titles. Limited gift offerings include museum-style notecards, tote bags and appointment calendars.

INSIDERS' TIP

If you take a side trip to Hilton Head during your stay in Savannah, don't miss Eggs N Tricities, (803) 757-3446. This unique upscale boutique, located in an old gas station in Bluffton, South Carolina, has hundreds of interesting things to choose from including women's clothing, jewelry, handbags, children's clothing, picture frames, cards, art, T-shirts and much more. It's at the corner of Calhoun and Bridge streets.

Stardust Books
11 W. York St. • 236-1441

This shop carries a wide range of new and used metaphysical books, along with lines of jewelry, cards, cassettes, incense and Tarot. (See the New Age section of this chapter for more on Stardust.)

Candy

When we travel and need a gift for a hostess, or when we want to send a present with regional flavor (pun intended), we often opt for pralines. No one can claim these super-rich candies (made of sugar, butter, cream and pecans) are good for you, but at $10.95 to $11.95 per pound, your purse will probably stop you before you do yourself too much harm. You can find them made and sold in two shops on River Street. Although the shops would scream to hear it, we can't taste any difference.

River Street Sweets
13 E. River St. • 234-4608

Pralines are made right here, in full view, and there's usually someone near the door to offer you a sample. Display cases showcase other store specialties — confections of chocolate and nuts, spiced pecans, divinity, etc. There's a wide array of gift baskets and special packaging and an efficient shipping service.

Savannah Candy Kitchen
225 E. River St. • 233-8411

Kids of all ages will run rampant in this large candy store, which fills several rooms. In addition to pralines and other store-made specialties, you'll also find gourmet jelly beans and a staggering selection of other mass-produced candy — the kinds you remember from childhood and assumed no one sold any more. Choose from a wide selection of decorative tins to fill with goodies. Again, this store offers gift shipping.

Clothing

Alberts
106 W. Broughton St. • 236-8070

Alberts is a hip boutique featuring urban wear for men and women. Walk inside and you feel like you could be in a trendy store in any major city in the country. What you won't find here, however, are overly expensive price tags. Most of the clothes are priced under $100, some even lower than $50. The day we stopped by, several items were on sale, including a black linen dress for $28 and a bright green skirt for $25.

Chutzpah & Panache
251 Bull St. • 234-5007

Enjoy an afternoon of shopping and dining at Chutzpah & Panache, a charming boutique and eatery in the heart of the Historic Downtown. Fine woven and handprinted women's dresses, blouses, pants and scarves are sold in the boutique. The clothes are flowing, pretty and very comfortable. (For more on the dining options, see our Restaurants chapter.)

EJ Scandal's
205 W. River St. • 236-6064

This elegant, feminine boutique on the western edge of River Street has one of the nicest selections of women's clothing in Savannah. Cut Loose, Kiki and Flax are some of the brands you will find here. Mixed in the lot you might even discover a Max Studio or other rather expensive and exclusive label. Jewelry and other accessories such as belts and scarves are also available.

Gaucho
250 Bull St. • 232-7414

This upscale ladies' boutique has things you might need for a night out or just touring around town — there are dresses, jewelry, hats, skirts and more. The shop is eclectic, and many of the clothes are perfect for weathering Savannah's humid weather. Gaucho is near a smattering of other shops on Bull Street in the heart of the Historic Downtown.

Jezebel
25 E. River St. • 236-4333
Twelve Oaks Shopping Center, 5500
Abercorn St. • 354-8889

This upscale ladies' clothing boutique features casual and formal clothing for the Southern woman. Comfortable linen pants, dresses and shirts perfect for weathering 90-degree temperatures are Jezebel hallmarks. Brands

include Flax and Cut Loose, among others. Long flowing dresses, pants and shirts with pretty prints are included in the mix, along with jewelry, shoes, hats and more.

Profiles Ladies' Accessories and Gifts
307 Bull St. • 233-3892

This elegant accessories shop will make costume jewelry lovers drool. The store designs and manufactures its own line of earrings and other pieces, so you may recognize the name from shopping elsewhere. A wide range of handbags, scarves, belts and gloves is also offered, along with gift items like lovely glass ornaments and perfume bottles. The costume jewelry is of good quality in a wide variety of styles, from fun to dramatic.

Dime Stores

Mack's 5 and 10 Cent Store
Medical Arts Shopping Center, 4800
Waters Ave. • 354-3025

You'll think this store is a time machine. This classic dime store opened in 1946 and moved to its present location in 1962, where not much has changed since. While this is a fun store for browsing, it has a practical side because, crammed into a tiny space, it somehow manages to have everything. When we needed pinwheels for a photo assignment, we knew without question we could find them here. People come here for stuff they still want but can't find elsewhere — things like hair nets, soft peppermint sticks or flyswatters with wire mesh flaps. There are all sorts of housewares, along with plastic flowers, inexpensive toys, greeting cards, embroidered hankies and cardboard cutouts for elementary school bulletin boards.

> **FYI**
>
> Unless otherwise noted, the area code for all phone numbers listed in this guide is 912.

INSIDERS' TIP

Roadside produce stands as well as regular grocery stores are good places to pick up Vidalia onions. These famous mild, sweet onions are grown only in and around nearby Vidalia and have acquired a dedicated national following of gourmets.

Willows...
Where imagination Starts...

For Your Home...
Furniture, lamps, mirrors, glassware, framed art, garden accessories, linens, pottery

The Unusual...
Kilim rugs, kimonos, antiques from afar

For Yourself...
Books, throws, pillows, candles, bedding, jewelry

For Your Friends...
New Surprises

912-233-0780
Mon.- Sat. 10-6
101 W. Broughton St., at corner of Whitaker

Willows

Contemporary merchandise isn't ignored: The store even stocks (when it can get 'em) Beanie Babies — not because they're hot collectible items, but because before collectors discovered them, they were nice, inexpensive toys that made great gifts for children in Memorial Medical Center across the street. By the way, Mack's can still legitimately call itself a five-and-dime: Look hard enough, and you can still find items for these prices. We spotted tiny plastic boats for a dime and plastic rings and individual candies for a nickel.

Gifts and Fun Shops

Arts & Crafts Emporium of Savannah
234 Bull St. • 238-0003

Hundreds of artisans from around the country rent spaces ranging from large areas to small shelves to show their wares in this gigantic arts and crafts store. Wander around and some of the thousands of items you will encounter could include Christmas decorations, original watercolor paintings, jewelry, handmade children's dresses, pottery, dolls, small furniture and much more. We like to go after Christmas when some artisans mark their Christmas items down, giving us an excuse to stock up for next year.

Baskets, Bears & T's . . . Oh, My!
305 E. River St. • 232-4546

The title of this cozy shop (previously known as The Basket Place) pretty well describes the stock. The collection of stuffed animals includes both collectors' treasures and high-quality children's toys. Look for brands like Ty, Russ, Boyd's Bears, Enesco and other, smaller lines. Upstairs you'll find 2,500 square feet devoted to baskets of every imaginable shape, size and material. T-shirts include both Savannah-themed versions and witty (but not vulgar) novelty shirts. Other stock includes dolls (such as the Susan Wakeen line) and plenty of furniture perfect for toys. Other gift and novelty items are scattered in among it all — items owner/manager Carol Devine describes as "silly stuff . . . things that strike me at the moment."

Beaucoup Beads
306 W. Congress St. • 232-1353

Just as the name says, you will find thousands of beads at Beaucoup. From exotic imports to the simplest of bead designs, it's all here in Savannah's only bead shop. You will also discover the supplies you need to design and make a necklace, earrings or other piece of jewelry.

Byrd Cookie Company and Gourmet Marketplace
6700 Waters Ave. • 355-1716

You can buy these well-known local cook-

Not everyone can shop 'til they drop, even on River
Street with its many stores and gift shops.

ies all over town, but the advantage of choosing them from this shop is that you can sample the wide range of flavors here — Key Lime Coolers, Benne Bits, raspberry, butter cookies and so on. They're sold in decorative tins that are excellent choices for those obligation gifts: One is sufficient for a solid token gift, or you can assemble a collection if you need something more impressive. If you show up during a production run, you can even watch the manufacturing process through a glass window. In addition to Byrd Cookies, this shop features an array of clever gifts (most with a culinary theme), a selection of other gourmet food items and fresh flowers. Note that it is closed on Saturday but open on Sunday.

Callaway Gardens Country Store
301 E. River St. • 236-4055

Everything you might expect to discover in a country store can be found at Callaway Gardens. This large shop on the eastern end of River Street sells hard candy, several brands of jewelry (including the antique-looking line 1928), Mary Engelbreit books, cards and writing paper and, yes, even Beanie Babies. The store also features gourmet food items like muscadine preserves, speckled heart grits, handmade candy and other Southern delicacies like Vidalia onion jelly and hot sauce.

The Cat House
310 W. St. Julian St. • 236-2287

Cat lovers shouldn't miss this City Market store. Owner Janet Waters advertises that her shop is full of "Feline Fancies for Feline Fanciers." Adorned with pictures of Julian and other felines owned by Waters, the shop features fuzzy stuffed cats, along with cat greeting cards, figurines, toys, books and more. For those having problems with a finicky cat, you can find books with advice on how to better understand and take care of your feline friends.

Charlotte's Corner
1 W. Liberty St. • 233-8061

This eclectic gift shop offers a little bit of everything, spread out over four rooms. There are lots of shirts — T-shirts, tank-tops, sleep shirts, sweatshirts. Fancy children's clothing featuring appliques and smocking — the things that grandparents buy — are well represented

in the stock. A line of fun clothes for adults is included, and there are plenty of toys. Woven afghans are offered in various motifs, including local ones. In addition to a line of *Midnight in the Garden of Good and Evil* merchandise, there are local souvenirs including other Savannah books, ornaments and prints by local artists.

Gypsy Moth
311 W. St. Julian St. • 232-6800

This City Market gift shop gained lots of attention when a local politician denounced it as demonic. Turns out he'd misinterpreted the Third World folk art it stocks, which includes some pretty graphic renditions of Christian martyrdom, Mexican Day of the Dead items and the like. We've bought molas, the reverse-applique fabric art produced by Central American Indians, here. There's also a line of clothing, some new and some vintage, as well as unusual postcards and jewelry.

The Little House
107 E. Gordon St. • 232-1551

This upscale gift shop features elegant presents, including fine china, lovely linens, unusual tableware, toys and children's books and fine paper goods. Some cookbooks, many by Savannahians, and a few books on Savannah are also featured. The shop is actually in a little house, set back from the street in a garden.

Midnight Star Pottery
213 W. St. Julian • 236-3473

This store is actually a pottery painting studio where the customers pick out pieces of pottery, then go to work painting a one-of-a-kind creation. There are hundreds of pieces of pottery to chose from including tiles, bowls, goblets and vases. Items start around $2. Besides purchasing the piece, you pay an additional $6 per hour ($5 per hour for children 10 and younger) for the studio fee, which includes all the paints, brushes, stencils, sponges and other supplies you'll need, plus glazing and firing. Many people make an outing to Midnight Star Pottery an event for family gatherings, wedding showers or birthday parties.

Nellie's Nook
19 E. River St. • 233-5401

This shop focuses mainly on major collectible lines, including what it calls the largest collection of Sheila pieces in the country. The Sheila line is made up of shallow, three-dimensional wooden representations of historic buildings, presented in limited editions. The collection includes several Savannah buildings, including Savannah City Hall. Other stock includes Boyd's Bears, the All God's Children figurines, Fenton Glass, Sandicast Dogs, the Herd line of elephant sculptures, Barlow knives and related faux scrimshaw jewelry from that company, Coca-Cola collectibles and other specific collections. The store handles mail orders as well.

Sails & Rails
423 E. River St. • 232-7201

It's hard to miss Sails and Rails on River Street. It's the shop with the brightly displayed kites, flags and wind socks blowing outside. This unique shop includes dozens of kites, along with flags from around the world and decorative ones for your front porch. Wind socks — ranging from those with pictures of snowmen on them to others shaped like whales — are also for sale, along with things for toy train enthusiasts.

Terra Cotta
34 Barnard St. • 236-6150

Wander by Terra Cotta, just outside of City Market, and you can't help but be lured in. The shop features an eclectic mix of items from fine silk and linen dresses to gigantic Portuguese soaps, inviting bath towels, cotton lingerie and delicate jewelry. Just about everything someone would need for a night of pampering can be found inside this very feminine boutique. Owner Christine DiNicola has chosen carefully and it shows. With soft blues music playing and the lavender scent of candles on the air, stepping inside Terra Cotta provides a respite from a hectic day of touring.

True Grits
107 E. River St. • 234-8006

This novel gift shop comes in two separate and distinct parts, and by the time you read this, the new nautical and Civil War section may have its own name, differentiating it from True Grits' more generic gift shop. Don't let the name game confuse you, however: The stores are right next door to one another, and there are interior isthmuses that connect them.

On the gifty side, choose from 250 different varieties of hot sauce, each label claiming to be deadlier than the other. You'll also see plenty of shirts, toys, mugs and plates with Savannah scenes. In the newer portion of the shop(s), you'll find items with nautical themes — lighthouse figurines and lighthouse needlework kits; large, realistic wooden ship models; tables made from hatch covers or using four-bladed brass props as bases; and antique telescopes. Civil War merchandise includes replica swords and hats, many history books and three different versions of Civil War-themed chess sets. (One set features President and Mrs. Lincoln and CSA President and Mrs. Jefferson Davis as the respective kings and queens, and William T. Sherman and Robert E. Lee in the role of bishops.)

Wild Birds Unlimited
Medical Arts Shopping Center, 4821 Waters Ave. • 692-0060

Bird enthusiasts can stock up on bird seed, feeders, houses, binoculars, toys, gifts and

---

INSIDERS' TIP

Savannah is home to a premier cigar manufacturing company. While traveling down Abercorn Street near Mall Boulevard, you may have noticed a gigantic military vehicle known as a Hummer. This marks the offices of Camorra Cigars, 355-5611, a company started by four young entrepreneurs. The firm also has cigar manufacturing operations overseas. Camorra's line of cigars has received praise in national magazines including *Cigar Aficionado* and *Smoke*.

CDs here. This shop is geared to those who want to watch birds in the wild (including their own backyards), so it doesn't handle pet bird supplies. Some of the feeders and birdhouses double as lawn sculptures, including ornate, copper-roofed models. You'll also find a small stock of educational toys, and such unique items as hummingbird feeders and houses especially designed for butterflies and bats.

Home and Food

Chili Chompers
30 Barnard St. • 234-1932
You'll can't miss Chili Chompers. The eye-catching window displays are usually full of everything a salsa-loving, chili-eating, spicy food-craving addict can't live without. This unique boutique that includes gifts and food touts itself as "The Cool Store with the HOT Stuff." Inside you will find all things Tabasco — from a plain old bottle of the stuff to Tabasco posters, earrings, neckties and even boxer shorts. Don't miss the salsa tasting bar, where you can try (if you dare!) before you buy. The Savannah store was the first to open in this fun chain that now can be found in cities around the country including Hilton Head and Charleston.

The Hammock Company
20 Jefferson St. • 232-6655
Audubon guides, bird feeders, wind chimes, plantation rockers, swings and (of course) hammocks can be found at this home and camping store. Their signature hammock is the Original Pawley's Island Rope Hammock that has been handcrafted by islanders for more than 100 years. Enjoy a relaxing turn in this hammock, while the rest of your group browses among the other related items in this unique store.

Kitchen Kaboodle
31 Barnard St. • 238-3474
Need a cappuccino machine? What about some fun dishes featuring flowers or fruit for that special occasion? Or a gift for that soon-to-be-wed couple? Come to Kitchen Kaboodle. Located just outside City Market, this shop has an eclectic mix of kitchen supplies, with a few gourmet foods thrown in. The selection is vast and varied and lives up to their motto, "The Kitchen Store with More." You will find everything here from the basics to silver platters with rabbits etched into them. The gourmet food selection features items like Vidalia onion and summer tomato salad dressing and raspberry salsa.

Peanut Shop of Savannah
407 E. River St. • 232-8612
Peanut brittle, roasted peanuts and plain ol' peanuts, along with hard candy and Key lime jelly, are just some of the many things you will find inside the Peanut Shop. If you aren't sure what kind of peanuts you want, don't worry, there are usually several samples out so you can try before you buy.

Willows
101 W. Broughton St. • 233-0780
This upscale boutique featuring home furnishings is one of the newer additions to the Broughton Street revival. Bamboo, wicker and other modern furniture, along with pottery, cotton and linen duvet covers, rugs and sheer window coverings are just some of the many items you will enjoy browsing through.

New Age

Moon Dance
306 W. St. Julian St. • 236-9003
This City Market shop, formerly known as Dreamweaver, carries books with mystical, women's and New Age themes, along with music, herbs, crystals, incense and gifts. It's also a center for classes, lectures and service sessions by various New Age practitioners.

Stardust Books
11 W. York St. • 236-1441
As mentioned in the Bookstores section, this shop is a great source for metaphysical books, jewelry, cards, cassettes, incense and Tarot. The shop's windows and walls are also a good information source, with handbills and posters about events and lectures in the local New Age community.

Thrifts and Flea Markets

This kind of shopping isn't for everyone, just the most dedicated bargain hunters. If you don't mind rolling up your sleeves, these places can be real treasure troves. Of course, you'll occasionally come away empty-handed, but if you are into the thrill of the chase, you won't mind a bit.

Goodwill Industries
2123 E. Victory Dr. • 352-2413
7220 Sallie Mood Dr. • 354-7423
23 Westside Shopping Center, U.S. Hwy.
80, Garden City • 966-0080

Chances are your community has these stores, with donated goods refurbished, sorted and stocked by the disabled. But you should definitely check ours out: With our large military and college populations (which tend to be mobile), Savannah's Goodwills see lots of merchandise turnover. We have friends who have furnished entire beach houses with stuff from these stores. The Sallie Mood Drive location is the best place for furniture: It's in the back, behind swinging doors and easy to miss if you aren't specifically looking for it. We've bought three-drawer pine dressers rescued from dormitories for $35, current hardback bestsellers for $2, glass ice buckets from the 1950s for $4 and so on.

Keller's Flea Market
5901 Ogeechee Rd. • 927-4848

Ever wonder where people buy velvet wall-hangings depicting the Last Supper, wild stallions and dogs playing poker? We've found them here ($10 each). In fact, if you go often enough and search diligently, we're convinced you can find just about anything in one of the 400-plus booths. Some are just tables under shed roofs; others are enclosed mini-stores. Don't expect anything fancy — this is the base of the food chain of retail shopping. Still, we've made some real finds here and had fun people-watching.

Among the booths you'll find the equivalent of yard sales, estate sales and salvage sales. Some have new merchandise, including designer-label stuff that doesn't appear very convincing, and pure junk that isn't masquerading as anything else. Handcrafters, small-scale importers and collectors set up

here. Go early on Saturday, and you'll see the antique dealers scouting for stuff they'll clean up (and mark up) for their own shops. Our finds here have included an IBM Selectric typewriter for $35 (in need of some repair, but still worth it), used books, carved onyx parrots and a possibly authentic (but probably not) poster from the 1955 World Series.

Other merchandise on a typical weekend includes fresh produce, house plants and plants for landscaping, sports cards, T-shirts and bumper stickers with politically incorrect slogans. One section features exotic birds, reptiles, puppies and chickens, but real animal lovers should give that section a wide berth. The market is open Saturday and Sunday. Ogeechee Road is also U.S. Highway 17, and the market is in the county's far southern section. About 2 miles past Savannah Mall, you'll spot the exit for U.S. Hwy. 17. Take the exit, turn left at the end of the ramp, and you'll soon see the market on your left. Dress casually: The parking field tends to be either a quagmire or a dust bowl.

Surfing/Beach Shops

High Tide Surf Shop
1401 Butler Ave. Tybee Island
• 786-4274

Surfboards, boogie boards, sunglasses, beach chairs, swimsuits and everything else needed for a day at the beach can be found at High Tide Surf Shop on Tybee Island. Women's and men's beachwear in many popular brand names are here, along with some traditional tourist finds like T-shirts with Tybee Island emblazed on the front.

Tobacco

The Tinder Box
244 Bull St. • 232-2650

This smoking specialty shop stocks tobacco in all its forms, and chances are you don't realize how many forms that is. There are between 180 and 200 different types of cigars in stock at any given time, along with 30 blends of pipe tobacco (including their own custom blend). Cigarettes include imported

Dunhills, Export A (Canadian) and the American-made additive-free Nat Sherman cigarettes in various sizes and shapes. The inventory even includes Indonesian clove cigarettes and Darsham Bidis, which is Indian tobacco wrapped in eucalyptus and flavored with strawberry or vanilla. Accessories include elegant lighters, cutters, punches, clippers and humidors in fine wood (the most expensive currently in stock is $1,250). They also stock books and magazines for cigar and pipe enthusiasts.

The most distinguishing feature at The Tinder Box, however, is the lounge, a small comfortable room at the rear of the store with leather sofas and big-screen TV. Here customers from Savannah's business district (and tourists, of course) can relax with their smokes. Individual locker-size humidors with full temperature and humidity control are available for rental to house customers' personal tobacco collections. The shop is part of a franchised chain of tobacco shops.

Verdery's Lamps and Ye Ole Tobacco Shop
131 W. River St. • 236-9384
280 Eisenhower Dr. • 691-0807

Lamps and tobacco might sound like a strange combination, but the way the shopkeepers see it, it gives them something for both male and female shoppers. It must work: They've been on River Street since that area was resurrected in the early 1970s, and they recently expanded to a Southside store. On the lighting side, they offer custom lamps and

shades, along with repairs and restorative work. For tobacco enthusiasts, there's a walk-in humidor with more than 100 brands and 200 sizes of cigars, ranging in price from 65¢ to $29.95 each. The pipe tobacco selection includes Verdery's own custom blends. In addition to the usual line of American cigarette brands, they have imported Dunhills, Gauloises and others, along with clove cigarettes and additive-free versions. The store also stocks pipes and leather goods for smokers.

Toys

Toy Smart
309 Eisenhower Dr. • 351-6060
2 N. Lincoln St., off River St. • 651-8888

Tired of violent-themed, over-advertised plastic toys? If so, this set of local toy stores is for you. We don't mean to imply that all the stock here is made by elves at the North Pole, but it is less schlocky than your run-of-the-mill toys. You'll find appealing educational toys (that don't come across as homework on the make), high-quality stuffed animals, Madame Alexander dolls, Thomas the Tank Engine merchandise and other items geared toward children whose parents pay close attention to what goes into the toy box. The Eisenhower Drive store (a few blocks east and north of Oglethorpe Mall) is roomier and better for browsing; the River Street store is smaller and crowded but features a small toy museum that will prompt aging baby boomers to remember, "I used to have one of those."

With most of the city's best-known attractions in the Historic Downtown, a walking tour seemed in order to give your personal trek some direction.

Attractions

Savannah is perfect for strolling, and we thought this chapter would be the perfect place to provide you with a little direction. With most of the city's best-known attractions in the Historic Downtown, a walking tour seemed in order to give your personal trek some guidance.

Here's the format: We provide detailed listings of many of the popular historic sites downtown, and in between we give explicit directions (in italics) on how to get from one location to the next. The tour takes in a little more than 2.5 miles; how long it takes depends on how fast you walk and whether you decide to take a detour or two and further explore some sites. We heartily encourage you to do so.

You will find many benches for leisurely breaks along the way. If you get hungry or have an urge to do some browsing, you will be passing by many restaurants and specialty shops. If you stumble on a place that catches your fancy and is not listed in this chapter, chances are you can find out more about it in our Restaurants or Shopping chapters. Another great dining option is to pack a picnic before setting out: Each square you encounter — and we will cover 10 — is perfect for relaxing near the magnolia trees while enjoying a good sandwich.

If you need a visual aid, several good maps of the Historic Downtown are available in shops around town and typically cost less than $5. The Savannah Area Convention & Visitors Bureau, 222 W. Oglethorpe Avenue, 944-0444, also provides a visitors guide that has a great map. And don't forget our own at the front of the guide.

Following our Insiders' Historic Downtown tour, we provide information on other guided touring options in the city, plus a variety of other interesting attractions to explore both in Savannah's downtown and the outlying areas — the Islands and West Chatham.

Doing the Historic Downtown

Whether you are coming to the Historic Downtown from the Talmadge bridge or you're already there and wandering around on foot, you can't miss the gold dome on top of City Hall. Because of this, we decided to start our tour at this landmark on Bay Street and the northern tip of Bull Street. So look up (or down, depending on your vantage point), and when you spot the gold dome, head in that direction. Once you arrive, don't be shy — wander inside for a quick look around. You will be glad you did, and the office workers don't mind a bit.

City Hall
Bay and Bull Sts. • 651-6410

Local architect Hyman Wallace Witcover designed and built City Hall in 1905 for an estimated $205,167. This price was to include statues of chariots and horses on top of the structure, but budget constraints prevented them from being built. The exterior is comprised of several materials including rough-hewn granite blocks, colored limestone and polished granite. The dome, rising 70 feet, was originally copper. However, in 1987 a local philanthropist donated $240,000 to the city, allowing the dome to be gilded with thin layers of 23-karat gold leaf. The gold was applied to the dome, cupola and clock hands.

Inside the foyer you will find small tiles on the floor having intricate and colorful patterns. Look up in the foyer, and you will see more detailed tiles. Go farther into the rotunda and look up for a pretty, circular view all the way up to the fourth floor and the stained glass in the dome. The original building directory is also in the rotunda on a giant tablet. Today,

Savannah city offices are located throughout the community, but the second floor of City Hall is much like it was when the building was originally built. It still houses the mayor's office, clerk of council offices and the council chambers.

After leaving City Hall head south on Bull Street. Look to your left while crossing Bay Street. The huge building on the corner opposite City Hall is the United States Custom House.

United States Custom House
1 E. Bay St.

The magnificent columns in front of the Custom House each weigh 15 tons. Across the street are cannon presented to the Chatham Artillery in 1791 by George Washington.

In 1972 the structure was designated a historic custom house by the U.S. Commissioner of Customs. As you walk by, notice the wonderful ironwork fencing that not only decorates the building, but also guards it. It is just one of many fine examples of wrought iron you will notice throughout your walking tour. Today the building houses U.S. Customs Service officials who process paperwork involving shipments in and out of the local port.

FYI

Unless otherwise noted, the area code for all phone numbers listed in this guide is 912.

Continue south on Bull Street in the direction of Johnson Square. You will note Morrison's Cafeteria, a downtown restaurant staple for nearly 40 years, on your right.

Johnson Square
Bull St., between Bryan and Congress Sts.

This is Savannah's first square. It is named for Robert Johnson, the governor of South Carolina who helped the Georgia colony get established. During the early days of the colony, this was the center of activity for the city. In the center is a monument to Revolutionary war hero Gen. Nathanael Greene, who died in 1786; his grave is here as well. Today the square is the center of banking in Savannah. Stand in the middle and you will be surrounded by several banks. If you need to pick up some cash, this is a good spot to find an ATM.

On the eastern side of the square, look for pairs of gigantic green doors and majestic columns. They belong to Christ Episcopal Church.

Christ Episcopal Church
28 Bull St. • 232-8230

Christ Church is known as Georgia's Mother Church. It was founded in 1733, on the exact spot where the first religious service in Georgia was held. The present church replaced two churches that were destroyed. In 1735, John Wesley, the founder of Methodism, served as pastor here and founded what is believed to be the world's first Protestant Sunday school.

Also interesting: Christ Church has one of the rarest church bells in the entire country. It is known as a Revere Bell and was built by Paul Revere and Sons, the company owned by the noted "British are coming" patriot. It is one of about 130 Revere bells, the majority of which are found in New England states; only a handful made it to the South. The bell in the tower is actually the third Revere Bell the church has owned. The first, purchased in 1816 for $716, cracked during shipment. The second cracked the second Sunday it rang. The third bell, as they say, was the charm. The church didn't have any significant problems with the third bell until 1995, when repairs needed to be made to the apparatus holding the bell. After a two-year repair job, the bell was rung again in early November 1997.

INSIDERS' TIP

The Rev. John Wesley's early Savannah ministry is remembered with a statue of him in Reynolds Square in the Historic Downtown.

Continue heading south on Bull Street, crossing Congress Street and proceeding to Broughton Street. This is Savannah's original business district. Look east and west to see many shops and restaurants. From trendy Italian eateries to a great place for a hot dog, Broughton Street offers it all — take a detour if you are hungry. If not, continue south on Bull Street to Wright Square, the second square on our trip.

Wright Square
Bull St., between State and York Sts.

Wright Square is named for Sir James Wright, the last royal governor of Georgia. The monument in the center is for William Washington Gordon, one of the founders of the Central of Georgia Railroad. (The railroad's offices used to be about a block away; you will pass the site on our walking tour.) The large boulder, taken from Stone Mountain in Atlanta, marks the grave of Tomo-chi-chi, the Yamacraw Indian chief who was instrumental in helping the founders get established in their new colony.

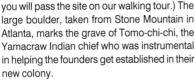

www.insiders.com

See this and many other **Insiders' Guide®** destinations online — in their entirety.

Visit us today!

Taking up the entire western side of the square is the U.S. Post Office, completed in 1898. Made of Georgia marble, its architecture is a conglomeration of many styles — Spanish, French, Italian Renaissance and Romanesque among them. Today it remains a working post office and houses U.S. district court offices. On the eastern side of the square, you'll see the old Chatham County Courthouse, a light-colored brick building designed in 1889 by noted Boston architect William G. Preston. On the same side as the courthouse is Lutheran Church of the Ascension.

Lutheran Church of the Ascension
21 E. State St. • 232-4151

Massive red doors lead into Lutheran Church of the Ascension, formed in 1741 by German settlers. The present church was built between 1875 and 1879 and was designed by George B. Clarke using Norman and Gothic styles. One of the church's most striking features is the Ascension Window, depicting the Ascension of the Lord.

Continue heading south on Bull Street. On the northeastern corner of Bull and Oglethorpe streets is the Juliette Gordon Low Center.

Juliette Gordon Low Center
142 Bull St. • 233-4501

The Juliette Gordon Low Center gives visitors an authentic glimpse of what life was like in the 1800s for one of Savannah's most prominent families — one that just happened to include Juliette Gordon Low, founder of the Girl Scouts.

But the Low Center isn't just about Girl Scouts. This beautifully restored home, Savannah's first National Historic Landmark, is full of the Gordon's original belongings — from Georgian Revival chairs in the dining room to a painting of Niagara Falls by moonlight, a souvenir the Gordons bought some years after their honeymoon. When entering the main hallway you will immediately notice the beautiful winding staircase with a rose-colored bull's-eye glass window in the background; it was installed in 1886 to give more light in the stairway. In the library is a brass chandelier original to the home. The south parlor, decorated in striking yellow, red and green, has a pier mirror installed in 1884.

Construction on the home began in 1818 in the newly fashionable English Regency style. William Washington Gordon and his wife, Sarah, were the first of four generations of the Gordon family to live in the home. William Gordon served as mayor of Savannah and is credited as a founder of the Central of Georgia Railroad. The house was eventually inherited by William Washington Gordon II and his wife, Eleanor Kinzie Gordon, the parents of Juliette Gordon. Juliette spend her childhood here.

After passing through another generation of Gordons, the house in 1953 was threatened with demolition. A concerned group of local Girl Scouts, including youngsters and adults, appealed to the national organization to save the birthplace of their founder, and the building was purchased by the Girl Scouts. It was restored and opened to the public three years later. Today thousands of Girl Scouts from around the world make the pilgrimage to

Photo: Kyle Cason

This trolley-style tour bus is one of many vehicles used for guided tours.

Savannah to visit the home of the group's cherished founder. The house is open from 10 AM to 4 PM Monday through Saturday (except Wednesday) and from 12:30 to 4:30 PM on Sundays. Cost is $5 for adults and $4 for students ages 6 to 18.

Continuing south on Bull Street, you will pass the offices for the local school district on the left and Independent Presbyterian Church on the right.

Independent Presbyterian Church
25 West Oglethorpe Ave. • 236-3346

This church was founded in 1755 and is considered one of the most important Federal-style churches in the country. The original was designed by John Holden Greene of Rhode Island. It burned in 1889. The current building has an elevated mahogany pulpit, and the four Corinthian columns of the sanctuary were made from a single tree trunk that was carefully selected through exhaustive searches in the South. Woodrow Wilson married Ellen Axson, granddaughter of the church's pastor, here.

Continue south to Chippewa Square.

Chippewa Square
Bull St., between Perry and Hull Sts.

Gen. James Oglethorpe is immortalized in bronze in the center of this square. First Baptist Church, organized in 1800, is on the northwestern corner of the square. Across the park on the northeastern corner is the Savannah Theater, which hosts many locally produced shows throughout the year.

For movie buffs, this is the square where Forrest Gump sat waiting for the bus. The bench was placed on the far northern tip of the square. Next time you see the film, notice that traffic in the square is moving in the wrong direction! The beautiful building on the southwest corner is known as the Philbrick-Eastman House and is a fine example of Greek Revival architecture. It served as home for many prominent families; today it houses a law firm. It was also a location for the movie *Now and Then*, which starred Demi Moore, Rita Wilson and Melanie Griffith, among others.

While walking south through the square, look to your left along W. Perry Street and you will notice a row of magnificently restored private homes — the first of many you will see on your trip today.

Continue south on Bull Street. After crossing Perry Street, notice a dolphin downspout on the home to your right. These interesting adornments to lovely houses are a common sight throughout Savannah. You'll pass the Six Pence Pub, a popular hangout year round, but especially on St. Patrick's Day (the parade passes right by; see our St. Patrick's Day chapter for details).

There are several boutiques, a coffee shop and a few lunch spots in this area. Duck into Arts & Crafts Emporium of Savannah, Gaucho, Chutzpah & Panache (which is both a quaint lunch spot and a boutique) and look for buys. Check the Shopping and Restaurants chapters for more information. Down Liberty Street is the DeSoto Hilton, built on the site of the DeSoto Hotel, which was razed in 1966. Next is Madison Square.

Madison Square
Bull St., between Harris and Charlton Sts.

Madison Square is named for James Madison, the fourth U.S. president. When entering Madison Square, you will notice the Sorrel-Weed House on the northwest corner of the square. It was completed in 1841 and is an example of Greek Revival architecture. In 1997 the home was purchased and underwent an extensive $2 million renovation that restored it to its original condition. This, however, included painting the home its original bright orange color, which did not please neighbors and members of a local historic review committee. However, the homeowner won out, as you will see when walking by.

On the northeastern corner is E. Shaver Bookseller, a popular locally owned bookstore. If you need a break, this could be a good place to take it. On the southeastern edge of the square is a gigantic red brick building that was the former Savannah Volunteer Guards Armory. This structure and the large building across the street on southwest corner of the square — the old Scottish Rite Temple — are owned by the Savannah College of Art and Design. The armory was the first building art school founders Paula and Richard Rowan purchased when they came to town in the late 1970s. At the time, there was an old greasy spoon inside, so complete renovation was needed. It was the first in a long list of buildings purchased and restored by the school; you'll find them throughout the Historic Downtown. Today, the armory houses classrooms and Exhibit A, an art gallery that features artwork by students and professors and, at times, work by famous artists. It is free and open to the public. (For more information on the Savannah College of Art and Design, see our Education and Child Care chapter.)

Look to the northwest corner of the square. The Gothic brick mansion is the Green-Meldrim House.

INSIDERS' TIP

If you're venturing south of the Historic Downtown to do some sightseeing, be sure to take a drive down portions of two streets in Midtown — Victory Drive between Abercorn Street and Waters Avenue, and Washington Avenue between Bull Street and Waters. You'll see stately homes set amid huge, graceful oak trees and, if you hit it just right during the springtime, medians and yards bursting with the color of azaleas in bloom. Palm trees were first planted along Victory Drive in 1906 when it was called Estill Avenue, and this thoroughfare — which starts at Ogeechee Road, runs to the Wilmington River and continues to Tybee Island as U.S. 80 — was once reputed to be the longest avenue of palms in the nation. When Estill Avenue was widened and extended in 1922, it was renamed Victory Drive in honor of the Americans who fought and died in World War I.

Green-Meldrim House
1 W. Macon St. • 233-3845

Built in 1853 by architect-builder John S. Norris for a wealthy cotton merchant, the Green-Meldrim House is best known as being headquarters for Gen. William T. Sherman, who gave the city of Savannah to President Lincoln as a Christmas present. The famous telegram to Lincoln, dated December 22, 1864, reads: "I beg to present to you as a Christmas Gift, the City of Savannah with 150 heavy guns and plenty of ammunition; and also about 25,000 bales of Cotton."

Today the home is owned by its neighbor, St. John's Church; it serves as the parish house. When you walk by, notice the beautiful and elaborate ironwork and the oriel windows that give light from three sides. Inside are American black walnut wooden floors, elaborate moldings, marble mantels and other original adornments. The home is open for tours from 10 AM to 4 PM on Tuesday, Thursday, Friday and Saturday. Admission is $4 for adults and $2 for students.

Continuing south on Bull Street you will pass Jones Street, considered one of Savannah's most picturesque roadways. Notice the brick streets and wonderfully restored homes. It is well worth a short detour. It is also home to one of Savannah's most noted restaurants, Mrs. Wilkes', which is known for its Southern fare (see our Restaurants chapter). Next is Monterey Square.

Monterey Square
Bull St., between Taylor and Gordon Sts.

This is the final square on Bull Street. Its name commemorates the Battle of Monterey in the Mexican War. The square was laid out in 1847. In the center is a monument honoring Casimir Pulaski, a Polish noblemen who was killed during the American Revolution. The monument has caused a lot of interest of late. In 1996 it was removed for repairs. When this occurred, a group of forensic scientists were also on hand to remove the body buried beneath the monument.

There is a longstanding debate among local historians regarding who is buried in Monterey Square. One side contends it's Casimir Pulaski, the war hero honored by the monument. Others argue that Pulaski was either buried at sea or elsewhere. The scientists are in the process of conducting tests on the remains to determine the identity of the corpse and put an end to the debate. Results aren't expected until sometime in 1998.

During filming of the movie *Midnight in the Garden of Good and Evil*, the monument was still being worked on, so the set designers brought in their own monument. Now when you see Monterey Square on the big screen, you'll know the monument is not the original. The square contains other significant sites used in the movie, including the home where the book's main plot unfolds — the killing of Danny Hansford. This occurred at the Mercer-Wilder House, commonly known as Mercer House, which is on the western edge of the square.

Mercer House
429 Bull St.

Cited by Historic Savannah Foundation as nationally significant for its architectural style, this home was designed by John S. Norris and completed in 1871. The striking ironwork — including cast-iron window pediments, eight cast-iron balconies and the sidewalk fence — is one of the house's signature features. The house was named for Confederate Gen. Hugh Mercer, songwriter Johnny Mercer's great-grandfather, but Gen. Mercer sold the house. He never lived there nor did any member of the Mercer family.

In 1970, after the house was neglected and empty for many years, Jim Williams, the antique dealer and central character in *Midnight in the Garden of Good and Evil*, finished a complete restoration of the home. It is also here that Williams shot his companion, Danny Hansford, which is detailed in the book. Today the private home is owned by Dorothy Kingery, sister of the late Jim Williams. In an interview with *Savannah Magazine*, she described how her life has changed since the book was published. "The publication of the book ended privacy as I had known it," she said. "Since then, privacy has been an ongoing concern." Thousands of tourists seek out the house every year. Most likely when you wander by, you will see a tour bus or two.

Looking past Mercer House, on the southwest corner of the square, you will notice rowhouses along Gordon Street. One of these homes — 7 W. Gordon Street — has also had a brush with celebrity. If you are a fan of the PBS show This Old House, you may be familiar with the renovation that took place here in 1996 at the home of Mills and Marianne Fleming. For several months, Norm Abram, Steve Thomas and the rest of the crew from the popular PBS series were in town helping restore the 1884 home, which made headlines when it was built for being one of the first homes in the city to have indoor plumbing. Across the square from Mercer House, on the eastern side of the square, is Temple Mickve Israel.

Temple Mickve Israel
20 E. Gordon St. • 233-1547

Temple Mickve Israel began with a group of Spanish Portugese Jews who came to Savannah in 1733, just five months after the founding of the colony. It is the site of the first Jewish congregation in the South and the third in the entire United States. It is also the only Gothic synagogue in the country. The temple was designed by Henry G. Harrison and houses the oldest Torah in America. There are also hundreds of documents, historical books and letters from presidents Washington, Jefferson and Madison in the museum adjoining the temple. Free tours of the sanctuary and museum take place Monday through Friday from 10 AM to noon and 2 to 4 PM.

Continuing south on Bull Street, you will pass the George Armstrong House on the northwest corner of Bull and Gaston streets. This massive building, constructed in 1920, was given to the city in 1935 and converted into Armstrong Junior College, predecessor to Armstrong Atlantic University, which subsequently moved to Savannah's Southside. (For more on Armstrong Atlantic, see our Education and Child Care chapter.) Today it houses a law firm.

Across the street, on the northeast corner of Bull and Gaston streets is the Oglethorpe Club, one of Savannah's most elite and private clubs. As detailed in The Book, the Oglethorpe Club is characterized as the place that separates the truly elite among the locals from the rest: "In Savannah we have our little way of drawing the line — of saying, You shall come this far and no farther, you are not really one of us. We have the Oglethorpe Club as our way of saying this. And we have the yacht club." Straight ahead is Forsyth Park.

Forsyth Park
Bull St., between Gaston St. and Park Ave.

This 30-acre park filled with azaleas, magnolia trees, walkways, park benches and more is one of Savannah's most beautiful spots. If you are in need of a break during the walking tour, don't miss a stroll through Forsyth Park; in fact, we suggest a picnic. The park was laid out in 1851. One of its most recognizable and often photographed features is the white fountain near the center. Visit on the weekend, and you might see a bride and groom getting pictures made here next to the ornate swans and other creatures in the fountain.

The monument in the center of the park was erected by the United Daughters of the Confederacy and honors those killed during the Civil War. The park is also home to a Fragrant Garden for the Blind and is surrounded by beautiful and elaborately restored homes, many of which are Victorian in style. Across from the northwestern corner of the park is the Georgia Historical Society. (For much more on Forsyth Park, see our Parks and Recreation chapter.)

Georgia Historical Society
501 Whitaker St. • 651-2128

Dr. William Bacon Stevens, a physician who later became the Episcopal Bishop of Pennsylvania, and attorney I.K. Tefft are generally credited with organizing the Savannah-based Georgia Historical Society. The pair were soon joined by Dr. Richard D. Arnold, a founder of the American Medical Association. In 1839 the group incorporated one of the country's oldest (and the Southeast's first) historical societies.

Nearly 160 years later, the realization of their efforts can easily be seen in thousands of historic documents, artifacts, newspapers and other source materials documenting Georgia's past. Visitors to the Society will find everything in its massive archives — from copies of letters Gen. James Edward Oglethorpe wrote to the Trustees of the Colony, to the grapeshot that killed Casimir Pulaski and was extracted from the Polish war hero's leg. There are minutes from the first Georgia Medical Society meeting, held in Savannah in 1804, photographs from the now-defunct YWCA and family letters such as the one written by Garnett Andrews about the cotton gin Eli Whitney had invented.

The Society also publishes, in cooperation with the University of Georgia, the highly acclaimed *Georgia Historical Quarterly*, a collection of scholarly articles. Entry to the Georgia Historical Society is free. The building is open to the public from 10 AM to 5 PM Tuesday through Friday and 9 AM to 3 PM on Saturday.

This is the midpoint of the walking tour. We will travel north for this portion of the tour, heading back in the direction of City Hall, where we started. Continue one block east on Gaston Street, crossing Drayton Street. Check out the many beautifully restored homes, including the Lions Head Inn, one of Savannah's fine bed and breakfast establishments (see our Bed and Breakfast Inn chapter for more details). Head north by turning left on Abercorn, and stay on this street until you reach Calhoun Square.

Calhoun Square
Abercorn St., between Taylor and Gordon Sts.

The first of the Abercorn Street squares on our tour was named for John Calhoun, a South Carolina statesman. It was laid out in 1851. When entering the square, you can't help but notice Wesley Monumental Methodist Church on the southwestern corner of the square. This Gothic Revival church was built as a memorial to John and Charles Wesley, founders of the Methodist movement. The sanctuary, built between 1876 and 1890, seats more than 100. It features a Wesley Window opposite the pulpit that contains the busts of the men for whom the church was named.

On the southeastern edge of the square is the Massie Heritage Interpretation Center.

Massie Heritage Interpretation Center
207 E. Gordon St. • 651-7380

Honored as Georgia's oldest school in continuous operation, the Massie Heritage Interpretation Center is also the only remaining original building from Georgia's oldest chartered school system. The Greek Revival structure is listed on the National Register of Historic Places. It was completed in 1856 and is known for its gable roof, wood cupola and cornice, among other features. Today an enrichment program is offered to increase student understanding of Savannah's historic and architectural heritage. The center is open to the public from 9 AM to 4 PM Monday through Friday. It's free, but a donation is requested.

Continue north on Abercorn Street. On your way, you will pass Clary's Cafe, a must for fans of The Book. It's the spot where Luther Driggers, the man rumored to have enough poison to kill the entire city, often hung out. You will also pass Jones Street before entering Lafayette Square.

Lafayette Square
Abercorn St., between Harris and Charlton Sts.

This square, which was laid out in 1837, was named for Marquis de Lafayette, who visited Savannah in 1825. There are several significant buildings on this square, but when you enter it you can't help but notice the Cathedral of St. John the Baptist, located near the northeast corner.

Cathedral of St. John the Baptist
223 East Harris St. • 233-4709

This magnificent Gothic cathedral, with its twin spires, is one of Savannah's most noted landmarks. It is also the oldest Roman Catholic church in Georgia and the seat of the Diocese of Savannah. The parish organized in the late 1700s and erected its first church on Liberty Square. It wasn't until 1876 that the cathedral was built; it was tragically destroyed by fire 20 years later.

When the cathedral was rebuilt the original designs were used. One of the cathedral's most striking features is its stained glass. Most of it was executed by Innsbruck Glassmakers in Austrian Tyrol and installed around 1900. Other features include an Italian marble altar, the Stations of the Cross (which were imported from Munich) and the Coat of Arms of Pope John XXIII.

The Andrew Low House
329 Abercorn St. • 233-6854

On the northwest corner of Lafayette Square is the Andrew Low House, built in 1848 by Low, a wealthy cotton merchant. Low's son, William McKay Low, married Juliette Gordon, founder of the Girl Scouts. In fact, the carriage house in back of the home is the first official headquarters of the Girl Scouts of the U.S.A. Juliette Low left the building to the organization following her death. (For more on Juliette Low, see the listing for the Juliette Gordon Low Center in this chapter.)

The stunning home, with its elegant front gardens and beautiful ironwork, is built of stuccoed brick. It is owned by the National Society of the Colonial Dames of America in the State of Georgia, whose members also donated its furnishings. Even the three-tiered fountain in the center of the square was donated by the organization. Some of the home's most noted guests have included Robert E. Lee and William Makepeace Thackeray. The home is open for tours from 10:30 AM to 4 PM Monday through Saturday and noon to 4 PM on Sunday. It is closed on Thursday. Cost to tour the house is $6 for adults and $3 for students, Girl Scouts and Girl Scout leaders.

The Hamilton-Turner House
330 Abercorn St.

The Hamilton-Turner house is a Second Empire chateau built in the 1870s by a former mayor of Savannah. The Lafayette-Square home was the first house in the city to get electricity and has many distinctive features including a mansard roof and cast-iron balconies. In 1969 it was scheduled for demolition, but those plans were abandoned after the Historic Savannah Foundation stepped in. It has changed hands several times since then.

Flannery O'Connor House
207 East Charlton St. • 233-6014

Noted Southern author Flannery O'Connor was born in this high-stoop 19th-century home on the outskirts of Lafayette Square. She lived here as a child until 1938. The parlor floor has been restored to its original appearance and houses a small museum dedicated to the author. The home is open from 1 to 4 PM on Saturday and Sundays, and there is no admission charge.

Continuing north on Abercorn Street, cross Liberty Street. On the east side of Abercorn Street is Colonial Park Cemetery.

Colonial Park Cemetery

Button Gwinnett, who signed the Declaration of Independence, and miniature painter Edward Green Malbone are two of the notable Georgians buried in this cemetery — the second public burial ground in Savannah. The cemetery, which takes up several blocks in the Historic Downtown, opened in 1750; it closed to burials 100 years later. Visitors are welcome to tour the cemetery and glimpse the old tombstones and inscriptions.

After exploring the cemetery, continue north on Abercorn Street, crossing Oglethorpe Avenue. As you cross Oglethorpe you will pass the city's fire department headquarters, then Southern Images Gallery — the studio of photographer Jack Leigh, who gained national fame for his picture of the "Bird Girl" on the cover of *Midnight in the Garden of Good and Evil. Leigh has captured Southern life in many of his photos, some of which have been published in a variety of books. Across the street from Leigh's studio is Nita's, a favorite eatery for Southern food; see the Restaurants chapter for more details. Next is Oglethorpe Square.*

Oglethorpe Square
Abercorn St., between State and York Sts.

Oglethorpe Square was named for Georgia's founder, James Edward Oglethorpe. It was laid out in 1742. On the northeast corner of the square is one of Savannah's most famous museum houses — the Owens-Thomas House.

Owens-Thomas House
124 Abercorn St. • 233-9743

Taking up an entire block on the eastern edge of the square is the Owens-Thomas House, considered to be one of the finest examples of English Regency architecture in the country. The home, with its columned entrance portico, brass inlaid staircase and more, was designed by architect William Jay from 1816 to 1819 for cotton merchant Richard Richardson.

The home is made largely of tabby — an indigenous, concrete-like material made of lime, oyster shells and sand. The exterior is English stucco. The interior, which includes

three rare built-in marble-top tables that belonged to the Richardsons, has many stunning features, including an entryway with a brass inlaid staircase and a drawing room with an unusual ceiling that gives the effect that the room is round. The carriage house, also open for tours, is one of the earliest intact urban slave quarters in the South and opens into an English-inspired parterre garden.

In 1830, after the home had been used as a boarding house, George Welchman Owens, a congressman and former mayor of Savannah, purchased it for $10,000. The property remained in the Owens family until it was bequeathed to what is now the Telfair Museum of Art. The home is open from 10 AM to 5 PM Tuesday through Saturday and from 2 to 5 PM on Sunday. It is closed Mondays. The cost to tour the house is $7 for adults, $4 for students and $3 for children 6 to 12. Children younger than 6 are free.

One of Savannah's other noted museum houses is just around the corner from the Owens-Thomas house on E. State Street. If you would like to detour to this house, head east on State Street and cross Lincoln. One block on your left will be the Davenport House.

Isaiah Davenport House
324 E. State St. • 236-8097

As you walk around today in the Historic

Photo: Kyle Cason

The Mighty Eighth Air Force Heritage Museum commemorates the exploits of these World War II heroes.

Downtown enjoying the beautifully restored homes and other sights, know that it was the Davenport House that was largely responsible for the preservation of the national treasure that is the Historic District. In the 1950s, when developers came up with a plan to demolish the house, sell the brick and put in a parking lot, seven local women banned together to stop it. That group, which later became the Historic Savannah Foundation, raised $22,500 to purchase the home; such were the beginnings of restoration efforts in Savannah.

At the time of the rescue purchase, the home was a tenement, divided into small apartments and full of people. The Federal-style home was originally built in 1820 by master builder Isaiah Davenport, who used the home as a kind of showcase for his work. One of the incredible features of the house is the delicate and ornate molding and plaster work found throughout the home. The detail is so incredible that in some cases it looks almost like a wedding cake border has been placed around the edge of the ceilings. There is also a lovely house garden and museum shop that sells period items, note cards, Savannah specialty items and more. The Davenport House is open from 10 AM to 4:30 PM, seven days a week. Cost is $5 for adults and $3 for students 18 and younger.

After viewing the Davenport House, head west on State Street to Abercorn Street. Again, travel north on Abercorn. As you cross Broughton Street, you'll notice a large department store on your right. It was purchased by the Savannah College of Art and Design in 1997 and is expected to become the school's library. Continuing along Abercorn Street, you will pass the Lucas Theatre.

Lucas Theatre
22 Abercorn St. • 232-1696

This Savannah landmark, built in 1921, served not only as a theater, but also as a general center of entertainment for the city. It had floors of imported marble, a dome ceiling surrounded by 600 incandescent lights and 36 ornate boxes. However, it deteriorated with the rest of downtown after World War II. A group of citizens — Lucas Theatre for the Arts Inc. — have banned together to reopen the

theater and have been raising the millions of dollars needed to complete the project. As part of their fund-raising efforts, when the crew filming *Midnight in the Garden of Good and Evil* was in town in 1997, it participated in a fund-raiser for the theater. Among those in attendance were director Clint Eastwood and actor Kevin Spacey. Once the restoration is completed, the theater is expected to be a venue for a variety of performing arts.

After passing the Lucas Theatre you will enter Reynolds Square, the last square on our trip.

Reynolds Square
Abercorn St., between Bryan and Congress Sts.

Reynolds Square was named for Capt. John Reynolds, who served as governor of Georgia in 1754. In the center is a statue of John Wesley, the founder of Methodism. On the northwestern corner of the square is The Olde Pink House, a popular eatery (see our Restaurants chapter for more information).

Continuing north on Abercorn Street you will reach Bay Street. Look to the west and you will once again see the dome on City Hall, where the tour began. Directly across Bay Street is Factors' Walk and River Street.

Factors' Walk and River Street

Bay Street Factors' Walk is named for the cotton brokers (or "factors") who brought, sold and shipped their wares along the banks of the Savannah River. This unique row of buildings, built on the bluff overlooking the water, rise two or three stories on the street side and three or more stories over the riverfront.

The focal point is the old Cotton Exchange, a red brick building with the name Cotton Exchange etched along the top of the facade. It was built in 1886 by William G. Preston, using the principal of air rights and was one of the first buildings in the United States to be erected entirely over a public street. At one time this building is where the world price for cotton was set. While the brokers set the price of cotton, the lower floors served as cotton and naval warehouses with entrances at several levels including River Street.

Today both River Street and Factors' Walk are full of shops, restaurants and galleries, all housed in the restored warehouses. It is a favorite spot for visitors. Take a stroll on the river for a fitting end to our tour.

Guided Tours

Savannah abounds with guided tour companies. Their offerings are varied — general history, ghosts and hauntings, African-American history, you name it. Modes as well as subjects vary: Travel by air-conditioned minibus, open-sided pseudo-trolley, horse-drawn carriage, riverboat or plain old shank's mare (walking, in other words).

This is a very fluid industry. New tours are added constantly, schedules and itineraries change, etc. This is not a comprehensive listing, but it will get you started. We have avoided naming any one set of tours "the best" — the quality of a given tour, we believe, really varies based on the guide more than the tour company. The City of Savannah requires guides to earn licenses by passing a test on local history and attractions every two years, so you can expect reasonable competence from any guide.

When you are making those required reservations, it's a good time to take advantage of the competitive nature of the industry. Ask specifically which sites are entered (most tours don't actually go inside buildings) and what perks are included. We've found a constantly changing array of extras — discount coupons, refreshments, etc. — are put into play in an attempt to stand out in an industry where everyone is selling essentially the same thing. Remember, all prices are subject to change and are likely to increase slightly when the tourists return in large numbers in spring 1998.

We can't overemphasize what we touched on in the last paragraph: Reservations are required. Call ahead. It's easy. We've usually managed to make same-day arrangements except at peak tourism times. (Don't push it on Book tours, however, which are extremely

trendy at the moment; see our chapter on The Book for more information on tours focusing on sites mentioned in *Midnight in the Garden of Good and Evil*.)

Boats

River Street Riverboat Company
9 E. River St. • 232-6404, (800) 786-6404

This hour-long cruise takes you up and down the Savannah River on a replica riverboat. It's really the only good way for a tourist to get a firsthand look at the industrial and shipping side of the city — the bread-and-butter for many of us who live here. You can also get a waterfront perspective on historic structures. River Street from the water makes good panoramic photos. Depending on river traffic, you may get to see some of the massive ships that make the Port of Savannah among the busiest in the nation.

The daytime sightseeing cruise is narrated. Wear sunscreen! This company also offers a variety of other cruises, keyed around dinner and dancing, Sunday brunch or even gospel music with a buffet dinner. The sightseeing cruise is $9.95 for adults and $7 for those younger than 12, plus tax. The moonlight dancing cruise goes to $10.95 for adults, and the meal cruises range from $23 to $33.

Buses

In this category, we've grouped together big buses, minibuses, vans and trolley-like vehicles — the whole motorized land travel thing. Reservations (again) are required and easily made by phone. Most tours make pickups at the visitors center at 301 Martin Luther King Boulevard, which has reasonably ample parking if you are vacationing with a car. The tour companies use the large parking slots near the front entrance, and each space is marked with a posted sign identifying and advertising the company that leases that space. Convenient pickup is also available at

---

INSIDERS' TIP

John Houston, a former governor of Georgia, was named Savannah's first mayor in 1790.

most downtown hotels and bed and break-fasts. In fact, you can probably make arrangements for most tours to pick you up anywhere you like downtown — this is a competitive business.

While most tours will take credit cards, some drivers do not have the means of processing them. If you plan on paying by plastic, mention that while making your reservations, since it may impact your selection of pickup locations. Also, prices don't include tips for the guide/driver, which most of the brochures and onboard signs shamelessly hustle for; they are strictly optional.

Coastal Georgia Tours
10 Silverstream Plantation, Richmond Hill • 727-4837

Offerings include a Historic District and Mansion Tour ($12.50), an afternoon ghost tour that includes dessert at the supposedly haunted Pirate's House Restaurant ($14), a Book Tour ($14) and a cemeteries tour ($14).

Gray Line Savannah
215 W. Boundary St. • 234-8687

This national tour firm offers both trolley-like vehicles and minibuses. The basic Historic District trolley tour runs 75 minutes ($15 for adults, $6 for children younger than 12). Add the house museum of your choice to that ticket for an additional $2 for adults and $1 for children. The longer Historic District and Mansion Tour runs just more than two hours, with rates set at $16 for adults and $6 for children younger than 12. A more extensive version includes the Victorian District and admission to two sites ($19 adults, $8 for children). A Low Country tour, which includes refreshments, goes to Bonaventure Cemetery, Bethesda Orphanage, Wormsloe Historic Site and the scenic bluff at Isle of Hope. It's $23

adults and $9 for children younger than 12. Gray Line also has a *Midnight* tour for $14.

Hospitality Tours
2610 Jefferson St. • 233-0119

This tour group offers Historic District tours that include admission to two historic sites (two-and-a-half hours, $17 for adults, $5 children for children younger than 12), one historic site (one hour and 45 minutes, $14 for adults and $5 children) or simply a driving tour (one hour, $10 for adults, $4 children). Sites vary depending on the operating days and hours. They also have a Book tour and a walking tour of haunted sites ($15 adults, $5 children). Groups can arrange African-American history tours and a tour that includes Bethesda Orphanage (now Bethesda Home for Boys), Wormsloe Historic Site, the scenic bluff at Isle of Hope and Bonaventure Cemetery.

Negro Heritage Trail Tour
502 E. Harris St. • 234-8000

This tour offers an African-American perspective of Savannah's history. Stops include the Ralph Mark Gilbert Civil Rights Museum, First African Baptist Church, the King-Tisdell Cottage and Beach Institute (see separate listings for all these attractions in this chapter). The tour runs 90 minutes to two hours, and the admission cost is $15 for adults and $7 for children younger than 12.

Old Savannah Tours
514 Berrien St. • 234-8128

White, trolley-style vehicles offer on-off privileges throughout the Historic District for self-paced tours. Tickets are $15 for adults and teens and $7 for children ages 5 to 12. There are also more conventional tours: a Historic Downtown overview (90 minutes; $13 for

Photo: Kyle Cason

Carriage tours cover the Historic Downtown.

adults and $6 for children), a Book tour ($12 for adults and $6 for children) and a "hauntings" tour ($14 for adults, $7 for children). Less conventional offerings take you outside the Historic Downtown. These include a pontoon boat expedition to look at local wildlife ($23 for adults; $13 for children) and a trip to Tybee Island that includes its lighthouse and museum, the beach, Fort Pulaski and the remnants of Fort Screven ($23 for adults, $12 for children). (For more on these island attractions, see our Tybee Island chapter.)

Old South Historic Tours
250 Martin Luther King Jr. Blvd. • 232-3859
Offerings include a 70-minute tour of local historic sites. Prices are $13 for adults and $6.50 for children younger than 12, and you can add house museum entrance for an additional $3. The Book Tour ($17 for adults, $11 for kids younger than 12) includes admission to the Telfair Museum of Art.

Old Town Trolley Tours of Savannah
234 Martin Luther King Jr. Blvd. • 233-0083
This 90-minute tour offers reboarding options throughout the Historic Downtown on orange and green trolley-style vehicles. Tickets

cost $17 for adults and $7 for children ages 4 to 12. Kids younger than 4 ride for free.

Horse-drawn Carriages

While children generally don't jump up and down at the prospect of a guided tour of historic sites, we've found horse-drawn carriages up the appeal significantly. Who knows? You may be lucky enough to see a chartered and decorated carriage ferrying a bride and groom from a wedding at one of the Historic Downtown churches.

Carriage Tours of Savannah
10 Warner St. • 236-6756
Narrated tours are about an hour in length. Options include a daytime historic tour ($14 for adults, $6 for those ages 4 to 11), evening historic or ghost story tours ($16 for adults, $8 for children) and private carriage tours for couples at $60.

Magnolia Carriage Company
8 Warner St. • 232-7727
These hour-long tour options include the Historic Downtown and a horse-drawn Book tour. It's $13 for adults and $6 for children ages 4 to 11. Private tours are $60.

Walking

A Saunter in Savannah
6 E. Liberty St. • 234-9255

Offerings include a tour of the Historic District and an evening hauntings tour. The tours cost $10 for adults and $8 for seniors and students; children 5 and younger are admitted free.

The Savannah Walks
123 E. Congress St. • 238-9255

This walking tour firm offers a varied menu with different meeting points — check that when you make your reservations. Fees are $13 for adults and $6.50 for children ages 6 to 16, with the Historic Homes Walk priced at $23 and $12.50 since it includes admission to attractions. Options include general tours, a Book tour, a ghost tour, a pub walk, one themed to women, a Civil War walk, a walk featuring churches and graveyards and even specialty tours you can set up individually to explore things like antiques and galleries or arts and literature.

Other Savannah Attractions

What follows are listings of several other terrific Savannah attractions. Some are in the Historic Downtown but weren't covered by our walking tour; others are in the city's outlying areas.

Historic Downtown

Beach Institute
502 E. Harris St. • 234-8000

The Beach Institute was established in 1865 by the American Missionary Association to educate newly freed slaves. It was the first school in Savannah for African Americans and became a public school in 1919. The institute is an African-American cultural center and houses art, sculpture and artifacts relating to the cultural contributions of black Americans. Lectures and other programs are frequently held. It is open from noon to 5 PM Tuesday

through Saturday. There is no admission charge.

First African Baptist Church
23 Montgomery St. • 233-6597

Overlooking Franklin Square is First African Baptist Church. This church, which is still active, is descended from the oldest African-American congregation in the United States. George Leile, a slave, began making missionary visits to plantations up and down the Savannah River as early as 1774. A permanent congregation was formed at Brampton Plantation in 1788 — the first black missionary Baptist church in Savannah.

Eventually, the congregation constructed the present building. It is the first brick building erected in Georgia by African Americans for African Americans; it was built by slaves, who worked on it at night after being in the fields all day. The sanctuary has beautiful stained-glass windows framing the back of the altar, which displays pictures of the founding pastors. In the balcony are original pews with markings left by the slaves who built the church.

Ralph Mark Gilbert Civil Rights Museum
460 Martin Luther King Jr. Blvd. • 231-8900

More than 40,000 people toured Ralph Mark Gilbert Civil Rights Museum during its inaugural year of 1996. The museum chronicles the story of Savannah's civil rights struggles during the 1940s, '50s and '60s. Along with traveling exhibits and special programming, it spotlights how Martin Luther King Jr. Boulevard, formerly known as West Broad Street, was once the center of the city's thriving black business community. Besides educating the community, the museum also serves as an educational resource for southeastern coastal Georgia.

Development of the museum took place during several years. More than $1.7 million went into the museum, which included the renovation of the Wage Earners Savings Bank building where the museum is housed. The Wage Earners bank is believed to be the second bank for African Americans in the nation. The museum is the brainchild of local historian and activist W.W. Law. It is named after the Rev. Ralph Mark Gilbert, a pastor at First African Baptist Church (see previous listing) who pioneered Savannah's modern civil rights movement. (For information on the museum's annual anniversary celebration, look under September in our Annual Events and Festivals chapter.)

Historic Railroad Shops
601 W. Harris St. • 651-6823

The Historic Railroad Shops are the oldest and most complete antebellum railroad manufacturing and repair facilities still in existence in the United States. Thirteen of the original structures, which were built beginning in 1859, are still standing. Included are the roundhouse and turntable (where the engines were turned around) and the 125-foot brick smokestack. The site is a National Historic Landmark. It is open from 10 AM to 4 PM Monday through Saturday and from noon to 4 PM on Sunday. Cost is $2.50 for adults and $2 for students. Children younger than 5 are free.

King-Tisdell Cottage
514 E. Huntingdon St. • 234-8000

Built in 1869 by W.W. Aimar, this cottage, with its original gingerbread ornamentation, is in the Beach Institute neighborhood of the Historic Downtown and serves as a museum dedicated to preserving the African-American history of Savannah and the sea islands. Inside the small home you will find art objects, documents and furniture of the 1890s. It is open by appointment only; cost is $3.

Savannah History Museum
Savannah Visitors Center, 303 Martin Luther King Jr. Blvd. • 238-1779

Delve into Savannah's colorful past at the Savannah History Museum, located in the old passenger station of the Central of Georgia Railroad that also houses the Savannah Visitors Center. The structure, a National Historic Landmark, features a variety of exhibits, including an 1890 steam locomotive that is still

sitting on the original Central of Georgia tracks. A genuine antique cotton gin is on display, along with artifacts from the Civil War and other eras. A small theater shows a film that provides an overview of the city's history. The museum is open from 9 AM to 5 PM seven days a week. It costs $3 for adults and teens, $1.75 for children 6 to 12. Kids younger than 6 are free.

Ships of the Sea Museum
41 Martin Luther King Jr. Blvd. • 232-1511

Viking ships, Chinese war ships and more than 75 ships in bottles are just some of what you will discover at the Ships of the Sea Museum. Learn about Savannah's maritime history while exploring this museum, which recently relocated to one of Savannah's historic old residences, the Scarbrough House. The home, built in 1819 for the principal owner of the *Savannah*, the first steamship to cross the Atlantic Ocean, was designated a National Historic Landmark in 1974. Cost is $5 for adults, $4 for children 7 and older (if you have a college ID you can get the discounted rate). Children younger than 7 get in free. The museum is open from 10 AM to 5 PM Tuesday through Sunday. It is closed Mondays.

Telfair Mansion and Art Museum
121 Barnard St. • 232-1177

The Telfair is the oldest art museum in the South. Its permanent collection of paintings, prints, sculpture and decorative arts is housed in a mansion designed by English architect William Jay for Alexander Telfair, son of Georgia governor Edward Telfair. The family lived here until 1875.

Among the museum's holdings are paintings by Childe Hassam, Frederick Frieseke and Gari Melchers, along with Robert Henri, George Bellows and George Luks. The museum also has a decorative arts collection that includes American and European objects from 1790 to 1840, including a rare Philadelphia suite of maple furniture, a secretary-bookcase

INSIDERS' TIP

The Pirates' House at 20 East Broad Street, which is now home to a restaurant (see our Restaurants chapter) featuring a mysterious maze of rooms, is a former seaman's tavern built in 1794.

Photo: Kyle Cason

The Owens-Thomas House is a house museum where - yes - George Washington once slept.

commissioned from Duncan Phyfe of New York and a dining table ordered from Thomas Cook of Philadelphia. The Telfair is open from 10 AM to 5 PM Tuesday through Saturday, 2 to 5 PM on Sunday and noon to 5 PM Monday. Cost is $6 for adults, $5 for seniors, $2 for students 12 and older and $1 for children 6 to 12. Children younger than 6 are admitted free.

Islands

Oatland Island Education Center
711 Sandtown Rd. • 897-3773

A visit to Oatland gives you a good idea of what Georgia's first European settlers might have seen when they landed in 1733. Walk the 1¾-mile trail through the center's 60-acre forest of oaks, pines and magnolias and you'll encounter enclosures providing natural settings for animals native to the state — shorebirds, alligators, panthers, otters, birds of prey, white-tailed deer, black bears, timber wolves and bison. The enclosures are large and wooded and the inhabitants are often hard to spot, but getting a look at them in their environment is worth the effort. The trail leads you to the Heritage Homesite area, where two log cabins (built in 1835, moved to Oatland and restored there) convey a feeling for life on the farm during pioneer days. Another Oatland feature is a barnyard where youngsters can see and feed farm animals.

Oatland, once cleared farmland where cotton was grown in the 18th and 19th centuries, was the site of a retirement home built in 1927 for railroad conductors. The home was in the center's main building, which later was used by the federal government until it was declared surplus in 1973. The Savannah-Chatham County School System (see our Education and Child Care chapter) took possession of the site for use as an environmental education center, and the main building now houses classrooms, offices and a conference center. Although Oatland's main focus is on teaching students from local and out-of-county public and private schools, it is open to the public from 8:30 AM to 5 PM Monday through Friday and 10 AM to 5 PM on Saturdays, except those following Thanksgiving and Christmas.

On the second Saturday of several months,

Oatland hosts special events such as its annual cane grinding and crafts festival, sheep shearing and crafts festival and cultural history celebration (see our Annual Events and Festivals chapter). Admission to Oatland is a cash donation used for care and veterinary treatment of the animals. Sandtown Road runs south off Islands Expressway 4 miles east of Historic Downtown. The tour of the center's animal habitats is self-guided and takes about 90 minutes.

Old Fort Jackson
1 Fort Jackson Rd. • 232-3945

Georgia's oldest standing brick fortification is an intriguing place. The fort perches right on the banks of the Savannah River — built there so its guns could fire on any vessel coming into Savannah — and chances are good you'll get an up-close view of an ocean-going ship during your visit.

Walk on the parapet of the fort and investigate the structure's many nooks and crannies. Two powder magazines and most of the casemates are open to the public, and they contain displays of weaponry and tools used at the fort and artifacts from the *Georgia*, a Confederate ironclad whose remains lay on the river bottom a few hundred feet away. Inspect eight cannon, five of which are authentic and three of which are reproductions; cannon-firing programs are presented during the summer. Call for more information.

Construction of Fort Jackson was begun in 1808 on the site of what had been an earthwork battery during the Revolutionary War. It was manned during the War of 1812 and expanded between 1845 and 1860. Confederate forces used it as headquarters of the Savannah River defenses during most of the Civil War, and it was garrisoned by Union troops after the city's surrender in December 1864. The only time it was fired upon was on October 1, 1862, when two Union steamers shelled it for about an hour during a reconnaissance mission.

The fort is not on an island, but we've placed it in this section because it's a couple of miles from the Historic Downtown on the way to the eastside islands. To get there, take President Street Extension (also known as Islands Expressway) east to Woodcock Road and turn north on Woodcock, which will lead you to Fort Jackson Road. The nonprofit Coastal Heritage Society operates the fort under a lease with the state of Georgia. Admission is $2.50 for adults and $2 for students, senior citizens and members of the military; there's no charge for children 5 and younger. The fort is open from 9 AM to 5 PM seven days a week but is closed on Thanksgiving, Christmas and New Year's Day. There are a variety of special programs available for groups and gatherings for a variety of fees; these include some after-hours events that the society will cater. The fort is also the site of special events including the annual Scottish Games and Highland Gathering (see our Annual Events and Festivals chapter).

Wormsloe Historic Site
7601 Skidaway Rd. • 353-3023

You'll find the last architectural remnant of the Oglethorpe era in Savannah at Wormsloe Historic Site, which is at the end of Skidaway Road on the doorstep of the Isle of Hope, about 10 miles south of the Historic Downtown. After driving under a large masonry arch at the entrance to Wormsloe, you'll travel down an "avenue of oaks," a wide, crushed-stone road lined with majestic live-oak trees. After 1.25 miles, the road narrows to a walking trail. At this point, you'll find a parking lot and the Wormsloe museum.

Continue on foot down the trail about a quarter-mile, and you'll be looking at the remains of a fortified house where construction was started in 1739 during the 10-year span James Edward Oglethorpe spent founding and nurturing the colony of Georgia (see our History chapter). The builder and owner of the house — a physician, carpenter and surveyor named Noble Jones — came to the new colony in 1733 with Oglethorpe and the first boatload of settlers. Three years later, Jones leased 500 acres from the Trustees of Georgia, land that would be part of a plantation he called Wormslow. The name was changed to Wormsloe in the mid-1800s by his great-grandson, and the plantation eventually grew to cover nearly 900 acres. Jones' descendants donated 822 of those acres to the Nature Conservancy in 1972, and the property was transferred to the state of Georgia, which manages the site via the Parks and Historic Sites Division of the Department of Natural Resources.

The house Jones completed in the mid-1740s was a five-room, one-and-a-half-story dwelling built into a fort-like, rectangular wall intended to protect its inhabitants from attack by the Spanish. The house and wall were made of tabby, a concoction of oyster shells, lime and sand mixed with water. You can see parts of the foundation of the house and large portions of the wall. Other points of interest at Wormsloe are the museum and theater, where you can learn more about the site and the early days of the colony; a stone monument marking the first Jones family burial plot; nature trails; and the Colonial Life Area, which contains re-creations of outbuildings characteristic of Wormsloe's early period. This area is also the site of living history demonstrations and programs presented during special events (see our Annual Events and Festivals chapter).

During your drive down the avenue of oaks, you may notice an elegant, two-story frame house on the eastern side of the road. This structure was built in 1828 and is home to the ninth generation of Jones' descendants; it is closed to the public. Wormsloe is open from 9 AM to 5 PM Tuesday through Saturday and from 2 to 5:30 PM on Sunday. It's closed on Mondays that are not legal holidays, Thanksgiving, Christmas and New Year's Day. Admission is $2 for adults and $1 for those 18 and younger; children 5 and younger are admitted free.

After you visit Wormsloe, take a few minutes to drive through nearby Isle of Hope, a community of narrow streets and beautifully preserved houses. Turn right after leaving Wormsloe and you'll be on Parkersburg Road, which meanders through Isle of Hope until it reaches Bluff Drive, one of the prettiest streets in the Savannah area. A jaunt down Bluff Drive, which runs alongside the picturesque Skidaway River, is worth the time it will take to make this short detour. (For more on Isle of Hope, see our Neighborhoods and Real Estate chapter.)

West Chatham

Bamboo Farm and Coastal Gardens
2 Canebrake Rd. • 921-5460

If you like digging in the dirt and growing things, you should love this spot in southwest Chatham County that was once an experimental station where the federal government introduced plants from throughout the world.

Called the Bamboo Farm through the years by Savannahians because of the groves of the tropical plant grown there, the facility has large collections of roses, day lilies, tropical hibiscus, cultivated herbs and, of course, bamboo — more than 200 varieties of it. The bamboo collection is the largest in the United States open for viewing by the public, and there's also a grove of giant timber bamboo — the reason the farm was purchased for the U.S. Department of Agriculture in 1918. The bamboo grove, where stalks can reach a height of more than 70 feet and a diameter of 6 inches, originated with three seedlings planted on the site in 1890; 25 years later, it attracted the attention of plant explorer David Fairchild, who bought the 46-acre farm where the bamboo grew and donated it to the government.

The plant introduction station was closed in 1978, and the property was deeded four years later to the University of Georgia, whose Cooperative Extension Service operates it today as a center for research and education. The farm offers a self-guided walking tour that will take you to (among other botanical treasures) the bamboo collection and grove; a bed displaying Savannah's 10 all-time favorite roses, as selected by the local rose society; beds of ornamental and turf grasses; a collection of crape myrtle trees that's probably the largest in coastal Georgia; and a variety of other interesting trees, including one whose fruit resembles popcorn.

The Bamboo Farm and Coastal Gardens holds a number of special events throughout the year, most of which require reservations, and makes available a 300-seat open-air pavilion and a 100-seat conference hall. The farm is open from 9 AM to 5 PM Monday through Friday and from 9 AM to 3 PM on Saturday; it's closed on Sunday, Thanksgiving, Christmas, New Year's Day, the Fourth of July and Labor Day. Admission is free, and donations are accepted. The facility is on U.S. Highway 17, about 13 miles south of the Historic Downtown.

Mighty Eighth Air Force Heritage Museum
175 Bourne Ave., Pooler • 748-8888, (800) 421-9428

It's not unusual for veterans of World War II aerial combat to leave this museum's Mission Experience exhibit with tears in their eyes. This re-creation of an Eighth Air Force bombing mission brings back vivid memories to those who flew over Europe — recollections of heavily defended targets, stricken aircraft and fallen comrades. The panoramic, eight-screen theater and its B-17 flight are a featured part of the 90,000-square-foot museum in Pooler near the intersection of Interstate 95 and U.S. Highway 80. In addition to the exhibit area housing the Mission Experience and other displays, the museum has a library stocked with books pertaining to aviation and air warfare, an art gallery, Memorial Gardens, gift shop and snack bar.

The museum opened in May 1996. It honors the more than 1 million men and women who have served in the Eighth since its creation in Savannah on January 18, 1942, at the Chatham Artillery Armory on Bull Street at Park Avenue. A small command force worked there for a few months before moving to England, where the organization manned bases from August 1942 until May 1945 and grew to have more than 350,000 members during World War II. The Eighth flew more than 600,000 sorties against Nazi Germany and dropped more than 700,000 tons of bombs on enemy targets. Today the building where the Eighth was born is the home of American Legion Post 135.

Besides the Mission Experience, the museum's exhibit area contains displays featuring numerous units that were part of the Eighth, a scale model depicting a World War II bomber base in England, Escape and Evasion and Prisoner of War areas and several other theaters. The museum is open from 9 AM to 6 PM daily except for New Year's Day, Easter, Thanksgiving and Christmas. Admis-

Photo: Kyle Cason

You'll find many interesting ships moored along River Street.

sion to the exhibit area is $7.50 for adults and teens and $5.50 for children 6 to 12, with those younger than 6 admitted free; tickets are not sold after 5:30 PM. There are discounts for members of the military, senior citizens and groups of 20 or more. There is no charge to visit the library, art gallery and Memorial Gardens. The library is open from 10 AM to 5 PM Monday through Saturday and from noon to 5 PM on Sunday.

Savannah-Ogeechee Canal Museum and Nature Center
681 Fort Argyle Rd. • 748-8068

The Savannah-Ogeechee Canal, which played a role in the commercial development of Savannah during the 1800s, lay virtually forgotten for a century until a group of Chatham Countians reclaimed a third of it from the tangle of foliage that had grown over it. These volunteers started their work in 1992 and now, organized as the Savannah-Ogeechee Canal Society, oversee the restoration and continued development of the waterway as a historic and recreational area.

The 16-mile canal, which is 58 feet wide at water level, was completed in 1830 and links the Savannah and Ogeechee rivers. It accommodated horse- and mule-drawn barges as much as 70 feet long along with boats poled by their occupants. These vessels carried lumber, cotton, rice, naval stores and other goods. Six 18-foot-wide locks, originally made of wood and later replaced with brick, controlled the hydraulics of the canal, which faded from usage in the early 1890s because it could not compete with the region's railroads and road system.

You can get a splendid idea of what the southern portion of the canal was like by visiting the society's museum and 184-acre na-

ture center, which is on Fort Argyle Road (better known as Ga. Highway 204), a little more than 2 miles from Exit 16 of Interstate 95. The museum, a converted bungalow, has two exhibit rooms, one depicting the history of the canal and another displaying reptiles and amphibians that inhabit the area the waterway runs through. Within view of the museum is Lock 5, which is on a trail you can follow for four-tenths of a mile along the canal south to Lock 6 and the Ogeechee River; this trail is the tow path that horses and mules trod while pulling barges more than 100 years ago. The tow path is one of several trails you can walk while at the nature center (see our Parks and Recreation chapter for more details). The museum and nature center are open from 9 AM to 5 PM each day of the year. There is no admission fee, but donations are accepted.

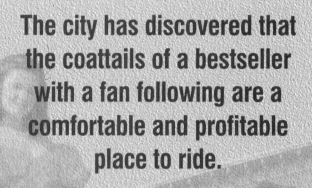

The city has discovered that the coattails of a bestseller with a fan following are a comfortable and profitable place to ride.

The Book

This chapter might not make much sense if you have not read John Berendt's *Midnight in the Garden of Good and Evil*. In fact, some of the whole *Midnight* phenomenon in Savannah doesn't make much sense to us, and we've read the book several times, remember many of the events it recounts and have met lots of the people portrayed in it. Why are readers all over the country (and beyond) captivated by this account of death, voodoo and card-playing etiquette (among other topics) in Savannah? And why do many Savannahians get such a kick out of a set of stories that portrays the city (however affectionately) as a wellspring of weirdness?

Perhaps the locals just want that promised 15 minutes of fame, which *Midnight in the Garden of Good and Evil* certainly gives to Savannah and its residents. Perhaps normally reticent people are willing to put up with the public airing of any amount of dirty laundry as long as it brings Clint Eastwood to town to film a movie about it.

The real answer, however, probably lies deep within a cash register. The city has discovered that the coattails of a bestseller with a fan following are a comfortable and profitable place to ride. The book has spawned no fewer that four guided bus tours of the sites mentioned in it, generated a souvenir output of great variety (if not of universally good taste), launched a gift shop that bears its name, made a drag show a regular — albeit unlikely — tourist attraction and boosted the fortunes of the eateries, watering holes and singers described in its pages.

In this chapter, we'll document the various opportunities fans of *Midnight in the Garden of Good and Evil* have to sample in person what they've experienced in print, and we'll try to explain to those who haven't read it why that little statue of a girl feeding birds keeps cropping up. For the duration, we'll follow local practice and just call Berendt's bestseller "The

Book" — shorthand we have all adopted in self-defense, since an eight-word title takes a while to say in a Southern drawl, and locals have trouble pronouncing Berendt's name.

A Little Background . . .

Midnight in the Garden of Good and Evil was published in January 1994. Berendt, a columnist and former editor at *Esquire*, had spent several years living off and on in Savannah, collecting the stories that make up the book. The unifying thread of the book is the four murder trials that followed the fatal shooting of a young man by self-made millionaire antiques dealer Jim Williams. Mingled in are the stories of a flamboyant drag queen, a tax lawyer who excels as a bad-check artist and a piano player, white socialites who play cards and black debutantes who dance the minuet, an odd-ball genius with a penchant for poisons, and so on.

Random House quickly had a hit on its hands. The Book hit *The New York Times* bestseller list in March 1994 and has pretty much stayed there ever since. As a result of its success in hardcover, it hasn't seen paperback despite its four years in print (not counting the soft-cover trade paper version that is the large-print edition).

Ah, but is the book as true as it claims? Well, that brings to mind what the character Huck Finn had to say about the Tom Sawyer story — "mostly true but with some stretchers." The timelines, for example, are a little out of sync, and the slant of the stories can still spark debate among locals. Several of the names of central figures are pseudonyms, and that told-as-true tale about the dead cat, the dinner party and the stomach pump is a classic urban belief tale — consider it modern folklore.

With book sales so brisk and a larger-than-life cast of characters on the page, it was inevitable that Hollywood would go Gardening. In May 1996, director Clint Eastwood began filming the screen version with Kevin Spacey in the Williams role, John Cusack as Berendt, and the Lady Chablis (the aforementioned drag queen) as the Lady Chablis. The story got a revision for the screen, and the city got an out-of-season facelift, as the squares involved in the shooting were decked out in Christmas greenery in a month that already qualifies as full summer in Savannah.

So now fans of The Book have had a refresher course, and those who haven't read it at least have an idea of what we are talking about. Let's move on to how visitors to Savannah can walk inside Berendt's pages.

FYI

Unless otherwise noted, the area code for all phone numbers listed in this guide is 912.

Tours

If you want to cover a lot of Book territory relatively quickly, the tour buses are your best bet. We're describing them in plural here because they offer essentially the same thing — a two- to two-and-a-half hour tour that is mainly a drive-by of important sites from The Book, capped off with a cemetery visit. Be aware that tours have a tendency to run longer than advertised, so allow plenty of time. All tours require reservations, which can be made by phone. If this is an important event for you, call well in advance — tours are often full or nearly full. The various tour companies take the major credit cards, but because tour drivers usually don't handle anything other than cash transactions, ask where you'll pay if you plan to use a credit card — it might affect which of the pickup locations you specify.

Tours pick up at the Savannah Visitors Center, 301 Martin Luther King Jr. Boulevard, which has reasonably ample parking. Stash your car and look for the large parking slots near the center's front door, marked with signs identifying the tour company that uses that spot — that's where you'll board. Major downtown hotels and some bed and breakfasts in the Historic Downtown also serve as pickup locations — get details when you make your reservations.

Remember that the Book-related tours are just part of a wider tour menu offered by each company. Others include ghost tours, walking tours, Civil War-themed tours, carriage tours, Savannah history tours and the like. (See our Attractions chapter for more on other types of guided tours.) The city of Savannah requires that tour guides pass a test and hold a license. On a typical tour, you'll drive by Mercer House, the mansion which was the site of The Book's fatal shooting; Club One, performance venue for the Lady Chablis (see our Nightlife chapter for details); various homes where lawyer and professional partier Joe Odom stayed, often without the owners' knowledge; the jail where Williams was incarcerated (now replaced by a structure outside town); the modern county courthouse where the first three trials were held; the ornate old federal courthouse that stands in for it in the movie version; and so on.

Along the way, you'll get a chance to see the city's more conventional attractions as well, and chances are the tour guide will throw in a few comments about those. The highlight of all the tours is a visit to Bonaventure Cemetery, which you can read about elsewhere in this chapter. But while you are welcome to visit the dead, don't expect to get inside any of the homes of the living. The tours don't go inside the buildings involved

in The Book, most of which are private homes. Mercer House, especially, is private territory: don't expect to see its fabled luxurious interior except in the movie scenes that were filmed there.

Coastal Georgia Tours
10 Silverstream Plantation, Richmond Hill • 727-4837

This Book tour includes day and night options, both at $14. The day tour includes Bonaventure Cemetery. The cemetery closes at night, so that stop is replaced by Hannah's East, atop the Pirate's House Restaurant, a jazz nightclub where Book character Emma Kelly often performs (see our Nightlife chapter).

Gray Line Tours
215 W. Boundary St. • 234-8687

This long tour includes a visit to Bonaventure and tends to spill over its adver-

tised two-hour length. Tickets are $14, and transportation is via minibus.

Hospitality Tours of Savannah
2610 Jefferson St. • 233-0119

This two-and-a-half-hour tour bills itself at the first of the bunch. Parts of this tour were featured in the *Midnight in Savannah* two-hour special that ran on the Arts & Entertainment cable channel in late 1997. Tickets are $15.

Old South Tours
250 Martin Luther King Jr. Blvd. • 232-3859

This tour, in addition to the Bonaventure visit, includes admission to the Telfair Museum of Art to see the Bird Girl statue from The Book's cover photo. Tickets are $17.

Seeing It On Your Own

If you want to see some of The Book sites

Bonaventure Cemetery: Good Fortune for Lovers of The Book

"Bonaventure" means "good fortune," which may strike you as a strange name for a graveyard. But once you visit this serenely beautiful place, chances are the name will seem more appropriate. Bonaventure Cemetery plays a prominent role in John Berendt's *Midnight*

in the Garden of Good and Evil. It is here in this lush Victorian graveyard that the book's narrator drinks martinis and gets his introductory course on Savannah society. The massive cemetery stands under the moss-draped shade of towering live oaks, is peopled by row upon row of elegant statuary and headstones, and commands a waterfront view that would make a condo developer drool.

The graves made famous in the book include the Aiken family plot. Here, the parents of Pulitzer Prize-winning poet Conrad Aiken — killed in a murder-suicide — are buried. Conrad Aiken's own grave, marked by a bench engraved with poetry, stands alongside. Not too far away, you'll spot the graves of famed Savannah lyricist Johnny Mercer and wife, Ginger.

This is the culminating point for the guided tours of Book sites. If you happen to be a non-fan of The Book, and you were swept along by a fervent spouse or group, hang in there. The 160-acre graveyard was well worth seeing in its own right well before the book was published, and it will be well worth seeing when all the hubbub dies down (assuming, of course, that it ever will). Fame carries with it drawbacks, for places as well as people. On our last visit to Bonaventure, we encountered an unseemly traffic jam of competing tour bus groups, with some guides quietly leading their charges to alternate sites until the crowd cleared; another guide brashly interrupted a national gourmet magazine's efforts to photograph two models posing with martinis on Aiken's grave-marker bench.

The tour companies have been cooperative in efforts to minimize impact on the cemetery, according to Terry Shaw, who heads up the 4-year-old Bonaventure Historical Society. One result is that the largest tour buses aren't allowed within the gates — instead, only Book tours using smaller minibuses can enter. In fact, the cemetery is even cashing in on The Book to some extent. Berendt named Bonaventure as one of three local nonprofits to receive his share of royalties from the sale of Byrd's cookies in the commemorative Book tin. The cash will come in handy for cemetery preservation and research efforts, Shaw said.

Bonaventure was once an elegant plantation, but the grand home burned down more than once. Local folklore has it that the roof caught fire during a dinner party, and the guests finished the meal outdoors by the light of the burning house. If you are looking for ghost stories, there's a tale that you can still hear the revelry and breaking glass of that party at certain times. You'll find these tales repeated in The Book. The property became a cemetery in the 1800s and was put into city hands in 1907. It is still an active cemetery with an occasional burial, but the few remaining spaces are taken — don't get attached to the place.

Many important figures from the history of Georgia and the nation are buried here. There's Noble Jones, who arrived with James Oglethorpe at the beginning of the colony; several members of Georgia's Liberty Boys; and a number of prominent

— continued on next page

Photo: Kyle Cason

Little Grace marks the grave of a young girl in Bonaventure Cemetery.

physicians including Brodie Herndon, chief surgeon of hospitals for the Confederacy and the first doctor to perform a Caesarean operation in the United States. John Walz, sculptor of many of the impressive funerary statues in Bonaventure and other local cemeteries, is buried here — ironically, there is no headstone at his grave.

You can get these and other interesting details in a brochure put out by the Historical Society and available at the front office just inside the cemetery gates. Shaw can provide more information about the Bonaventure Historical Society; Write to him at 1317 E. 55th Street, Savannah, GA 31404. If you are interested in joining the society, the $15 annual membership fee includes a subscription to a monthly newsletter with stories on Bonaventure's significant residents. Shaw said the group has more than 100 members, including 30 who live out of state. The membership even includes folks from Canada and Hungary.

If you want to visit Bonaventure Cemetery without a tour, here are some fairly detailed instructions. How you get there depends, of course, on where you start. Since we reasoned most visitors would be starting from the Historic Downtown, we launch our trek at the intersection of Bull and Liberty streets, right beside the DeSoto Hilton Hotel. Set your trip odometer there; you have about 3.5 miles to go. Liberty Street is a major east-west thoroughfare downtown. Follow it east. You'll quickly leave the Historic District and pass through areas that include low-income housing and small industry. Don't be distracted by the large cemetery to your left shortly after you leave downtown

— continued on next page

— that's Hillcrest. The road forks just beyond that, so bear right: It will be fairly obvious in doing so that you are staying on the same road. The road assumes different names as you travel — from Liberty to Wheaton to Skidaway.

Immediately past a complex five-way intersection, you'll see the only real turn you'll make — a left onto 36th Street. It's identified by a street sign hanging between double traffic lights, and there's a turn arrow to help you make the turn in the increasingly heavy traffic you'll encounter. A McDonald's stands on the right just past this intersection; if you go past it, you've gone too far. Just after you get on it, 36th Street merges into Bonaventure Road so seamlessly you probably won't even notice. Bonaventure Road is a narrow, two-lane road that winds through neat, modest housing and is lined by massive trees that are literally on the edge of the road. Pay attention!

In just under a mile, you'll see the cemetery gates, where the road curves away to the right. Don't be distracted if a Forest Lawn Cemetery billboard is still in place in the vicinity: The sign on the gate identifies Bonaventure. There's a large, framed map just inside the entrance, but it gives locations by grave site number, not name. Instead, depend on the small wooden signposts stationed along the lanes between the plots. Book fans are looking for the sign marked "Aiken" and the nearby "Mercer." The wooden marker signs are easy to follow.

Park with care, as there is a lot of tour bus traffic. There's a small lot behind the office building just inside the gates if you are the hiking kind; there's also a grassy parking area for a few cars that's near the water and not far from the Aiken plot. While we haven't heard of any trouble, it's an isolated spot between tours, so it's probably a good idea to lock your car and bring a friend.

Meanwhile, let's clear up some misconceptions in parting. Jim Williams, The Book's central figure, isn't buried at Bonaventure — or anywhere else in Savannah, for that matter. Instead, he was put to rest in his hometown of Gordon, Georgia. And Bonaventure is not the graveyard from which the Minerva character dug up the dirt for her voodoo spells, so leave the soil where you found it. It's history, not dirt.

---

but don't fancy tours, you can get to many of them on your own. After all, the Historic Downtown itself is a character in the book. Here are some tips on what you can see solo. There's no shortage of maps in Savannah (hardly surprising in a city with a thriving tourism industry), and there's a good one in this very book. With a copy of The Book in hand and the map of the Historic Downtown you'll find at the front of our guide, you can find major Book sites such as Monterey Square. If you seek more precise instructions, we can steer you to at least two maps specially produced for Book followers.

Mapping Midnight

The Midnight Newsletter
After Dark Publishing, P.O. Box 30267, Savannah, GA 31410
This occasional newsletter, which is pub-

lished on no particular schedule, features stories about The Book, its characters and the ongoing phenomenon. The most recent edition we've seen includes a detailed *Midnight* map, along with a photo-illustrated map key. While you can order by mail at the $4 cover price, the newsletter is for sale at several Savannah bookstores and souvenir shops. We got ours for $3.50 at Media Play.

The Savannah Map of Good & Evil According to Mandy
Backyard Publishing Co., P.O. Box 8343, Savannah, GA 31412
This map to book sites includes some breathless prose by Nancy Hillis, who describes herself as the inspiration for the Mandy character. You can get it for about $5 in bookstores and Book souvenir shops. This publication came out in 1995, and it's showing its age a little — the Hamilton-Turner Mansion described as a tour house was in the process

of being sold in late 1997 and is expected to reopen as a bed-and-breakfast.

Easily Accessed Sites

Now that you have a map, we'll list a few of the most easily found sites. We'll start with two general outdoor sites, where you can stand on the sidewalk and gaze, then move on to places you can actually get into.

Monterey Square
400 block of Bull St., bounded by Taylor and Gordon Sts.

This square is home to many of the central events in The Book, but it's worth a good look on its own merits. The massive central monument to Polish Count Casimir Pulaski, a hero of the American Revolution, was removed in 1997 for essential repairs. Its return date is linked to completion of those repairs, which in turn is linked to the discovery of funding. At any rate, the monument base was standing bare when the *Midnight* film crews arrived. The statue got a stand-in for the

movie, not nearly as nice as the original. Maybe by the time you arrive, the original will be back in place.

Mercer House
429 Bull St.

The famous house looks out on the square from Bull Street. This is where Williams lived and threw his famous parties, and where he shot his companion to death. It remains a private residence. Mercer House had claims to fame well before Williams' misfortunes. While lyricist Johnny Mercer ("Moon River," "That Old Black Magic," etc.) never lived there, he had close family ties to it. Jackie Kennedy Onassis once showed up to tour it, and The Book claims she concluded that tour with a request for directions to the nearest Burger King. (It's a cute story, true or not, and if you believe it and want to follow in the footsteps of the rich and famous, there are two nearby Burger Kings, one in the 600 block of W. Oglethorpe and one in the 600 block of Martin Luther King Boulevard.)

Next to Mercer House, across narrow

INSIDERS' TIP

The script for the movie of *Midnight in the Garden of Good and Evil* involved some significant revision from the book. Where the two conflict, believe the book first.

Wayne Street, stands the home of the neighbors Williams feuded with. He gets in some sharp digs on them from beyond the grave, thanks to The Book. Again, this is a private house — no tours. Directly across the square from Mercer House stands the historic Temple Mickve Israel synagogue, whose congregation, along with many other Savannahians, was affronted when Williams hung a Nazi flag from his balcony in an attempt to disrupt filming of a movie.

Intersection of Bull and Gaston streets

Remember, The Book maintains nothing counts unless its North of Gaston Street (NOGS, for short). This is where Bull Street hits that great divide. The sweeping white brick building on the western side of Bull is Armstrong House, which crops up in the book several times, most prominently as the offices of the lawyer who handled Williams' defense. On the eastern side you'll see the Oglethorpe Club, which also turns up in said Book. This is the city's most exclusive private club, with rigid membership requirements that include white skin, blue blood and money that's yellowed with age.

Clary's Cafe
404 Abercorn St. • 233-0402

Clary's was the setting where Berendt first encountered the Luther Driggers character who tried to make goldfish glow and enjoyed toting about a bottle of poison. At the time, Clary's was a drugstore with a lunch counter. The drugstore is long gone, but the restaurant has grown. Read more about it in our Restaurants chapter.

Club One Jefferson
1 Jefferson St. • 232-0200

The Lady Chablis performs in the drag show here periodically. For more details, check out the Close-up in our Nightlife chapter.

Hannah's East
20 East Broad St. • 233-2225

This comfortable nightclub isn't in The Book, but it's here you are most likely to find Emma Kelly ("The Lady of 6,000 Songs"), who definitely is a charming character both in print and real life. She's a regular performer here, but call ahead to make sure she's on if she's the main reason you are going. Even on nights she's not there, the music is pretty good. The bar is upstairs at the popular Pirates' House Restaurant.

Southern Images Gallery
132 E. Oglethorpe Ave. • 234-6449

The black-and-white work of photographer Jack Leigh is displayed in this gallery, and his range goes well beyond The Book's oddly hypnotic cover shot. You'll see other examples of his published work here. You can buy a Bird Girl poster (economy version about $35; embossed and signed specialty print just over $80) or pick up a Windows screen saver ($16) featuring Leigh's work, including the Bird Girl.

Telfair Museum of Art
121 Barnard St. • 232-1177

This local art museum is the new home for the Bird Girl statue pictured on the cover of The Book. The figure once stood guard over the Trosdal family plot in Bonaventure Cemetery, and neither the statue nor the Trosdals are in the print version of the story. Family members had the statue removed when Book tourists overran the family plot to pose for photos beside it. (By the way, photography is not allowed inside the Telfair, a common enough prohibition by museums.) The Telfair is worth a visit in its own right — see our Arts and Culture chapter. If you time your visit for Sun-

INSIDERS' TIP

Uga V (pronounced UGH-uh), who portrayed The Book's Uga IV (his sire) in the movie, made the cover of *Sports Illustrated* as the nation's best mascot in 1997. For the uninitiated, Uga is THE Georgia Bulldog, seen on the sidelines at every University of Georgia football game.

Photo: Kyle Cason

SAVANNAH 9 OCT. 1779

The Pulaski Monument graces Monterey Square, in front of Mercer House.

day, admission is free. Otherwise, admission costs $6 for adults, $2 for older children and $1 for elementary school students.

Souvenirs

The variety of Book souvenirs is impressive. Here's a very partial list, just to give you a taste: a woven afghan featuring book scenes, bookmarks picturing one of Joe Odom's rubber checks, paintings of Mercer House, a video "tour" with interviews of some of the real-life characters, coffee mugs and jewelry featuring the Bird Girl figure, a limited-edition candle shaped like the cover statue, postcards depicting the Lady Chablis, and miniature cookies in a tin patterned after the book cover. Several T-shirts are on the market, and for $4 you can even get a photocopy of Jim Williams's will.

The ultimate souvenir is, clearly, The Book itself. Of course you'll find it in local bookstores, but you'll also spot it in local stores that have never sold any other book before.

Great Savannah Books on the Other Side of Midnight

Close-up

John Berendt's *Midnight in the Garden of Good and Evil* is not the first book to be set in Savannah, although you might get that impression the way some folks carry on. If you want to read more Savannah-as-a-setting books, we have some suggestions.

Savannah bookstores tend to have their regional sections prominently displayed near the front. There you'll find predictable stuff like cookbooks from area restaurants (some of which are quite good) and coffee-table books displaying beautiful homes. But look closer: The collections usually include plenty of unexpected things as well. Here's a sample, starting with two books that have at least a passing Berendt connection, then moving on to more general topics

Hiding My Candy: The Autobiography of the Grand Empress of Savannah, by the Lady Chablis and Theodore Bouloukos ($22 hardback, $14 trade paperback), tells the story of the drag queen Berendt made famous. It includes pictures of the performer.

To Live and Die in Dixie, by Kathy Hogan Trocheck ($4.99 paperback), is an installment in her mystery series about a housekeeper/sleuth. Trocheck was a newspaper reporter in Savannah before moving on to Atlanta, where most of her books are set. This 1993 mystery (published a year before The Book) features a rich antiques dealer implicated in the murder of an employee-house guest. He's known for disrupting movie filming with a Nazi flag and feuding with his Jewish neighbor over gentrification versus rehabilitating housing for the poor. The plot diverges from there, but Book fans will still catch the allusions.

Savannah Lore and More, by Tom Coffey (hardback, $24), is a second compilation of the veteran newsman's pithy essays on Savannah. The first is "Only in Savannah."

Photo: Kyle Cason

The Mercer House was the home of Jim Williams, a major player in The Book.

Instead of Berendt's social/sexual tales, you'll read about the political side of the city, which can be similarly outrageous. In addition to local bookstores, this one can be bought at the cashier's department at the Savannah Morning News, 111 W. Bay Street.

Savannah Spectres and Other Strange Tales, by Margaret DeBolt ($9.95, trade paperback), is a collection of local ghost stories that has become sort of the standard reference work on the topic hereabouts. Williams, of *Midnight* fame, crops up as the restorer of one of the more vigorously haunted structures in this collection.

Hooligans, by William Diehl (paperback), was published in 1984. It never attracted as much attention as Diehl's more successful works such as *Sharkey's*

— continued on next page

Machine and *Primal Fear*, which became movies. This tale of political corruption is set in a thinly veiled Savannah — "Oceanby" for Tybee, "Isle of Sighs" for Isle of Hope and so on. Diehl is part of a productive writers' colony on St. Simons Island, about 90 miles south of Savannah as you near the Florida border.

Savannah, by Eugenia Price ($6.99 paperback), is a historical romance distinguished by Price's research and a literary approach that stands far above the genre's norm. If you like what you read, you're in luck: This is the first of a four-volume saga set in Savannah. Price, who died in 1997, was another St. Simons Island author.

Direct Hits and Cheap Shots, by Mark Streeter ($11.95 trade paperback), is a compilation of editorial cartoons by the *Savannah Morning News* cartoonist. The city-specific portion of this compendium will be lost on non-locals, who won't understand the digs at the foibles of local politicians, but Streeter takes plenty of shots on the national and international fronts. One of our favorites features King of Pop Michael Jackson gripping his newborn son and saying "He doesn't look a thing like me . . . But then again, neither do I!" There are even a couple of Book cartoons (there's just no escaping that topic lately). In addition to bookstores, you can also buy this one at the newspaper's offices.

You'll find a huge supply of books that have been autographed by the author. Early in the phenomenon, there was a scandal about faked autographs at one supplier, and Berendt himself came forward to get that stopped. The book lists for $25. Some of the downtown souvenir places jack the price for an autographed copy. You'll find bestseller discounts of 30 to 40 percent at the major book chain stores on the city's Southside, which you'll find described in our Shopping chapter. All the local independent booksellers also carry the book, and we encourage you to keep your copy close at hand. (We ran into Emma Kelly in the frozen food section at the grocery store.) By all means, bring your book along if you want to seek autographs. Kelly signs the book at breaks in her performances, and the Lady Chablis holds an autograph session after her set. You'll never get a complete set of character autographs, however, since several central characters have died.

Random House also has produced audio versions, both abridged and unabridged. If you haven't gotten around to reading it, these might be good options for car listening if you are driving into Savannah from some distance. Beware, however: The unabridged version runs more than 11 hours.

Basically, the same items are available at all stores that carry Book souvenirs. We've listed two stores that devote a large percentage of their stock to Book items, but you can find the same stuff in any number of general gift shops along River Street and even in scattered suburban and mall stores. The only specific recommendation we make on these things concerns the cookies. If you want Byrd Cookie's Key Lime Coolers in the Byrd Girl commemorative tin, check out our Shopping chapter. Byrd Cookie operates a gift shop as part of its bakery, and it stands to reason this would be the cheapest place to get the cookies. We've seen them as expensive as $3 per box higher elsewhere. Besides, at Byrd's you can sample the Key Lime Cooler and the other flavors available.

INSIDERS' TIP

If you can't get enough of The Book, try the Internet. Run a search involving the words Berendt, Midnight and Savannah, and you'll be busy for quite a while.

Photo: Kyle Cason

Temple Mickve Israel is shown in silhouette.

"The Book" Gift Shop
127 E. Gordon St. • 233-3867

This shop occupies the garden floor (which is what we in Savannah call the ground floor of a building, topped by the parlor floor, followed by a second floor, which is really the third floor, and so on) of a building at Abercorn and Gordon streets. Wander through several rooms to see a mix of Book souvenirs and general gifts. You'll find elements of a Book shrine along with the merchandise. The back room boasts some not-for-sale items such as a painting by Williams, a chair he once owned, a large collection of clippings about the phenomenon, etc.

INSIDERS' TIP

Savannah got its first look at the movie version of The Book on November 20, 1997, at a benefit for the Lucas Theatre restoration and the Frank Callen Boys and Girls Club.

Hospitality Tours and Gifts
141 Bull St. • 233-0119

The tour company of the title drops its patrons off here during a break in its bus tour so they can shop among the souvenirs, but the shop is open to the general public as well. The place is small, with the stock in a single room, but there are bathrooms.

St. Patrick's Day Parade Route

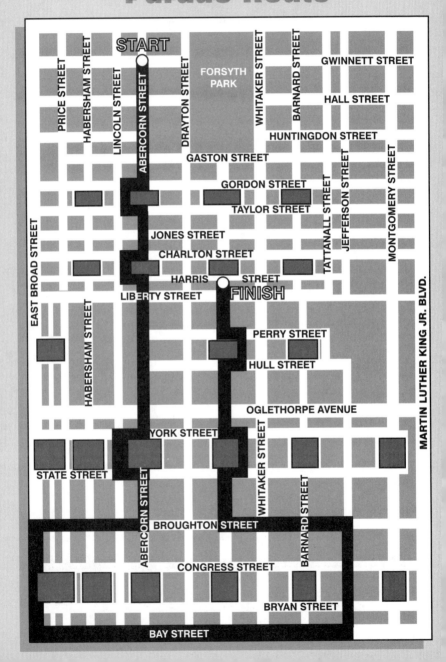

St. Patrick's Day

Kermit the Frog of Muppets fame occasionally croaks out a melancholy little ditty stating "It's Not So Easy Being Green." Obviously, Kermit has never hopped into the midst of St. Patrick's Day in Savannah, where it's not only easy being green, it's darn near mandatory.

On St. Patrick's Day in Savannah, people clothe themselves in outfits featuring every shade of green imaginable. They decorate themselves with green accessories, such as green beads, green-and-white-striped *Cat in the Hat* headgear and green-and-white buttons conveying a variety of messages, the most prevalent being "Kiss Me, I'm Irish." The revelers color their hair, beards and mustaches green and affix little green shamrock appliques to their faces. They even dye their dogs and the water of the city's fountains green.

On St. Patrick's Day in Savannah, people eat green grits and drink green beer, which tends to make some of them feel a wee bit green at the gills. On St. Patrick's Day in Savannah, people give themselves over to a wonderful green giddiness that permeates the atmosphere. Is this the work of the mischievous leprechauns — the little people of Irish lore? We're not sure, but we know it's there, wafting through the soft air of springtime, transforming human beings into creatures of whimsy.

Why St. Patrick's Day?

You might be wondering why St. Patrick's Day has evolved as the most festive day of the year in Savannah, and why a city of fewer than 150,000 people has ended up playing host to some 500,000 celebrators on that day.

These are good questions — ones on which we can only speculate. It's not enough to say that a large segment of Savannah's population is or has been Irish or of Irish descent. That's true of lots of cities that don't make anywhere near the fuss over St. Patrick's Day as does Savannah. (According to the Associated Press, 10 percent of Savannah's population is of Irish ancestry, the same percentage as San Francisco and Dallas and less than that of Kansas City, Seattle and St. Louis.)

Part of the reason for the popularity of the day might stem from the fact that it's been celebrated here for a long time — longer than in most American cities. According to the late William L. Fogarty, who wrote a history of the local observance entitled *The Days We've Celebrated*, the first celebration here was in 1813 when the Hibernian Society, formed by Irish Protestants seeking to help their impoverished countrymen, held a private procession. The city's first public procession, which is recognized as Savannah's first St. Patrick's Day parade, was also held by the Society and took place in 1824.

The observance was for many years mainly an Irish Catholic religious celebration aimed at honoring Patrick, the priest who brought Christianity to the Emerald Isle in the fifth century. While the celebration remains religious in nature (many Savannahians begin the day by attending Mass at 8:30 AM at the Cathedral of St. John the Baptist on Lafayette Square), the observance has become more

INSIDERS' TIP

Be sure to make a note of where you park your car. There will be vehicles parked all over the place, and it will be easier to lose track of yours than you might think.

secular over the years and has been adopted by other segments of the population, leading to the saying that "everyone's Irish on St. Patrick's Day."

Another reason for celebrating the day in a big way might have to do with its occurrence at a time of year when Savannah is blessed with some of its best weather. It seldom rains on St. Patrick's Day, the normal high temperature is 70, and the normal low is 49. The often dreary days of winter are over, and folks are just itching to get outside and cut loose. What better way to do so than with a citywide party?

FYI

Unless otherwise noted, the area code for all phone numbers listed in this guide is 912.

It's More Than Just a Day

The celebrating that is part of St. Patrick's Day festivities in Savannah occurs over a span of three or four days. St. Patrick's Day is observed on March 17, and the annual parade is held on that day except when the 17th falls on Sunday — in that case, the parade is on Saturday, March 16. Some people celebrate by holding parties or get-togethers in their homes or by attending the invitation-only functions of Savannah's Irish societies. The public partying occurs at watering holes throughout the city, but the bulk of the celebrating takes place on River Street, in City Market and along Bay Street.

Most of the merrymaking happens on the day of the parade and the weekend closest to it. When the parade is on a Monday, Tuesday or Wednesday, the partying will be on that day, the weekend before and the day or days before. When the parade is on a Thursday or Friday, the celebrating will be on that day, the day before and the weekend following. On parade days and weekends, River Street and City Market are packed with celebrators. Bands pump out the rock and roll, and the beer flows from an endless array of taps (see our Annual Events and Festivals chapter for more details).

The St. Patrick's Day holidays are also a time of traditional events such as the investiture of the parade grand marshal on the first Sunday in March, the gathering of Irish descendants at the Celtic Cross on the following Sunday and the laying of a wreath at the Sgt. William Jasper Monument on the afternoon before the parade. There are also family-oriented events emphasizing Irish heritage and culture such as the Savannah Irish Festival at the National Guard Armory and the Tara Feis festival in Emmet Park on Bay Street. For the athletically inclined, there's the St. Patrick's Day Rugby Tournament, held in Daffin Park on the weekend closest to the big day. For more about all these, see our Annual Events and Festivals chapter. The focal point of the festivities, however, is the St. Patrick's Day parade.

The Parade

Savannah's St. Patrick's Day parade is the third-oldest and one of the largest in the United States. It dates back to 1824, and only New York City's (1762) and Philadelphia's (1780) have been in existence longer. In 1997, there were more entries — 250 — in Savannah's parade than those in Chicago (200), Philadelphia (101), Boston (100) or New York (75). With 10,000 marchers, Savannah had fewer than New York (150,000) and Chicago (20,000)

INSIDERS' TIP

One of the best places to view the parade is from Lafayette Square, which is on Abercorn Street between Charlton and Harris streets. This is where the folks who judge the marching bands sit, so you'll see the bands performing at their best if you hang out here. Another good spot is the steps of the U.S. Custom House on Bay Street at Bull Street. The steps here are like bleachers, perfect for sitting and watching the festivities.

Kids and adults go a little crazy over St. Patrick's Day in Savannah.

Photo: Phyl M. Gatlin

but as many as Boston and more than Philly (9,700).

Savannah's parade covers a lot of pavement: specifically, 3.2 miles, making it as long in distance as the parade in Boston and longer than Philadelphia's (2.6 miles), New York's (1.5) and Chicago's (1). As you can imagine, given the number of people who march and how far they have to walk, the local parade takes quite a while to unfold — three-and-a-half to four hours. That being the case, it's a good idea to bring lawn chairs or stadium cushions so you can be as comfortable as possible while you watch, particularly if you arrive early and stake out a viewing spot closer to where the parade ends than where it begins. The farther you are from the starting point, the longer you'll have to wait for the first marchers to reach you, maybe as much as an hour.

Speaking of beginnings and endings, the parade starts at 10:15 AM at Abercorn and Gwinnett streets and ends at Bull and Harris streets. The route of march is north on Abercorn to Broughton Street, east on Broughton to East Broad Street, north on East Broad to Bay Street, west on Bay to Jefferson Street, south on Jefferson to Broughton, east on Broughton to Bull and south on Bull to the finish line (see accompanying map). We think you'll find this event to be as enjoyable and festive as you can imagine, but don't go expecting to see something akin to the Tournament of Roses parade or Macy's Thanksgiving Day bash. There are floats in Savannah's parade, and they seem to be more numerous and elaborate each year, but you won't see anything that remotely resembles what you'd watch in Pasadena, California, on New Year's Day or on the streets of New York during the Christmas holidays.

What you'll see in Savannah on St. Patrick's Day is more like a small-town parade that has

INSIDERS' TIP

The water of the Forsyth Park fountain is traditionally dyed green each year for St. Patrick's Day, but don't expect the Savannah River to be treated in similar fashion. The last and only attempt at turning the river green occurred in 1961 with less than desirable results. A thousand pounds of the chemical Uranine was used, and the outcome was a striped effect.

During St. Patrick's Day festivities, Savannah's fountains flow green.

Photo: Phyl M. Gatlin

grown to the point that it's burst clean out of its Kelly green britches. The down-home flavor of the parade is a big part of its appeal; one of the reasons we Savannahians keep going back year after year is to watch our relatives, neighbors and co-workers as they march or ride by, and to wave and yell at each other. You'll see a lot of folks stepping out of or into the line of march as they shake hands and hug necks. And you're likely to see a woman or two dash from the sidelines to plant kisses on the cheeks of marchers, particularly those in uniform and especially members of the U.S. Army Ranger and Benedictine Military School aggregations.

What you'll see are lots of high school marching bands, numerous glad-handing politicians riding in convertibles, some beauty queens, several military color guards, the parade grand marshal, a gaggle of past grand marshals and a multitude of men, women and children of Irish descent, all dressed up in their best greenery and marching in family groups or as members of Savannah's many Irish societies. Keep your eyes peeled for one of our favorite entries, the "Irishman At Large." You'll see college cheerleaders and dance teams, officials of the Catholic church, bagpipers and detachments of soldiers, sailors, Marines and veterans groups. In 1997 there were nearly 30 floats representing a variety of organizations and businesses and an appearance by the

101 Dalmatians, a group of local canines walking their owners.

Among our favorite parade units are those of the Shriners of Savannah's Alee Temple. The most outlandish of the Shriner groups is the Oriental Band, which consists of a group of pillars of the community clad in colorful burnooses, jackets and pantaloons and wearing shoes that have been spray-painted gold, turned up at the tips and decorated with tiny bells. As the band members tootle and bang away on their recorders, cymbals and drums, they are led by the least-inhibited of all the outgoing St. Patrick's Day parade marchers. He wears a turban, pantaloons and a vest, an outfit exposing to spectators a belly that appears to have seen more than a few beers pass its way. In his navel is a huge "gem," reputed to be a ruby. Swinging a scimitar over his head, the leader of the band pauses periodically to perform a bump-and-grind routine that would put most Bourbon Street strippers to shame. He is often joined by female onlookers unable to resist the temptation to dance in the middle of one of the city's main streets.

Other crowd pleasers from the Shrine are its Dunecat Unit, whose members zip around in souped-up go-karts, and the Keystone Kops, who hand out tickets to spectators amid much frenzied whistle-blowing and scurrying around. In short, what you'll see at Savannah's St. Patrick's Day parade are lots of enthusiasm, a world of pride in being Irish and the smiles of thousands of people having one heck of a good time.

Parking on St. Patrick's Day

If there is a downside to St. Patrick's Day, it's might be finding a place to park. Metered spaces are free on this holiday, but they won't be easy to find unless you get to town real early. The least frustrating thing to do might be to park in one of the city's garages or lots, which you can do all day for $5. The garages are at State and Abercorn streets, at Montgomery and York streets and at Bryan and Abercorn streets, and the lot is at Liberty and Montgomery streets.

On a recent St. Patrick's Day, we drove into town about 8 AM, parked in the garage on State Street, ate a leisurely breakfast at one of the downtown restaurants and had plenty of time to find a spot on Abercorn Street from which to watch the parade. An option to parking downtown is to park away from the area and take a Chatham Area Transit bus into the city. There are regular bus routes to and from downtown (see our Getting Here, Getting Around chapter), and there will be an express St. Patrick's Day shuttle from a staging area on the Southside that will offer continuous service all day and into the night. As of this writing, the location of the staging area had not been determined; you can call 233-5767 for information on this shuttle service.

Whatever you do, don't park in a lot or space that's designated for use by a business or private individual. If there's a sign saying your car will be towed, that's probably what will happen, and you'll have to pay $50 to get your vehicle back.

Savannah is a city that's ideal for walking, and your stroll to and from a festival could be one of the most enjoyable parts of your day.

Annual Events and Festivals

Savannahians love to party. They love their history. They also love getting outdoors and taking advantage of coastal Georgia's congenial climate. Is it any wonder, then, there's almost always something going on in Savannah? The something might be a festival attracting thousands of people or the commemoration of a historic event drawing a few hundred, but a week seldom passes in which there's nothing to do in Savannah.

We admit things slow down a tad during the summer months because of the heat, but that doesn't mean you can't get out and enjoy yourself. Grab your suntan lotion, cooler and lounge chair and head for a day at the beach on nearby Tybee Island, just as Savannahians have been doing for more than a century.

Savannah's biggest party is its celebration of St. Patrick's Day, a green-hued blast bringing up to a half-million visitors to the city in mid-March. It's such a big deal we've devoted an entire chapter to it. But because we want to be sure you don't miss any of the fun, we've included in this Annual Events and Festivals chapter brief looks at significant happenings on that great day for the Irish and the days leading up to it.

As we indicated earlier, finding a parking space in Savannah can be a hassle, and the problem intensifies when a festival is held in the downtown area. It's a good idea — particularly if you're attending an event on River Street, where parking is extremely limited — to arrive early, find a spot on a street or in a lot a few blocks from the festival, then hoof it to your destination. Savannah is a city that's ideal for walking, and your stroll to and from the

festival could be one of the most enjoyable parts of your day.

We need to mention one other thing before taking you through our month-by-month rundown of events and festivals: Dates, times and admission fees can change, so it's best to call ahead for the most current information. The telephone numbers included with the following writeups are the numbers of the individuals, organizations or agencies sponsoring or coordinating the events.

January

Historic Downtown

Emancipation Day Service
Location varies • 234-6293

Savannah's Emancipation Association commemorates the signing of the proclamation that freed the slaves by holding a special church service on New Year's Day. During the 11 AM gathering, held at a different church each year, a student reads the Emancipation Proclamation, a mass choir sings hymns, and a speaker delivers an address concerning the significance of that historic day.

Martin Luther King Jr. Observance Day Activities
Various locations • 236-4898

This month-long tribute to civil rights leader Martin Luther King Jr. culminates with a parade through downtown on the third Monday in January, the national day of observance for

King Day. The parade, starting at 9 AM at Forsyth Park, follows a busy weekend featuring a gospel festival on Friday, a breakfast for the business community at the Savannah Marriott Riverfront hotel on Saturday morning, an educational program and career fair at Savannah Technical Institute from 10 AM until 2 PM on Saturday and a citywide memorial worship service at the Savannah Civic Center at 11 AM on Sunday. On the second weekend of the month, the Dr. Martin Luther King Jr. Observance Day Association presents the Freedom Ball on Friday, the Women's Unity Luncheon at the Marriott at noon on Saturday and an interfaith service at the Cathedral of St. John the Baptist at 7 PM on Sunday. Tickets to the Freedom Ball are $15, and you can reserve a seat at the Unity Luncheon for $25.

FYI

Unless otherwise noted, the area code for all phone numbers listed in this guide is 912.

ing pine-cone bird feeders. The center's nature trail is made available to visitors. The 1.75-mile trail takes you through Oatland's maritime forest to large, fenced-in enclosures housing animals native to coastal Georgia — alligators, panthers, bobcats, foxes, deer, bears, wolves, bison, eagles, owls and hawks. A petting zoo in the center's barnyard gives children the opportunity to touch and feed cows, sheep, goats, rabbits, pigs and fowl. Admission is $2 for persons 4 and older, free for those 3 and younger.

Heart Ball
Savannah Marriott Riverfront, 100 Gen. McIntosh Blvd. • 355-0233
The American Heart Association's premier fund-raiser has a different theme every year and is held in late January or the first part of February. Tickets are $125 per person and include a reception with open bar and dinner with wine. The North Tower Band of Atlanta plays popular dance music, and there's a silent auction of a variety of high-quality items such as jewelry, wines from private cellars, trips and getaways and works by local artists.

Islands

Birds of Prey Program
Oatland Island Education Center, 711 Sandtown Rd., Oatland Island • 897-3773
Conservationist Doris Mager presents two 45-minute talks about eagles, owls and other birds of prey during this educational event on the second Saturday of January. Mager, known nationwide as "The Eagle Lady," brings four to five birds with her to liven up her lectures at 11:30 AM and 1:30 PM in the conference room of the center. The event runs from 11 AM until 5 PM and offers activities for children such as building birdhouses and creat-

February

Historic Downtown

Georgia Week
Various locations • 233-7787
This period celebrating Georgia's founding and heritage usually begins on the first Monday in February and runs through the 12th of the month — the day on which the first colonists landed in 1733 — so it's a week that can last as long as 12 days. Georgia Week opens with a ceremony presented by the Georgia Historical Society featuring portrayals of significant state historic figures. An interdenominational church service is held at a downtown location one evening during the week, and there are wreath-layings at monuments throughout the city. On the morning of Georgia Day, February 12, school children dressed as colonists and the Native Americans who welcomed them walk in a procession from Forsyth Park up Bull Street to City Hall on Bay Street. The Georgia Day Luncheon follows and features a speaker who usually addresses an aspect of historic preservation. Tickets to the luncheon were $17 in 1997; the other events are free. Historic Savannah Foundation and the public school system's Massie Heritage Center co-sponsor Georgia Week.

Super Museum Sunday
Various locations
More than 20 of the area's museums open their doors and invite the public in at no charge

on the first Sunday of Georgia Week observances (the Sunday that falls before February 12). To determine if a specific museum participates in this program and to ascertain hours of operation, contact the museum ahead of time. You can find museums and their telephone numbers in the Attractions chapter. Also note that the local transit district, CAT (233-5767), offers free rides to all the museums.

Telfair Ball
Telfair Museum of Art, 121 Barnard St.
• 232-1177

The Telfair Museum creates an elegant evening of dining and dancing in an artistic setting by hosting the Telfair Ball on the last Saturday in February. Guests sip cocktails in the rotunda of the museum, then venture outside to partake of a gourmet dinner served under a tent in Telfair Square. They can bid on 25 luxury items at a live auction in the square before returning to the museum and dancing to the music of a black-tie orchestra. The evening closes with champagne and dessert served in the sculpture gallery. Tickets to this largest of the Telfair's fund-raisers are $500 per couple.

Islands

Georgia's Cultural Heritage Program
Oatland Island Education Center, 711 Sandtown Rd., Oatland Island • 897-3773

The Oatland Island staff gives visitors the chance to celebrate Georgia's founding and Black History Month via this program on the second Saturday in February. At the log cabins of the Heritage Homesite, deep in the center's maritime forest, jazz musicians perform and discuss their art, and Civil War re-enactor Murry Dorty describes the lives of African-American soldiers who fought with the Union during the War Between the States. Staff members dressed in costumes like those worn on Georgia farms in the early 1800s help children prepare corn bread and make candles by dipping string in wax and water. Visitors can also walk the center's nature trail (see Birds of Prey Program listing in January events) and spend time at a petting zoo during the program, which runs from 11 AM until 5 PM. Admission is $2 for persons 4 and older, free for those 3 and younger.

Wormsloe Celebrates the Founding of Georgia
Wormsloe Historic Site, 7601 Skidaway Rd. • 353-3023

Historical re-enactors clad in the garb of Georgia's colonists demonstrate crafts such as making candles and musket balls at this program, held in an open area near the marsh overlooking the Skidaway River. At the visitors center, you can view artifacts excavated from Wormsloe's tabby ruins and watch an audiovisual show about the founding of the 13th colony. The program takes place from 11 AM until 4 PM on the second Saturday in February, and admission is $2 for adults and $1 for folks 6 to 18.

Southside/Midtown

Savannah Irish Festival
National Guard Armory, 1248 Eisenhower Dr. • 234-8444

This family-oriented event uses song, dance and recitation to emphasize the heritage of the Irish and the contributions of Irish immigrants here and throughout the United States. In addition to the main stage, where much of this activity takes place, there are stages for children's entertainment and workshops in Celtic art, poetry and music. Vendors market Irish clothing, jewelry and artifacts, and

INSIDERS' TIP

Wear comfortable shoes to outdoor festivals, especially those on River Street, where you'll be walking on cobblestones and uneven pavement. Be careful if you use the steps leading from Bay Street to River Street — they seem to have been designed for people with long legs and short feet.

members of 13 local Irish organizations prepare and sell food, including shepherd's pie and corned beef and cabbage. The festival is in early to mid-February from 11 AM until 10 PM on Saturday and from 11 AM until 9 PM on Sunday. On Friday night there's a party called a ceilidh (pronounced "KAY-lee") that's similar to a square dance. Admission to the festival in 1997 was $6 for adults and $4.50 for students, senior citizens and military personnel. Children 10 and younger are admitted free.

March

Historic Downtown

First Saturday
Rousakis Plaza, River St. • 234-0295

Browse through the wares of artisans and crafts people from throughout the Southeast and listen to light jazz or folk music during First Saturday on the plaza on River Street. While enjoying the breeze blowing off the Savannah River, you might find yourself staring at a large cargo ship as it glides along the waterway, so close you'd swear you could reach out and touch it. The 50 to 70 open-air arts and crafts booths on the plaza offer a variety of treasures — everything from oil paintings and watercolors to rocking horses fashioned from wood scraps. If you can't turn up something that catches your fancy among the artists' booths, visit the shops in the renovated cotton warehouses lining River Street.

Hungry? You have your choice of restaurants dishing up a variety of cuisines. The Savannah Waterfront Association presents First Saturday festivals from 9 AM to 6 PM on — what else? — the first Saturday of each month, with the exception of January and February. First Saturdays in May, October and December are part of expanded, more distinctive festivals: the Savannah Seafood Festival in May, Oktoberfest on the River in October and Christmas on the River in December (see subsequent listings for more details on these festivals). Admission is free.

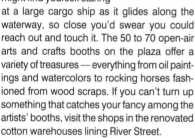

www.insiders.com

See this and many other **Insiders' Guide®** destinations online — in their entirety.

Visit us today!

Spring Herb Festival
City Market, Jefferson and St. Julian Sts. • 236-9003

Vendors sell from 75 to 100 varieties of herbs at this event in City Market on the first Saturday in March. There are also lectures about herbs and sales of items related to growing herbs. Sponsored by the Moon Dance shop (see our Shopping chapter), the festival runs from 9 AM until 4 PM and is free.

Savannah Onstage International Arts Festival
Various locations • 236-5745

Savannah Onstage enhances the beauty of the city with nine to 11 days of classical music and cultural arts starting the first weekend in March. The cornerstones of this steadily growing festival are the World Class Concert Series and the American Traditions Competition. Each year a third major component is incorporated into the festival — in 1997 Savannah Onstage premiered a new musical by Charles Strouse, the composer of *Bye, Bye, Birdie* and *Annie*. The festival also reaches out into the community by serving as a vehicle for more than two dozen "offstage events" including a juried art exhibit and noonday organ recitals in downtown churches.

The Concert Series presents the winners of many of the world's most prestigious music competitions performing at Savannah's historic churches and synagogues. The American Traditions Competition features solo vocalists singing music that has played a significant role in forming the cultural heritage of the United States. Ticket prices range from $10 to $40, with discounts for students. Several events sell out quickly, so you'd do well to call early to reserve seats and obtain details about performers and venues.

Grand Marshal Investiture Ceremony
DeSoto Hilton Hotel, 15 E. Liberty St. • 233-4804

The St. Patrick's Day Parade Committee presents the parade grand marshal with his sash and recognizes civic dignitaries at this

Columbia Square in the Historic Downtown looks festive in holiday decorations.

ceremony in the ballroom of the DeSoto Hilton Hotel. The event takes place at 3 PM on the first Sunday in March, one week after the committee elects the leader of the parade. There is no charge for admission.

Celtic Cross Ceremony
Emmet Park, Bay and Price Sts.
• 233-4804

Members of the city's Irish organizations gather at the Cathedral of St. John the Baptist for Mass at 11:30 AM on the second Sunday of the month, then march in procession to Emmet Park, where they lay a wreath at the Celtic Cross and listen to a speech about their heritage. The Cross, officially named the Irish Monument, was carved from a single piece of Irish limestone in County Roscommon, Ireland. The Savannah Irish Monument Committee erected the Celtic Cross in 1983, the 250th anniversary of the founding of Savannah and Georgia, to commemorate Georgians of Irish ancestry. The ceremony starts about 1 PM, and it's open to the public.

Tara Feis
Emmet Park, Bay and Price Sts. • 651-6417

The City of Savannah's Department of Cultural Affairs puts the emphasis on family-oriented activities at this Irish festival on the Sat-

urday before St. Patrick's Day. Irish music, dancing and crafts fill the spotlight, and youngsters can participate in hands-on activities with a Celtic touch such as making Irish flags and building castles out of sugar cubes. Alcoholic beverages are prohibited in an effort to enhance the family-day atmosphere. The event, in sun-dappled Emmet Park, runs from 11 AM until 5 PM, and it's as free as the Irish mist on a day in Killarney. In case you're wondering, Feis is pronounced "fesh."

Sgt. William Jasper Memorial Ceremony
Madison Square, Bull St. between Harris and Charlton Sts. • 233-4804

On the eve of the St. Patrick's Day Parade, the parade grand marshal and his aides recognize the contributions of the military by walking from Johnson Square down Bull Street to Madison Square, where they lay a wreath at the monument honoring Revolutionary War hero William Jasper. They are usually accompanied by a band or two that will be participating in the parade. A 21-gun salute is fired during the ceremony, which occurs about 4:30 PM.

St. Patrick's Day Parade
Various downtown streets • 233-4804

Savannah's biggest annual event lasts upwards of four hours and involves thousands of participants. Some 250 units take to the streets for the parade, including marching bands, floats and the city's numerous Irish organizations. The parade starts about 10 AM at Forsyth Park and winds its way around several of Savannah's squares and down its main thoroughfares. (For more information, see our St. Patrick's Day chapter.)

St. Patrick's Day on the River
Rousakis Plaza, River St.
• 234-0295

The Savannah Waterfront Association sets up food booths on the plaza and brings in rock-and-roll bands to perform on the center stage, but the main attraction of St. Patrick's Day on the River isn't eating or listening to music — it's being part of the crowd that jams River Street. This nine-block party is free, and it's the place to be during St. Patrick's Day festivities if you like to rub elbows with people — literally. The merry-making is at its peak on St. Patrick's Day and the weekend closest to the holiday; the party cranks up about 10 AM and doesn't wind down until 3 AM on most nights, although food sales and scheduled entertainment end at midnight.

St. Patrick's Day Street Party
City Market, Jefferson and St. Julian Sts.
• 236-4903

City Market celebrates the big day with live music and dancing in the courtyard. The party occurs over a span of time that includes St. Patrick's Day and can last as long as five days depending on when the holiday falls. It's free.

The Savannah Tour of Homes and Gardens
Parish House of Christ Church, 18 Abercorn St. • 234-8054

This granddaddy of Savannah's seasonal tours offers a different tour of private homes and gardens on each day of its four-day run. Each three-hour, self-guided walking tour takes you to six to eight sites in the Historic District. The homes and gardens on the tours are open from 10 AM until 5 PM, and participants are

encouraged to stroll from site to site at their own pace and in any order they choose. On one of the four days, there is a twilight tour and a tour of an area outside the district. Special events such as luncheons, boat rides and picnics are also presented, and they vary from year to year. The tour is held on a Thursday through Sunday in late March. Begun in 1935, the event is sponsored by the Episcopal Church Women of Christ Church, along with Historic Savannah Foundation, and proceeds benefit outreach ministries of the church and the foundation's preservation efforts. The fee for each walking tour is $25, and it's wise to order tickets for the tours and other activities ahead of time. You pick up your tickets at tour headquarters, the Parish House of Christ Church.

FYI
Unless otherwise noted, the area code for all phone numbers listed in this guide is 912.

Kids Day
Savannah Civic Center, Liberty and Montgomery Sts. • 355-8111

One of the organizers of Kids Day is fond of saying the event gives children an opportunity to receive some education with a little "e" while having fun with a capital "F." Kids Day exposes youngsters to career choices and the arts and sciences via hands-on activities such as decorating pottery, making hats from newspapers, delivering mock television weather reports and listening to storytellers. Staffed primarily by volunteers of the Jewish Educational Alliance, the event is free for adults and 50¢ for kids (or free with a donation of a can of food). We've placed Kids Day in our March events listings, but it's just as likely to be held in April or May. However, it's always on a Sunday from noon to 4 PM.

Islands

Sheep to Shawl Crafts Festival
Oatland Island Education Center, 711 Sandtown Rd., Oatland Island • 897-3773

While musicians of the Savannah Folk Music Society fiddle and strum up a storm on the porch of a log cabin built in 1835, visitors watch an old-fashioned sheep shearing. This activity on the second Saturday in March takes place at the education center's Heritage Home-site, where there is also a fair featuring 55 to 75 artists and crafts people. Oatland empha-sizes the sale of handmade items at the fair, and shoppers are likely to find a variety of unique pottery, jewelry and baskets in addi-tion to paintings and stained-glass artwork.

The main events occur about 11:30 AM and 2 PM, when workers clip the sheep with hand-operated shears. Members of the Fiber Guild of the Savannahs card wool from the previous year's shearing, spin it into yarn and, using a 150-year-old loom, weave yarn spun beforehand into a shawl. The shawl is raffled off, and the winner is announced near the end of the festival, which runs from 11 AM until 5 PM. The center invites youngsters to try their hands at carding and spinning wool. Folks interested in viewing Oatland's wild and barn-yard animals can walk the facility's nature trail and visit the petting zoo. Admission is $2 for persons 4 and older, free for those 3 and younger.

Southside/Midtown

St. Patrick's Day Rugby Tournament
Daffin Park, Victory Dr. and Bee Rd.
• 234-5999

Billed as the largest tournament of its kind in the Southeast, this event is staged by the Savannah Shamrocks rugby club on the week-end closest to St. Patrick's Day. Fifty-six teams participated in 1997. There's no charge for roaming the sidelines and learning about this sport that's akin to American football and has been called "a ruffians' game played by gentle-men." The action starts about 8 AM on both days of the tourney.

April

Historic Downtown

First Saturday
Rousakis Plaza, River St. • 234-0295

See our March listing for more information on this monthly event.

A Night in Old Savannah
Historic Railroad Shops, 601 W. Harris St.
• 651-6840

The Girl Scout Council of Savannah pre-sented the first A Night in Old Savannah festi-val as a bicentennial project in 1976. The cel-ebration of music and ethnic foods was held in Johnson Square and attracted national at-tention and huge crowds. After several years, the Shriners of the Alee Temple became spon-sors of the festival and staged it in the parking lot of the Savannah Visitors Center on Martin Luther King Jr. Boulevard. The event is now presented by the Coastal Heritage Society in the roundhouse area of the Historic Railroad Shops a block south of the visitors center.

The two-night celebration continues to pro-vide festival-goers with an opportunity to hear distinctive music and enjoy a variety of cuisine — the emphasis lately has been on blues and barbecue. Intended as a "gathering of neigh-bors and visitors," the festival offers several performers, including a headliner who fits into a distinct musical niche or is an up-and-comer: Recent headliners included singer Maria

---

INSIDERS' TIP

Pick up some bargains at the Junior League Thrift Sale or the Landlovers Flea Market. The Landlovers, residents of The Landings residential community on Skidaway Island, load up about 90 tables with sale items on a Saturday in mid-March. The event at The Village shopping center on Skidaway runs from 11 AM until 2 PM. The Junior Leaguers fill the arena of the Savannah Civic Center with good deals on a Friday and Saturday in early October. There's a $2 admission fee to the thrift sale on Friday but no charge on Saturday. For specifics on the thrift sale, call the Junior League at 352-4433.

Muldaur and Chubby Carrier and his zydeco band. The music is played and the food from more than a dozen booths is served rain or shine, because there is cover for 2,000 people at the roundhouse. Parking is available in nearby lots at the visitors center and the Savannah Civic Center (at Montgomery and Liberty streets). The festival runs from 6 PM until midnight, and admission is $5 for adults and teens, $2 for children ages 6 through 12, and kids younger than 6 are admitted free.

NOGS Hidden Gardens of Savannah Tour
Green-Meldrim House, Madison Square • 238-0248

For more than 20 years, the members of the Garden Club of Savannah have, via this tour, enabled folks to glimpse a part of the city they would not otherwise see. As its name implies, this self-guided walking tour is your chance to get a look at some of the elegant gardens hidden behind the walls and gates of downtown homes. Chosen because of their beauty and unusual arrangement, the eight gardens are opened to the public by their owners for only the two days of the tour.

You buy your tickets in front of the Green-Meldrim House, just west of Madison Square on Bull Street between Macon and Charlton streets, and then off you go at your own pace. A splendid way to end your walk is by finishing at the Green-Meldrim House and attending the tea served there, a treat included in the $18 ticket price ($15 for members of groups of 20 or more). A visit to the Massey Heritage Center and its garden is included on the tour, which is presented on a Friday and Saturday in mid-April, about the time Savannah is in full bloom. The gardens are open from 10 AM until 5 PM, and light refreshments are served at the tea from 1 to 5 PM. By the way, NOGS stands for North of Gaston Street, the locale of all the gardens on the tour.

Sidewalk Arts Festival
Forsyth Park • 238-2487

The normally sedate squares of the sidewalks leading through Forsyth Park pulsate with color in late April, when the Savannah College of Art and Design stages its Sidewalk Arts Festival. SCAD students, alumni, prospective students, children and pre-teens cover the concrete with chalk drawings, creating an immense art exhibit on the ground. You'll see everything from reproductions of famous masterpieces to the flights of fancy of 5-year-olds as you stroll through the park. Some 1,500 artists participated in 1997, the 17th year for the event. The festival starts at 11 AM and ends at 5 PM. Other attractions include the music of various bands, interactive booths manned by student organizations and the horseplay of wandering actors clad in Renaissance-period costumes.

Confederate Memorial Day
Forsyth Park • 651-6840

An observance that began in 1866 with women decorating the graves of husbands, sons and brothers who fell while wearing the gray and butternut of the Confederacy continues in Savannah with a gathering at the Confederate Memorial monument in Forsyth Park on the Sunday closest to April 26. Civil War reenactors fire a 21-gun artillery salute, and there is a performance by a fife and drum corps consisting of students from Old Fort Jackson's spring Field Music School. The solemn ceremony takes place in early afternoon.

Savannah Shakespeare Festival
Forsyth Park • 234-9860

"The play's the thing" at the Savannah Shakespeare Festival in Forsyth Park on a Friday, Saturday and Sunday in late April or early May. A different work of William Shakespeare is presented outdoors each year by the City Lights Theatre Co. (see our Arts and Culture chapter), with the curtain rising at 8 PM. There is music, singing and dancing beforehand. It's a free event, and many play-goers use the festival as an opportunity to have a picnic in the park. Recent productions have included *Othello* and *The Tempest*.

May

Historic Downtown

Savannah Seafood Festival
Rousakis Plaza, River St. • 234-0295

Fresh seafood prepared at booths on River

Photo: Rick Lott

River Street plays host to numerous seasonal events including Oktoberfest.

Street's Rousakis Plaza is the main attraction of this event on the first weekend in May. Menus feature shrimp, crab and crayfish — much of it caught in local waters. Festival-goers munch away as they check out sales of arts and crafts and boogie to the beach and Cajun music provided by bands playing on the plaza's main stage. Hours are 9 AM to 11 PM on Friday and Saturday and 9 AM to 6 PM on Sunday. Admission is free.

Savannah Duck Race
Rousakis Plaza, River St. • 236-9536

If horse racing is the sport of kings, rubber duck racing could be the pastime of . . . you, maybe. You'll spend a fortune to buy a race horse but a mere $5 for a little yellow entrant in the Savannah Duck Race on the first Saturday of May. OK, OK, if your synthetic fowl triumphs in this race, you won't wind up in the winner's circle at Churchill Downs, but a win, place or show will earn you a nifty prize. Among those awarded in 1997 were a 55-inch television and a three-day stay at a villa on Jekyll Island, Georgia (see our Daytrips chapter). The Savannah Symphony Women's Guild presents this fundraising event in conjunction with the Savannah Seafood Festival. The ducks — usually 8,000 to 10,000 of them — bob their way to

the finish line of a one-eighth-mile course in the Savannah River alongside the plaza on River Street. Starters dump the ducks in the water between 3 and 4 PM, depending on when the tide is right for racing. If you wanna buy a duck, call the listed number or purchase a ticket on the day of the race. If you just want to watch, you can do that for free.

Big Savannah Bridge Run
Various downtown streets • 944-0444

Participating in this 10-kilometer race will give you a unique view of Savannah — on foot from the Eugene Talmadge Memorial Bridge, a 1.4-mile span that rises 196 feet above the Savannah River. The race — which is for runners or walkers — takes entrants from the starting line at Broughton and Lincoln streets through downtown Savannah, over the bridge and back into the city. You can register ahead of time for $15 or enter for $20 on the first Saturday in May, the day of the race. In 1997, a total of 963 people took part in this event, which is sponsored by the Savannah Sports Council.

Kirkin' O' the Tartan
Independent Presbyterian Church, 25. W. Oglethorpe Ave. • 236-3346

The Kirkin' O' the Tartan service begins

with a procession of bagpipers and Scottish descendents bearing tartan banners representing their clans. After their entry into the church, the reading of scripture, the presentation of the banners and a special sermon, there is more piping on the green outside the church. The service is at 11 AM on the second Sunday of May, and it's an occasion when many worshipers, Scottish and otherwise, rededicate themselves and their families to God.

Scottish Games and Highland Gathering
Old Fort Jackson, 1 Fort Jackson Rd.
• 964-4951

Although tests of strength and dexterity are the focal point of the Scottish Games, there's more to the event than brawny laddies tossing long poles ("cabers") and heaving sheaves of hay into the air. Aye, there are winsome lassies performing the dances of the Highlands and stouthearted bagpipers playing their melancholy tunes. Also, members of more than 50 Scottish clans bring a touch of plaid to the green fields of Old Fort Jackson as they gather to parade, socialize and celebrate their heritage during this festival on a Saturday in mid-May. If you're not feeling Gaelic enough by the end of the afternoon, you can attend an evening party featuring Scottish entertainers at the Savannah Marriott Riverfront hotel. The entry fee to the games in 1997 was $8 for adults and teens and $3 for children younger than 12. Admission to the party, which is called a ceilidh (again, it's pronounced "KAY-lee"), was $8.

Arts on the River
River St. and other locations • 651-6417

Presented on Mother's Day weekend, Savannah's celebration of fine arts begins on Friday night with a reception for a juried competition and continues on Saturday and Sunday with an artists' street market on Rousakis Plaza and performances by the Savannah Symphony Orchestra in Morrell Park. The juried show attracts more than 300 entries, with the winners displayed in a different gallery each year. Call ahead for information on the location. You can view the winning entries at the reception or the following two days of the festival. The street market on the plaza along River Street runs from noon until 9 PM — ceramics, hand-blown glass, fine crafts, jewelry and yard sculptures fill more than 70 booths beside the Savannah River. The symphony performs in the evening in the park at the east end of River Street. Admission to the festival, a project of the city's Department of Cultural Affairs, is free.

Savannah Asian Festival
Savannah Civic Center, Montgomery and Liberty Sts. • 651-6417

A response to the contributions of Savannah's growing Asian community, this one-day event features displays and entertainment reflecting the heritage of people of Chinese, Filipino, Indian, Japanese, Korean, Thai and Vietnamese descent. The festival runs from noon until 9 PM on the last Saturday in May, and it's sponsored by Savannah's Department of Cultural Affairs.

Memorial Day at Old Fort Jackson
Old Fort Jackson, 1 Fort Jackson Rd.
• 651-6840

One of several observances held throughout Chatham County on the last Monday of May to honor those who died while serving the nation, the Fort Jackson ceremony involves the playing of "Taps" and the firing of a huge cannon by Civil War re-enactors clad in the uniforms of the North and South. The activity occurs at noon. Admission to the fort is $2.50 for adults and $2 for senior citizens, military personnel and students. Children 5 and younger are admitted free.

Islands

War of Jenkins' Ear Observance
Wormsloe Historic Site, 7601 Skidaway Rd. • 353-3023

Wormsloe emphasizes the military aspect of life in the Georgia of the 1740s with living history demonstrations on the last Saturday in May. In a program running from 11 AM to 4 PM, members of the Wormsloe militia depict the lives of soldiers who fought in the War of Jenkins' Ear — England's struggle with the Spanish for possession of the Southeastern portion of North America between 1739 and 1742. Admission is $2 for adults and $1 for children ages 6 to 18.

West Chatham

Stand Up for America Day
Various locations, Port Wentworth • 964-4379

Residents of the west Chatham County town of Port Wentworth show their red, white and blue colors from 9 AM until 5 PM on a Saturday in early May devoted to patriotism and fun. A parade featuring go-carts and bicycles decorated by youngsters starts at 10 AM, with a rally near City Hall following at noon. A 5-kilometer run, a 1-mile fun walk, a street dance, craft sales and activities for children round out the day, with much of the action occurring on Ga. Highway 25, which is blocked off for the celebration.

June

Historic Downtown

First Saturday
Rousakis Plaza, River St. • 234-0295

See our March listing for more information on this monthly event.

City Market Blues Fest
City Market, Jefferson and St. Julian Sts. • 232-4903

Local bands play early in the evening and bigger-name groups perform later on during Blues Fest, which is presented free of charge by City Market on the second Friday and Saturday in June. The music starts about 5 PM and continues until about 1:30 AM, with performances at 8:30 and 10:30 PM by regional headliners such as Ella Speed, Playing for Keeps, EROK, Red House and The Blues Daddies.

July

Historic Downtown

First Saturday
Rousakis Plaza, River St. • 234-0295

See our March listing for more information on this monthly event.

Tall Ship Festival
Rousakis Plaza, River St. • 944-0456

Tall-masted sailing ships will rendezvous at Savannah during the weekend of July 4, 1998, for the start of an Atlantic Ocean race to Long Island, New York, that's part of Americas' Sail '98. The ships will parade up the Savannah River to the city's harbor on July 3 and will be open to the public free of charge along Rousakis Plaza on the 4th and 5th. The race begins July 6. Twenty-three ships took part in the inaugural Americas' Sail in New Haven, Connecticut, in 1995. The event is an effort to celebrate friendly ties among participating nations and to recognize the brotherhood of the sea.

The Great American Fourth of July
Rousakis Plaza, River St. • 234-0295

The sky above the Savannah River explodes in fireworks as folks gather on the plaza to celebrate the nation's birthday on July 4. Technicians shoot off shells 3 to 6 inches in diameter from nearby Hutchinson Island or a barge in the river during a 30-minute, computer-synchronized "pyro-musical." Come early to stake out a good spot for viewing the show, and bring lawn chairs and a picnic supper to participate in what resembles a gigantic tailgate party. While you're waiting for the fireworks, you can listen to live music and people-watch. The free event opens about 5 PM, and the rockets start bursting in air about 9:30 PM.

Reds, Whites and Blues Festival
City Market, Jefferson and St. Julian Sts. • 236-4903

City Market enlivens the Fourth of July holiday with a winetasting that raises money for local charity. A $15 donation gets you a T-shirt and a wine glass that's your passport to tasting the wines on display and munching on food provided by City Market restaurants. While you're sipping the reds and whites, your children will be enjoying cookies and blue-colored drinks. Entertainment is provided by groups playing some of the music associated with the nation's heritage — folk music, marching band music and Dixieland. The festivities occur on the Fourth and the day before and the day after, with activities on all three days starting at 3 PM.

August

Historic Downtown

First Saturday
Rousakis Plaza, River St. • 234-0295

See our March listing for more information on this monthly event.

Old Fort Jackson Auction and Crab Boil
Old Fort Jackson, 1 Fort Jackson Rd. • 651-6840

If you're going, you need to call ahead for tickets to this evening of fun, history and food at the oldest standing fort in Georgia. The easy-going event takes place within the brick walls of the structure, which was manned during the War of 1812 and used during the Civil War as a headquarters for the Confederacy's de-

fense of the Savannah River. After visitors chow down on boiled crabs, fried fish and all the trimmings, a live auction is held. Although there are no special activities for children, the young-sters enjoy themselves scampering around in what amounts to a walled playground. Admission is $7 for adults and teens and $3.50 for children 6 to 12. Children younger than 6 are admitted free.

Islands

Tools and Skills That Built the Colony
Wormsloe Historic Site, 7601 Skidaway Rd. • 353-3023

Wormsloe staff members in Colonial attire demonstrate carpentry, blacksmithing and other skills essential to the development of Georgia. This living history program is offered from 11 AM until 4 PM on the Saturday of Labor Day weekend. Admission is $2 for adults and $1 for children 6 to 18.

September

Historic Downtown

Ralph Mark Gilbert Civil Rights Museum Anniversary Celebration
Ralph Mark Gilbert Civil Rights Museum, 460 Martin Luther King Jr. Blvd. • 231-8900

Workshops and lectures inside the museum and a festival outside the building emphasize its founding in 1996. The workshops and lectures deal with aspects of African-American heritage and so does the festival, which features activities for children and entertainment by dancers and musicians. Another major part of the celebration, which takes place the first weekend of September, is a fund-rais-

INSIDERS' TIP

Get a unique view of activities on River Street and stay out of the crowds by renting a hotel room facing the Savannah River, but be prepared for some late-night noise from musicians and merrymakers.

ing banquet. Admission to the museum is $4 for adults, $3 for senior citizens and $2 for students. Tickets to the banquet are $35.

First Saturday
Rousakis Plaza, River St. • 234-0295

See our March listing for more information on this monthly event.

Savannah Jazz Festival
Various locations • 232-2222

Forsyth Park and other downtown venues heat up with the sounds of jazz on the last weekend in September when nationally and internationally famous musicians come to Savannah. These entertainers, along with local and regional talents, play their special brand of American music in the park from 6 to 11 PM on Friday and 2 to 11 PM on Saturday. The festival continues on Sunday with an event for children at Rousakis Plaza on River Street and a jazz brunch at a different restaurant each year. Among the jazz greats who've performed at past festivals are singers Nancy Wilson and Joe Williams, organist Jimmy Smith and vibraphonist Lionel Hampton. The festival is funded by the city's Department of Cultural Affairs and organized by the Coastal Jazz Association, a nonprofit, community organization that depends on vol-

unteers to run the event. Sessions presented outdoors are free, and tickets to the jazz brunch run from $25 to $35.

Southside/Midtown

Savannah Folk Music Festival
Daffin Park • 927-1376

The focal point of this three-day musical jamboree is a concert in Daffin Park in Savannah's midtown area. The concert consists of four to five acts featuring nationally recognized musicians. In recent years, the stage has been graced by folks such as blues singer and guitarist Etta Baker, Cajun music makers Coz Fontenot and the Metro Playboys and Appalachian Mountain-style singers Norman and Nancy Blake. The free concert, funded by Savannah's Department of Cultural Affairs, lasts from 1 to 6 PM on the Sunday of the festival. The event starts on Friday evening of the third weekend in September with performances of local musicians at City Market in downtown Savannah and continues Saturday night with a square dance, usually at the Oatland Island Education Center. The whole shebang is presented by the Savannah Folk Music Society.

Photo: Phyl M. Gatlin

Thrills are plentiful at the annual Coastal Empire Fair.

October

Historic Downtown

Oktoberfest on the River
Rousakis Plaza, River St. • 234-0295

If you happen to have a dachshund handy, you might want to enter it in the Wiener Dog Race, a comical competition that's become a featured part of the Savannah Waterfront Association's Oktoberfest event. Some 200 low-slung pooches "sprint" down the 50-foot race course as they seek to win prizes for their masters. The race — run in heats of four to six dogs until an overall winner prevails — benefits the local Humane Society and costs $5 to enter. Watching is fun even if you don't have a dog running: Some pups never get out of the starting gate, and others wander around instead of heading for the finish line. The race, the brainchild of Waterfront Association Director Rick Lott, is staged on the Saturday morning of the festival, which occurs during the first weekend of the month.

Oktoberfest also serves up German food and music and plenty of beer. Booths manned by employees of River Street restaurants sell wiener schnitzel, sauerbraten, bratwurst and German chocolate cake, but there is also food for those whose tastes aren't Teutonic. Oompah band members decked out in lederhosen and Tyrolean hats provide much of the music, and festival-goers are invited to join them in doing the arm-flapping, head-bobbing "Chicken Dance." Also, a headline entertainer usually performs at Oktoberfest. Admission is free, but the food is not. Hours of operation are 9 AM to 11 PM on Friday and Saturday and 9 AM until 6 PM on Sunday.

Fall Herb Festival
City Market, Jefferson and St. Julian Sts. • 236-9003

From 75 to 100 varieties of herbs are sold at this event in City Market on the first Saturday in October. There are also lectures about herbs, and vendors sell items related to growing herbs. Sponsored by the Moon dance shop (same as the Spring Herb Festival in March),

the festival runs from 9 AM to 4 PM and is free of charge.

Revolutionary War Memorial Celebration
Historic Railroad Shops, 601 W. Harris St. • 651-6840

The Coastal Heritage Society uses this celebration to commemorate the Siege of Savannah, which was fought about a block from the Historic Railroad Shops. A fife and drum corps from Old Fort Jackson's fall Field Music School provides music for the ceremony, held about 2 PM on the Sunday closest to October 9, the day of the battle. Admission is free.

Telfair Art Fair
Telfair Square, 121 Barnard St. • 232-1177

The Telfair Museum's annual fair attracts about 60 artists from throughout the United States. They compete for cash awards and sell their creations to the public from displays under tents set up in Telfair Square. You can find paintings, sculpture, photographs, fabric, jewelry and other fine arts at this juried exhibition, which takes place on a weekend in mid-October. Hours are 10 AM until 5 PM on Saturday and 12:30 to 4 PM on Sunday. The fair is free, as is admission to the museum.

Historic Savannah Foundation Gala
Location varies • 233-7787

Historic Savannah Foundation's major fund-raiser starts with cocktails in private homes and moves to a downtown square for a black-tie dinner party. The event is always held in October, but the date and location vary. Tickets are $100.

Picnic in the Park
Forsyth Park • 236-9536

Sip wine under the stars and enjoy the music of the Savannah Symphony Orchestra at Picnic in the Park in mid-October. The more elaborate your picnic meal, the better. Judges select the best table settings, with awards for the most elegant and most creative. One year, some enthusiastic picnickers rigged up a chandelier to add some sophistication to their dinner. If you prefer to simply sit on a blanket and nibble on a sandwich, that's OK too. The concert and your seats on the grass are free of charge.

The Tom Turpin Ragtime Festival
Various locations • 233-9989

Held during five days in late October, this festival celebrates ragtime music by offering seminars and performances at a variety of venues including downtown theaters and the parlors of homes in the Historic District. The event is named for Tom Turpin, who was born in Savannah and was a mentor to major writers of ragtime such as Scott Joplin. When Turpin wrote "Harlem Rag" in 1897, he became the first African American to have a piece of ragtime music published. Concerts presented during the festival, which runs from Wednesday through Sunday, feature entertainers from throughout the United States. Tickets for the concerts range from $15 to $25.

Black Heritage Festival
River St. and other locations • 651-6417

During the portion of the festival occurring on River Street, various musical groups entertain with performances of gospel, reggae and jazz music, and crafts people at a marketplace on the plaza sell items related to African culture. The W.W. Law Lecture Series kicks off the festival at the Ralph Mark Gilbert Civil Rights Museum with a guest speaker discussing a topic concerning the heritage of African Americans. The event is in late October, and admission to events on River Street is free. Admission to the museum where the lecture series is held is $4 for adults, $3 for seniors and $2 for students.

Hard Lox Cafe Jewish Food Festival
Monterey Square, Bull St. between Taylor and Gordon Sts. • 233-1547

Congregation Mickve Israel presents this opportunity to sample Jewish foods such as blintzes, potato latkes, matzo ball soup, knishes and bread called challah. These delectable items are sold from booths set up in Monterey Square across from Temple Mickve Israel. Live entertainment and activities for children add to the event, which runs from 11 AM until 4 PM on a selected Sunday in October. Admission is free, and you purchase food by buying tickets at the square.

Halloween on the River
Rousakis Plaza, River St. • 234-0295

Too old to go trick-or-treating but still enjoy dressing up for Halloween? You might consider joining the procession of costumed merrymakers walking the length of River Street from 7 to 11 PM on that enchanted evening. The Savannah Waterfront Association gives prizes for the best get-ups, and there is entertainment on the main stage of the River Street plaza. The prizes — including vacation packages and cash awards — inspire some exceedingly creative costumes. On a recent Halloween a winning entry involved two men, one of whom was dressed as a waiter with a cloth-covered table suspended from his midsection. When he lifted the lid of a serving dish affixed to the table, an unusual entree was revealed — his partner's head. Admission to Halloween on the River is indeed a treat: It's free.

Southside/Midtown

Savannah Greek Festival
St. Paul's Greek Orthodox Church, 14 W. Anderson St. • 236-8256

When we think of the Savannah Greek Festival, we can taste the baklava and loukoumades melting in our mouths. Those scrumptious pastries are two of the tasty concoctions offered for sale at the Hellenic Center adjacent to St. Paul's church in midtown Savannah during the third Thursday, Friday and Saturday in October. Among other favorites of the patrons of the festival are the Greek

INSIDERS' TIP

You can walk around in public in Savannah with an alcoholic beverage in your hand without fear of being arrested as long as the drink is in a plastic cup or mug. However, drinking beer, wine or other spirits from bottles, cans and glasses is prohibited.

salad, baked chicken seasoned with oregano and lemon juice and a spinach pie called spanakopita. While you're enjoying the food, sit back and watch the Hellenic Center's dance group perform. You can also tour the church and browse through the Greek grocery store. Festival hours are 11 AM until 9 PM. A $2 admission fee is charged on Saturday and after 4 PM on Thursday and Friday.

FYI

Unless otherwise noted, the area code for all phone numbers listed in this guide is 912.

Coastal Empire Fair
520 W. 63rd St. • 354-3542

During late October and early November when the weather turns chilly, the Coastal Empire Fair comes to town. The fairgrounds off Montgomery Street glow and throb with the lights and sounds of thrill rides, sideshows and game booths. The 60-odd rides include about a dozen for children. This Exchange Club Fair Association extravaganza also features livestock shows, flower shows and home demonstrations in skills such as canning and quilt-making. The $10 admission fee allows you to hop on as many rides and attend as many shows as you wish, and the price is reduced to $8 for special occasions such as days dedicated to students.

November

Historic Downtown

First Saturday
Rousakis Plaza, River St. • 234-0295

See our March listing for more information on this monthly event.

Islands

Cane Grinding and Crafts Festival
Oatland Island Education Center, 711 Sandtown Rd., Oatland Island • 897-3773

Get a glimpse of pioneer life in the Georgia of the 1830s and do some early Christmas shopping by ambling through the Oatland forest and visiting the Heritage Homesite on the second Saturday in November. At the end of your walk through a wood thick with oak, magnolia, pine and vines of the muscadine grape, you'll find yourself in a small clearing where sugar cane is being processed and an arts and crafts fair is in progress. Farmers grind the cane into juice at a mill powered by a horse, then boil it into syrup. You can watch the entire operation, then buy a bottle of the sweet-smelling nectar to pour on your Sunday-morning pancakes.

As many as 75 artists and craftsmen will have their handmade creations on sale, and you can pick and choose while strolling amid the displays and snacking on a chunk of cane, a funnel cake or a chocolate-covered apple on a stick. You might also want to poke your head into the cozy interiors of the two log cabins at the site and watch weavers at work and costumed women preparing corn bread, or you might hunker down on a bench and listen to members of the Savannah Folk Music Society as they perform songs from Georgia's past. Complete your day at Oatland by walking the nature trail to the wild-animal habitats and visiting the barnyard petting zoo. If you need to get off your feet for a while, take a ride through the forest in a horse-drawn hay wagon. The festival opens at 10 AM and closes at 5 PM. Admission is $2 for persons 4 and older; those 3 and younger are admitted free.

December

Historic Downtown

Christmas on the River
River St. • 234-0295

Usher in the Christmas season on the first Saturday in December by shopping for gifts created by artists and craftsmen and watching a parade starring Santa Claus. The arts and crafts vendors start selling at 9 AM on the riverfront plaza, and the parade begins at 10 AM on the western end of River Street. A highlight of the parade are the "Newfies," 50 to 60 Newfoundland dogs from throughout the United States. Newfoundlands are huge ca-

Photo: Kyle Cason

Although the live oaks remain green all year, Savannah does have displays of fall color.

nines used in rescue operations in cold climes, and the large gathering of these animals is quite a sight. The parade lasts from an hour to 90 minutes and also includes high school bands, color guards, floats, dance troupes, antique cars and, last but most important, St. Nick riding in a carriage. After the parade, Santa sits on the main stage of the plaza and listens to children recite their Christmas wish lists. Enjoy the parade but keep an eye out for flying candy flung from the floats to youngsters lining the route. Arts and crafts booths remain open until 6 PM. In keeping with the

spirit of the season, there is no charge for admission to this holiday festival.

Christmas 1864 Program
Old Fort Jackson, 1 Fort Jackson Rd.
• 651-6840

On the first Saturday evening of the month, Civil War enthusiasts portray what might have occurred at Fort Jackson on December 20, 1864, when Confederate troops defending Savannah evacuated the city. On that night, Lt. Gen. William J. Hardee, outnumbered six-to-one but refusing to surrender to Union commander William T. Sherman, led 10,000 troops safely out of Savannah and into South Carolina. Fifty to 60 re-enactors dramatize the strategic retreat in the glow of firelight and torches. Admission is free.

Historic Inns of Savannah Annual Holiday Tour
Various locations • (800) 379-0638

The owners of 15 festively decorated inns open their doors to tour-goers, serve refreshments and discuss the histories and furnishings of their establishments during this weekend event in December. The inns are available for self-guided visits from 1:30 to 4:30 PM on the Saturday of the tour and from 1:30 to 4:30 PM and 6 to 8 PM on Sunday. Tickets, which were $15 in 1997, are good for both days and can be purchased at any participating inn (call the toll-free number for a rundown). The sponsoring Historic Inns of Savannah Association donates the proceeds to charity.

Jazz Up Your Sunday Afternoon
Ralph Mark Gilbert Civil Rights Museum, 460 Martin Luther King Jr. Blvd. • 231-8900

Jazz musicians cook up their distinctive style of music in the theater of the Ralph Mark Gilbert Civil Rights Museum each Sunday afternoon of the month from 3 to 5 PM. Featured performers include local favorites such as pianist/trombonist Teddy Adams, bassist Ben Tucker and pianist Percival Williams. Admission to the museum is $4 for adults, $2 for students and $3 for senior citizens.

Christmas Open House
City Market, Jefferson and St. Julian Sts. • 232-4903

On a weeknight in early December, the courtyard at City Market glows with the soft light of luminarias as shop owners open their doors and offer complimentary refreshments to visitors. Strolling carolers sing yuletide classics while Father Christmas — resplendent in his green velvet robe and red velvet cape and hat — talks with children about the spirit of the season and their plans for the holidays. This festive atmosphere takes place at City Market's Christmas Open House, which starts at sun-

down with the lighting of the luminarias and ends about 9 PM.

Downtown Neighborhood Association Holiday Tour of Homes
DeSoto Hilton Hotel, 15 E. Liberty St. • 236-8362

Many of the homes on the tours offered during this mid-December event are decorated for Christmas in ways reflecting the lifestyles of their owners. The self-guided walking tours are on Saturday afternoon and evening and Sunday afternoon, with a different set of eight to 10 homes featured on each day. The sponsoring Downtown Neighborhood Association selects homes in the Historic District that present a diversity in architectural design and decor. The Saturday evening tour runs from 5 to 7 PM, and candles light the interiors and exteriors of many of the residences visited. Afternoon tours are from 1 to 4 PM both days. Tickets were $18 in 1997. They can be picked up in the lobby of the DeSoto Hilton Hotel on the days of the event. The association returns tour revenues to the community in the form of projects aimed at maintaining and improving the quality of life downtown.

Festival of Trees
Savannah Civic Center, Liberty and Montgomery Sts. • 238-2777

This event features more than 75 trees and wreaths decorated for the holidays by professional designers, florists and community groups. There's also a nativity scene, a display of menorahs and special events such as a gingerbread-house decorating contest, a tea for senior citizens and a black-tie gala dinner. Parent and Child Development Services, a private, nonprofit agency, sponsors the festival, which begins during the second week in December and continues through the remainder of the month. Hours are from 10 AM until 8 PM, and admission to the display of trees is free.

Holiday Family Sunday
Telfair Museum of Art, 121 Barnard St. • 232-1177

The Telfair gets into the holiday spirit by

offering demonstrations by local artists, musical performances, storytelling and activities for children such as making holiday cards and spice balls. To top all this off, Santa Claus pays a visit, and admission is free. The Sunday on which the festival is held varies from year to year, but the hours are set at 2 to 5 PM.

Christmas for Kids
City Market, Jefferson and St. Julian Sts. • 232-4903

It's been said that Christmas is for children, and City Market takes that to heart by offering a program for young people from 11 AM until 2 PM on the Saturday before the holiday. This event gives youngsters the opportunity to visit with Father Christmas and make ornaments representative of Christmas, Hanukkah and Kwanzaa. The entertainment varies from year to year, with puppet shows and performances by youth choirs in the mix. It's all free.

New Year's Eve at City Market
City Market, 232 W. St. Julian St. • 232-4903

Bands or a band and a disc jockey create a party atmosphere at City Market during the hours leading up to midnight on New Year's Eve. When the clock strikes midnight, hundreds of balloons strung across the courtyard are dropped amid the merrymakers. The event is free, and the partying starts about 7 PM and lasts until 1 or 2 AM.

Islands

Colonial Christmas at Wormsloe
Wormsloe Historic Site, 7601 Skidaway Rd. • 353-3023

While a yule log is burned, carolers sing to the accompaniment of musicians playing a zither and flutes at this celebration of Christmas as it was during Colonial times. Sip some hot cider and munch on cookies as you enjoy the festivities. This holiday program on the second Sunday in December runs from 2 to 5:30 PM, and admission is $2 for adults and $1 for those 6 to 18.

Southside/Midtown

Christmas at Bethesda
Bethesda Home for Boys, 9250 Ferguson Ave. • 351-2040

The boys of Bethesda present a re-enactment of the Magi's visit to the baby Jesus and sing Christmas carols during a program at their chapel. The boys and their guests then move to the gymnasium for cookies and punch, the bringing in of a yule log and a visit from Santa Claus, who has gifts for the residents of the home. This celebration occurs on the Friday two weeks before Christmas and gets started about 6 PM. The event is free and open to the public; donations are accepted.

There are dozens of things for the young and young at heart to do while in Savannah. Best of all, most won't drain Mom and Dad's wallets or patience.

Kidstuff

Hey kids, there are ghosts in Savannah. And dolphins and lions. Look closely enough and in the right places and you just might find them. If art is more your thing, that's OK, too. Become an artist for the day by spending time creating brightly colored pottery. You can also fish or swim or parasail, if you prefer.

There are dozens of things for the young and young at heart to do while in Savannah. Best of all, most won't drain Mom and Dad's wallet or patience with hefty admission charges or long lines. So when your kids start uttering the infamous declarative, "I'm bored," take a look here for some nifty ideas.

Stretch Your Legs

For outdoor fun, get moving with one or more of these options. Savannah offers everything from ghosts and goblins to dolphin tours and downtown parks.

Take a Tour

Coastal Georgia Tours
10 Silverstream Plantation, Richmond Hill • 727-4837

You'll learn why they call it the Goosebumps ghost story tour when you join in this excursion offered by Coastal Georgia Tours. While driving around the historic city, you'll see dozens of spots that are said to be haunted and hear about ghostly encounters. These aren't folktales, the people at Coastal Georgia Tours say, but real stories from real people who are otherwise quite rational and ordinary folk. The kids fare is $5 (it's $10 for adults) for the 90-minute tour.

Bull River Marina
8005 Old Tybee Rd. (U.S. Hwy. 80 E.), Tybee Island • 898-9222

Float down Bull River for a 90-minute, nar-rated nature cruise and who knows, you might encounter some bottle-nosed dolphins. Enjoy the scenery while hearing about nature aboard a 40-foot pontoon boat. Trips are made daily from spring through fall. The cost is $14 for adults and teens, $12 for seniors and $10 for children 12 and younger.

Lazaretto Creek Marina
U.S. Hwy. 80 E., just across Lazaretto Creek Bridge, Tybee Island • 786-5848

While enjoying the scenery of Fort Pulaski and the North Beach of Tybee Island, see friendly bottle-nosed dolphins playing in their natural habitat. The 90-minute tours cost $12 for adults and teens and $5 for children 12 and younger.

Fish or Fly

Bull River Marina
8005 Old Tybee Rd., (U.S. Hwy. 80 E.) • 898-9222

Parasail over Bull River from the *Island Gypsy*, a 30-foot aerial pro parasail boat. The 90-minute session includes about 10 minutes of flight time for each passenger. There is on-boat launch and recovery, and the cost is $45 per flier and $15 for observers, with a six-passenger limit. Kids must be at least 85 pounds to fly alone; smaller children can fly with adults. All equipment is included. Daily departures April 15 through October are at 10 AM, noon and 2, 4 and 6 PM.

Tybee Pier
16th St., Tybee Island • 786-7574

Grab your pole and head out to Tybee Pier where you will join other anglers hoping to catch the big one. If you don't have a pole, don't worry; you can rent one at the pier. Fishing rods are $3 per hour and $10 a day. The pier is open 24 hours a day.

Go On Safari

Savannah Safari

Savannah Safari, written by Polly Wylly Cooper and Emmeline King Cooper, takes young readers on a trip through the Historic Downtown in search of frogs, lions and flowers. Young readers get a choice of a one- or two-hour parent-guided tour while they fill in the blanks with answers to questions in the workbook. It's great for coloring, so bring some Crayolas. See if your child can find the great blue herons keeping cool in Forsyth Park or the lounging lions in Lafayette Square. When we looked, the book was selling for $4.95 in local bookstores.

Savannah National Wildlife Refuge
S.C. Hwy. 170 • 652-4415

Take a coastal safari through the 26,349-acre Savannah National Wildlife Refuge. It's full of freshwater marsh, tidal rivers, creeks and bottomland hardwood swamps. While driving through the refuge, see if you can spot alligators, owls, hawks, turtles, snakes or maybe even a bald eagle. The refuge is owned and managed by the U.S. Fish and Wildlife Service. It is open seven days a week during daylight hours (except federal holidays), and visiting is free. The refuge is about 9 miles from downtown; for more information and directions, see our Parks and Recreation chapter.

Play the Day Away

Forsyth Park
Bull St., between Gaston St. and Park Ave.

Thirty acres perfect for letting off some steam are set aside in the Historic Downtown. There are swing sets, slides and other con-

traptions for youngsters needing to get rid of some energy, along with plenty of open space to just plain run around. There are lots of benches, beautiful magnolia trees and scenery for Mom and Dad to enjoy too. May we suggest a picnic?

Skidaway Island State Park
52 Diamond Causeway, Skidaway Island
• 598-2300

Camping sites, picnic areas, trails, playgrounds and a swimming pool can be found at 533-acre Skidaway Island State Park, the only state park in Chatham County. Maps of the park and trails are available at the park office. If you don't want to tackle the trails alone, free guided hikes are available with advance reservations. The pool is open Memorial Day to Labor Day. Cost to enter the park is $2 per car. (For more information, see our Parks and Recreation chapter.)

The Playground
1127 Fulton Rd. • 925-7529

Save your quarters then head to The Playground, a giant playland for kids filled with video games, tunnels for crawling in, special prizes and much more. Across the street from the Savannah Mall on the Southside, The Playground could keep kids busy and happy (provided the quarter-provider's pockets don't empty out too soon) for hours. Admission is $3.99 for children ages 1 to 3 and $5.99 for kids 4 and older. It is open 10 AM to 8 PM Monday through Thursday, 10 AM to 9 PM Friday and Saturday and noon to 8 PM on Sunday.

Lake Mayer
Montgomery Crossroad and Sallie Mood Dr. • 652-6786

Bring your bike and take a spin around the

FYI

Unless otherwise noted, the area code for all phone numbers listed in this guide is 912.

Photo: Kyle Cason

Oatland Island features native animals in natural habitats.

1.5-mile trail at Lake Mayer, located in the 75-acre community park of the same name. While there, you can also play tennis or basketball or feed the ducks swimming in the lake.

The Ol' Ball Game

Savannah Sand Gnats
Grayson Stadium, Daffin Park, 1401 E. Victory Dr. • 351-9150

If you happen to be in town during the Sand Gnats season (early April through the end of August), round up the kids and take them to a ball game. Besides being entertained by the Gnats, the single-A affiliate for the Texas Rangers, kids and parents will have fun watching the dueling mascots and between-inning contests (including the classic one in which two people spin around dozens of times with their heads on the ends of bats, then try to make it to first base), munching on barbecue and boiled peanuts and getting caught up in the atmosphere of this old-time ballpark. Games start at 7:15 PM on weekdays and Saturdays and at 2 PM on Sundays until mid-June, when Sunday games begin at 6:15 PM. General admission is only $3.75 for adults and $3 for students and children. Parking is free around the stadium. (For much more on the Sand Gnats, see our Spectator Sports chapter.)

Open Your Mind

Midnight Star Pottery
213 W. St. Julian St. • 236-3473

Paint a bowl for your grandmother or a water dish for your favorite kitty at Midnight

---

INSIDERS' TIP

Another famous Savannah youngster is noted Southern author Flannery O'Connor. Mary Flannery O'Connor was born in Savannah on March 25, 1925, and grew up at 207 E. Charlton Street on Lafayette Square. She left Savannah when she was about 13 years old.

Star Pottery, a unique and enjoyable pottery-painting studio in City Market. Kids can spend hours choosing among the dozens of pottery pieces — included are plates, picture frames, pasta sets, tiles, napkin rings, even dog and cat dishes — and creating masterpieces. It's a lot of fun for Mom and Dad too. Costs include the pottery items, which start at $2 for a tile and go up from there, and an hourly studio fee. Children 10 and younger pay $5 per hour for studio use; adults pay $6 per hour. The fee includes all creative materials (paints, brushes, glazes), firing and instruction. The clock doesn't start ticking on the studio fee until you've picked out your piece of pottery, colors and designs and have sat down to paint. In other words, if your child takes an hour trying to figure out just the right present to create for his or her teacher, it won't cost you anything.

Saturday Art Colony
Tybee Arts Association, P.O. Box 2344, Tybee Island, GA 31328 • 786-5920

Make a puppet, create art out of sand or just paint and draw during this class offered by the Tybee Arts Association. The association offers Saturday Art Colony year round. It runs from 10:30 AM to noon and costs $6 per session for Tybee residents and $8 for non-residents. A different medium is featured each Saturday, with kids involved in activities such as working with clay, painting or creating sand sculptures.

The Aquarium at Skidaway Island
30 Ocean Science Cir. • 598-2496

Scout out Georgia's marine life at The Aquarium at Skidaway Island. This small facility, operated by the University of Georgia Marine Extension Service, also includes a picnic area and a walking trail. See 200 live animals including fish of all shapes and sizes, turtles and maybe even a small shark in the many wall tanks lining the exhibit hall. Then go outside for a stroll along the Jay Wolfe Nature Trail, which passes by scenic marshes. The aquarium is open from 9 AM to 4 PM on weekdays and noon to 5 PM on Saturdays. It is closed on Sundays and holidays. Cost is $1, with children younger than 6 admitted free.

River Street Train Museum
315 W. River St. • 233-6175

See dozens of model trains chug and whistle around the track at the River Street Train Museum. Mom and Dad might also enjoy checking out model trains dating to the 1930s. Everyone agrees, however, the best part is watching them make their way around the track that takes up the center of the museum. Cost is $1.50 for adults and 50¢ for youngsters 5 to 12; children 5 and younger get in free. The River Street museum is open Monday through Saturday from 11 AM to 6 PM and Sunday from 1 to 6 PM.

Ships of the Sea Museum
41 Martin Luther King Jr. Blvd. • 232-1511

The kids can learn all about Savannah's maritime history at this museum, which recently relocated to one of Savannah's historic old residences. The Scarbrough House, built in 1819 for the principal owner of the *Savannah*, the first steamship to cross the Atlantic Ocean, now houses the museum. There are 75 ships in bottles to widen those little eyes, along with Viking ships. Cost is $5 for adults, $4 for children 7 and older (if you have a college ID, you can get the discounted rate). Children younger than 7 are fee. The museum is open from 10 AM to 5 PM Tuesday through Sunday and is closed on Mondays.

---

www.insiders.com

See this and many other **Insiders' Guide®** destinations online — in their entirety.

Visit us today!

INSIDERS' TIP

Like roller skating? In 1997, Chatham County authorized funding of a roller hockey rink for in-line skating and roller hockey enthusiasts. The rink, to be located in Lake Mayer on the city's Southside, is expected to be finished sometime in 1998.

Photo: Kyle Cason

Nature walks over Savannah's well-known marshes are popular for kids.

Surf's up!

Photo: Phyl M. Gatlin

Tybee Island Marine Science Center
14th St. parking lot, Tybee Island • 786-5917

Stroll the beach, toss a net into the ocean, then learn about what you find during a beach discovery walk held daily at the center. A tour guide leads the way and explains about Tybee's marine life. Don't forget to check out the stuff inside the center too — you'll find a touch tank, aquariums and shark displays. There's no admission charge, but donations are requested. (See our chapter on Tybee Island for more information.)

Oatland Island Education Center
711 Sandtown Rd. • 897-3773

See alligators, buffalo and other animals while walking along Oatland Island's nature trail. This self-guided outdoor hike takes you through marshes and around to the different animal and plant exhibits. Admission is any cash donation. The center, which hosts many popular annual events and festivals (see our Annual Events and Festivals chapter), is open from 8:30 AM to 5 PM Monday through Friday and 10 AM to 5 PM on Saturdays. (For more on the center, see our Attractions chapter.)

INSIDERS' TIP

Going to be in town July 4th weekend in 1998? Check out America's Sail 98. Tall ships from around the world are expected to call on the port of Savannah and will be open free of charge on July 4 and 5.

Tybee Island Lighthouse
30 Meddin Dr. • 786-5801

Hike 154 feet to the top of Tybee Lighthouse for a great view of Tybee and Savannah. You'll also be learning a few things about one of America's historic light stations. From April 1 to Labor Day, the lighthouse is open daily except Tuesdays from 10 AM to 6 PM. After Labor Day it is open from noon to 4 PM on weekdays and is closed on Tuesdays. On winter weekends it is open from 10 AM to 4 PM. Cost, which includes admission to the Tybee Museum, is $3 for adults, $2 for seniors and $1 children.

Savannah College *of* Art *and* Design

Premier Galleries

Pinnacle
318 East Liberty Street

Exhibit A
340 Bull Street

West Bank
322 Martin Luther King Jr. Blvd.

Recent exhibitions have included works by Jasper Johns, Robert Rauschenberg, Jacob Lawrence, Adrian Piper, Laurie Simmons, Romare Bearden, Dale Chihuly, and Bill Viola.

*For more information, please call 912-239-1486
or visit our website at www.scad.edu.*

Arts and Culture

Savannah prides itself on its arts and culture scene, and justifiably so. The city is not only a consumer of the arts, but with the advent of Savannah-based art colleges of growing repute, it is also a producer of art. Music, drama and the visual arts are all well represented here, both in the form of outlets for local talent and in venues for touring artists of greater renown.

You can take your arts and culture on various levels in Savannah. You can don your designer duds and shop in ultra-chic art galleries, picking up pieces by artists who never set foot on these shores; you can dress in jeans and pick up a sketch from a sidewalk artist on River Street; or you can rent a garret, buy a backpack and enroll in art classes yourself. You can also work through the same type of strata musically as a symphony concertgoer, a jazz follower in smoky nightclubs, or as a community band or civic orchestra performer bent on honing your talents. As for theater, you'll find two active local theater groups, thriving secular performance venues in some local churches and, for those who prefer the role of spectator, the occasional national touring troupe.

With this chapter, we outline the major cultural organizations and venues of Savannah for you. We provide plenty of telephone numbers and instructions on how to tap into specific schedules. You might also want to check out our Annual Events and Festivals chapter for further suggestions for an artsy afternoon or evening. Keeping abreast of the local cultural scene is fairly easy. The *Savannah Morning News* (see our Media chapter) offers its most comprehensive arts coverage in a Sunday Arts and Travel section. The *Morning News'* Friday Diversions section also contains event listings, but the coverage there tends to be more club- and concert-oriented. Diversions can be picked up free at various downtown and Southside shopping centers and restaurants after it appears as part of Friday's edition, but if you want to get your hands on a Sunday section during the week, you either have to pay full face value at the newspaper's offices (111 W. Bay Street in the heart of the Historic Downtown) or swing by a library.

Among the weekly papers, the *Georgia Guardian* (which has an affiliation with the Savannah College of Art and Design and, hence, a vested interest in the subject) and *Creative Loafing* are good sources. Again, check our Media chapter for suggestions on where to find these publications.

Venues

Savannah Civic Center
Montgomery and Liberty Sts. • 651-6556

This is a place, not an entity like a symphony or a drama group, but we list it here because it is the major performance venue in the city. The city of Savannah owns and operates this major facility, but groups, including private ventures and touring companies, stage the shows here.

The Civic Center has two main components, not including various meeting rooms and a ballroom. The arena, named for the late Dr. Martin Luther King Jr., can seat up to 9,000, depending on the event configuration. The theater, which seats about 2,500, is named in honor of Johnny Mercer, the famed Savannah-born lyricist. By and large, the more formal events such as dramatic presentations or one-person shows play in the theater, with the arena going for large-scale, pack-'em-in audiences for such events as Ringling Bros. and Barnum & Bailey Circus, rock or country music concerts, wrestling matches and monster truck shows. But that isn't a hard and fast rule: When Mikhail Baryshnikov danced in Savannah with the touring experimental group White Oak Dance Troupe, they filled the arena.

The offerings at the Civic Center vary, depending on the tastes and daring of various promoters. A full Broadway touring production of *Les Miserables* was one recent feature, and you can expect a handful of the better-known touring shows to pass this way. The concert scene has become more lively with the continued growth of the Savannah College of Art and Design, with its built-in audience potential. To keep up with what might be available during your visit, check the media sources mentioned at the opening of this chapter, or simply check the large billboard on the Liberty Street side of the building. The number listed here is for the box office, and tickets generally are on sale well in advance of performances.

The Civic Center consumes an entire block between Oglethorpe and Liberty streets, with entrances on Montgomery Street and facing the parking lot. A word of warning about parking is in order. Popular events at the Civic Center put parking at a premium. The closest lots associated with the center fill quickly. Because it is easier to get out of a street-side parking space, many patrons prefer to park along the surrounding streets. While you don't have to feed the meters at night, be sure not to block the crosswalks leading to the squares or make up any imaginative parking spaces — lots of parking tickets get handed out on the evenings of big performances. Also, avoid the temptation to whip into the vacant parking lots of obviously closed businesses: Many businesses choose to defend that space at night and will have after-hours parkers towed. There is ample parking in the city's parking tower a few blocks away at 132 Montgomery Street, and it is usually scheduled to be open the nights when the Civic Center is in action.

FYI

Unless otherwise noted, the area code for all phone numbers listed in this guide is 912.

The Roundhouse Complex
601 W. Harris St.

Adjacent to the old Central of Georgia Railroad Station that now serves as the Savannah Visitors Center, this old railroad yard where trains used to turn around is becoming one of the most popular concert venues in the city. While you most likely won't find the hottest new acts here, you can see old rock-and-roll favorites like Hall and Oates and Joan Jett playing in this unique outdoor arena. It isn't unusual to find a few thousand people coming out to watch one of their favorite acts perform. Again, check the local papers when you're in town (see our Media chapter) to see if there is anything going on at the Roundhouse that sounds worth checking out.

Music

Savannah Symphony Orchestra
225 Abercorn St. • 236-9536, (800) 537-7894

The Savannah Symphony Orchestra is the crown jewel of Savannah's cultural collection. Before turning up your nose at smaller city orchestras, consider this — the Savannah Symphony was rated the best in the state in 1995 by the Georgia Council for the Arts. That field included Augusta, Columbus . . . and Atlanta.

The orchestra has a core of 37 permanent performers, supplemented by additional musicians who come in from around the Southeast when their services are needed for the Masterworks Series, Pops and other large-scale programs. The symphony gives more than 300 performances in a season that begins in September and runs through May.

INSIDERS' TIP

If you are looking for arty souvenirs at low prices, the Telfair Museum of Art has a limited selection of posters, postcards and the like for sale at token prices. For something even cheaper (i.e., free), look for the postcard reproductions that SCAD uses to announce gallery openings. We've found them stacked for giveaway in the college galleries and downtown coffeeshops and eateries.

Many feature smaller subdivisions of the group — say, a string quartet or a brass ensemble. Others are in-school performances as part of an exceptionally active outreach program to young people.

The real mainstays of the schedule, however, are the Masterworks and Pops series, regularly scheduled performances held in the Savannah Civic Center's Johnny Mercer Theatre on Saturday nights. See the previous listing for more information on the Civic Center. The Masterworks series describes itself with its title. The program runs to Beethoven, Verdi, Brahms, Mozart and their peers. Nationally and internationally known guest performers join the symphony for these performances. During the 1997-98 season, guest artists were to include Itzhak Perlman, along with Marko Ylonen, Eugene Fodor, Martin Hebert, Alberto Reyes and others of similar caliber. The Pops series is also pretty self-descriptive — lighter fare and a slate of guest artists who will be recognized outside the circle of classical music aficionados. For 1997-98, these included Crystal Gayle, Skitch Henderson, bluegrass fiddler Mark O'Connor, the Preservation Hall Jazz Band and the Empire Brass Quintet.

The symphony derives about 60 percent of its $2.5 million operating budget from ticket sales, so it's hardly surprising that guests will find an efficient and professional ticketing operation. The symphony handles its own ticket sales at its offices up to the day of performance, only then shifting it to the box office at the Civic Center. The easiest way to get tickets is to order by phone, pay by credit card and pick them up at the "will call" window at the Civic Center (just give yourself a few extra minutes before curtain to do so).

The best ticket deals come in series and packages, but visitors will hardly need those. Single tickets run $10 to $40 for Masterworks performances and $15 to $35 for the Pops. What to wear? Business attire is sufficient.

People tend to dress more formally for the Masterworks than the Pops, but you really don't have to. As long as guys wear a jacket and tie, they're dressy enough. (In other words, shelve the tux unless you are just dying to wear it). Women can stop at the semiformal level, and they certainly don't have to go that far unless after-concert plans dictate it.

The symphony also stages a number of free-admission concerts in other settings, predominantly outdoors. Foremost among these are the Picnic in the Park in Forsyth Park, held on a Sunday evening each October, and the Arts on the River weekend, which culminates in an outdoor concert on River Street in May. Definitely build your weekend around these events if you are lucky enough to be in town when they are staged: They show Savannah at its best, with large crowds turning out for good-natured enjoyment of a light classical program in two of the city's most attractive settings. (For more on both of these happenings, refer to our Annual Events and Festivals chapter.) The symphony maintains the listed toll-free line for information and ticket orders.

Theater

Savannah has two full-time drama groups, but the theater scene is larger than that infers. Several churches have recently launched highly successful productions of secular works such as Gilbert and Sullivan offerings, and there are also collegiate theatrical groups. Check the event pages of the newspapers cited above for schedules and further information.

Savannah Theatre
222 Bull St. • 233-7764
The home base for this group is billed as the oldest continuously active theater in the

country. Of course, the building burned down a few times over the years, but the location and foundation are the same. Before its conversion to serve the local theater group, this was the last of the once-plentiful downtown movie theaters.

Look here for a varied schedule of community theater productions — light musicals, mysteries, dramas and what have you. You want examples? How about *The Almost Ed Sullivan Show*, *Nunsense* and its sequels, *Arsenic and Old Lace* and others. The quality of the productions will vary from show to show, but these are generally fun evenings that tap into local talent. The *Savannah Morning News* usually reviews the opening night performance if you are looking for guidance. Ticket prices are $15 for musicals and $12 for dramas, with reduced rates for students and seniors.

City Lights Theater
125 E. Broughton St. • 234-9860

Offerings here tend to be a little heavier, though City Lights will do the occasional musical or comedy as well. In the 1997-98 season, the schedule included *One Flew Over the Cuckoo's Nest*. The theater setting is more intimate, and the approach is a little more risk-taking. City Lights, for example, hosts a local playwrights' festival. Again, performances are generally reviewed by the daily paper after opening night performances, and ticket prices vary.

Visual Arts

Telfair Museum of Art
121 Barnard St. • 232-1177

Savannah boasts many museums, but most are either themed museums (like the Ralph Mark Gilbert Civil Rights Museum) or house museums — interesting homes whose main attraction is the historical significance of

---

www.insiders.com
See this and many other **Insiders' Guide®** destinations online — in their entirety.
Visit us today!

---

the building itself, backed up by the re-creation of a bygone lifestyle through period furnishing. You can find out more details about these places in our Attractions chapter.

The Telfair, however, is a true art museum, although the house museum description certainly applies to a portion of the Telfair mansion. Housed in the Neoclassical Regency mansion designed by English architect William Jay for the prominent Telfair family (a Georgia governor was among the family members), this is the oldest art museum in the South. Think of it as having three elements: It's part house museum, part permanent collection, part gallery for visiting exhibitions and programs.

The permanent collection includes paintings, sculpture, prints and decorative arts. The collection includes examples of American impressionism, Ash Can Realists and classical sculpture casts. Included are works by Childe Hassam, Frederick Frieseke, Gari Melchers, Robert Henri, George Bellows and George Luks. The museum also holds the largest existing collection of the works of Lebanese mystical poet and artist Kahlil Gibran, best known for *The Prophet*. His patroness, Mary Haskell, made her home in her later years on Gaston Street in Savannah. Because of the fragile nature of the artwork (it was done predominantly in pencil), it is only on display occasionally. On a more contemporary note, the Telfair is the new home for the Bird Girl sculpture featured on the cover of John Berendt's *Midnight in the Garden of Good and Evil*. Fans of the book hounded it out of its original setting in a family plot at Bonaventure Cemetery (see our chapter on The Book for details).

Admission to the Telfair is $6 for adults, $5 for seniors, $2 for students ages 12 and older and a dollar for children 6 to 12. Younger children are admitted free. No admission is charged on Sunday afternoons. Hours (subject to change) are 10 AM to 5 PM Tuesday through Saturday, 2 to 5 PM Sunday and noon to 5 PM Monday.

INSIDERS' TIP

Got symphony tastes but a student pocketbook? Relax. A half-hour before the Masterworks and Pops series concerts at the Civic Center, remaining tickets (known as "rush" tickets) go on sale for $5.

Photo: Kyle Cason

Ironwork on Monterey Square homes is particularly distinctive.

Savannah College of Art and Design
345 Bull St. • 238-2480, 239-1486, (800) 869-SCAD

This growing art college's campus is scattered throughout Savannah's Historic Downtown and Victorian District. Among its holdings are multiple on-campus galleries featuring rotating displays in a variety of media. Some feature the work of students, both graduate and undergraduate, or the college's faculty. Frequently,

Savannah: Style Central for Architecture Buffs

Stroll along the streets of Savannah's Historic Downtown, and you'll be looking at a blend of buildings reflecting architectural styles prevalent in America during the 19th and late-18th centuries. Among these types  were Federal, which was in vogue from 1790 to 1838; English Regency, 1811 to 1830; Greek Revival, 1820 to 1875; Gothic Revival, 1830 to 1885; Italianate, 1830 to 1900; Romanesque Revival, 1850 to 1890; and Victorian, 1860 to 1915.

Probably the city's most outstanding example of the Federal style is the Isaiah Davenport House, with its central hallway and arched fanlight doorway. This brick and brownstone house at 324 E. State Street "reflects the balance and symmetry" of the Federal style, says Roulhac Toledano in *The National Trust Guide To Savannah*, and its double-entry stairway "must have set the standard for future graceful curving entry staircases leading to high stoops that dot the city in houses of all styles." The Davenport House, one of Savannah's many museum houses, was built in 1820; a successful effort to save it from demolition in the mid-1950s brought about the creation of the Historic Savannah Foundation preservation group. (Read more about the house in the walking tour section of our Attractions chapter.)

The Regency style is best typified by the work of English architect William Jay and two of his designs, the Owens-Thomas House at 124 Abercorn Street and the Scarbrough House at 41 Martin Luther King Jr. Boulevard, both of which are open to the public. The porches and columns of these buildings are prime examples of the Regency style. A commission to build the former house for cotton merchant Richard Richardson is what brought Jay to Georgia and he "went on to create a series of buildings that qualify as the state's first architectural masterpieces," says Tom Spector

— continued on next page

Photo: Savannah Area Convention and Visitors Bureau

The Isaiah Davenport House, built on E. State Street in
1820, is a fine example of the Federal style.

in his book, *The Guide to the Architecture of Georgia*. These two houses "rank among the best works produced in America" during the early 1800s. The Owens-Thomas House, which Toledano deems "probably the finest example of English Regency architecture in America," was constructed in 1819 and the Scarbrough House was completed in the same year.

Greek Revival-style buildings are reminiscent of the temples of Greece with their long front porches supported by towering columns. To see two fine models of this style, take a look at the Aaron Champion House at 230 Barnard Street and the Sorrel-Weed House at 6 W. Harris Street. Both houses were designed by Charles Cluskey; the Champion House was built in 1844 and the Sorrel-Weed House in 1841. Cluskey was Georgia's premier architect during the 1830s and '40s.

Walk over to Madison Square for a look at what Toledano calls Savannah's "foremost Gothic-style house." The Green-Meldrim House at 1 W. Macon Street, which can be toured by visitors, was designed by John S. Norris and built in 1853. Exterior features are the crenelated parapet, oriel windows and heavily detailed iron porch. (See our Attractions chapter for more on the Green-Meldrim House.)

The Mercer House at 429 Bull Street is another Norris design, but it is an example of the Italianate style, which has the look of Italian villas — low-pitched roofs, wide eaves, long porches and cast-iron balconies. The house was designed before the outbreak of the Civil War but was completed in 1871 by two former assistants of Norris. (For more on the Mercer House, see our chapters on Attractions and The Book.) Another Italianate-style residence (and another of the city's house museums) is the Andrew Low House at 329 Abercorn Street (see our Attractions chapter).

The Romanesque Revival style is embodied by two Savannah landmarks, the Cotton Exchange at 100 E. Bay Street and the Chatham County Courthouse at 124 Bull Street. Both were designed by William G. Preston. The Cotton Exchange, with its brick and terra cotta facade and turned wooden posts, was constructed in 1886. Preston came to Savannah to build the courthouse three years later.

An interesting example of the gingerbread style of the Victorian period is the King-Tisdell Cottage at 514 E. Huntingdon Street, which now serves as a black cultural museum. It dates to 1896.

however, these galleries host works of internationally known artists such as Jasper Johns, Robert Rauschenberg and Dale Chihuly. The flagship galleries, most likely to feature professional work, are Exhibit A and West Bank. These exhibits are free and open to the public. Times vary, particularly in keeping with the academic year, so call one of the numbers above for hours and information on what is currently on exhibit. Also, check out the media outlets discussed earlier in this chapter for exhibit details. Following is a rundown of SCAD's galleries.

Exhibit A Gallery

This gallery, housed in an old armory building in the center of the Historic Downtown at 340 Bull Street, was among the first of the college's now-significant real estate holdings. This gallery concentrates on visiting national and international exhibits and is among the easiest of the SCAD galleries for a visitor to find. If you are only doing one SCAD gallery, and the details on current exhibits don't give you a reason to pick one over another, do this one. A look at the Rococo building is worth the trip by itself.

Bergen Hall Galleries

This gallery, located at 101 Martin Luther King Jr. Boulevard, concentrates primarily on exhibiting photographic work.

Eichberg Hall Gallery

This is another general gallery that will fea-

Savannah on the Silver Screen

Jodie Foster, Robert Mitchum, Tom Hanks, Demi Moore, Julia Roberts, Kenneth Branagh, Clint Eastwood — they've all been Savannahians, at least temporarily, thanks to the appeal our city holds for filmmakers.

Savannah has hosted at least 38 film or television projects since 1975, and it formalized the whole process by establishing a film liaison office at City Hall in 1995. Some of those productions have been among the most critically acclaimed movies of our day. Some have starred the biggest names on the silver screen. Some have launched catch-phrases into the lexicon of popular culture ("Life is like a box of chocolates . . ."). Some of them . . . well, some of them were *Return of Swamp Thing* and the like.

Examples of the outstanding include *Glory*, a saga involving African-American soldiers in the Civil War that won three Oscars; *Forrest Gump*, which claimed six Oscars and solidified Tom Hanks' superstar status; and *Roots*, filmed here in part, which became the standard against which all miniseries are still measured. Going back even further, to 1962, when location shoots were rarer, the original *Cape Fear* was filmed here in part; City Hall and the downtown business district were on display. This original movie, since remade, featured Robert Mitchum at his creepiest.

Life as a location can be, well, interesting. The idea of having famous people spending money in your town sounds great, but production demands and daily life can occasionally conflict. We still remember a forgettable TV movie whose producers wanted to remove all the Spanish moss from one of the squares so it would look more like New England. Tree-lovers and purists wondered why New England didn't look enough like New England — it's just up the road a piece on I-95 — but the city fathers

— continued on next page

Photo: Kyle Cason

This side of the Chippewa Square is where the movie-prop bench for *Forrest Gump* sat.

sided with the production company (the square eventually recovered). A similar clash, and one that became more famous, resulted during the filming of *The Ordeal of Dr. Mudd*, a Civil War drama about the physician who treated Lincoln's assassin. Jim Williams (of *Midnight* fame) hung a Nazi flag outside his house — and directly across from a historic synagogue — to disrupt the filming when he became upset with the production crew.

Things usually go more smoothly. When *Forrest Gump* came to town in 1993, the production crews settled into the Board of Education headquarters parking lot and arranged for a chartered bus to ferry displaced employees from more distant asphalt to work. The new microwave oven and refrigerator in the employee lounge are gifts that *Gump* gave. By the way, don't waste time looking for Gump's famous bench. While the squares are well-equipped with benches, that one was a prop, positioned to face down Bull Street on the square's northern face. You can still spot an occasional fan there, hovering with his or her backside perched on empty air, "sitting" on the nonexistent bench for a Kodak moment.

Once a movie company came and went through Savannah so quickly the local media didn't even notice. When the movie showed up in theaters many months later, it also came and went quickly, thanks to the court system. Seems the saga of a giant shark plaguing a resort community was familiar enough to inspire a copyright complaint that resulted in an injunction against further showings.

Midnight in the Garden of Good and Evil drew the biggest local response, including breathless live TV coverage of the local premiere. Critics didn't exactly embrace the movie version, but Savannahians were quick to point out the scenery was beautiful.

Savannah Filmography
1975-1997

(Note that accompanying dates are filming dates, not necessarily release dates.)

1997: *The Gingerbread Man*; *Midnight in the Garden of Good and Evil*; *Claudine's Return*

1996: *Wild America*

1995: *Something to Talk About*

1994: *Now and Then*

1993: *Forrest Gump*; *Camilla*

1990: *Goldenboy*; *Love Crimes*

1989: *The Rose and the Jackal*; *Flight of the Intruder*; *Glory*

1988: *The Return of Swamp Thing*; *The Judas Project*

1987: *My Father, My Son*; *1969*; *War Stories*

1986: *Pals*

1983: *Solomon Northup's Odyssey*

1981: *All My Children*; *Tales of Ordinary Madness*

1980: *The Slayer*; *White Death*; *Scared to Death*; *When the Circus Came to Town*; *Fear*; *East of Eden*; *Mother Seton*

1979: *Gold Bug*; *The Ordeal of Dr. Mudd*; *Orphan Train*; *Hopscotch*; *Carny*

1978: *The Double McGuffin*

1977: *The Lincoln Conspiracy*

1976: *Roots*

1975: *Gator*

Photo: Kyle Cason

Savannah College of Art and Design has adapted many historic structures, including this old armory, for its scattered urban campus.

ture the work of students and professionals on rotating schedules. It is located at 229 Martin Luther King Jr. Boulevard.

Ex Libris Third Floor Gallery

Atop the college-operated book and supply store at 228 Martin Luther King Jr. Boulevard, this gallery sells the work of SCAD faculty, students and alumni. (See more on Ex Libris in the Bookstores section of our Shopping chapter.)

Hamilton Hall Gallery

This building at 522 Indian Street houses the college's video department. The gallery hosts both student and faculty work and traveling exhibits.

Henry Hall Gallery

This gallery at 115 W. Henry Street showcases painting and fiber arts works.

Pinnacle Gallery

The college describes this gallery (located at 320 E. Liberty Street) as "dedicated to celebrating multiculturalism through the arts." Most of the featured artists are from outside the states.

Rapid Transit Gallery

This dark, basement, Bohemian-style gallery at 342 Bull Street exhibits graduate student thesis shows. It's right alongside the Exhibit A Gallery.

West Bank Gallery

SCAD devotes this gallery to contemporary cutting-edge art. When you are finished inside at 322 Martin Luther King Jr. Boulevard, check alongside the building for one of the more interesting entries in the SCAD gallery collection, the Garden for the Arts. This outdoor sculpture garden has four sections: the African-American Garden, Asian Garden, English Garden and French Garden.

Other Galleries

Savannah has a large stock of art galleries. We listed those with collegiate connections separately: These are independent. This is only a very small sample to get you started. We recommend that you check *Arts and Antiques Monthly*, a free monthly newspaper distributed at restaurants and shops in the Historic Downtown, for updated lists of which artists are showing where. The Sunday arts section of the *Savannah Morning News* also offers a current listing of shows.

All African Art Gallery
323 W. Broughton St. • 944-0955

The collection here ranges from imported collector-quality sculptures to small carved animal figures you can stock up on for the kids. There is a full line of character dolls displaying traditional African roles, along with paintings and prints. One eye-catching piece we noted was a chess set with carved wooden pieces in African images.

Checkered Moon
422 Whitaker St. • 233-5132

This gallery features regional work, much of it with a folk art flavor, but there is fine art represented as well. In addition to paintings, you'll find sculpture and wearable art, along with an attractive and unusual line of cards.

Gallery 209
209 E. River St. • 236-4583

This River Street gallery is the place to start your search for local artwork. Stuff here varies in quality, from some wannabe artists to the real thing. We especially like the enamel jewelry, such as a jewel-tone seahorse. In addition to paintings that run the gamut from very good to not very, you'll find fiber art and interesting and affordable ceramics.

Off the Wall
412 Whitaker St. • 233-8840

This colorful, cheerful gallery features a mix of work by area artists and others and includes some very reasonably priced pieces. Paintings account for most of the art, but there are a few other pieces as well, such as jewelry and, when we last went by, some whimsical sculpture.

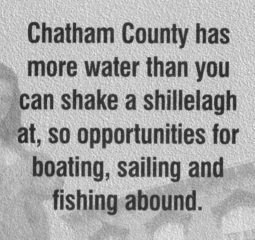

Chatham County has more water than you can shake a shillelagh at, so opportunities for boating, sailing and fishing abound.

Parks and Recreation

From time to time we hear local residents say, "There's nothing to do in Savannah." A look through this chapter will prove those folks don't know what they're talking about, at least as far as outdoor activities are concerned. Chatham County has more water than you can shake a shillelagh at, so opportunities for boating, sailing and fishing abound. We're blessed with parks and park-like areas of every description and in every jurisdiction — national, state, regional, county and city — and these provide settings for picnics and play and trails for hiking, biking and jogging. Golfers and tennis players will find numerous venues that are open to the public.

Those who like their recreation organized can participate in a variety of team sports offered for adults and youngsters by the county, city, YMCA and the recreation departments of the smaller municipalities; athletes 18 and younger can keep busy playing practically year round, and many do. Much of this organized activity takes place at facilities comprising Bacon Regional Park, a 500-acre complex in Southside/Midtown. This is the site of Memorial Stadium, where many of the area's high school football games are played; Lake Mayer Community Park; and public facilities for golf (Bacon Park Golf Course), tennis (Bacon Park Tennis Complex), youth baseball and softball (Ambuc Park and Guy Minick Youth Complex), adult softball (Allen E. Paulson Softball Complex), soccer (Chatham County Soccer Complex), swimming (Chatham County Aquatic Center) and weightlifting (Paul Anderson-Howard Cohen Weightlifting Center). All of these venues are included in individual write-ups in this chapter.

On the following pages, you'll also find information concerning the parks and activities we mentioned earlier. While you're reading, kept in mind that a big part of the beauty of the area's recreational offerings is that, because of Savannah's mild climate, they're available to you just about every day of the year.

Parks and Nature Trails

Historic Downtown

Forsyth Park
Drayton and Gaston Sts. • 351-3841
This downtown park on the southern boundary of the Historic District has sort of a split personality, but it's a delightful one. The northern portion consists of 11 acres filled with trees and shrubs and has an ornate fountain as its focal point. Splashing waters and shady sidewalks make this part of the park, which was laid out in 1851, a wonderful spot for strolling, relaxing on benches and just plain goofing off.

The southern portion has a more active persona. Here you'll find a large playground, basketball and tennis courts and wide open spaces often used by folks engaged in softball, team Frisbee and other athletic pursuits. The southern portion, a drill field for local military units before it was made part of the park in 1867, is also the site of monuments commemorating the Confederacy and honoring Georgians who served in the Spanish-American War. The city's Bureau of Leisure Services maintains the 19 acres of the southern part of the park, and the Park and Tree Commission looks after the northern portion.

Two dummy forts, structures built in 1909 and used for military exercises before World War I, straddle the line dividing the two areas. The fort on the western side of the park was renovated in 1963 as the Fragrant Garden for the Blind; the eastern fort is used as a storage shed.

FYI

Unless otherwise noted, the area code for all phone numbers listed in this guide is 912.

The park was laid out on the site of a pine forest that was at the southern reaches of the city, a wood that made "sad and sea-like music, when stirred by the breeze," according to a historian of the late 1800s. Over time, the pines were removed, died out or were uprooted by storms. Of the park's numerous existing trees, a few are pines, but you'll see many more oaks, sycamores and magnolias when you visit. Particularly impressive are the live oaks that line the central walkway stretching from the park's northern end at Gaston Street to its southern end at Park Avenue.

The monuments are on this wide promenade, as is the much-photographed fountain, which features a female figure surrounded by water-spouting swans and tritons (men with the lower bodies of fish). The fountain, said to be the largest in the United States when it was unveiled in 1858, is modeled after one in the Place de la Concorde of Paris. Forsyth is bordered by a sidewalk that's much favored by walkers and joggers who live or work downtown. According to the city, the distance around the park is 1.5 miles. The park is also the site of several major annual events, including the Sidewalk Arts Festival, the Savannah Shakespeare Festival and Picnic in the Park (see our Annual Events and Festivals chapter).

Islands

Old Savannah-Tybee Railroad Historic and Scenic Trail
U.S. Hwy. 80 E. • 652-6780

When you walk, jog or bicycle on this 6.5-mile trail, you're traversing the roadbed of a railroad that took passengers from eastern Savannah to Tybee Island for nearly 50 years starting in the late 1800s. The palm-lined, limestone-rock trail on McQueen's Island is maintained by Chatham County and was created beginning in 1991 as part of the Rails Into Trails program, an effort to transform abandoned railroad rights of way into recreational areas. Besides what it offers in the way of exercise, the trail presents visitors with picnic tables, vistas of marshland and the south channel of the Savannah River, glimpses of wildlife indigenous to the marsh and opportunities for fishing and crabbing.

The railroad was built over 17.7 miles of salt marsh, rivers and tidal creeks by a group of investors led by Savannahian D.G. Purse, who in 1885 owned a good portion of Tybee Island and was trying to find a way to transport people there that was faster than the two-hour ride by steamboat. His solution was to build a railroad, and the idea was considered a harebrained scheme by local folks; they were convinced it was an engineering feat that couldn't be accomplished. But Purse persisted, and his Savannah and Tybee Railway began making regularly scheduled runs in July 1887.

A few years later the line became part of the Central of Georgia Railway system and was operated from then on as the Savannah and Atlantic Railroad. The last passenger excursion was in July 1933; by then, the advent of the automobile and the construction of a road to Tybee (now U.S. Highway 80) had made the railway obsolete. But in its heyday, the little railroad carried thousands of Savannahians and out-of-towners to Tybee for days of sunning and swimming at the beach and nights of dancing at the Tybrisa Pavilion. The entrance to the trail places you at its midpoint and is on U.S. 80 just east of the Bull River bridge. The highway is well-traveled, and there is not much space at the trail entrance, so be careful when you pull off the road to park. The trail is off limits after darkness falls. (For much more on Tybee's interesting past and present, see our Tybee Island chapter.)

Skidaway Island State Park
52 Diamond Causeway • 598-2300

Get back to nature on the Big Ferry or

Chatham County's many parks offer treats to kids and birds alike.

Photo: Phyl M. Gatlin

Sandpiper trails at Skidaway State Park. Walking either will give you a good look at a maritime forest and the salt marsh, their plants and possibly some of their animals, including fiddler crabs, egrets, deer and alligators. The trails also take you to earthwork fortifications built as Confederate defenses during the Civil War and the remains of a moonshine still. Big Ferry can be hiked in either a 2- or 3-mile loop, with the latter taking about 90 minutes to walk; Sandpiper is a mile long, takes about 20 minutes and can be traversed by people using wheelchairs (with a little help) and parents pushing baby strollers.

The 533-acre park, created during the early 1970s and opened in 1975, is in the western portion of Skidaway Island and borders a stretch of the Intracoastal Waterway called the Skidaway Narrows. Other features of the park are a pool, picnic sites and campsites (see the Camping section of this chapter). The 75-by-40-foot pool is open from Memorial Day to Labor Day, and the entry fee is $2. In addition to the picnic sites, there are five covered shelters available on a first-come, first-served ba-

sis. If you don't want to take a chance, you can rent one at $30 a day; a group shelter accommodates 150 people and rents for $100 per day.

The park is open from 7 AM to 10 PM seven days a week. There's a $2 parking fee on all days except Wednesday, when admission is free. If you're planning to come here often or visit other state parks and historic sites in Georgia, you might consider purchasing an annual Georgia ParkPass for $25 ($12.50 for those 62 and older). That will get you unlimited admission to all state parks.

Southside/Midtown

Daffin Park
1301 E. Victory Dr. • 351-3841

When Savannah's Park and Tree Commission members conceived plans for Daffin Park in 1908, the recreational area was on the outskirts of the city. Now, Daffin is in the middle of Midtown, and it's a drawing card for residents of that area. The park covers 77 acres bounded by Victory Drive, Waters Avenue, Washington Avenue and Bee Road.

Opportunities for enjoying the outdoors in a residential setting abound at Daffin, which has a large playground; grassy fields that accommodate softball, baseball, football, soccer, rugby and, on occasion, cricket; basketball courts; nine tennis courts; a pool; a 4-acre lake where you can fish for bass, bream and catfish; and a pavilion on the lake that can be rented for a variety of gatherings (call 351-3837 for reservations).

The eastern portion of the park is the site of Grayson Stadium, home of the city's minor-league baseball team (see our Spectator Sports chapter), and a picnic area shaded by towering pine trees. The playing fields on the southern side of the park — once the site of polo matches and a landing strip for airplanes before the city built its first airport in 1929 — are also fine for flying kites, driving golf balls and exercising Rover, when the fields are not otherwise occupied. If you're into walking or jogging, you'll find room to roam on the wide sidewalk surrounding the park, which is maintained by the city of Savannah's Leisure Services Bureau.

Lake Mayer Community Park
Montgomery Crossroad • 652-6786

As the name implies, the centerpiece of this 75-acre park on the Southside is the lake, but there's more here than recreational offerings involving water. Lake Mayer is surrounded by a 1.5-mile walking and jogging track dotted with 18 fitness stations. The park grounds provide space for eight lighted tennis courts, two basketball courts, a ball diamond, a conditioning course for people using wheelchairs and a remote-control auto race track. Picnic tables are sprinkled throughout the park, and two covered areas accommodate large groups — a pavilion with space for as many as 500 people and a shelter with room for 80 to 100. These can be reserved at fees of $100 for five hours of usage and $125 for more; otherwise, they are available on a first-come, first-served basis.

Getting back to the 35-acre lake: Swimming is prohibited, but you can fish for bass, bream, catfish and crappie if you have a freshwater license. The possibilities for boating abound; the lake is the site of the Savannah Sailing Center (see this chapter's Sailing section), which offers instruction to young people and adults, and of Red Cross classes in kayaking and canoeing. Windsurfing is permitted on the lake, and paddleboats holding a maximum of four people are available for rent at a fee of $1.50 per person for 30 minutes.

And lest we forget, the park is the home of numerous ducks and geese that are more than happy to take stale bread off (and out of) your hands. The park — created in 1972 and operated by Chatham County's Department of Parks, Recreation and Cultural Affairs — is on Montgomery Crossroad at Sallie Mood Drive. It's open from 8 AM to 11 PM in the spring and summer and 8 AM to 10 PM in fall and winter.

Southside Community Park
Science Dr. • 351-3841

Developed by the city of Savannah in cooperation with Armstrong Atlantic State University (see our Education and Child Care chapter), this 28-acre wooded area on the Armstrong campus features a nature walk that's two-thirds of a mile long. A playground and picnic tables round out the facility. The park opens at dawn and closes at dusk.

West Chatham

L. Scott Stell Community Park
383 Bush Rd. • 925-8694

Helicopter pilots once prepared for war on the site of this 108-acre park southwest of Savannah. Now Chatham Countians come here to play ball on the four lighted diamonds of the Jim Golden Sports Complex, shoot hoops on the basketball courts, pedal paddleboats on the 15-acre pond, jog and walk on the 1-mile fitness trail and picnic under the pines. During the early 1970s, the park site was Cu Chi Stage Field, a training area for South Vietnamese helicopter pilots stationed at nearby Hunter Army Airfield. Later in the decade, the county planted the seeds, literally, for the park by making garden plots at the site available to local residents free of charge. You can still farm one of these 30-by-60-foot plots (there's no cost involved; participants simply sign an agreement stating they will be responsible for their plot) in addition to taking advantage of the other recreational opportunities offered here since the park's completion in 1984. The fun includes fishing for bream, catfish, bass and crappie in the pond. The park is open all year long, from 8 AM to 10 PM during fall and winter and from 8 AM to 11 PM during spring and summer.

Savannah National Wildlife Refuge
S.C. Hwy. 170 • 652-4415

By traveling the Laurel Hill Wildlife Drive, you can see some of the refuge's 26,349 acres of freshwater marshes and hardwood islands, which are known locally as "hammocks." This 4-mile gravel road is open to hikers, bicyclists and motorists, and it takes you along dikes built during the late-18th and early 19th centuries by rice planters. The U.S. Fish and Wildlife Service, which manages the refuge, maintains 3,000 acres of freshwater pools created by the dikes, areas that serve as feeding grounds for wading birds and waterfowl. All the dikes are open to foot travel, as is the Cistern Trail, a winding path that runs off the Wildlife Drive; however, if you're planning on leaving the Drive to hike or bike, call ahead to ascertain the condition of the dike system.

The Wildlife Drive is open from sunrise to sunset throughout the year, except for one weekend during the fall, usually in October, when it's closed to the general public to allow a deer hunt by people using wheelchairs; you should check to see if this event falls at a time when you intend to visit the refuge. The Drive and the dikes are great places from which to observe wildlife, in particular birds and alligators. A marvelous time for bird watching is late December and early January, when the refuge is visited by as many as 13 different types

of ducks in concentrations of as many as 1,000 birds. The best times for viewing gators are in March and April and in October, when the big reptiles crawl onto the banks of the refuge's canals to bask in the sun.

Laurel Hill Wildlife Drive and most of the refuge are in South Carolina but right across the Savannah River from Chatham County; the entrance to the Drive is only a couple of miles from the West Chatham town of Port Wentworth on S.C. Highway 170, which is Ga. Highway 25 south of the river. The Drive is not far from downtown Savannah. To get to it from downtown, about a 15-minute trip, take U.S. Highway 17 north across the river to its intersection with S.C. Highway 170, then turn south on S.C. 170.

You can fish in the refuge's freshwater pools from March 15 to October 25, but the fishing there isn't anything to write home about, and you'll need a South Carolina license. You'll get better results fishing in the Savannah River along the refuge's boundaries, and a Georgia license will suffice if you stay in the main channels. The refuge manages hunts for deer, feral hogs, squirrels and turkeys during the fall and winter. Permits to hunt there are required and can be obtained by mailing requests or applications to Savannah Coastal Refuge Hunts, 1000 Business Center Drive, Parkway Business Center, Suite 10, Savannah, GA 31405.

Savannah-Ogeechee Canal Museum and Nature Center
681 Fort Argyle Rd. • 748-8068

The 184-acre nature center and its several trails will give you a look at three environments — pine woods, hardwood river swamp and sand hills. Two of the trails start in the pines at the museum and follow the southern portion of the canal, which dates to 1830, faded from usage near the end of the 19th century and has recently been cleared of brush and other growth. These trails — the Tow Path and the Heel Path — are each four-tenths of a mile long and lead you past Locks 5 and 6 of the canal to the Ogeechee River. The only bridge across the canal is at Lock 5 near the start of the paths, so don't expect to walk down one path and back on the other.

You can also reach the river from the museum by hiking the half-mile Jenkes Road, which was once a thoroughfare for wagon traffic. The road and the paths take you through the swamp; you can see the sand hills by walking the half-mile Holly Trail. The nature center is open from 9 AM to 5 PM daily. There's no admission fee, but donations are accepted. (For more on this site and the history of the canal, see our Attractions chapter.)

Recreation

Recreation Programs

What follows are listings for three Savannah groups that help organize a wide variety of sports activities for youth and adults. Note that most of the smaller municipalities in Chatham County have recreation departments as well, some of which are extremely active. To register to play on teams sponsored by these agencies or to find out about their programs, call their representatives in Bloomingdale at 748-0970, in Garden City at 966-7788, in Pooler at 748-5776, in Port Wentworth at 966-7428, in Thunderbolt at 354-5537 and on Tybee Island at 786-4573.

Chatham County Department of Parks, Recreation and Cultural Affairs
Montgomery Crossroad • 652-6780

Operating out of offices at Lake Mayer Community Park on Montgomery Crossroad at Sallie Mood Drive, the department's Sports Division provides league play for youngsters in a variety of sports. These include basketball (January through March for boys ages 8 through 12 and girls 9 through 14); soccer (March through May for boys and girls 6 through 19); baseball (April through July for boys 6 through 14); softball (April through July for girls 6 through 18); and football (October

FYI

Unless otherwise noted, the area code for all phone numbers listed in this guide is 912.

through December for boys 6 through 10). The division also sponsors swimming and weightlifting complexes near Lake Mayer. Entry fees are $50 a team for participation in basketball and $100 per team for participation in soccer, baseball, softball and football.

City of Savannah Department of Recreation Services
7171 Skidaway Rd. • 351-3852

The city provides team athletic competition for youngsters and adults throughout the year. Youth sports include basketball (January through March for kids ages 8 to 18); baseball (April through July for boys 6 to 18); football and cheerleading (September through November for kids 6 to 12); and soccer (September through November for girls and boys 6 to 19). For adults, there are leagues in softball in the fall and in spring/summer, basketball from January through March and flag football from September through November. Entry fees for youth sports are $100 per team. Fees for adult teams can run anywhere from $250 to $450, depending on how many games are played in the sport involved and the expenses incurred by the city in providing the program.

YMCA of Coastal Georgia
6400 Habersham St. • 354-5480

Besides the programs you'd expect to find at the Y such as those involving swimming and other types of physical fitness for individuals, the YMCA of Coastal Georgia, through its three branches in Chatham County, offers youngsters opportunities to participate in youth basketball, baseball, softball, soccer and in-line hockey. Participants are registered and teams are formed at the branches, and leagues are set up and scheduled by the Y's central office. For the most part, games are played at facilities owned or leased by the Y.

Programs are open to non-members at fees slightly higher than those charged to members, and scholarships are available. Basic fees for individuals participating in under-6-year-old divisions in all sports are $30 for members of the Y and $40 for non-members. For all other age divisions, fees are $45 for members and $68 for non-members. To enroll your child in a program, contact the Y branch nearest you. The facilities are the Islands Branch on Wilmington Island at 250 Penn Waller Road, 897-1192; the Habersham Branch in Southside/Midtown at 6400 Habersham Street, 354-6223; and the West Chatham Branch in Pooler at 605 U.S. Highway 80 W., 748-9622.

Basketball

The county offers basketball for boys ages 9 through 12 and girls ages 9 to 14 at a variety of sites between January and March. The city runs basketball programs for adults 18 and older and for youngsters 8 to 18 during January, February and March. Teams play at gyms in community centers and public schools, and the youth program puts 80 to 90 squads on the floor.

The YMCA hoops program attracts about 1,200 youngsters, making it bigger than either the county's or city's. Teams of boys and girls play in leagues starting at under-6 and progressing to under-18, and they do their dribbling and shooting at gyms at the Y's three branches, previously listed.

Baseball/Girls' Softball

In April, the fancy of many a youngster in the Savannah area apparently turns to . . . baseball and softball. The city's baseball program involves from 150 to 160 teams in 8-and-under, 10-and-under, 12-and-under, 14-and-under, 16-and-under and 18-and-under leagues. The county fields in the neighbor-

hood of 35 teams in 8-and-under, 10-and-under, 12-and-under and 14-and-under competition, and the YMCA's program accounts for 55 teams in those age groups, plus an under-6 category. Some city and county teams play into July, while the Y program ends in May. City teams play at numerous locations including the Guy Minick Youth Complex, and on diamonds in parks and at public schools.

Diamonds are also the best friends to many local young women: The county's softball program for girls ages 6 to 18 will field close to 100 teams between April and July, and the Y has leagues for under-10 and under-12 teams during April and May. The county schedules its baseball and girls' softball games at the Charles C. Brooks Sports Complex in the Islands, Ambuc Park in Southside/Midtown and the Jim Golden Sports Complex in West Chatham. Y teams play at the Y branches, at the Brooks complex and on local school fields.

Ambuc Park
Sallie Mood Dr. • 351-6754

This sports complex in Southside/Midtown has four lighted diamonds for baseball and girls' softball. Maintained by Chatham County, it's also the site of youth football games.

Charles C. Brooks Sports Complex
Johnny Mercer Blvd. • 898-7430

If you hear locals talk about this county facility on Wilmington Island, they'll probably refer to it as "the landfill" because that's what it's built on. The complex has four lighted fields for baseball and softball and a football field. The road leading to the complex is on Johnny

INSIDERS' TIP

While you're at Skidaway Island State Park, consider visiting the University of Georgia Marine Extension Service aquarium on the north end of Skidaway. The aquarium has 14 tanks ranging in size from 30 to 1,600 gallons and containing fish indigenous to Georgia's coastal and offshore waters. Admission is $1, with children younger than 6 admitted free, and the aquarium is open from 9 AM to 4 PM Monday through Friday and from noon to 5 PM on Saturday. To get there after leaving the park, take Diamond Causeway east to McWhorter Drive, turn left on McWhorter and stay on it until you reach the Skidaway Marine Science complex, the site of the aquarium.

Mercer near that street's intersection with Quarterman Drive.

Guy Minick Youth Complex
Eisenhower Dr. and Sallie Mood Dr.
• 351-3858

This city facility is the site of many of the baseball games played by teams in city leagues. Four lighted fields are also used for soccer games played by teams in the younger age groups in the city's fall program.

Jim Golden Sports Complex
383 Bush Rd. • 925-8706

The Golden complex has four lighted fields for baseball and girls' softball and an unlighted T-ball field. It's part of L. Scott Stell Community Park in West Chatham.

Boating

Chatham County has about 86,700 acres of tidal marshlands laced by approximately 420 miles of navigable tidal waters. In other words, the area is a paradise for boaters.

Three of the most accessible, scenic waterways are the Wilmington, Bull and Skidaway rivers, and they'll lead you to Wassaw Sound and the protected beaches of Wassaw and Beach Hammock islands, where you can picnic, swim, sunbathe and look for shells. The 7 miles of beach at Wassaw, a barrier island that's part of a national wildlife refuge and accessible only by water, are most inviting, particularly the "boneyard" on the northeast end where the bleached remains of toppled trees present opportunities for taking intriguing photographs. These basically pristine beaches are about a 25-minute trip from the marinas in Thunderbolt.

When you make a landing you shouldn't have to worry about rocks, but be aware of what the tide is doing — if it's running out, you could get stranded for several hours if you're not careful. Also, be sure you're wearing shoes when you jump out of your boat into the water so you won't be injured by oyster shells, broken glass or the occasional stingray.

The county maintains boat ramps at several locations that will provide you with access to local waterways. In the Islands area, there are two double ramps at Skidaway Narrows

on the Diamond Causeway, and double ramps at Lazaretto Creek on U.S. 80 E. at Tybee Island and on the Islands Expressway just east of the bridge over the Wilmington River. In West Chatham, there are two double ramps at the Houlihan Bridge on Ga. Highway 25 and the Savannah River and at Kings Ferry on U.S. 17 S. and the Ogeechee River; and there is a single ramp at Salt Creek on U.S. 17 S. All of the ramp facilities have restrooms, and all but Skidaway Narrows have wooden docks. You'll find picnic areas at all the ramps (with the exception of Lazaretto Creek), and Kings Ferry has a swimming area and a playground.

Downtown Via Boat

You can reach River Street and its shops, restaurants and other attractions by boat via the Savannah River, but make sure to stay well clear of the commercial vessels using the shipping channel. These are huge ships, and they throw huge wakes. The city has a 60-foot-long floating dock at the foot of the Abercorn Street ramp to River Street and a pier of vertical pilings at the western end of Rousakis Riverfront Plaza. The dock is intended for short-term use by craft up to 35 feet long, and the pier accommodates vessels from 35 to 250 feet long.

Rates at these public facilities are 50¢ per foot. There are no services at the dock and limited services at the pier (water, refuse and electrical), available on request. If you plan to stay more than two hours, you must register with the city's Revenue Department, which can be contacted by calling 651-6451. There's also a dock at the Hyatt Regency hotel that's 366 feet long and available for boats 25 feet or longer. The fee for using the hotel dock overnight is $2 per foot, and electricity and water is provided.

Marinas

If you're traveling to Savannah by boat and are looking for a place to dock during your visit, or if you need somewhere to store your boat, you can choose from several marinas.

Fountain Marina
2812 River Dr., Thunderbolt • 354-2283

Tie up at Fountain Marina and you're within walking distance of the restaurants on the bluff at Thunderbolt. This facility, on the Wilmington River near Intracoastal Waterway mile marker 583, offers 30 wet slips and 148 dry racks, plus a bait house, store, bathrooms and showers. The marina has served local boaters since 1980.

Hogan's Marina
36 Wilmington Island Rd. • 897-FISH

Situated on Turner Creek about three-fourths of a mile from the Wilmington River — the Intracoastal Waterway, Hogan's has more than 1,100 linear feet of dock space and 272 dry-rack spaces. Name it and they've got it at this marina on Wilmington Island, which opened in the spring of 1991. You'll find a store with nautical gear and fishing tackle, gasoline, restrooms and showers, live and frozen bait, a fish-cleaning facility and ice and beverages. Hogan's also repairs engines.

Isle of Hope Marina
50 Bluff Dr. • 354-8187

On a picturesque bend of the Skidaway River sits the Isle of Hope Marina, which was established here in 1926. The marina was the first dealer of Cris Craft boats in the nation and was the site of the dock scenes in the original production of the movie *Cape Fear*, the first in a long line of films made in the Savannah area. There are 85 wet slips and a lot in which boats on trailers can be parked. Gas and diesel fuel are available, as are showers, and you can rent kayaks and power boats. It's at Intracoastal Waterway mile marker 590.

Palmer Johnson Marina
3124 River Dr., Thunderbolt • 356-3875

Yacht owners docked at this marina, next to the Palmer Johnson boat works in Thunderbolt, get complimentary newspapers and donuts delivered to them in the morning. If you're staying here, you can arrange to take a tour of the boat yard, where world-class yachts are refitted and serviced. Palmer Johnson has

60 wet slips, with about half of them available for transient boaters. The marina offers a convenience store and gift shop, has gas and diesel fuel and provides a laundry and showers. Rivers End Restaurant is on the premises. Palmer Johnson is on the Wilmington River at Intracoastal Waterway mile marker 583.

Savannah Bend Marina
Old Tybee Rd., Thunderbolt • 897-DOCK

Call ahead to the boat valet at Savannah Bend and order fuel and provisions to have them awaiting your arrival at this marina on the Wilmington River at Intracoastal Waterway mile marker 582. Savannah Bend has 45 wet slips and a dry storage building containing 262 racks for boats up to 32 feet long. The ship's store carries nautical gifts and apparel, and the Wheelhouse Cafe serves deli-style sandwiches and beverages. After you've eaten, you can relax and get a fine view of the river from one of the rocking chairs lining the porch of the restaurant/store. Savannah Bend offers fuel service 24 hours a day and has showers and restrooms. The marina is in Thunderbolt near the eastern end of the bridge over the Wilmington River.

Sail Harbor Marina
618 Wilmington Island Rd. • 897-2896

As the name implies, Sail Harbor caters mainly to owners of sailboats, but this marina on Turner Creek near the Wilmington River will also accommodate power boats. For more on this facility, see this chapter's Sailing section.

Camping

Skidaway Island State Park
52 Diamond Causeway • 598-2300

The park has 88 pull-through campsites set amid the serenity of a maritime forest on

Skidaway Island. Each has water and electrical hookups, and elevated tent pads, grills and tables are provided. You can build campfires but not on the pads. The park is a popular spot because of its natural beauty and also because it's only about 35 minutes from the Historic Downtown (see the state park's listing in the Parks and Nature Trails section of this chapter). Many campers use the park as a "bedroom" while they visit the city, so the sites tend to fill up on major holidays and the weekend closest to St. Patrick's Day. If you're planning to stay at the park during those times, make a reservation by calling (800) 864-7275. Fees for campsites between March 1 and November 1 are $17 for motor homes and most pull trailers and $15 for tent campers. They're $2 less the rest of the year.

FYI

Unless otherwise noted, the area code for all phone numbers listed in this guide is 912.

Fishing

If you like to fish, you've come to the right place. Year round, there's somewhere in Chatham County or offshore in the Atlantic Ocean where you can wet a line and catch something. Basically, we're talking about three types of fishing — inshore and offshore, which involve fish that live in salt water and doesn't require a license in Georgia, and freshwater, for which you will need a license.

The inshore area stretches from the beachfronts into the tidal rivers and creeks and includes Wassaw Sound. This is where you'll find spotted sea trout, red drum (also known as spot-tail bass), flounder, sheepshead, tarpon in the summer and whiting in the spring and summer. If you're visiting or new to the area and want to do some inshore fishing, hire a guide to show you some good fishing holes, which local folks call "drops." There are countless drops in Chatham's inshore waters, and it pays to know where they are; if you don't, you might find yourself sitting in a boat doing nothing while anglers in a vessel less than 50 feet away are hauling them in.

It's also a good idea to consult the local tide charts before you go fishing inshore; Chatham County has a high tidal range and when the tides are "springing" — rising to 8 to

10 feet — the fishing isn't good because the bottom is churned up and the water is muddy. Go fishing when the tides are in the 6- to 7-foot range and the water is clear. You can find tide charts on the weather pages of the *Savannah Morning News*.

When you fish offshore, you'll either be bottom fishing or trolling for sport fish. Bottom fishing will net you black sea bass, red snapper and grouper. The sport fishing is seasonal, starting in spring with bluefish, followed by cobia, king mackerel, bonito, wahoo, marlin, sailfish, amberjack, tuna and Spanish mackerel. The sport fishing is good into November, and some veteran anglers say the optimum time to venture out is after Labor Day. Offshore angling is best in the Gulf Stream and at a particularly fishy live bottom called the Snapper Banks. The Snapper Banks are about 40 miles out, and a trip there from Wilmington Island will take about two hours; the Gulf Stream, the warm ocean current that flows from the Gulf of Mexico along the U.S. coast to New England, is about an hour farther.

If you're after freshwater fish in Chatham County, head for the Ogeechee River above Kings Ferry and the Savannah River above Port Wentworth. That's where you'll encounter largemouth bass, shad, bluegill bream, redbreast bream, shellcracker bream and crappie. Make sure you have a Georgia fishing license; you'll be fined if you get caught without one. Licenses can be purchased just about anywhere you can buy fishing tackle, including discount department stores. One-day licenses cost $3.50, licenses good throughout the year are $9 for residents and $24 for non-residents, and seven-day licenses for non-residents run $7.

OK, now gather up your gear and bait and go fishing. To help you get started, we've listed a few charter services and marinas that cater to anglers. Also, the marinas included in our section on Boating can hook you up with charter captains and fishing guides.

Amick's Deep Sea Fishing
8005 Old Tybee Rd. • 897-6759

Amick's offers mostly offshore fishing trips

and can accommodate from six to 20 people on its 41-foot, custom-built Morgan, the *Scat II*. Full- and half-day trips are available for private parties or individuals, and the company also has a 31-foot Morgan, the *Scamp*, for offshore fishing. A third boat, a 17-footer, can be chartered on weekends for inshore fishing. Amick's is based at Bull River Marina, which is just off U.S. 80 E. at the western end of the Bull River bridge. Open-boat trips to the Snapper Banks aboard the *Scat II* are $75 per person. Private charters on the *Scat II* are $695 for six passengers and $985 for 10 passengers.

Bona Bella Marina
2740 Livingston Ave. • 355-9601

Bona Bella Marina rents out 14- and 16-foot johnboats to anglers and offers guide service for inshore fishing. Boat storage and 400 feet of dockage are available at this facility, which is on Country Club Creek about 100 yards from the Herb River. Anglers can buy live and dead bait here, purchase snacks from the store and gas up their boats. Owner Matt Starling conducts fishing tournaments each month and holds a crabbing tournament for kids 12 and younger during the summer; it's scheduled for June in 1998. Boats rent for $70 a day, which includes gas and oil, and you can hire a guide for $275.

Chimney Creek Fish Camp
40 Estill Hammock Rd., Tybee Island • 786-9857

Located adjacent to the Crab Shack restaurant and operated by the restaurant's owners, this fish camp sells live and dead bait and launches boats up to 24 feet long. Chimney Creek leads to Tybee Creek and the Atlantic Ocean, which is only 10 minutes away. The camp also has a dock for fishing and offers boat storage in the water and yard. You can purchase fishing tackle and other gear in the camp store.

Coffee Bluff Marina
14915 White Bluff Rd. • 925-9038

Even if you didn't take advantage of the services offered by Coffee Bluff Marina, the ride out to the end of White Bluff Road would be worth making just to get the panoramic view of the Forest River and the wide expanse of adjacent marsh. Anglers who make the trip will also find the marina's large convenience store with a supply of fishing tackle and equipment, a boat hoist, gas, oil, bait and ice. The marina also offers boat storage in the water and in sheds, but there are no rentals. This facility is closed on Tuesdays.

Miss Judy Charters
124 Palmetto Dr. • 897-4921

Go fishing and have fun doing it with Miss Judy Charters. Why is it fun? Owner Judy Helmey, who started skippering boats in the mid-1960s at the age of 14, says it's because her company caters to customers by making them aware of their surroundings during trips, answering their questions, showing them rod and reel operations and swapping a fish story or two. "They get to do everything that's fun and we take care of the hard stuff," she says. The Wilmington Island-based company — started in 1947 by Judy's father, the late Sherman I. Helmey — provides inshore and offshore fishing via the *Miss Judy Too!*, a customized 33-foot Morgan, and the *Miss Judy Four*, a 21-foot, center-console Sportscraft. Each boat carries as many as six passengers.

INSIDERS' TIP

Crabbing is a favorite pastime of many Savannahians. It's a recreational pursuit that's relatively inexpensive, and you don't need a boat to do it. All you do need is a basket net, some bait (chicken parts, such as the necks, will do fine) and a tidal creek in which to crab. If you don't want to buy the basket net, you can affix your bait to a line with a lead weight attached, but you'll probably need a dip net for getting the crabs you catch out of the water. You can buy the items you'll need at bait shops or most hardware stores.

Trips leave from the company's dock on Turner Creek; the entrance to the road leading to the dock is on Wilmington Island Road about a mile south of Johnny Mercer Boulevard. Rates for fishing parties of up to six people are $299 for a four-hour trip, $389 for a six-hour trip and $499 for an eight-hour trip.

Neva-Miss Charters
Old Tybee Rd., Thunderbolt • 897-2706
One local expert on fishing says the Neva Miss outfit is appropriately named because owner Billy Shearin and his skippers will always find you some fish. Based at Savannah Bend Marina in Thunderbolt (see previous listing in our Boating section under Marinas), the company takes anglers on offshore fishing trips to the Snapper Banks aboard a 43-foot Morgan that can accommodate 17 people, a 34-foot Luhrs and a 33-foot Morgan, the latter two carrying six passengers each. The big boat is for private parties, and all three vessels are powered by twin-diesel engines. Rates for parties of up to 10 people are $898 Monday through Thursday and $998 Friday, Saturday and Sunday.

Flag Football

City of Savannah Department of Recreation Services
Daffin Park • 351-3852
Via its flag football program, the city gives adults a chance to relive their glory days on the high school gridiron, sans pads, helmets and tackling. The season starts in September and runs through Thanksgiving, and about 10 teams take part. Entry fees in 1997 were $260 per team.

Youth Football

The county provides facilities and support for 8-and-younger and 10-and-younger football teams that play games during October, November and December at Ambuc Park, the Charles C. Brooks Sports Complex (see previous listings for these venues) and Memorial Stadium. The city's youth football program is for 8-and-younger, 10-and-younger and 12-and-younger teams. From 30 to 45 squads participate, playing games at Daffin Park (see previous listing) starting in mid-September and finishing just before Thanksgiving.

Golf

If golf is your game, you have several public and semi-private courses from which to choose — one on the islands, four in Southside/Midtown and two in West Chatham. The following listings will give you an idea of what's available; greens fees include cart rentals.

Islands

Sheraton Savannah Resort & Country Club
612 Wilmington Island Rd. • 897-1615
Set amid the oaks, pines and palms of southwestern Wilmington Island, this par 72 course rambles over 6876 yards. Raised, undulating greens are planted in Tifton and bermudagrass, and there's water on 10 holes, including No. 7 and No. 14, two of the course's four well-bunkered par 3s. The signature hole is No. 15, a 385-yard par 4 with two ponds on the left side and bunkers on the right.

Donald Ross designed the course, which opened in 1927 as part of a resort, the centerpiece of which was the eight-story General Oglethorpe Hotel on the Wilmington River. In the mid-1960s, the hotel was refurbished and renamed the Savannah Inn and Country Club, and the golf course was rebuilt and improved by Willard Byrd. The resort was later purchased by the Sheraton corporation, which gave the property its current name. The hotel is now vacant, but the golf club continues to thrive.

This semiprivate club offers golfers a pro shop, driving range and two practice greens. Aura Belle's, a full-service restaurant with a lounge, is next to the pro shop and serves breakfast and lunch. Only club members are allowed to walk the course, and only after 4 PM. Greens fees are $32 Monday through Thursday; on Friday, Saturday and Sunday, they are $48 in the morning and $37 after noon.

Southside/Midtown

Bacon Park Golf Course
Shorty Cooper Dr. • 354-2625
Bacon Park's 27-hole layout presents golf-

Photo: Kyle Cason

Chatham County is a boater's paradise.

ers with three nine-hole courses — Cypress, Live Oak and Magnolia — featuring narrow, tree-lined bermudagrass fairways and elevated greens. Each course carries a par of 36, and the combined length of any pair of the courses is more than 6500 yards. Donald Ross designed the layout, which is in the midst of suburban Savannah; it's owned by the city and operated by American Golf Corporation. The clubhouse contains a pro shop and self-service snack bar, and a driving range and practice green are available. You can walk the course on weekdays and after 1 PM on Saturdays and Sundays. Playing 18 holes costs $21.25 on weekdays and $23.25 on weekends.

Cypress Course

The shortest of Bacon Park's three courses at 3256 yards, Cypress has water on seven holes, including No. 8, the signature hole. This 161-yard par 3 has a narrow green with bunkers on both sides; the water is on the left side of the green.

Live Oak Course

The first hole is long and narrow, a 402-yard par 4 with a green that's well-bunkered. The ninth hole is the longest at Bacon Park, a 581-yard par 5 with a fairway that is crossed by a canal past midpoint; there's plenty more water along the remainder of the fairway and in front of the green. The course runs 3423 yards.

Magnolia Course

This course starts with a long hole, a 530-yard par 5 whose green has lots of water on the right. Another interesting hole is No. 8, which is crossed near midpoint by a canal that runs down the lefthand side of the latter half of the fairway. Total length of Magnolia is 3317 yards.

Henderson Golf Club

1 Al Henderson Dr. • 920-4653

Henderson, opened in March 1995 and owned by Chatham County, offers a good mix of lengths among its 18 holes, ranging from just 127 yards on the 15th to 522 yards on the first hole. The course was built on farmland in southwest Chatham that contained 240 acres of wetlands, so there's plenty of water to look

at. In most cases, however, the water is an intimidation factor rather than a sheer hazard.

In laying out the 6273-yard, par 71 course, designer Mike Young took advantage of the wetlands and an abundant number of native trees by weaving them in with fairways and greens. Some of the holes eventually will be overlooked by homes; a private investment group is developing the area as a golf community where 350 residences in the $135,000 to $200,000 range are planned.

Rapidly gaining a reputation as Henderson's signature hole is the 18th, a par 4 that's 416 yards long. Accuracy is paramount here because there's water on the entire lefthand side of the hole and to the right of the green. The sixth hole also presents a worthy challenge; it's a long (437 yards) par 4 that plays more like a par 5 because of the usual prevailing winds from the southwest. This is the hole where the ability to hit long counts most. Henderson has a pro shop, driving range, practice green and a grill serving hot food and sandwiches. Walking is permitted anytime on weekdays and after 1 PM on weekends. Fees are $34 on weekdays and $40 on weekends. The course is off Ga. Highway 204 just east of the Interstate 95-Ga. 204 interchange.

West Chatham

Mary Calder Golf Club

West Lathrop Ave. • 238-7100

Owned by Union Camp Corporation and located on the grounds of the company's kraft paper-manufacturing plant just east of Garden City, this par 35, nine-hole course exists mainly for the enjoyment of Union Camp employees but is open to the public. Play 18 holes, and you'll cover about 6000 yards on a course that's not difficult but does present some challenges because of its tight, elevated greens. On the par 4, 385-yard fourth hole, for example, you're faced with a green that's narrow in front and has a slight swale in the middle that can keep your ball from getting to the back. The course's three par 3s are well-bunkered and can be tough, particularly the finishing hole, a 179-yarder with a small green.

The course, opened in 1937 on the site of Hermitage Plantation, has a pro shop, snack bar and two putting greens. You can walk the course anytime. Because of its semiprivate nature, the club does not schedule tee times for non-members. Fees for 18 holes are $18 on weekdays and $20 on weekends. You reach Mary Calder from downtown Savannah by driving west on Bay Street, turning north on West Lathrop Avenue and entering the Union Camp manufacturing complex at Blue Gate 1.

Southbridge Golf Club
415 Southbridge Blvd. • 651-5455

Rees Jones designed this 6458-yard, par 72 course, blending in the tall pines, graceful oaks and wetlands of the West Chatham woodlands. Water comes into play on 11 holes on the course, opened in 1988 as part of the Southbridge residential community. The signature hole is No. 4, a par 3, 179-yarder involving a shot over water to an elevated green cut into three sections. The 13th hole is also challenging; it's a long par 5 typical of holes on the back nine. No. 13 was carved out of a thick forest. Water on the left side is involved in every shot on this 492-yarder, and the right side is guarded by bunkers.

Southbridge is off Dean Forest Road at Interstate 16, making it about five minutes from downtown Savannah. An antebellum-style clubhouse adorns the semiprivate course, and the building houses a pro shop and the Southbridge Grill, a full-service dining room. The course has a driving range and putting green and is the home of the Georgia School of Golf, a facility that provides instruction to players of all skill levels. Use the same phone number for information on the school. Greens fees at Southbridge, which has co-hosted the Georgia Open several times, are $35 on weekdays and $45 on weekends and holidays. Walking is allowed after noon on weekdays and after 2 PM on weekends.

In-line Hockey

YMCA of Coastal Georgia
6400 Habersham St. • 354-5480

This sport — hockey played on in-line roller skates — is new to the area but growing in popularity. The Y started its first leagues in the fall of 1995 and offers the sport during two seasons — in the spring during April and May and in the fall during October and November. From 20 to 25 teams are formed, and they play in leagues for under-8, under-10, under-12 and under-16 age groups. The majority of participants are boys, but girls are welcome to take part. The Y stages its games at parking lots at its Habersham Branch, on the south end of Tybee Island at the end of 16th Street and at the Savannah Festival outlet mall at I-95 and Ga. 204.

Sailing

Sailing is smooth in Savannah, as you might expect from the venue for the yachting events of the 1996 Summer Olympics. The best sailing is in Wassaw Sound, which is where the Olympic competition was staged. The sound has lots of deep water and few hazards, and you can bank on getting a tradewind breeze in the afternoon. Another good place for sailing is the Wilmington River, which is the site of several local regattas. The following facilities are great places to get started.

Sail Harbor Marina
618 Wilmington Island Rd. • 897-2896

Sail Harbor is on Turner Creek, right around the corner from the Wilmington River and about 7 miles from Wassaw Sound. This marina has 140 wet slips, 10 of them for transients; a ship's store offering a variety of sailing merchandise; and a laundry, showers and restrooms. You can step off your boat and into The Lightship restaurant, which serves lunch and dinner (see our Restaurants chapter).

Sail Harbor offers sailing charters, either skippered or bare boat, and is the site of a sailing school providing instruction in the basics of the sport and in coastal piloting. Contact the school, Sail Harbor Academy, by calling the marina. Sail Harbor was the 1996 Olympic yachting marina, meaning it served as a shore base for officials coordinating the sailing events. The actual sailing was done from a floating marina in Wassaw Sound that was dismantled after the Olympics. Bare-boat charter fees range from $140 to $500 for the first day of sailing, depending on the size of the boat rented. Hiring a skipper will cost about

$125 more. The basic sailing course is $250 for four five-hour lessons.

Savannah Sailing Center
Lake Mayer, Montgomery Crossroad at Sallie Mood Dr. • 231-9996

Youngsters and adults can learn to sail and sharpen their skills by participating in the various programs offered by this community-based, nonprofit organization. The center began operations in 1993 and trained all of the volunteers who served on the water for Olympic yachting. Courses are taught at the boathouse at Lake Mayer. The center will accept children as young as 7 if they know how to swim. Rates for 1997 for the center's spring programs were $45 or $10 per session for junior sailors and $80 or $20 per session for adult sailors; summer program rates were $75 per session for junior sailors and $20 per session for adult sailors.

Soccer

Youth soccer is huge here, so big that there are spring and fall seasons. The county handles the spring program from March through May and typically has 60 teams in leagues for youngsters 6 to 19. The city coordinates play for a total of about 160 teams in those ages during September, October and November. Most matches are played at the county's soccer fields on Sallie Mood Drive, but the city also stages matches at Guy Minick Sports Complex on Sallie Mood at Eisenhower Drive and in Daffin Park.

Teams participating in city and county leagues are members of either the Coastal Georgia Soccer Association (691-2472) or the Savannah Magic Soccer Club (232-2791). Register your child to play by contacting these groups. The YMCA of Coastal Georgia runs its own fall soccer program, fielding about 55 teams in the under-6, under-8, under-10, under-12 and under-14 age groups. Matches are played at the three Y branches in the county between September and November.

Chatham County Soccer Complex
7221 Sallie Mood Dr. • 356-2503

Local youngsters get their kicks on eight lighted fields at this 50-acre complex on Sallie Mood Drive near Eisenhower Drive. There are three fields that are 64-by-110 yards, three that are 60-by-105 yards and two that are 75-by-115 yards. On occasion, the larger fields are divided into smaller fields to accommodate matches being played by the youngest participants.

Adult Softball

Allen E. Paulson Softball Complex
7171 Skidaway Rd. • 351-3852

Winter is the only time you won't find softballs flying at the city's Allen E. Paulson Complex, one of the finest facilities of its kind in the Southeast. Other times, the place is jumping with slow-pitch activity. From 125 to 130 teams compete in Savannah's open, church and co-ed leagues during the spring and summer season, which ends around Labor Day. In September, the fall leagues crank up, and from 75 to 80 teams hit the five lighted, 300-foot fields; play ends around Thanksgiving. Paulson hosted two national tournaments in 1997, and there are tourneys of some description scheduled on most weekends during softball-playing months.

Swimming

Chatham County Aquatic Center
Sallie Mood Dr.

Chatham County opened this state-of-the-art facility in late December 1997. A dome suspended by air covers an area containing an eight-lane, 50-meter pool and a six-lane, 25-yard warmup and instructional pool. In addition to accommodating recreational swimming, the large pool will be used for district, regional, state and national swim meets; there's seating for 976 spectators. The building also has men's and women's changing rooms, a pro shop, a concession stand, several offices, a meeting room and a lounge.

Tennis

About 1,500 tennis players participate in the USTA league program here, making it the second largest program in the state next to Atlanta's. A total of 150 of the teams in the program, more than a third of those involved, play at public courts. That number has grown from 50 teams in 1987. There are courts at city and county parks throughout the area, but the biggest public tennis complexes are at Bacon and Daffin parks.

Bacon Park Tennis Complex
6262 Skidaway Rd. • 351-3850

Tucked into a wooded area on Skidaway Road, this complex has 16 lighted hard courts open from 9 AM to 9 PM Monday through Saturday and from 9 AM to 5 PM on Sunday. A pro shop sells tennis merchandise and beverages. Fees are $1.75 per hour during the day and $2.25 per hour at night.

Daffin Park Tennis Courts
1001 E. Victory Dr. • 351-3851

Daffin's six clay courts and three hard courts sit near the park's lake, so you can occasionally catch a breeze off the water. You can play for free on the lighted hard courts (available from 6 to 8:30 PM); there's a fee of $2.25 an hour for using the soft courts, which don't have lights and are open from 9 AM until an hour before dark.

Weightlifting

Paul Anderson-Howard Cohen Weightlifting Center
7232 Varnedoe Dr. • 351-3500

Work out for free at the Weightlifting Center, which is adjacent to Memorial Stadium in the Southside and is part of Chatham County's recreational setup. The center is geared toward Olympic-style weightlifting and strength training for local sports teams, but it's open to the public from 9 AM to 9 PM Monday through Saturday.

At the center, you can lift free weights or train on the strength-building machines, and coaches are on hand to answer questions. Separate showers and saunas for men and women are available. The facility opened in February 1995 and is home to Team Savannah, the largest Olympic-style weightlifting team in the United States.

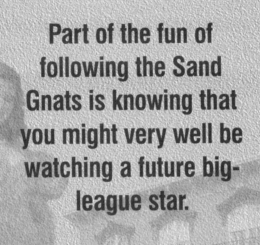

Part of the fun of following the Sand Gnats is knowing that you might very well be watching a future big-league star.

Spectator Sports

The professional sports scene in Savannah falls into the minor-league category, but as one local entrepreneur put it, there's nothing bush league about it.

The Savannah Sand Gnats of the Class A South Atlantic League are affiliated with the Texas Rangers, one of the most stable organizations in big-league baseball, and the local team and the city of Savannah have made continuous improvements to Grayson Stadium, the city's gem of an old-time ball park.

The staging of the first Savannah Grand Prix in 1997 marked the return of road-course auto racing to the city after an 86-year hiatus. Back in 1908, 1910 and 1911, famed drivers such as Ralph DePalma and Louis Chevrolet zoomed over the roads of Chatham County at speeds of up to 85 mph as Savannah stepped to the fore of the racing world with its Grand Prize and Vanderbilt Cup competitions. In 1997, Helio Castro Neves, Clint Mears and other up-and-coming drivers hit 165 mph as they gunned their open-wheel racers around a newly built circuit on Hutchinson Island.

Unfortunately, the road-racing return has been sidetracked, at least for the time being, and the Indy Lights temporarily snuffed. Colonial Motorsports, the organization that brought the competition to town in hopes that it would help pave the way for Savannah to join the Indy Car circuit, was in bankruptcy proceedings as we went to press. The Hutchinson Island circuit and facilities remain in place; only time will tell if big-time racing will ultimately get the green light in Savannah.

On the football front in 1997, the Savannah Chiefs played their second season of minor-league pro football, and the Savannah Rug Ratz brought indoor soccer to the city. In addition to those endeavors, Savannah has top-flight operations in minor-league basketball, stock-car racing and drag racing.

This wide range of spectator sports should be enough to keep any rabid fan busy, but if you're hankering for some big-league action, you can find it within comfortable driving distance. Atlanta, with its Falcons of the National Football League, Braves of Major League Baseball and Hawks of the National Basketball Association, is five hours to the northwest. The NFL's Jaguars of Jacksonville, Florida, are even closer — about two-and-a-half hours south on Interstate 95. Nearer still is Hilton Head Island, the site of two major sporting events in the spring: the MCI Classic PGA golf tournament and the Family Circle Magazine Cup women's tennis tourney (for more on each of these events, see our Hilton Head chapter).

If you're into intercollegiate sports, you'll find a lot to choose from close to home at the city schools, or you can hit the road for Georgia Southern University in Statesboro (about an hour away), the University of Georgia in Athens (four-and-a-half hours) or Georgia Tech in Atlanta.

Baseball

Savannah Sand Gnats
Grayson Stadium, 1401 E. Victory Dr.
• 351-9150

If you believe there's nothing as American as spending an evening or Sunday afternoon at the old ball park, a visit to Grayson Stadium to watch the Savannah Sand Gnats is for you.

The city's Class A minor-league baseball team plays 72 regular-season games at Grayson, where the brick grandstand was built in 1941. Located at the eastern end of Daffin Park, the stadium stands amid tall pines and oaks dripping with Spanish moss, and it's a great place to sit back, relax and enjoy the national pastime while sipping a cold beer and devouring some peanuts — the boiled variety being the most popular in this part of the world.

Savannah began fielding a professional baseball team in 1903 and is a charter member of the South Atlantic League. Following lengthy affiliations with the Atlanta Braves and St. Louis Cardinals, the local club became part of the Los Angeles Dodgers organization in 1996, adopting the name Sand Gnats (see the Close-up on these pesky critters in our Area Overviews chapter) and the unique team colors of burgundy, forest green and tan. In November 1997 the team again changed its big league organizational affiliation: In '98 the Sand Gnats players will be working to get the call up to the American League's Texas Rangers. The local club's most recent management regime — headed by General Manager Ric Sisler, grandson of Hall of Fame first baseman George Sisler — has developed a winning tradition: Savannah teams captured Class A SALLY League championships in 1993, '94 and '96. Part of the fun of following the Sand Gnats, regardless of their affiliation, is knowing that you might very well be watching a future big-league star.

Grayson's covered grandstand seats 5,000 people, and there's room for 2,500 in the bleachers. Most of the viewing area is screened from foul balls. If you can't resist eating while watching the old ball game, you can find plenty to munch on — in addition to the usual ball-

FYI

Unless otherwise noted, the area code for all phone numbers listed in this guide is 912.

park fare, Grayson in past years has offered Philly cheesesteaks, chicken fingers and beef kabobs. The Sand Gnats organization schedules numerous special events and promotions. In 1997, there were four game-night fireworks shows; performances by those zany mascots, The Famous Chicken and Sport (portrayed by the creator of the Philly Fanatic); and giveaways of items such as caps, helmets, seat cushions and jerseys.

Games start at 7:15 PM on weekdays and Saturdays and at 2 PM on Sundays until temperatures start to climb in mid-June; thereafter, Sunday contests begin at 6:15 PM. General admission is $3.75 for adults and $3 for children, senior citizens and military personnel. Reserved seats are $4.50, and box seats go for $5.50. You can reserve tickets by calling the number listed, or you can pick them up ahead of time at the team's offices at Grayson from 9 AM until 10 PM on game days and from 9 AM until 5 PM when the team is out of town. Parking is free in the mostly unpaved areas under the oaks of Daffin Park.

Auto Racing

Oglethorpe Speedway
Jesup Rd. off U.S. Hwy. 80 • 964-RACE
This speedway gives the green flag to stock-car drivers competing in the NASCAR Winston Racing Series every Friday night from April until early September, and special racing events are held on Friday evenings during October and November. You'll see at least 100 entries competing each week on the half-mile dirt track in Winston Series mini-stock, street-stock and late-model division events. NASCAR celebrities such as Sterling Marlin and Derrike Cope participate in races once or twice a sea-

Photo: Savannah Sand Gnats

It might be. . . It could be. . . It is! Home run Sand Gnats!

son, and enduro events are held every six weeks.

The racing is handled by NASCAR officials, who keep things moving at a brisk pace. Oglethorpe Speedway is on Jesup Road off U.S. 80 in West Chatham County. The 5,000-seat aluminum grandstand was built in 1995 and is accessible to the handicapped. Tickets are sold at the gate and are $8 for adults and teens and $6 for senior citizens and persons in the military. Children 12 and younger are admitted free if accompanied by an adult. Parking is also free. The gates open at 6 PM, and racing starts at 8 PM.

Savannah Dragway
U.S. Hwy. 17 • 234-1965

The drag racing is legal at this 0.8-mile track in West Chatham. The Dragway own-

ers hold "grudge" night competitions on Thursdays starting at 5:30 PM for racers who want to challenge each other, and there are National Hot Rod Association-sanctioned races on Saturdays. On NHRA race days, the gates open at 4 PM, time trials take place from 4:30 to 6:30 PM, and the races start at 7:30 PM. Admission is $5 on Thursdays and $10 on Saturdays, with tickets purchased at the gate.

The grandstands seat about 3,500 people. Concessions are available, but you can bring your own grill and food and cook out if you want. The racing season runs from the end of February until late November, with special events in December and January. The dragway entrance is on the north side of U.S. Highway 17, about 1 mile west of Chatham Parkway.

INSIDERS' TIP

The native Savannahian who had the most notable career in major-league baseball is Ken "Hawk" Harrelson. The Hawk, who was known for his flamboyant attire and outspoken ways, played 900 games for a variety of American League teams during 1963-71. Harrelson, who participated in the first Little League game ever staged in Savannah, hit 35 home runs and led the American League in runs batted in with 109 while playing outfield and first base for the Boston Red Sox in 1968. Since his playing days, he has worked in the big leagues as a broadcaster and executive.

Football

Savannah Chiefs
P.O. Box 30206, Savannah GA 31410
• 826-4182

The Savannah Chiefs became part of the upper echelon of minor-league professional football in 1997 by joining the 36-team International Football League. The Chiefs won nine of 11 games before dropping out of the IFL because of differences with the way the league was being run, then won another game while playing as an independent team. As of early December, Chiefs officials were in the process of determining how the team would be affiliated in 1998.

The Chiefs maintain a 53-man active roster comprised of players hoping to make the jump to the National Football League, the Canadian Football League or Arena Football. The Chiefs play Saturday home games at Memorial Stadium on Skidaway Road at John J. Scott Drive and at Garden City Stadium on Wheathill Road off Ga. Highway 21. The regular season runs from early August through early October. Game times are at 7 PM, and tickets were $8 at the gate last season. To order tickets in advance or obtain information on games, call the number listed.

Indoor Soccer

Savannah Rug Ratz
Savannah Civic Center, Montgomery and Liberty Sts. • 232-2892

The Rug Ratz introduced Savannahians to indoor soccer in 1997. This fast-paced game is played on carpet — hence the team's nickname — in an area 200 feet long and 80 feet wide (an outdoor soccer field measures 360 by 225 feet). Indoor soccer tends to be more physical and higher-scoring than the outdoor game — on average, 14 or 15 goals will be scored during an indoor game, as opposed to two to three outdoors. The Savannah team participates in the Eastern Division of the Eastern Indoor Soccer League along with Charleston, South Carolina, and Daytona Beach and Tallahassee in Florida. The purple-and-white-clad Ratz play their home games at 7 PM at the Savannah Civic Center arena during a regular season that runs from mid-June through August. Tickets range from $5 to $9 and can be purchased at the Civic Center box office, 651-6556.

Basketball

Plans call for Savannah to have a franchise in the Continental Basketball Association during the 1998-99 season. The local entry would be one of 12 teams in the CBA, which predates the National Basketball Association and is the official minor league for the NBA.

The new team is the brainchild of Dean Schoenewald, who runs Nashville, Tennessee-based Mascot Mania, which creates mascots for college and professional sports teams and conducts a school for mascots. Schoenewald promises the 28 home games his team will play in the Savannah Civic Center from November through mid-March will be more than athletic contests — they'll be entertainment

---

INSIDERS' TIP

If you attend a football game at the University of Georgia in Athens, you'll get a chance to see the mascot *Sports Illustrated* calls the best in the nation. He's UGA V (that's "UGH-uh Five"), a white English bulldog who lives at the home of Savannah attorney Sonny Seiler. UGA V, who portrays his sire, UGA IV, in the movie *Midnight in the Garden of Good and Evil*, appeared on the *SI* cover for April 28, 1997, promoting a feature story titled, "America's Top 50 Jock Schools."

Photo: Kyle Cason

This waterfront sculpture commemorates Savannnah's
role as the yachting venue for the 1996 Olympics.

events. If you attend a game, he says, you might expect to see fireworks over the Civic Center, a Ferris wheel in the parking lot and a Calypso band playing in the arena. Tickets are expected to run from $6 to $10 and will be sold at the Civic Center box office and outlets throughout Savannah.

Big-league Sports

Sports fans in Savannah have for years been making daytrip and overnight pilgrimages to Atlanta to watch the Braves, Falcons and Hawks in action and enjoy the big-league surroundings. However, Savannahians no longer have to drive five hours to Georgia's capital to witness sports at a top level — at least not during football season. The Jacksonville Jaguars, of Florida and the NFL, play eight home games in a recently refurbished, state-of-the-art stadium that's half the traveling time of the Savannah to Atlanta junket. The Jags, in existence since only 1996 but a contender in their second year of play, have become a hot ticket here and have put a decided dent in the Falcons' local fan base. To order tickets to Braves, Falcons and Hawks games, call Ticketmaster in Atlanta at (404)

Photo: Kyle Cason

This Sand Gnats southpaw might someday make it to the parent club - the Texas Rangers.

249-6400 or (800) 326-4000. You can obtain Jaguars' tickets by calling (904) 633-2000 or (800) 618-8005.

Intercollegiate Sports

You can witness competition on various intercollegiate levels in football, baseball, men's and women's basketball and women's volleyball and stay in town while doing so. Armstrong Atlantic State University, Savannah State University, the Savannah College of Art and Design and Savannah Tech all compete in basketball, Savannah State plays football and Armstrong and SCAD field baseball and volleyball teams.

You'll have to do some driving to see the big-time college athletes compete. Georgia Southern University in Statesboro (a one-hour drive west) plays Division I-AA football and has four won national championships since 1985. The GSU men's basketball team has been to the NCAA Division I playoffs twice since 1987, and the women's team has gone two times since 1993. The college's baseball team had 14 consecutive winning seasons through 1997, and Coach Jack Stallings was the winningest active skipper in Division I with 1,209 victories.

But the really big shows are in Athens at the University of Georgia, where the Lady Bulldogs and Bulldogs compete in the Southeastern Conference, and in Atlanta, where Georgia Tech's Rambling Wreck participates in Atlantic Coast Conference play.

Billionaire auto pioneer Henry Ford revitalized the Richmond Hill area in the 1920s, '30s and '40s, transforming an area where moonshining was one of the major occupations.

Daytrips

You obviously will find plenty to occupy your time in Savannah, but if you want to go roaming a bit, you'll discover lots to see and do in the rest of coastal Georgia. To get you started on your explorations of the territory to the south of Savannah, we've mapped out trips to Richmond Hill-Liberty County and to Jekyll Island. The sites in the Richmond Hill-Liberty County area that we've spotlighted are within an hour's driving time of Savannah. It will take a little longer to reach Jekyll, which is about a 90-minute jaunt from our city. For those inclined to range considerably farther, we've thrown in a tour of Atlanta's newest attraction, Turner Field, the home of baseball's winningest franchise of the '90s, the Atlanta Braves. Happy wandering!

Richmond Hill- Liberty County

Lovers of history and nature will enjoy a tour of Richmond Hill and Liberty County, an area of extensive marshlands, lush forests and meandering rivers, where the past is rich in significant people and events. To adequately visit all the spots we'll be sending you to, you'll probably need more than a day. That said, you might want to split this tour into a couple of daytrips, or pick a few places that sound the most appealing and spend a day visiting those.

Begin your tour of the area by driving to the Bryan County municipality of Richmond Hill, a fast-growing town that's become a bedroom community of Savannah during the past 20 years. This one-time stomping ground of industrialist Henry Ford is 19 miles southwest of downtown Savannah and can be reached by heading west on Interstate 16 to Interstate 516, south on I-516 to the Southwest Bypass (Veterans Parkway), south on the Southwest Bypass to Ga. Highway 204, west on Ga. 204

to U.S. Highway 17 and south on U.S. 17 to the highway's intersection with Ga. Highway 144. Turn left from U.S. 17 onto Ga. 144 and head east through the heart of Richmond Hill; it's 1 mile to your first stop, the Richmond Hill Historical Society and Museum. The museum building, which once housed a kindergarten that was a project of Ford and his wife, is on the right on the corner of Ga. 144 and Timber Trail Road.

Richmond Hill Historical Society and Museum
Ga. Hwy. 144 • 756-3697

You'll learn the fascinating story of Richmond Hill's Henry Ford era (1925-1951) when you visit this museum. The billionaire Ford purchased 85,000 acres in Bryan County in the mid-1920s, in effect buying the town of Richmond Hill, which was then known as Ways Station. He spent his winters there, living on a plantation that accommodated a laboratory where chemists attempted to transform agricultural products into goods that could be used by the automobile industry.

Ford revitalized an area where moonshining was one of the major occupations; he put people to work on his plantation and at a sawmill that he refurbished, and he built medical clinics, houses, chapels and the town's Community House. Ford also improved existing schools and built a trade school for boys and a grammar and high school for African-American youths. A museum staffer will tell you about Ford's accomplishments and their impact on the community while you look at photographs and artifacts from the period.

Other sections of the museum depict the area's plantation era and offer displays of photos and some of the furniture used in the county's one-room schoolhouses. You'll also find out about sites from the Ford era that you can visit, such as the Community House, which is now a funeral home, and one of the chapels, now a Catholic church. The museum is open from 9 AM to 3 PM on Monday, Thursday and Friday and from 10 AM to 4 PM on Saturday and Sunday. An admission fee is not charged, but $2 donations are accepted.

After you've looked at the displays at the Richmond Hill Museum, hop in your vehicle and head east on Ga. 144 to Fort McAllister State Historic Park. To reach the park, you'll drive 4 miles into the country-side on Ga. 144 to Ga. Spur 144, then turn left onto Ga. Spur 144; the entrance to the park is 4 miles ahead, and the drive to it will take you past upscale Lowcountry- and ranch-style homes, some of them with back-yard boat docks on the beautiful and fast-flow-ing Great Ogeechee River, which can be seen on your left.

FYI

Unless otherwise noted, the area code for all phone numbers listed in this guide is 912.

plenty of rustic-looking playground equipment for the kids in this area, which borders the main road leading to the fort.

If you plan on making your visit to Richmond Hill-Liberty County last longer than a day and you like roughing it, consider staying at the park's Savage Island Campground, which has 65 campsites — 50 for recreational vehicles and 15 with tent pads, and all with water and electrical hookups, grills and tables. Two comfort stations provide campers with toilets, heated showers and washer/dryers, and the campground also has a playground, nature trail and dock and boat ramp on Red Bird Creek. The RV sites rent for $14 a night, and the tent pads are $12 a night, with rates for senior citizens dropping to $11.20 and $9.60 respectively.

Fort McAllister State Historic Park
3894 Fort McAllister Road • 727-2339

This 1,700-acre park between the Ogeechee and Red Bird Creek has two alluring identities: It's a recreational area featuring amenities for campers and picnickers, and it's also the site of an earthen fort where much of the Savannah area's most significant Civil War action took place.

Prior to 1980, these two attractions existed as Richmond Hill State Park and Fort McAllister Historic Site; that year, they were combined to form Fort McAllister State Historic Park, which today is operated by the Georgia Department of Natural Resources. There's a $2 parking fee to enter the park, which is open daily from 7 AM to 10 PM; admittance is free on Wednesdays. To keep things as simple as possible, we'll discuss the recreational area and the historic site separately.

The Recreational Area

For daytrippers, the main attraction here is the tree-filled picnic ground running along a high bluff overlooking the Ogeechee River. Tall pines and hardwoods make this a shady, serene spot for walking or sitting in a glider-type swing and watching the river flow by. You'll find 50 sites with picnic tables and grills, a fishing pier that extends out over the river and

The Historic Site

Fort McAllister is one of the best-preserved earthwork fortifications built by the Confederacy during the Civil War. The southernmost of the defenses ringing Savannah, the fort withstood several attacks by Union warships before being overpowered by Federal forces on December 13, 1864, at the end of Gen. William T. Sherman's March to the Sea. The site was once owned by Henry Ford, who began an extensive restoration in the late 1930s, and the fort eventually fell into the hands of the state of Georgia, which restored it to its 1863-64 appearance.

You can wander around the walls and through the interior of the fort and look inside its central bombproof, but be careful not to climb on these earthen structures, which are extremely susceptible to erosion from foot traffic. Take the self-guided tour of the fort and check out a 32-pounder smoothbore gun that fired red-hot cannonballs and the furnace where these projectiles were heated; the reconstructed service magazine, which held shells, powder and fuses for the Rebels' 32-pounder rifled gun; and the fort's northwest angle, where the attackers placed the first U.S. flag planted on the parapets.

The fort site also has a museum containing Civil War shells and weapons; implements such as those used in the construction of the fort; artifacts from the Confederate blockade runner *Nashville*, which was sunk in the Ogeechee by the Union ironclad *Montauk*; a diorama of the assault on the fort; and a display depicting life at the fort as experienced by its 230 defenders. The fort is open from 9 AM to 5 PM Monday through Saturday and from 2 PM to 5 PM on Sunday. Admission is $2 for adults and $1 for youngsters 5 to 18; children younger than 5 are admitted free.

After visiting Fort McAllister State Historic Park, head back to Richmond Hill on Ga. 144 and then south to Liberty County and the Historic Liberty Trail. The first attraction on this tour of the trail is Fort Morris State Historic Site, and you can get there from Richmond Hill by turning left onto U.S. 17 from Ga. 144 and driving 2 miles to I-95, heading south on I-95 for 11 miles and leaving the interstate at Exit 13. Next, turn left onto U.S. 84/Ga. 38 (Fort Morris Road) and stay on it for 7 miles until you come to the entrance to the site.

Fort Morris State Historic Site
2559 Fort Morris Rd. • 884-5999

This peaceful little spot on a low bluff on the Medway River was the scene of one of the classic rejoinders in American history. During the Revolutionary War, the British besieged the American earthworks of Fort Morris and the nearby town of Sunbury, and the Redcoat commander demanded a surrender. The fort's commander, Col. John McIntosh, answered the demand in this defiant manner: "We, sir, are fighting the battles of America, and therefore disdain to remain neutral till its fate is determined. As to surrendering the fort, receive this laconic reply, 'Come and take it!'" Lack-

ing some expected support from another British force and the exact knowledge of the strength of the troops at Fort Morris, the Redcoats did not follow McIntosh's suggestion; instead, they retreated. Fort Morris, however, eventually fell to the British and was dismantled.

A smaller earthen fort, called Defiance in honor of McIntosh's reply, was built during the War of 1812 from the remains of Fort Morris, and you can explore it by visiting this site. Strolling around the walls of the fort under the majestic oaks towering over it, you have a wonderful view of the Medway and its marshes, and you might even get a glimpse of a shrimp boat trawling in the river. The interpretive center/museum at the site tells the saga of the fort and of Sunbury, the town it was built to protect, and there's also a 1-mile nature trail through marsh and scrub oak forest.

The Georgia Department of Natural Resources, which maintains the 70-acre site, offers special events three times during the year — a program on "Artillery Through the Ages" on the last Saturday in April, the "Come and Take It!" re-enactment on the first Saturday in October and a "Christmas in the Colonies" presentation on the first or second Saturday of December. Admission to the site is $2 for adults and $1 for youths 6 to 18; entry for children younger than 6 is free. Fort Morris is open from 9 AM to 5 PM Tuesday through Saturday and from 9:30 AM to 5:30 PM on Sunday. It's closed on Monday.

While you're at the interpretive center at Fort Morris State Historic Site, be sure to view the award-winning, 12-minute video, Sunbury Sleeps: The Forgotten Town of Sunbury, Ga. This hauntingly beautiful tribute to one of

INSIDERS' TIP

After leaving Fort McAllister State Historic Park on Ga. Spur 144, you might notice a historical marker on the left side of the road 1.7 miles from the entrance to the park. This marker denotes the site of the town of Hardwicke, which in 1755 was chosen to be the capital of Georgia by the colony's first royal governor, John Reynolds. Six years later a new governor, James Wright, decided against removing the capital from Savannah to Hardwicke, and the town "became little more than a trading village," according to the marker. Eventually, it vanished.

Georgia's "lost towns" serves as the perfect introduction to the next stop on our daytrip, the *Sunbury Cemetery*. The cemetery is a little more than a mile from the entrance to Fort Morris. After leaving the fort, turn right onto Fort Morris Road and keep to your left until you reach Sunbury Road. Turn left onto this dirt road and drive to Dutchmans Cove Road, then take a right and follow this unpaved lane a short distance to the cemetery.

Sunbury Cemetery
Dutchmans Cove Rd.

This small cemetery is all that remains of the once bustling town of Sunbury, which in 1764 had 80 dwellings, three stores, several wharves and a trio of town squares. By 1773, Sunbury was a seaport beginning to rival Savannah as a place of commerce; that year, the town saw 56 vessels clear port as compared to Savannah's 160. Sunbury also had another claim to fame: All three of Georgia's signers of the Declaration of Independence had a connection to the town — Lyman Hall lived there, Button Gwinnett resided on nearby St. Catherines Island, and George Walton was confined there when Sunbury was made a military prison after its capture by the British during the Revolutionary War.

By the end of the war, most of Sunbury had been destroyed, and the town never recovered. There were fewer than eight families living there by 1855, and all evidence of the town eventually disappeared — everything but the cemetery and the 34 grave markers that remain standing. When we visited Fort Morris, we knew when we left there wouldn't be a great deal to see at the cemetery. But after viewing the Department of Natural Resources video about Sunbury, we felt compelled to take a look and pay our respects, so to speak. Maybe you will, too.

Now it's time to get back on the Historic Liberty Trail and head to the town of Midway. We recommend, though, that while you're on the way, you visit Seabrook Village, which you can find by turning right off Fort Morris Road onto Trade Hill Road.

Seabrook Village
660 Trade Hill Rd. • 884-7008

This 104-acre site portrays the history and culture of African Americans living in coastal Georgia during 1865 to 1930. Using authentic buildings and displays of artifacts, Seabrook brings that period to life. Among stops on guided and self-guided tours of the village are Bowen's Farm, with its rice fields and a barn containing tools used in farming, gathering oysters and making turpentine; the Ripley Corn Crib, where corn is ground into grits and meal; the Seabrook School, with its original wooden blackboard and desks made by former student John Stevens; the Gibbons-Woodward House, in which you can see a rural kitchen, a featherbed and a replica of the original clay chimney; a mill and boiler house where stalks of sugar cane are ground by horse power and cooked into syrup; and the Delegal-Williams House, with its family photographs and local furnishings.

While you're visiting Seabrook, be sure to see the unusual artwork of Cyrus Bowen, with which he adorned local grave sites. Seabrook is open from 10 AM to 4 PM Tuesday through Saturday. Group tours lasting three hours and conducted by costumed guides are available, as are one-hour guided tours in the afternoon. Admission is $5 for adults, $3 for youngsters 6 through 18 and $1.50 for 5-year-olds; children younger than 5 are admitted free.

The next stop on the tour is Midway, which was established in 1754 by a group of Congregationalists from Dorchester, South Carolina. Their Midway Society produced governors, cabinet members, U.S. senators and congressmen, numerous ministers and foreign missionaries. The parish they settled, St. John's, was a hotbed of patriotic fervor during the years leading up to the American Revolution, and two of its residents, Lyman Hall and Button Gwinnett, were among Georgia's three signers of the Declaration of Independence. To get to Midway, head west on U.S. 84 back to I-95 and stay on U.S. 84 until you reach U.S. 17, which is about 4 miles west of the interstate. Turn right onto U.S. 17. Clustered just up the road are the Mid-

way Museum, Midway Congregational Church and the Midway Cemetery.

Midway Museum
U.S. Hwy. 17 • 884-5837

This museum gives visitors an idea of what life was like for landowners in coastal Georgia during the late 18th century and early 19th century. The museum building is an elegant, raised cottage-style house erected in 1957 and based on a sketch made in 1828 of a home in nearby Riceboro. The rooms of the house are filled with original 18th-century furnishings; among the more unique items on display are a walking cane-gun that fired a .45 caliber slug and a set of musical glasses that are played by rubbing vinegar around the rims. A museum staff member will tell you about many of the items in the three first-floor rooms of the house and will play a tune on the glasses; you're free to look at the upper-floor bedrooms and displays in the ground-floor rooms on your own.

This attraction, which is operated by the Midway Museum Board of Governors, is open from 10 AM to 4 PM Tuesday through Saturday and from 2 to 4 PM on Sunday; it's closed on Monday. Admission, which includes access to nearby Midway Congregational Church, is $3 for adults and $1 for youngsters 6 through 14; children younger than 6 are admitted free.

Midway Congregational Church
U.S. Hwy. 17

Built in 1792, this stately church reflects a style reminiscent of Colonial New England (some of the founders of Midway were descendants of Puritans from Massachusetts who had settled in South Carolina). The existing building replaced a church that was burned by the British in 1778. The church is a short walk from the Midway Museum, and you can obtain a key from a museum staff member and take a look inside. The church has no heating system or artificial lights, but services are conducted there each April by the Midway Society.

Midway Cemetery
U.S. Hwy. 17

Researchers believe Midway Cemetery was laid out in the late 1750s and that it contains about 1,200 graves. Among those buried there are James Screen, a brigadier general in the American army who was killed in November 1778 in a skirmish with the British about a mile south of his resting place, and Daniel Stewart, who attained the rank of brigadier after fighting in the Revolution and Indian Wars and was the great-grandfather of President Theodore Roosevelt; Fort Stewart, the U.S. Army's military reservation at nearby Hinesville, is named after him. The cemetery is open to the public, and a brochure featuring a map and self-guided tour of the site is available at the Midway Museum for 25¢.

Midway Cemetery is also the burial site of Louis LeConte, who owned a rice plantation south of Midway where he created a botanical garden of great renown. You can reach the plantation by driving south on U.S. 17 for 3 miles to the Barrington Ferry Road. Turn right onto Barrington Ferry and follow it for 5.5 miles to the entrance to the plantation site.

LeConte-Woodmanston Plantation
Barrington Ferry Rd. • 884-6500

In its heyday during the early 1800s, Woodmanston Plantation covered more than 3,300 acres and was the largest inland rice plantation in Georgia. Louis LeConte came

INSIDERS' TIP

Some of the attractions on our Richmond Hill-Liberty County daytrip are in somewhat remote areas that aren't near restaurants, so you might consider packing a lunch for the day. You can dine in relative comfort at picnic areas at several stops on this tour, including Fort McAllister State Historic Park, Fort Morris State Historic Site and the Midway Museum. Each of these picnic areas has tables and pleasant surroundings.

into possession of Woodmanston in 1810, and the garden he planted there gained fame throughout the United States and Europe.

The plantation was abandoned in 1869, but a restoration of a 63.8-acre site was begun in the late 1970s as a project of The Garden Club of Georgia. The project, being carried on now by the LeConte-Woodmanston Foundation, is a work in progress that so far has resulted in the creation of a 1-acre botanical garden featuring plants that LeConte might have grown and a 1-mile nature trail along a network of rice dams. The garden contains more than 100 different plants, including beds of older varieties of camellias and roses. Plans for early 1998 call for the growing of rice in a 2-acre demonstration area and the start of construction of an interpretive center near the entrance to the site.

The plantation is open to the public during the spring and summer (when plants in the garden are in bloom) from 9 AM to 5 PM each day except Monday, and admission is $1 a car. Because LeConte-Woodmanston is in a somewhat remote spot, you are advised to call ahead to the listed number or 368-7002 to make arrangements for a visit. Also, be aware that the last 1.6 miles of the drive to the plantation is over dirt roads.

The last attraction on this tour is the Fort Stewart Museum, a military museum just inside the main entrance to Fort Stewart, the huge U.S. Army post at Hinesville. From LeConte-Woodmanston, drive back to the intersection of U.S. 17 and U.S. 84 and head west on U.S. 84 about 7 miles to Hinesville. Turn right onto General Stewart Way, which will take you to the entrance to Fort Stewart. The museum is on-post at the corner of Wilson Boulevard and Frank Cochran Drive.

Fort Stewart Museum
2022 Frank Cochran Dr. • 767-7885

Displays of photographs, uniforms, weapons and other military equipment at the museum focus on the history of Fort Stewart and its current occupant, the 3rd Infantry Division (Mechanized). Fort Stewart, now the largest Army installation east of the Mississippi River, was established in the summer of 1940 as Camp Stewart and served as an antiaircraft

artillery training center during World War II and the Korean War. During the early 1960s, the post was the site of a variety of tests and training by military units, and in the latter half of the decade it served as a training area for Army helicopter pilots.

In the mid-1970s, the 24th Infantry Division (Mechanized) was activated at Fort Stewart, and the unit was based there until April 1996, when the post became the home of the 3rd Infantry. The story of the 3rd Division's service in the two world wars and Korea is related at the museum, portions of which are also devoted to the 24th Infantry and the military history of coastal Georgia. Entry to Fort Stewart is open to civilians, and admission to the museum is free. Hours of operation are from 10 AM to 4 PM Tuesday through Sunday.

Jekyll Island

Georgia's coastline is a fascinating and varied one. Savannah, which snugs up to South Carolina, marks its northernmost point. At the southern extremity, up against the Florida line, you'll find St. Mary's, with its access to Cumberland Island. And in between you'll find the Golden Isles.

Four islands make up this cluster, accessible from Brunswick, a port and industrial city that retains a small historic district. It is the jumping-off point for the Golden Isles, reachable by causeway with one exception. St. Simons Island is the biggest and most developed of the Isles, with beaches, motels, restaurants and historic sites. Little St. Simons is accessible only by boat, open to a limited number of guests (by arrangement) to largely undeveloped beaches and marshlands — it's a real treat for environment-minded tourists. Sea Island, largely residential, is home to the extremely tony resort known as The Cloister.

Jekyll Island is the southernmost of the four Golden Isles. It's the one we've picked to feature as a daytrip option because we think it is likely to appeal to the same type of traveler who is attracted to Savannah. You'll find places to eat and sleep there, but development has not run wild. In fact, the state of Georgia owns the place, and the business and residential ventures there are really long-term leases. Enjoy the beaches (which are all public) and consider a trip along the extensive network of bike paths a must-do (bike rental places abound; check the lobby of larger motels). Jekyll, like the rest of the Golden Isles, is also covered up with golf courses, most of which are accessible to the public at large.

The Brunswick & The Golden Isles Visitors Bureau, 4 Glynn Avenue, Brunswick, 265-0620, and the Jekyll Island Welcome Center, P.O. Box 13186, Jekyll Island, GA 31527, 635-3636, (800) 841-6586, are two general sources that can provide additional information, including lodging details and how to get onto the golf courses. Expect to pay a $2 "parking fee" as you drive onto Jekyll.

To get there, head south on I-95. It takes about 90 minutes. While it's not that long a trip (we know people who commute there from Savannah for work daily, in fact), it can be harrowing: This is the corridor that runs between the Northeast population centers and Florida, and it is always heavily traveled by time-conscious vacationers. Exits are clearly marked.

Jekyll Island Historic District Museum Visitors Center
Stable Rd. • 635-2119

Georgia was originally founded as a refuge for debtors. (It didn't work out that way, as you know from reading our History chapter). Jekyll Island was originally developed by the richest and most powerful men in America. They bought the island in 1886 and made it into a private resort where you need not apply unless your annual income included at least seven figures, all to the left of the decimal point. Names that are synonymous with American fortunes were among the Jekyll Island Club's members — Rockefeller, Gould, Morgan. And they didn't stay in rented quarters, although the club was (and now is again) a fine hotel. Instead, they built "cottages" — mansions that took advantage of beautiful views, cooling breezes and balmy weather. This was, indeed, the playground of the rich and famous.

That era lasted for 55 years of Jekyll's history, and you can still see its vestiges. The "cottages" personify a lifestyle most of us have trouble imagining. They've been fixed up (coastal climate and humidity require diligent upkeep) and are now open to the public. Tours are available via open trams (which look like golf carts linked together) at a cost of $10 for adults and $6 for those ages 6 to 18. Children younger than 6 are free. Tours depart on the hour from 10 AM to 3 PM from the visitors center. (Later tours are often available during the summer.) There's bad news for independent-minded travelers: Only the guided tours get inside the choice buildings. The Goodyear Cottage, which houses the offerings of Jekyll Island Arts Association, and Mistletoe Cottage, again with artwork, are the only houses open to the non-paying public, but there is a good selection of shops.

Atlanta

Well, given that it's 250-plus miles away, you can't really call Atlanta a daytrip from Savannah. Still, if you traveled any major distance to get to Savannah, chances are your route took you through or near Georgia's storied capital city. If you don't get to this part of the country very often, you might want to take advantage of your visit to at least sample one of the world's great cities on your way home.

Atlanta offers attractions that obviously exceed the scope of a few pages. In fact, they fill a whole book — *The Insiders' Guide® to Atlanta* — a third edition of which is due out in early 1998. With that ultimate resource at hand, you don't need us babbling on about historic attractions, the amazing zoo, great shopping, etc. . . . Hey, we're tourists ourselves in Atlanta.

That said, however, we wanted to share a little bit about Atlanta's newest attraction with you. We're talking Turner Field, home of the Atlanta Braves. The new baseball-only park opened in 1997 (freshly refitted from its original Olympic stadium format), so we figure even experienced travelers to the area might not have seen it yet. Besides, we'll admit it — we're

---

INSIDERS' TIP

If you plan on eating at the stadium, you might want to try a Turner Field specialty — buffalo. Really.

baseball fans, and we've made the trek to the Ted (Atlanta slang for Turner Field, named for maverick media magnate and sports franchise owner Ted Turner) a couple of times already.

Getting to Atlanta from Savannah requires patience but no particular navigational skill. You can fly. You can take a bus, although that probably takes too much time and lacks the ambiance the average vacationer wants. Rail travel isn't an option, not since the demise of the old Nancy Hanks train. Given these options, most Savannahians just drive.

Your route is simple. Take Interstate 16, which begins in downtown Savannah, and travel west until it ends in Macon. This stretch of the journey will cover 165 miles, and it is lightly traveled, for the most part. As I-16 enters Macon, there's an easy merge onto Interstate 75 North, where traffic picks up enormously. From there, it's a straight shot to Atlanta. How long does it take? Of course, it depends on where in Atlanta you are going. Still, figure four-and-a-half hours minimum. It takes us a little longer.

Heading to a Braves game? You're looking for Exit 91 (Fulton Street/Stadium) off Interstate 75/85. If your travels around Atlanta have gotten you onto the east-west interstate, it's Exit 22 (Windsor Street/Stadium) from I-20 East, and Exit 24 (Capitol Avenue) from I-20 West.

The parking situation was in flux the last time we were there, with construction still to come on new parking at the site of the demolished old stadium. We paid $10 to park on the abandoned tennis court of a nearby motel, and similar informal arrangements abound to back up official parking — just make sure that whoever sells you a parking space actually has some connection with the business that owns that space.

Atlanta Braves
755 Hank Aaron Dr. • (404) 522-7630

This fan-friendly baseball park offers activities that would appeal to even those who aren't dedicated baseball fans, making it a good family destination. If you aren't interested

Atlanta's new Turner Field has already been nicknamed "The Ted."

Photo: Turner Field

in the game and the perennial National League East powerhouse Braves, leave the fans you accompanied to watch it in peace while you roam the attractions, play interactive games, shop for souvenirs and eat from a variety of food outlets that exceed tradition's peanuts and Cracker Jacks.

If you do want to see the local heroes in action (including multiple Cy Young Award winner Greg Maddux, Chipper Jones, John Smoltz, Javier Lopez and Tom Glavine), come early to sample the attractions, visit the Braves Museum and, most importantly, take the Turner Field tour. For Atlanta Braves tickets, you can reach TicketMaster at (800) 326-4000. Plan in advance, as games often sell out. The 1998 ticket prices did not change from 1997. They range from $5 to $30. If you are adventurous, $1 Skyline seats go on sale just before the game.

Tours are offered year round. In the off-season, tours are offered every half-hour from 9:30 AM to 3 PM Tuesdays through Saturdays, and 1 to 4 PM on Sundays. The tour schedule gets tricky during the season, for obvious reasons: Call (404) 614-2311 for schedules. For $7 for adults and $4 for children, you can get a guided tour of the Coca-Cola Skyfield, pressbox, a luxury suite, the visitors' dugout and the museum.

In the museum you'll find more than 200 artifacts, including the ball and bat that Hank Aaron used to break Babe Ruth's home run record. The Babe did a stint with the Braves himself when they were in Boston, so you'll find some relics of his career too, like the tiny baseballs he gave out to appease autograph seekers. The 1995 World Series trophy is on display, along with championship rings. The museum also traces the team's lean and hungry years in the 1970s and '80s, which have made the fat and happy years of the '90s particularly joyful for longsuffering Braves fans.

Until recently, many
people had never heard
of Savannah . . . . The
secret is definitely out.

Neighborhoods and Real Estate

Savannah was a well-kept secret for many years, according to local real estate experts. While places like Charleston and New Orleans garnered national attention as the "in" Southern hotspots, Savannah stayed quietly out of the spotlight, content in restoring its Historic Downtown, developing its suburbs and going about its daily business.

How things change. Since the late 1980s and early 1990s, factors ranging from media attention generated by a certain book to low interest rates have helped fuel a relatively solid market, resulting in steady sales and in some areas — especially the Historic Downtown and Tybee — significant jumps in housing prices, according to several local real estate experts. "It used to be that Savannah was the best-kept secret in the Southeast," said Realtor David Byck, who has been selling real estate in Savannah for 40 years. "Now we aren't that way."

Take the Historic Downtown. In the mid-1970s, Realtor Celia Dunn remembers selling a four-story home with a carriage house, off-street parking and side garden for $150,000. In 1997, the selling price for the same home, since restored, is $850,000. Another home she sold for $60,000 around 1976 is selling for $475,000 a little more than 20 years later. "When you have a finite commodity, once they are gone they are gone," said Dunn.

It is hard to believe, but there was a time when it seemed as if you couldn't give property away in the Historic Downtown. In the late 1950s, this area was full of dilapidated, abandoned and neglected buildings. Like several places around the country, many residents had slowly left the city core for the suburbs. Resto-

ration didn't become a priority until 1955, when a historically significant building (the Isaiah Davenport House; see our Attractions chapter) was going to be demolished to make room for a parking lot. This prompted the formation of the Historic Savannah Foundation and the beginning of Savannah's resurrection.

By the mid-1970s, the restoration effort had received a boost when a couple from Atlanta decided to move to Savannah and start an art school. In 1979, Paula and Richard Rowan launched the Savannah College of Art and Design in a massive old building, part of which was once a greasy spoon cafe. The college continued acquiring and restoring buildings, many of them gigantic behemoths sprinkled throughout the Historic District. Because of years of neglect, these eyesores taking up huge chunks of space were often homes only for pigeons. As the college grew, it attracted more students needing places to live, which in turn fueled more restoration efforts as investors saw potential profits. Prices slowly started creeping upward, while the number of available houses to restore began to decline throughout the '80s.

Then came The Book.

Since hitting the book stands in 1994, John Berendt's *Midnight in the Garden of Good and Evil*, with more than 1.1 million copies in print, has brought hordes of tourists to Savannah. In fact, it is responsible for spawning an entire cottage industry of tourism. There are The Book walking tours, The Book bus tours, The Book T-shirts and The Book tourist shops. Magazines like *Condé Nast Traveler* were suddenly in town writing about Savannah. And, of course, The Book resulted in The Movie, directed by Clint Eastwood and starring Kevin Spacey and John Cusack, which premiered in November 1997. (See our chapter on The Book for more on this literary-fueled phenomenon.)

But The Book wasn't the only attention Savannah was getting in the mid-1990s. In 1996, Savannah was in the limelight hosting Olympic yachting during the Summer Olympic Games in Atlanta. Again, the city was being introduced to thousands of people who might never have heard of Savannah. That same year Savannah's historic beauty was spotlighted when PBS's popular series *This Old House* came to town to capture the renovation of a Monterey Square home. "The Olympics and *This Old House* made a lot of people aware of Savannah as a comfortable place to live," said Dunn, who has been selling homes in the Historic District for several decades. "Until then many people had never heard of Savannah."

The secret is definitely out. On Tybee, prices in some cases have risen as much as 50 percent in the last few years, according to Judy O'Neill of Tybee Island Realty. People were finding an all-too-scarce commodity — affordable beachfront property; it was just a matter of time before the laws of economics kicked in. "If you are looking for a bargain you are about five years too late," said O'Neill. "Tybee used to be a vacation spot where people had second homes. More and more people want to live here year round now."

A two-bedroom, two-bath condo with a view will cost around $135,000, while a newer home with three-bedrooms and no view will cost around $160,000. Classic old beach houses and oceanfront homes are becoming harder to find, as more people realize their value and sit on them, O'Neill said. If you do find one, it could cost $500,000 or more. (For more on Tybee Island neighborhoods and real estate, including realty company listings, see our Tybee Island chapter.)

Elsewhere in the county, especially the other islands and outlying suburbs, development has been on the rise. In fact, since 1980 permits for single-family homes have more than doubled in unincorporated areas of Chatham County, which includes the islands, according to the county permit office. In 1980, the number of permits issued for single-family homes was 409. In 1996, the county issued 823 single-family home permits. With development on the rise, prices in many cases have also steadily increased. "I think we are seeing areas going up in value throughout the county," said Gary Udinsky, chief appraiser for Chatham County. "We live in a very desirable part of the country. The force of supply and demand drove prices up."

However, prices haven't outpaced people's wallets. First-time home buyers will have no problem finding a home in most areas of the city, while those with significantly more money to spend shouldn't have any problem either. "We can take care of people who want a $60,000 home up to a $600,000 home," said Realtor Charles Lamas, who has been selling real estate on Savannah's eastern islands for several decades. "We have got the hardworking blue-collar workers up to the very rich, which makes it a neat community."

FYI

Unless otherwise noted, the area code for all phone numbers listed in this guide is 912.

Savannah Neighborhoods

There are stories about people coming to Savannah for a visit, only to return a few months later in a U-Haul. One couple, after a weekend getaway, went back to New York, quit their jobs and were back in town in a few

INSIDERS' TIP

There are dozens of neighborhood associations in Savannah. To find out information about a neighborhood group you are interested in, call the City of Savannah's Community Services Department at 651-6520.

Photo: Kyle Cason

Available houses in the Historic Downtown area are becoming increasingly difficult to find.

months. They fell in love with the romance of the city, they said. That was more than 20 years ago.

Soon after arriving, our newcomers face a very difficult decision — where to live. Savannah offers many choices — there is the beach, tree-lined suburbia and, of course, the Historic Downtown. Each neighborhood is as distinctive as those who call it home. As one Realtor said of living in the Historic Downtown, it is as much a way of life as a place to live. Outside your doorstep are coffee shops, art galleries and history. And it's the same story no matter where you are in the city. Each neighborhood provides a glimpse into people's lives and lifestyles. Travel through Midtown's Ardsley Park, and you will see kids playing in front of wonderfully colorful craftsman bungalows — wood-frame homes, typically with front porches and interesting architectural touches like archways and wood floors.

On the Islands, new homes sprawl out next to pristine golf courses, while special garages are tacked on just to make room for golf carts. Young professionals a few years out of college can often be found in new developments on the Southside, near the hustle and hurry of shopping malls, restaurants and everything commercial.

People are very proud of their neighbor-

hoods in Savannah and don't mind bragging about what makes their choice of location clearly the only place to live in the city. There are literally hundreds of neighborhoods in Savannah. To show their loyalty, in the Historic Downtown area alone there are more than 40 neighborhood associations.

Obviously, we can't list every Savannah neighborhood, but we have attempted to spotlight a few. It should provide a good cross-section to help determine where you want to sink your roots.

The Historic Downtown

The Historic Downtown is a miniature city within a city. Inside the 2.5-square-mile area you will find restaurants, churches, antique shops, museums, banks, government buildings, art galleries and even some wildlife — that is, if you count the hundreds of squirrels who call the many squares and parks home. (See the maps at the front of the guide for a close-up look at the Historic Downtown.)

Of course, there are also the houses. Hundreds of homes painstakingly restored to their original 19th-century splendor fill the area. Within a few steps in the Historic Downtown, you are apt to encounter wrought-iron balconies, bricked courtyards and other architectural delights like historic downspouts shaped like dolphins that empty water into the street.

No doubt you will also encounter tourists. It isn't unusual to find visitors wandering with John Berendt's *Midnight in the Garden of Good and Evil* in hand, asking directions to Mercer House or Bonaventure Cemetery — two places where significant parts of the plot unfold. Prior to the book's publication, these sights were just another beautiful historic house and another beautiful historic cemetery in another beautiful historic Southern city. In a South full of such charms, Savannah was one of many. Not any more.

The Historic Downtown is also an area of great diversity. Some of Savannah's wealthiest and oldest families live a door or two away from art students who came to town from California or Ohio or some international destination. In the Beach Institute area on the eastern edge of the district, many longstanding African-American families raise their children in homes that have been in the family for generations.

Home prices vary in the area, but because of the interest in living in the Historic Downtown, it is becoming increasingly difficult to find a home for less than $250,000. First-time buyers will find duplexes starting around $150,000, while a few condos are available for less than that. Glance through a local real estate book, and you will see listings in the Historic District ranging from as much as $499,000 for a renovated two-bedroom townhouse with a garden apartment, carriage house and courtyard to $112,000 for a small, frame, two-bedroom townhouse on the outskirts of the district.

Islands

Dutch Island

Dutch Island, an exclusive, gated enclave 20 minutes from downtown Savannah, is a popular choice for young professionals or those looking to move up to a larger home. The first neighborhoods on the island opened up 15 years ago. Today, it is home to about 300 families and is expected to reach its maximum capacity of 500 homes within the next few years. Spacious homes with pristine lawns and traditional architecture can be found throughout Dutch Island. Home sizes range from 2,400 square feet up to 12,000 square feet, while prices fall between $164,000 and $600,000.

Providence Plantation is the island's newest neighborhood. Half-acre lots start at $39,000, and homes begin at $225,000. Gourmet kitchens, hardwood floors, screened porches and fireplaces are just some of the many amenities available. There is also a pool, playground and lagoons stocked with fish for anglers. There are no recreation fees charged to use these facilities.

Isle of Hope

This peninsula in southeast Chatham County was an early summer resort for tourists. Situated with the Herb River on the west and the Skidaway River on the east, the community is one of Savannah's most picturesque. Beautiful old cottages with white picket fences and massive oak trees in the front yards overlook the waterways, while newer homes scatter throughout other neighborhoods. The very old and very new mix together nicely.

There is a small-town feel even though large developments and the hustle of Savannah are just 20 minutes away. Longtime residents live on Isle of Hope as well as young families and professionals. Home prices vary from modest, older two-bedroom bungalows lower than $100,000 to new three- and four-bedroom homes with all the amenities for $250,000 or more.

Long Point

More than 130 new homes have been built since 1992 at this popular Whitemarsh Island development. Conveniently located on Johnny Mercer Boulevard, it comfortably puts homeowners a short, 15-minute drive away from downtown or the Southside. Homes range in price from $229,000 to $450,000 and include many amenities like hardwood floors, cathedral ceilings, gourmet kitchens and more. Styles differ throughout the development from sprawling single-story brick homes with circular drives to two-story stuccos with large front porches. Wide streets circulate through the community, and there is a guard gate that is typically occupied during the evening hours. According to local real estate agents, when the most recent section of interior and lagoon lots opened at Long Point, 25 were sold within the first 60 days.

The Landings on Skidaway Island

Spend any time in Savannah and no doubt you will hear someone refer to "The Landings." This massive, gated community takes up approximately 4,450 acres on Skidaway Island and is considered among Savannah's premier developments. Started in 1972, The Landings is currently home to 6,500 residents from 45 states and 15 foreign countries.

Since debuting more than 20 years ago, four phases have been built at The Landings, providing a diversity of architectural styles in a variety of prices ranging from $200,000 to $900,000. In Midpoint, one area of the development, you will find Colonial, Federal and Southern Lowcountry homes, while traditional, ranch-style wooden homes can be found elsewhere. Corian countertops, custom cabinets, hardwood floors, cathedral ceilings, terraces and bay windows are just some of the many amenities available in homes at The Landings.

All the homes are on nicely landscaped lots that are often filled with trees, giving the feeling that you're living in the country, not a development with thousands of homes. The Landings' other main selling points include six golf courses, designed by such golfing luminaries as Arnold Palmer and Tom Fazio, 34 tennis courts, two marinas and a yacht club. At the Oakridge Fitness Center there is a pool, plus fitness and exercise rooms. At the Franklin Creek Activity Center, there is a pro shop, clubhouse, 25-meter pool with hydrospa and a snack bar. Membership fees are required to use the various facilities. After paying a substantial initial fee, monthly membership can cost between $100 and $300.

Although nearly all the original lots have been sold, there are usually about 100 listings, including resale homes and homesites, available at any one time, according to Gerrit Albert, marketing manager for The Landings. Many interested people purchase a lot a few years before retirement in anticipation of eventually building a home, Albert said. All development at The Landings is closely monitored and must be approved by the Architectural Review Board.

Southside/Midtown

Ardsley Park

Ardsley Park is Savannah's original suburb. Laid out in 1911, the development is south of the Historic Downtown and Victorian District in Savannah's Midtown. Although it was designed as a single residential subdivision, over the years it has grown to include a large area loosely bounded by Victory Drive on the north, 55th Street on the south, Bull Street on the west and Waters Avenue on the east.

Ardsley Park offers wide, tree-filled streets with many sizes and styles of older homes. Drive around and you will see large four- or five-bedroom mansions with elegant entrances, sun porches and several fireplaces selling for around $400,000. In other blocks, first-time home buyers with small children live in very nice craftsman-style bungalows with big backyards that they purchased for under $100,000. Because the area appeals to such a wide section of the community — from professionals to young families — it is a popular place to buy. Another major selling point is its Midtown location, which puts residents about

10 minutes away from either the Historic Downtown or the edge of the Southside. This desirability means it isn't unusual for homes in Ardsley Park, especially the good deals, to be snapped up the first day they hit the market.

Gordonston

Gordonston is a small neighborhood nestled into Savannah's eastside. It is made up of both longtime residents and newcomers and, according to local Realtors, is a popular spot for many local professionals including professors and others working in education.

Bordered by Skidaway Road, Gwinnett Street and Pennsylvania Avenue, it was developed in the 1920s by the brother of Juliette Gordon Low, the founder of the Girl Scouts, on property that was once part of the family farm. In some ways it is like a miniature Ardsley Park. Similar to its bigger cousin, throughout the development you will find tree-lined streets filled with a variety of older homes on large properties with front and back yards. Home styles include bungalows, cottages and large mansions, and they tend to be less expensive than those in Ardsley Park. First-time home buyers might be able to find a two- or three-bedroom bungalow for around $70,000, while someone needing more space could find a large three- or four-bedroom home for $150,000.

The Victorian District

Just south of the Historic Downtown, the Victorian District is several blocks roughly bounded by Victory Drive, Gwinnett Street, Martin Luther King Jr. Boulevard and East Broad Street. There you will find two- and three-story Victorian frame houses, many in various stages of disrepair.

Despite appearances, this residential area is increasingly becoming a popular spot for those interested in renovation work, especially as the number of houses needing work in the Historic Downtown continues to decline. It isn't

FYI

Unless otherwise noted, the area code for all phone numbers listed in this guide is 912.

unusual to find a very large Victorian home dating back to the 1800s, with porches, fireplaces, three or four bedrooms and other unique features for well under $100,000. It will, however, need a lot of work if not a complete overhaul. Restoration in the area is sporadic. On one block you may find two or three houses that have been restored, while a block away the entire area may be filled with abandoned homes.

Georgetown

Although Georgetown debuted in 1974 and is one of the oldest developments on Savannah's Southside, you will still find homes going up there. More than 1,600 homes have been built throughout the development, located off the far southern reaches of Abercorn Street on King George Boulevard. There are nine subdivisions in total in the community offering a variety of home styles and prices. First-time home buyers should be able to find a two-bedroom home in Georgetown for around $70,000. Others wanting to move up to a larger house with many amenities like gourmet kitchens, Corian countertops and hardwood floors, will be able to find what they are looking for in Georgetown for $250,000 and up.

West Chatham

Southbridge

Southbridge is a 1,100-acre planned community 8 miles west of the Historic Downtown. Developed by Hall Development of Myrtle Beach, South Carolina, it is the first community of its size to open in West Chatham. But as the area continues to grow, it is not expected to be the last.

More than 350 families, including a mix of retired residents, young families and professionals, have moved to Southbridge since its opening in 1987. As its literature explains, Southbridge is "a residential golf community blending Southern tradition with the amenities of a country club." Traditional Southern architecture is the development's hallmark. Drive around the neatly landscaped neighborhoods, and you will see classic Georgian and Federal-style wooden, brick and stucco homes nestled among trees or along fairways on the golf course. Inside are many extras including modern kitchens, high ceilings, parquet floors, formal dining rooms, fireplaces and breakfast nooks.

Two-, three- or four-bedroom home options are available from roughly 1,600 to 2,400 square feet; prices range from $140,000 to $500,000. Homeowners' association fees for 1997 were $342. One of the newest additions to the development is Steeple Run, offering three-bedroom townhouses of roughly 2,000 square feet. These run $165,000 to $185,000 and include such features as vaulted ceilings, hardwood floors and skylights. If you prefer, you can purchase a lot for $30,000 to $100,000 and have a home built to your specifications. You pick the home style, wallpaper, where you want it on the lot, and the builders do the rest.

Golf architect Rees Jones designed Southbridge's 18-hole course, which is rated one of Georgia's 25 best courses by *Golfweek Magazine*. The semiprivate Southbridge Golf Club includes a 6,000-square-foot clubhouse with a pro shop, dining room and lounge. Besides golf, there is the Southbridge Racquet and Swim Club, featuring 12 clay tennis courts, two hard courts, a swimming pool and spa. Membership dues are required to use these facilities.

Real Estate Companies

Regardless of the area or price range you are considering, there are hundreds of local Realtors ready to help you with your real estate needs. What follows is a rundown of some of the best in the area, but remember that this is a small sample. Companies are listed in alphabetical order.

Barroll and Barroll Realty Company
101 W. Liberty St. • 235-5665

Since returning to Savannah from Philadelphia in 1981, Margery and Larry Barroll have formed a family real estate business that includes their two sons. Together, the husband and wife team have been in the real estate

Photo: Kyle Cason

Washington Avenue, divided by a heavily forested and azalea-decked median, runs through Ardsley Park.

business since 1975. Although the Barroll's live in Ardsley Park and, in fact, have purchased many homes there themselves, they don't limit their business to that area — but it is one of their areas of expertise. Their listings are throughout Savannah and include Tybee.

David Byck Realty Company
13 E. York St. • 233-1276

Commercial and residential sales and property management are what this 25-year-old company concentrates on. While its commercial and residential departments often specialize in the Historic Downtown, its rental apartments and homes are located throughout the city including the Southside. The company's commercial department is affiliated with a national network specializing in commercial and industrial leasing. They also work with a national relocation group with more than 900 agents throughout the country. According to owner David Byck, who has been selling real estate for 40 years, the company's 10 agents strive to meet all the needs of someone relocating to Savannah, whether the person requires rental property or wants to buy a home.

Century 21 First Realty
4700-B U.S. Hwy. 80 • 897-2121

Charles Lamas, a licensed Realtor for 26 years and president-elect of the local Board of Realtors, is one of nine agents in this Century 21 office, which specializes in the eastern islands including Wilmington, Whitemarsh and Talahi, among others. This is one of several Century 21 offices throughout Savannah and the surrounding communities including Southside/Midtown and West Chatham. The various offices offer a variety of specialties and services including property management, commercial sales and relocation assistance.

Celia Dunn Realty Company
9 W. Charlton St. • 234-3323

Celia Dunn has been selling real estate in

the Historic Downtown for 20 years. In fact, her offices take up the bottom floor of a beautifully restored three-story home overlooking Madison Square. Besides specializing in the historic area, she and her six licensed agents sell in several other areas of Savannah including Ardsley Park, Habersham Woods, Tybee and Thunderbolt.

Konter Realty
5801 Abercorn St. • 354-9314

Konter Realty is one of Savannah's largest real estate companies, with 30 to 50 agents selling throughout the city and surrounding counties. It is also one of the oldest. Husband and wife team Lawrence and Harriet Konter founded the company 36 years ago in a small, two-room office in the Historic Downtown. Today, the family-run company occupies a 9,300-square-foot office building on Savannah's Southside. There are six individual divisions under the corporate umbrella of Konter Realty including real estate, construction and property management. The company also manages more than 500 residential units, along with 600,000 square feet of commercial/office space. Konter builds between 50 and 60 homes each year and is also involved in light commercial development including apartments, offices and retail buildings.

The Landings Company
P.O. Box 13848, Savannah, GA 31416
• 598-0500, (800) 841-7011

This real estate company is part of The Landings on Skidaway Island — Savannah's largest development and one of its most exclusive (see listing for The Landings in this chapter). Ten agents are in the office, which, of course, specializes in selling homes, lots and condos at The Landings.

Mopper-Stapen Realtors
22 E. Liberty St. • 238-0874

Mopper-Stapen has been in downtown Savannah for 15 years. During this time, the

---

INSIDERS' TIP

Residents of the Historic Downtown are issued free-parking stickers, which allow them to park their vehicles at meters near their homes without getting tickets.

company has been involved with many properties requiring renovation — sometimes entire neighborhoods with dozens of vacant houses. Besides specializing in historic properties, the company also concentrates on commercial real estate and property management. There are six agents in the company, which is located in a beautiful historic apartment building in the Historic Downtown.

Judy Nease Realty
7505-F Waters Ave. • 345-9966

Judy Nease's specialty is her own backyard: She has called Savannah's eastern islands home for the past 30 years. This is also where she sells the majority of her real estate. Nease has been in the business since 1978 and started her own company around the beginning of 1996. There are seven agents in the office, all of whom have been selling real estate for many years and have built up their own areas of expertise. The company also offers relocation services for people moving to the area.

The Prudential S. East Coastal Properties
1 Diamond Causeway • 355-4171

There are 28 agents in this office, which is the only Prudential affiliate in Savannah. Reva and Bob Laramy started the company in 1982 and offer many services including relocation, property management, short- and long-term rentals and commercial sales. The company sells real estate throughout the city from West Chatham to the Southside. However, one of their main areas of expertise is The Landings on Skidaway Island.

RE/MAX Professionals
6813 Johnny Mercer Blvd. • 897-1955

RE/MAX Professionals has 10 agents specializing in Wilmington, Tybee and other islands. Owner Lynda Werntz has been in real estate since 1978. The office is one of three RE/MAX offices is Savannah, each with its own area of expertise and services.

Shore, Bell and Seyles Realty
401 Mall Blvd., Suite 102B • 356-1653

Relocation is the specialty of Shore, Bell and Seyles Realty. As part of their relocation efforts, owners Carey Shore, Nick Bell and Charles Seyles, who each have 25 years of real estate experience, will send you a relocation packet, give you a tour of Savannah and even pick you up at the airport if you need a lift. They handle individual and corporate moves involving several employees. The company's main areas of concentration are Dutch Island and Long Point, two high-end island developments with properties ranging in price from $200,000 to $750,000.

Cora Bett Thomas Realty
24 East Oglethorpe Ave. • 233-6000

Drive around the Historic Downtown and more likely than not, you will see several Cora Bett Thomas Realty signs. Fifteen agents are in this office, which specializes in historic properties.

Apartments

Several apartment complexes complete with pools, recreation rooms and clubhouses are available in Savannah. Most have been built within the last 10 to 15 years, if not sooner, and will be found on the Islands and Southside/Midtown. The complexes are listed in *Apartment Finders*, a free publication found at newsstands and local supermarkets all around Savannah.

The Historic Downtown also has a healthy apartment rental market. Many residents have converted all or part of their private homes into apartments, and there are also a few apartment buildings to chose from. With the influx of art students wanting to live downtown, finding an apartment in this area has become more of a challenge. Demand in some cases outpaces supply, so prices have been on the rise. Typically, you can find a one-bedroom apartment starting around $600 a month, while a two-bedroom will rent for around $650. However, depending on the apartment's size, quality and amenities, monthly rents can go for more than $1,000 in some cases.

One of the best ways to find apartments in the Historic Downtown is to check local newspapers including the *Savannah Morning News* and the *Georgia Guardian* (see our Media chapter). However, many owners don't bother advertising and simply post a "For Rent" sign on their apartment — a walk or drive around town is a good way to get leads.

Photo: Phyl M. Gatlin

The Historic Downtown is not just a tourist attraction — it's
also a home for many Savannahians.

You will also find houses for rent in several areas of Savannah including Southside, Midtown and the Islands. The homes vary from area to area and can include everything from older bungalows to new homes in gated developments. Like apartment rentals, many of the owners simply post a "For Rent" sign or advertise in a local newspaper. Some list their homes with local Realtors. Prices ranges from about $500 to $800 a month.

Real Estate Publications

Along with the periodicals listed below, check the *Savannah Morning News,* which carries regular real estate listings.

Homes & Land
(800) 240-2157

This nationwide publication, distributed free in newspaper racks around town, lists several dozen area homes for sale. In general, it tends to concentrate on listings for Tybee Island and the Historic Downtown.

Savannah Area Real Estate Today
1800 East Victory Dr. • 238-2040

This fat publication is created by Morris Newspaper Corporation, which also publishes Savannah's daily newspaper. Distributed every other week, it includes hundreds of listings (updated regularly) from all over the city and the surrounding area.

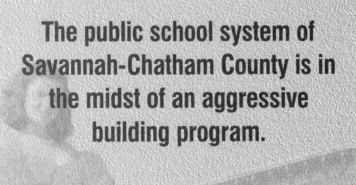

The public school system of
Savannah-Chatham County is in
the midst of an aggressive
building program.

Education and Child Care

Education

Savannah and Chatham County offer a wide spectrum of educational opportunities. In addition to the forward-looking public school system, there are a variety of private high schools, a technical school, two universities and the largest art school in the United States. This chapter presents overviews of all these plus a broad look at what's available in the area of child care.

Public Schools

Savannah-Chatham County Public Schools
208 Bull St. • 651-7000

The public school system of Savannah-Chatham County is in the midst of an aggressive building program that will result in the opening of seven new schools between the summer of 1997 and the year 2000. Coastal Middle School opened on Whitemarsh Island in August 1997; it's the first middle school built in the county in 40 years and one of five being constructed as part of the program. The adjacent Marshpoint Elementary School opened at the same time.

The new Savannah High School, being built on the city's east side and scheduled to be ready for the 1998-99 school year, will replace its namesake in Midtown on Washington Avenue. The old Savannah High, which was built in 1937, will house a magnet school dedicated to the arts and might become the home of a teacher-training center.

The Savannah-Chatham school system serves 35,000-plus students in pre-kindergarten (4-year-olds) through 12th grade. They are enrolled at 44 schools and participate in six alternative programs. As of fall 1997, there were 29 elementary schools, nine middle schools and six high schools in the system.

Among the alternative programs are the Coastal Georgia Comprehensive Academy, for students with severe emotional and/or behavioral disorders and autism; the Pearl Smith Learning Center, for students being disciplined for violating school policies; the Savannah Corporate Academy, which provides education for dropouts and potential dropouts by combining job skills training with academic instruction; and the Westside Academy, which uses small classes and computer-assisted instruction to allow at-risk students to work at their own pace.

The system has an extensive Magnet Academy program that enables students to concentrate on special talents and interests. Twenty-two magnet programs are available at 20 elementary, middle and high schools, including academies for the fine and performing arts, writing/communications technology, biological sciences, computer science, international studies, foreign language, military science/aviation and engineering and robotics. These academies use enhanced facilities and offer intensive curricula taught by specially trained teachers. There is also a SEARCH program for gifted students; participants are involved in a curriculum that's more advanced, mature and sophisticated.

The average class size at schools in the system is 25. There is an emphasis on computer technology, and the system has more than 6,000 computers in its classrooms and access to the Internet at each school. The system has 160 partnerships with the business community through which business people voluntarily assist individual schools in areas such as mentoring, accomplishing building projects, cleaning up campuses and raising funds.

FYI

Unless otherwise noted, the area code for all phone numbers listed in this guide is 912.

Two unique features of the local system are the Massie Heritage Interpretation Center and the Oatland Island Education Center (see our Attractions chapter). Massie, which is at 207 E. Gordon Street, is the oldest standing school in Georgia. The school does not hold regular classes, but programs on the history of Georgia are offered. Teachers arrange for their classes to attend programs at Massie. Oatland, at 711 Sandtown Road, covers 175 acres, and its 1.75-mile Discovery Trail takes visitors through woodlands, past marshes and to specially constructed habitats of endangered and protected animals of the state — wolves, bison, panthers and birds of prey among them. There's a recreation of a Colonial settlement and a barnyard where youngsters can get a feel for life on the farm, past and present. The Oatland staff holds several special events throughout the year, including a festival featuring sheep shearing in March and a crafts festival in November (see our Annual Events and Festivals chapter).

Private Schools

Savannah's private high schools provide teenagers and their parents with alternatives to what's offered by the public school system. Most of the private schools are Christian-based, and all are focused on preparing their students for college.

These are co-ed schools for the most part, but there is a school for girls and one that admits only male students. There's at least one private high school in each section of the city, with the majority being centrally located in the Midtown area.

Benedictine Military School
6502 Seawright Dr.
• **356-3500**

This Catholic high school for boys dates back to 1902, when it was founded on Bull and 33rd streets as Benedictine College. Having sons become "BC boys" is a tradition in many Savannah families, a circumstance that has led this military school for 9th through 12th graders to have an extremely faithful and active group of alumni. Sixty percent of those who attend the school are Catholic, but the remainder of the student body is as diverse as the faculty, which is composed of Benedictine priests and monks, laymen and laywomen and military retirees. Enrollment is about 450, and the ratio of students to faculty members is 16-to-1.

Benedictine is a college prep school, and 94 percent of graduates attend college. The school is housed in large, contemporary-style buildings on 90 acres in the Southside. It was moved there in the early 1960s; until that time, students received military training during all four years of school. Since then, however, Junior ROTC classes have been mandatory only for freshmen and sophomores and optional for juniors and seniors. Fifty to 55 percent of upperclassmen continue to participate in JROTC, training that can give them an advan-

INSIDERS' TIP

Several of Savannah's private schools compete athletically as members of the Georgia High School Association, which means they play against public schools as well as other private institutions. Calvary, Country Day and Savannah Christian participate in Class A, the division for the association's small schools, and Benedictine and St. Vincent's are in Class AAAA along with the largest schools in the state.

Photo: Kyle Cason

Children from Savannah's public schools celebrate the
arrival of spring with the traditional Maypole dance.

tage should they elect to attend a military college or enter the armed forces out of high school.

The school's mission calls on its faculty to "value all individuals as children of God with emphasis on the Benedictine principles of prayer, work and hospitality." The school offers opportunities for students to compete in a full range of sports, including a couple not normally encountered in this part of the universe — wrestling and team rowing. There are also rifle and drill teams. Extracurricular activities at Benedictine start an hour after the end of school so that participants can avail themselves of the after-school tutoring program.

Bible Baptist School
4700 Skidaway Rd. • 352-3067

The administration and faculty of Bible Baptist seek to educate the whole child while emphasizing the spiritual side of students' development. Bible is taught in every class of this traditional Christian school, which has an enrollment of 250 students in 4-year-old kindergarten through high school. The co-ed, college-prep school is a mission of Bible Baptist Church, and it's located on a 19-acre church-school complex that includes a football stadium and a gymnasium with two full basketball courts. Although the school is open to students of all faiths, the teaching of Christian values is stressed.

Spacious classrooms give teachers plenty of room for learning centers and computer corners, and the average class size is 16 to 17 students. Ninety percent of graduates attend college. Among school traditions are the ceremony at which juniors are presented their senior class rings, where students receive their rings from parents or friends and attend a social gathering afterward, and the Thanksgiving feasts held in each classroom on the Wednesday before the holiday, with parents, grandparents and siblings invited to join in. Bible Baptist, which was founded in the mid-1960s in reaction to the ban on prayer in public schools and what was seen as a lack of discipline there, has a full program of varsity athletics supplemented by the church's recreational program, which provides opportunities to participate in sports to students ages 14 and younger. The school is a member of the Georgia Christian Athletic Association.

Calvary Day School
4625 Waters Ave. • 351-2299

This co-ed school in Savannah's Midtown is a ministry of Calvary Baptist Temple and is open to students of all faiths and creeds. The school and church occupy 22 acres at Waters Avenue and 63rd Street. The school started downtown with a kindergarten class in 1961 under the leadership of the Rev. John T. Tippitt Jr., and a grade was added each year. Calvary, which moved south to Midtown in 1964, now provides Christian-based education to some 800 students in its elementary, middle and high schools.

According to school officials, academics are blended with a strong program of athletics and other activities to help students evolve into well-rounded citizens. The student-teacher ratio is 17-to-1. The curriculum is designed to prepare students for college, and 95 percent of Calvary's graduates attend institutions of higher learning. Among the tools used in accomplishing the goal of readying students for life after high school are five computer labs and a Resource Center. The three teachers of the Resource Center help students who might be struggling academically to build the skills they need to progress in their classes.

Calvary grants its oldest students senior privileges such as allowing them to buy lunches that are brought in from nearby restaurants, wear blue jeans to school on certain days and finish their last year a week ahead of students in lower classes. The school offers a full program of athletics and has its own football stadium and track, a complex named M.C. Anderson Field. In addition to providing day care for young children through the 2nd grade and an after-school program for kids in grades 3 through 6, the school has an early-morning program that starts at 6:45 AM.

Memorial Day School
6500 Habersham St. • 352-4535

Memorial, an all-faith, co-ed school, was founded in 1971 by Memorial Baptist Church and had its first graduating class five years later. Although the school shares its Midtown location at the corner of Habersham Street and Stephenson Avenue with the church, the school is independent and has its own board of directors. Memorial is a college prep school for students in pre-kindergarten (age 4)

through high school and also provides care for children as young as 6 weeks.

Memorial aspires to prepare students for college and adult life by tending to their spiritual, social, emotional and physical growth. There are about 360 students in pre-kindergarten through 12th grade, and average class sizes are 14 students in the lower school, 18 in the middle school and 22 in high school. From 90 to 95 percent of graduates continue their education by attending college. Seniors at Memorial who qualify academically can participate in a joint enrollment program with Armstrong Atlantic State University (see subsequent listing) that enables them to take courses at the school and receive college credit for doing so. As a member of the Georgia Independent Schools Association, Memorial provides its students with a full range of athletic and extracurricular activities. There are before- and after-school programs for kids up through the 6th grade.

St. Andrew's School
601 Penn Waller Rd. • 897-4941

The upper school at St. Andrew's is the only high school on the eastside islands. In addition to the upper school, which is for grades 6 through 12, St. Andrew's has a preschool for 2 and 3-year-olds and a lower school for pupils in 4-year-old kindergarten through 5th grade. About 300 children are enrolled at the co-ed, college prep school, which is on 25 tree-filled acres on Wilmington Island.

According to Headmaster Larry Berry, St. Andrew's seeks to "inspire passion for learning," prepare students to be leaders in the community and develop their personal integrity. The student-teacher ratio is 12-to-1, and all graduates attend college. A series of scholarship seminars, an online counseling office and school-arranged tours of various colleges assist students in making their post-secondary decisions. St. Andrew's is also attempting to help younger students begin thinking about careers by starting a school-to-work program that allows 8th graders to "shadow" people in the work force over a two-week period during the school year. The school offers a broad range of extracurricular activities, including participation in nine varsity sports, with St. Andrew's competing in the South Carolina Independent School Association because of its proximity to similar-size schools in the Palmetto State.

St. Andrew's has its roots in a day school that was begun downtown in 1947 by Independent Presbyterian Church. During the 1970s, the session of the church formulated plans for a larger institution, and the result was St. Andrew's, which was founded on Wilmington Island in late 1978. Although the school is no longer affiliated with Independent Presbyterian, St. Andrew's retains aspects of its Scottish heritage, including a field day in the fall when the school holds its own Scottish games.

St. Vincent's Academy
207 E. Liberty St. • 236-5508

St. Vincent's — a Catholic, college-prep school for girls — is the only private high school in the Historic District. The three main buildings of the school cover a city block on the south side of Liberty Street between Abercorn and Lincoln streets, the school's location since its founding in 1845 by the Sisters of Mercy. That religious order still operates the school although the majority of the faculty is composed of lay teachers. The school also has a gymnasium on Harris Street and a library at Liberty and Lincoln streets.

St. Vincent's, which teaches grades 9 through 12, is open to students of all faiths; about two-thirds of the student body of 365 is Catholic. Class sizes average about 15 students, and between 95 and 100 percent of graduates attend college. St. Vincent's places an emphasis on Christian values and "the acceptance of individuals as God's gift to the world," says the principal, Sister Helen Marie Buttimer. The administration feels being downtown is a plus because it enables students to experience an urban environment and brings them in contact with Savannah's history and culture. St. Vincent's competes in seven varsity sports — volleyball, softball, basketball, tennis, track, soccer and swimming.

The school has a long tradition of graduates sending their daughters to their alma mater; a member of the Class of 1997 represented the fifth generation of one family whose women had attended St. Vincent's. Another tradition is the school's elaborate commencement ceremony, which is held at the Cathedral of St. John the Baptist.

Savannah Christian Preparatory School
1599 Chatham Pkwy. • 233-9607

Savannah Christian offers a college pre-

Benedictine Military School, a parochial high school for boys, stages a Pearl Harbor memorial.

Photo: Kyle Cason

paratory curriculum in a nondenominational, Christian atmosphere at two campuses. The heavily wooded, 300-acre campus on Chatham Parkway in West Chatham is the site of the upper school (grades 9 through 12), a lower school (kindergarten through 5th grade) and a preschool and day-care center (for children 6 weeks to 4 years old). A 25-acre campus at 2415 DeRenne Avenue accommodates a smaller lower school and a middle school (grades 6 through 8). Each campus has dining facilities, a gymnasium and computer labs. The Chatham Parkway campus is also the site of a new science building that opened in September 1997 and of EDEN (Ecological Diversity for Educational Networking), a 125-acre outdoor education center that provides a wetlands laboratory for science students.

FYI

Unless otherwise noted, the area code for all phone numbers listed in this guide is 912.

The emphasis at Savannah Christian is on the basics of education and teaching students responsibility. Just about all of the graduates go on to college. The ratio of students to teachers ranges from 20- to 25-to-1. A wide variety of athletics is available, and the middle school has its own football field. The co-ed school has its roots in the Emanuel Bible School, which was started in 1951 on the West Chatham site by the Rev. George Akins, a Presbyterian minister who founded Savannah's Union Mission. In its early days the school served the children of the city's homeless; it became Savannah Christian School in the 1960s, when ties with Union Mission were severed, and assumed its current name in the late '70s. The DeRenne campus, former site

of Hancock Day School, was acquired in the 1980s. Savannah Christian's projected enrollment for the 1997-98 school year was 1,385.

Savannah Country Day School
824 Stillwood Dr. • 925-8800

Country Day strives to fulfill its motto — "Searching for the excellence in each of us" — through a college prep program that emphasizes top-flight performance in academics, the arts and athletics. The student-teacher ratio at the school is 16-to-1, and all of the graduates attend four-year colleges. The average SAT scores of students at Country Day are among the highest in Georgia, and the co-ed school offers 13 Advanced Placement courses. Six members of the Class of 1996 were National Merit finalists.

Country Day has 980 students enrolled in its schools: pre-kindergarten for 4-year-olds, kindergarten for 5-year-olds, and lower, middle and upper schools. A broad range of athletics and extracurricular activities is offered. In 1997 Country Day was in the midst of accomplishing a long-range plan that included the completion of the $1.1 million Lewis Leadership Center, the $1.2 million renovation of the Charles Gay Library, the building of a third gymnasium and the doubling of its endowment fund for need-based financial aid to $500,000 by the year 2000. The Leadership Center houses facilities for the upper school student body such as the college placement center, one of the school's two computer labs, a student center and classroom space. The renovation of

INSIDERS' TIP

There's Hope for Georgia residents entering their freshmen years at the state's colleges and universities. The Hope Scholarship, that is, which pays tuition and up to $100 per quarter for books to students who have earned a B average in high school. B students attending eligible private colleges in Georgia can receive Hope in the amount of $3,000 per academic year. Students can renew these scholarships in their sophomore, junior and senior years by maintaining 3.0 grade-point averages in college. Hope is funded by the Georgia Lottery for Education. For more information on the Hope program, call (770) 414-3085 or (800) 546-HOPE.

the library converted it into a fully electronic media center with 47 computers.

The Country Day campus is on 65 wooded acres tucked away in the Windsor Forest subdivision on the Southside. The school moved there in 1957 from a building on Forsyth Park that had been the home of the Pape School for Girls from 1905 until 1955, the year Country Day was chartered.

Technical Schools

Savannah Technical Institute
5717 White Bluff Rd. • 351-3662

Savannah Tech seeks to provide the local business and industrial community with highly trained workers — a service it has rendered since its founding by the Savannah Chamber of Commerce as the Opportunity School in 1929. Back then, the school turned out mainly stenographers and clerks; these days, the emphasis is on producing workers who are well-versed in the technological aspects of modern business and industry and are able to function as part of a team.

From the mid-1940s until the summer of 1997, the school was governed mainly by the Savannah-Chatham County Board of Education. Savannah Tech is now governed solely by the Georgia Department of Technical and Adult Education and is part of a statewide network of 33 post-secondary schools The school provides instruction for 2,000 students earning credit toward certificates, diplomas and associate degrees in 40 fields of study and for 2,500 noncredit students who are upgrading their job skills or taking part in industry-specific programs.

Students working toward certificates that would enable them to work in jobs such as aircraft structural assembler or certified nurse assistant should expect to spend from three to six months taking courses; to earn a diploma in fields such as marketing management or electronic technology, 12 to 15 months; and to obtain an associate degree in areas such as accounting or biomedical engineering technology, 24 months. Savannah Tech serves the four-county area of Chatham, Bryan, Effingham and Liberty from its main campus on the Southside and a satellite center in Liberty County. The main campus consists of four separate buildings on 37.5 well-manicured acres that were once part of Hunter Army Airfield. There are 60 full-time and 60 part-time instructors, and the average class size is 18 students.

Colleges and Universities

Armstrong Atlantic State University
11935 Abercorn St. • 927-5277, (800) 633-2349

Armstrong provides 75 fields of study through its College of Arts and Sciences, College of Education, School of Health Professions and School of Graduate Studies. The university's teacher education program has gained national recognition, and its computer science and chemistry programs are also particularly strong. Master's degrees are offered in history, criminal justice, nursing, health science, education and physical therapy. Armstrong has an abundance of evening and weekend classes.

INSIDERS' TIP

The Savannah-Chatham County public school system allows individual schools to adopt a policy enabling students to wear uniforms on a voluntary basis. Three-quarters of the faculty and three-quarters of the parents of students at a school must vote in favor of uniforms for the policy to be placed in effect. Students at these schools are not required to wear uniforms, but they have opted to do so in most cases. Uniforms were worn at about 25 schools during the 1996-97 school year. Private high schools where uniforms are worn are Benedictine, St. Vincent's and Savannah Christian.

A total of 5,100 undergraduates and 500 graduate students attend the school, and they are taught by 250 instructors, including mathematics professor Anne Hudson, who was the Carnegie Foundation's 1997 National Teacher of the Year at the senior college and university level. The great majority of students are commuters, and most hold full-time or part-time jobs. Armstrong has a somewhat mature student body: The average age is 27. The school is situated in the Southside on 250 acres dotted with pine trees and azalea bushes, and the campus recently has been graced with the addition of a sports center (in 1995) and University Hall, an 85,000-square-foot classroom and office building (in fall 1997).

Armstrong moved to the Southside in 1966 from Bull and Gaston streets in the Historic Downtown, where it was founded in 1935 as Armstrong Junior College, which was then a city-supported school. It became a part of the University System of Georgia in 1959, gained college status in 1964 and achieved university status in 1996, when its name was changed from Armstrong State College to Armstrong Atlantic State University. The school fields NCAA Division II teams in men's basketball, baseball, tennis and cross-country and in women's basketball, fast-pitch softball, cross-country, volleyball and tennis (the 1995 and '96 teams were national champions). Armstrong hosts more than 200 cultural events each year including a faculty lecture series, concerts and dramatic presentations, all of them open to the public and most of them free. The university is also the site of a criminal justice training center providing instruction to law enforcement officers from 19 surrounding Georgia counties.

Savannah College of Art and Design
345 Bull St. • 238-2483, (800) 869-SCAD

The Savannah College of Art and Design has grown tremendously since its founding in 1979 by Richard and Paula Rowan, who came from Atlanta and started the private, co-ed school with one building and 71 students. Today, SCAD is the largest art school in the country with its enrollment of 2,400 undergraduates and 1,100 graduate students. The college has 47 buildings spread throughout the

Historic and Victorian districts, many of them of historic significance and beautifully renovated by the school. The college's restoration efforts have been so striking that the National Trust for Historic Preservation awarded SCAD the National Honor Award for Historic Preservation in 1994.

The college offers bachelor's degrees in fine arts and architecture and master's degrees in arts, fine arts and architecture through its schools of building arts, fine arts, communications and media arts and three-dimensional design. Among fields of study are historic preservation, interior design, painting, photography, furniture design and industrial design. Programs involving computer art and graphic design attract scads of students, if you'll pardon the expression. The student-teacher ratio is 16-to-1.

The median age of students is 20, and they come from throughout the United States and from 83 foreign countries; only about 12 percent of the student body hails from Georgia. Thirty percent live in the school's six residence halls, several of which are former hotels, inns or apartment buildings. SCAD has more than 30 student organizations and an intercollegiate athletic program fielding teams in basketball, tennis, volleyball, crew, baseball, softball and soccer. The school competes in NCAA Division III, and its women's basketball and volleyball teams reached the playoffs in 1997.

Savannah State University
B.J. James Dr., Thunderbolt • 356-2186

Savannah State University has three colleges — Science and Technology, Business Administration and Liberal Arts and Social Sciences — offering a total of 23 undergraduate degrees, and two master's degree programs (social work and public administration). The campus in the town of Thunderbolt covers 165 acres, many of them shaded by large oak trees festooned with Spanish moss. The eastern portion of the campus is bordered by salt marsh and the Wilmington River; that and the school's proximity to the Atlantic Ocean (about 8 air miles) led to its sobriquet of "College by the Sea," which it was called for many years before its upgrade to university status by the Georgia Board of Regents in 1996. Now it's known, not surprisingly, as the "University by the Sea."

The school was founded in 1890 as Georgia State Industrial College for Colored Youths and retained that name until 1950, when the Regents dubbed it Savannah State College. It has been known as a traditionally black institution, and Savannah State has a student body that is 90 percent African American, but university officials say the student population and faculty become more diverse each year. There are 2,800 students, with 130 of them in graduate programs, and 165 instructors, 75 percent of whom hold doctorates.

Savannah State has a full-scale athletic program and competes intercollegiately in football, baseball, track and field and men's and women's basketball. There are 75 student organizations, including honor societies for high-ranking students in every major field of study, a theater group, concert choir, gospel choir and marching band. The school also has its own FM radio station, WHCJ, which broadcasts 14 hours a day.

South College
709 Mall Blvd. • 691-6000

This small, four-year commuter college offers bachelor of business administration degrees in four areas of concentration — finance, hospitality management, management information systems and organizational communications — and associate of science degrees in accounting, business administration, computer information systems, medical assisting and paralegal studies. The school is attended by about 400 students, 85 percent of them women. The average age of students is 28, but the student population has been getting younger since the college attained four-year status in 1996. The average class size is 12.

The school dates to 1899, when it was founded as Draughon's Practical Business College. The college was situated in various downtown locations prior to 1980, when the 4.5-acre main campus was established on Mall Boulevard in the Southside. The school also has a conference center, with offices and classrooms on nearby Mall Court, and operates its nursing assistant program at a building on Forsyth Park. The college was purchased by the South family in 1975, renamed Draughons

Junior College two years later and became South College in 1986. There is no athletic program, but the college does have a student government organization and several clubs related to specific fields of study.

Child Care

The state of Georgia regulates the businesses of people who provide care for more than two children at a time. To comply with state law, a person who provides care for from three to six children in his or her home — officially called a family day-care home — must obtain a certificate from the Child Care Licensing Section of the Georgia Department of Human Resources.

Persons operating businesses caring for more than six children must obtain licenses. Such businesses fall within two categories: group day-care homes, which provide supervision and care for seven to 18 children either in a home or another location, and day-care centers, which provide care and supervision for 19 or more children. To be certified or licensed, the operator of a child-care business must be at least 21 years old, have a high school or general equivalency diploma and pass criminal background and fingerprinting checks. They must have completed training in first aid and in infant and child cardiopulmonary resuscitation, and must annually undergo 10 hours of continuing education in health and safety and child development.

When you're shopping for child care, make sure the provider you're dealing with is registered with or licensed by the state. Take a good look at the facility you're visiting; ascertain that the inspection data on the fire extinguisher is current, that the smoke alarm and telephone operate properly and that rooms are in good repair, well-lit and spacious. Check to see if instructions involving fire drills and other emergency procedures are posted. Ask about the program offered — it should provide age-appropriate toys and activities that encourage children to use their five senses.

As of the summer of 1997, there were 432 family day-care homes and a total of 113 group day-care homes and day-care centers operating in Chatham County. They offer a wide variety of care — everything from the legal minimum to operations featuring state-funded and private pre-kindergarten programs, field trips and other extracurricular activities, plus food programs that serve balanced meals.

Caregiver Connections
10 W. 31st St. • 238-0002, (800) 281-9343

A great way to start your search for the child care that meets your needs is by calling Caregiver Connections, a child-care resource and referral service of Lutheran Ministries of Georgia. This child placement agency is licensed by the Department of Human Resources and serves 10 counties in coastal Georgia including Chatham. Tell the Caregiver representative about your requirements involving child care; you will be given five or six referrals to check out. You will be charged a fee for this service, but it is income-based and won't exceed $25.

Parent counseling is also available from Lutheran Ministries, which administers the A+ Parenting program. This program provides support for people striving to be good parents and is a collaborative effort involving Lutheran Ministries, the University of Georgia Cooperative Extension Service, Memorial Medical Center's Community Health Education Program, the Housing Authority of Savannah and the Georgia Council on Child Abuse. For more information on the program, call 652-7981 or 238-0599.

Babysitting Services

Vacationers in need of babysitting or drop-in child-care services should speak to the con-

Photo: Kyle Cason

School children celebrate the state's founding during the annual Georgia Day celebration.

cierge or desk clerk at their hotel, motel or inn. Most establishments have lists of child-care providers who offer short-term services. Among these are Angel's and Imp's Babysitting Agency, 355-1655, and The Savannah Nannies, 925-1776.

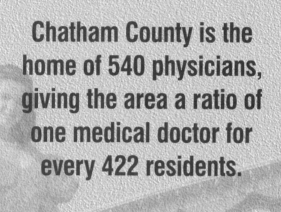

Chatham County is the home of 540 physicians, giving the area a ratio of one medical doctor for every 422 residents.

Healthcare

Savannah has experienced the good fortune of being a magnet for medical care almost since its founding in 1733. According to historians Preston Russell and Barbara Hines, the city's "first civic hero" was a physician, Dr. Samuel Nunes Ribeiro, who was among a boatload of Portuguese Jews who came to the town about five months after Savannah was settled. Georgia's founder, James Oglethorpe, credited Nunez, as he became known, with saving the colonists from the fevers that had killed several of them, including the only other doctor, William Cox.

The city was the site of Georgia's first hospital, a facility incorporated in 1808, and since the mid-1950s Savannah has been served by three large hospitals, two of which merged into a single healthcare system in the spring of 1997. The other hospital, Memorial Medical Center, is the regional tertiary medical center, a circumstance that draws many medical specialists to the area.

The latest available statistics involving healthcare indicate that Chatham County is the home of 540 physicians, giving the area a ratio of one medical doctor for every 422 residents. Georgia's first public health agencies were established in Savannah more than 100 years ago to combat yellow fever and improve the health of poor children. Since then, public health services have been expanded to offer preventive health services to all residents of the area and to provide primary care to those who do not have private physicians.

Hospitals

Memorial Medical Center
4700 Waters Ave. • 350-8000

This 530-bed hospital in Savannah's Midtown offers tertiary care to residents of 35 counties in southeast Georgia and southern South Carolina. In this role, Memorial provides the region with several one-of-a-kind facilities and services including the area's only pediatric intensive care unit (part of The Backus Children's Hospital); the only perinatal testing center; the only emergency helicopter service (LIFESTAR); the only ambulance specially equipped for sick newborns (Angel 3); and the only Level I trauma center, meaning the medical center offers extensive, immediate, round-the-clock services for emergency, life-threatening needs.

Memorial's Women & Infants center is one of only six perinatal centers in Georgia, and the Neonatal Intensive Care Nursery is among only five in the state. The hospital's Center for Cancer Care is southeast Georgia's referral source for cancer treatment and its Heart Institute is the regional coordinator of comprehensive cardiovascular services. Memorial's 50-acre campus is also the site of the Georgia Eye Institute, the Georgia Ear Institute, the Georgia Neurological Institute and the Rehabilitation Center, which provides a comprehensive regimen of services for people recovering from illnesses and injuries.

Memorial opened in 1955 as a 300-bed general hospital. As a regional referral center, it now ranks in size among the top 5 percent of hospitals in the United States and employs more than 4,000 people, with about 1,300 of those working for CareOne, Memorial's home care organization. CareOne brings home care to patients in 34 counties throughout southeastern Georgia and southern South Carolina, with its nurses providing services ranging from giving simple medications to highly technical care. Memorial is also a teaching hospital, being affiliated with the Medical College of Georgia, Mercer University School of Medicine and Emory University School of Medicine. Another feature of the medical center is its physician network of 36 practices for family doctors, internists and other specialists.

St. Joseph's/Candler Health System

This healthcare system was created in April 1997 as the result of the merger of Savannah's two oldest hospitals, 305-bed St. Joseph's on the Southside and 335-bed Candler in Midtown. The system has four Centers of Excellence — The Birthplace at Telfair, the Center of Orthopaedic Excellence, the Neurosensory Center and the HeartCare Center — and also offers services involving gastro-enterology, women's health, sports medicine, geriatrics, wellness, cancer care, diabetes treatment and management and outpatient surgery.

FYI

Unless otherwise noted, the area code for all phone numbers listed in this guide is 912.

Beyond these hospital services, the system maintains a presence in almost every community in southeast Georgia via its network of 55 primary-care physicians representing St. Joseph's Health Center, the SouthCoast Medical Group and the Candler Medical Group.

St. Joseph's Hospital
11705 Mercy Blvd. • 925-4100

This general acute-care hospital dates to 1875 when the Sisters of Mercy of the Roman Catholic Church took over operations of the Forest City Marine Hospital, a facility in downtown Savannah that specialized in the treatment of sick seamen. A year later, the operation was moved to more spacious facilities at Taylor and Habersham streets and renamed St. Joseph's Infirmary. It was named St. Joseph's Hospital in 1901 and expanded several times before a new facility was built on the Southside in 1970.

In the years between the move south and the merger with Candler, St. Joseph's accomplished a $7 million expansion of its Emergency and Outpatient Building and opened its Sports Medicine Center, Multiple Sclerosis

Clinic and Diabetes Management Center. The hospital is sited on 28 acres and is affiliated with the Mayo Clinic Jacksonville and Neumors Children Hospital in north Florida.

Candler Hospital
5353 Reynolds St.
• 692-6000

One of the longest continually operating hospitals in the United States and the first in Georgia, Candler was founded in 1805 and chartered in 1808 as the Savannah Poor House and Hospital. A new facility of the same name was built on Gaston Street in 1819, used as a Confederate hospital during the Civil War and renamed Savannah Hospital in 1872. The first school of nursing in Savannah was established there in 1902, and 28 years later the Methodist Episcopal Church purchased the hospital from the city and renamed it Warren A. Candler Hospital in honor of one of its bishops.

During the 1960s, the hospital was renamed Candler General Hospital and expanded through the purchase of the Telfair Hospital (which became its obstetrical unit) and the Central of Georgia Railway Hospital. Construction of a new hospital at DeRenne Avenue and Reynolds Street began in fall 1978, and it was opened in late 1980. Its name was changed to Candler Hospital in 1992, with the word "General" being dropped to reflect the hospital's growth in specialized healthcare services. Candler is affiliated with the Emory University System of Health Care.

Physician Referral Services

Savannah has three services you can contact for help in finding doctors and obtaining

---

INSIDERS' TIP

Free blood pressure checks are available at the City of Savannah's nine fire stations, at the Southside Fire Department's stations and during business hours (Monday through Friday from 8:30 AM to 4 PM) at the office of the Community Cardiovascular Council at 1900 Abercorn Street.

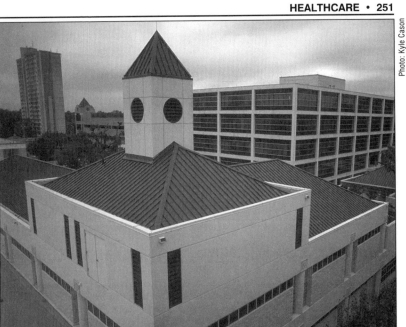

Photo: Kyle Cason

Memorial Medical Center is Chatham County's largest hospital.

free information about hospital services and your health. They are ASK-A-NURSE, 921-8827, (800) 622-6877; Candler Physician Finder, 353-2220, (800) 203-8413; and Memorial WellNet, 350-WELL.

Walk-in Clinics

If you find yourself in need of medical care during your visit to Savannah, there are clinics where you can obtain treatment without having an appointment. These facilities are in addition to the emergency rooms at the three local hospitals.

Immediate Med
2014 E. Victory Dr. • 234-8466
10410 Abercorn St. • 927-6832

Immediate Med handles emergencies and comprehensive family medical care at its two offices — one in Midtown on Victory Drive and the other in the Southside on Abercorn Street. These clinics are open from 9 AM to 9 PM seven days a week. Major credit cards are honored, but Medicare and Medicaid are not accepted.

Emergency Services

If you have an emergency or need general information about community resources, here are agencies you can contact. For emergencies requiring ambulance, police or fire departments, call 911.

ALANON	354-0993
Alcoholics Anonymous	354-0993
First Call for Help	232-3383
Georgia Medical Society	355-6607
Helpline Georgia	
(crisis line)	(800) 338-6745
Narcotics Anonymous	(800) 334-3322
Poison Control Center	(800) 282-5846
Rape Crisis Center	233-7273
Safe Shelter	234-9999
Silent Witness	234-4048
Tidelands Mental Health Center	
(24-hour crisis line)	356-2916

Photo: Kyle Cason

Savannahians — shown here at the annual St. Patrick's Day parade — are a hardy lot blessed with fine healthcare options.

Hospice Care

Several organizations in Savannah offer specialized care for the terminally ill and assistance to members of their families, such as respite care and bereavement counseling. One of them, Hospice Savannah, which introduced this type of care to the area in 1980, provides living quarters for patients who cannot be cared for at home. The four local options for hospice care provide essentially the same services. They are American HospiceCare, 340 Eisenhower Drive, 356-9090; Hospice Savannah Inc., 1352 Eisenhower Drive, 355-2289; United Hospice, 132 Stephenson Avenue, 691-2877; and Vencare Hospice, 340 Eisenhower Drive, 691-1476.

**For a city Savannah's size,
there are a surprising number
of choices on the radio dial.**

Media

The Savannah area ranks No. 100 in the national television market, placing the city smack dab in the middle of the pack for the country as a whole. There are about 100 bigger markets and 100 smaller. The city's two primary news stations, WSAV (NBC) and WTOC (CBS), were recently purchased by the same company — Raycom Media. Because of various laws prohibiting such dual ownership, one of the stations was in the process of being traded when we made inquires about the sale. There are also several cable companies in Chatham County, which makes for an interesting jumble of locally produced programming.

However, the most prominent media outlet in the area is the *Savannah Morning News*, the city's daily newspaper. With a circulation of 75,900 on weekdays and 84,399 on Sunday, it is widely read and even imitated. Pick up the paper in the morning, and you will often see the same stories that night on the 6 PM news. The relationship between the *Morning News* and the Savannah community at large can sometimes get dicey (as evidenced on the paper's editorial page), but it's no more so than in most cities.

There is a small, eclectic mix of other publications in town from weekly newspapers geared toward the African-American community to two nationally recognized magazines — one covering art, design, literature and music; the other tackling scuba diving.

For a city of Savannah's size, there are a surprising number of choices on the radio dial. Tune in during the day, and you are apt to hear gospel, jazz, rock or country music, among other forms. Some of the stations have a tendency to change their format frequently, making it a little difficult to keep up with what's where — just move the dial a little more to the left or right, and you're likely to find what you're looking for.

Newspapers

Dailies

Savannah Morning News
111 W. Bay St. • 236-9511

The *Savannah Morning News* was founded in 1850 and is Savannah's only daily newspaper. It is part of the Morris Newspaper Group, which also owns papers in Athens, Georgia, and Jacksonville, Florida, among other cities. Until a few years ago, it was one of the few newspapers left in the country that printed both a morning and afternoon edition.

Ask just about anybody in Savannah about the *Morning News,* and they usually have an opinion — sometimes quite a strong one — to share. Although on most issues it takes a generally conservative stance, the paper does allow for diverse voices on its editorial pages through nationally syndicated columns by the likes of Molly Ivins, David Broder and others. Cartoonist Mark Streeter adds yet another perspective with his insightful, fun cartoons dealing with local, regional and national issues and personalities. Like them or not, they keep people talking around the water cooler at work. Columnist Jane Fishman is another popular voice among locals. While keeping readers apprised of some of the simpler things in her life — tending her garden, hearing from an old friend, taking a trip to see relatives — she manages to find a lesson and passes it along.

If you want to get the pulse on local issues or find out what is really on people's minds, check out Vox Populi. Appearing on the cover of the Accent section, it is one of the newest and most popular additions to the paper. People call in to the paper and leave anonymous messages about everything from the guy who cut them off in traffic to why they don't agree with a decision made by a local politician. Diversions, a tabloid that runs every Friday, includes listings on everything from what movies are playing in local theaters to concerts, gallery exhibits and more.

Other Newspapers

Creative Loafing
1800 E. Victory Dr. • 231-0250

This alternative weekly newspaper (yes, it's related to the *Creative Loafing* publication in Atlanta) covers what is happening around town in arts, dining, music and more. It is a good resource for events and also offers some interesting voices such as columnist Mark Thomas. His fun and interesting perspective on the city can't be found anywhere else. In Savannah, *Creative Loafing* is published on Tuesday and can be found on racks all over town.

Georgia Guardian
528 Indian St. • 238-2440

Owned and produced by the Savannah College of Art and Design, the city's art school, the *Guardian* is a weekly newspaper emphasizing what is going on at the college while covering a smattering of local issues. Because the college often offers exhibits, classes and other events that are open to the public (often free), it is a good source for this type of information. It is distributed at many off-campus outlets.

Savannah Herald
1803 Barnard St. • 232-4505

Savannah Mayor Floyd Adams Jr. is the editor and publisher of this weekly newspaper, which was founded in 1945 by Adams' father. The *Herald's* motto is, "Publish Positive News For and About Savannah's African-American Community." Inside you will find local news stories, church news, sports and editorials. In Around Town, columnist Jettie Adams fills people in on a variety of subjects like who is having a birthday and the accomplishments of local children. The *Savannah Herald* is published on Wednesday, when 8,500 copies are distributed all over town.

Savannah Business Journal
6203 Abercorn St. • 354-5553

Founded in 1990, the *Journal* is a monthly tabloid covering everything from who was promoted at local businesses to topics like how to market products on the Internet. It also lists conferences, lectures and other issues of interest to the business community. It comes out early each month and is distributed throughout Savannah.

The Savannah Tribune
916 Montgomery St. • 233-6128

The Tribune, as it is known, is Savannah's other weekly newspaper devoted to the black community. Publisher and Editor Shirley B. James includes local, state and sometimes national items pertaining to African Americans. Pick it up and you could learn who Georgia's May Day queen is or news from Savannah State University, the city's predominately African-American school. *The Tribune* is distributed all over town on Wednesdays.

The Yokel
22 W. Bryan St. • 233-1009

The Yokel is a free monthly newsletter found in local coffee shops, video stores and the like. It offers an irreverent and alternative view of what is happening in Savannah. You never are quite sure what you might find. A recent issue contained a contest about worried rats and a horoscope advising, "Get a parrot."

Magazines

Contents
129 W. Gordon St. • 232-9889

This nationally acclaimed and distributed magazine covers Southern art, literature, design and music. Publisher and Creative Director Joseph Alfieris returned to his native Savannah in 1987 after spending time in New York and France. A National Endowment for the Arts fellow, Alfieris studied at the School of Visual Arts in New York City and designed book covers for Random House and other

---

FYI

Unless otherwise noted, the area code for all phone numbers listed in this guide is 912.

While you're in the area, sample our diverse menu of entertainment...

The Adventure Radio Group
offers
A Radio Menu to Satisfy Every Taste

The perfect recipe for good times and great memories. The ingredients: Standards of the past 50 years served on the sunny side - no matter what the weather. Daily Sunny Silver Card Specials: Money-saving discounts and reduced admissions on Hilton Head, Savannah and throughout the Lowcountry - ideal for those with a taste for saving money!

A tantilizing combination of smooth and bright favorites seasoned with stock reports, community news and events. Also on the menu: The Joy Forever Card - your daily recipe for saving money wherever you go. Joy 106.9 - a popular choice with the locals - and visitors too!

Classic rock and roll served fresh and piping hot. For added flavor: Beach, fishing and NASCAR reports, concert information - and just plain fun. Start your day having Breakfast with Bondo and stay tuned throughout the day. Jacksonville Jaguars Football in season. Try it, you'll like it!

Super-size your radio selection! An all-you-can-hear smorgasbord of the best music of the 50's and 60's. Carl Anthony and Nancy Brooks get your weekday mornings off to a powerful start. A great music format broadcast on two frequencies doubles the power!

Continuous Country! If you have a taste for today's best country and your all-time favorties, sample our new "sound-sation" - Gator 104.9! One taste and you'll know why country is the most listened to format in America.

Sports served round the clock for those who can't get their fill. Insightful sports commentary and the Fabulous Sports Babe. Exclusive Carolina Panthers Football in season. All sports, all the time!

Accompanying each selection, complimentary news and reliable weather forecasts from WTOC-Channel 11.

major publishers. He also created record sleeves for A&M Records before returning to launch *Contents* which is produced in a townhouse in the city's historic downtown. In 1994, Vanity Fair magazine called *Contents* "one of the most striking new independent magazines in America." Recent contributors have included author Laren Stover and photographer Shelby Lee Adams. If you see one, grab it; *Contents* isn't easy to find because it sells out quickly.

Rodale's Scuba Diving
6600 Abercorn St. • 351-0855

Savannah's other nationally distributed magazine is *Rodale's Scuba Diving*. Published nine times a year, it covers anything and everything about scuba diving. There are articles about such topics as diving health and fitness, adventure travel and marine environment.

Savannah Magazine
111 W. Bay St. • 652-0291

Savannah Magazine is owned by the Morris Newspaper Group, which also owns the city's largest newspaper, *Savannah Morning News*. This slick city magazine is published every two months and targets upper middle class and professional residents. While it is owned by the same company that owns the local newspaper, the magazine strives to present a fresh, unique voice in its publication. Stories run the gamut from a look at the most eligible bachelors and bachelorettes in town to profiles of the city's top lawyers. *Savannah Magazine* often includes helpful, lengthy looks at some of the city's charity festivals and other annual events, and it also carries a regular listing of city events of all types.

Television

Like many media outlets, there are strong local personalities filling up Savannah small screens. Many have been around for several

This home was renovated for *This Old House* on PBS.

years and are well-established in the community. During hurricane months, locals look to and depend on seasoned anchor persons and meterologists with sophisticated tracking equipment to guide them through the often-tense times. You will notice that in the following listings channel numbers are not included. That's because numbers differ depending on what area of the city you are in. Two cable companies serve the Savannah area: Jones Communications, 5515 Abercorn Street, 354-7531, and U.S. Cable Coastal Properties, 203 Second Avenue, Tybee Island, 786-5277.

WJCL-ABC
WTGS-Fox
10001 Abercorn St. • 925-0022

Although technically not owned by the same company, you will notice that the same anchors regularly switch from station to station. Newscasts on these stations seem less produced than those on the more established affiliates, and the anchors are generally young and working their way up the television news circuit.

INSIDERS' TIP

Savannah's only Spanish-language radio broadcast features Latin favorites every Thursday from 5 to 8 PM on WHCJ 90.3 FM. The locally produced show is broadcast from the campus of Savannah State University.

WSAV-NBC
1430 E. Victory Dr. • 651-0300

WSAV is the city's other major news station. Since 1996 this NBC affiliate has shuffled its cast of news anchors trying to find just the right fit. To fill one of their main 6 PM anchor chairs, they hired Jim Carswell, who formerly worked with the station's main competitor, WTOC (see subsequent listing). A huge advertising campaign was splashed around town announcing his arrival. Meteorologist Brad Huffines leads the weather team, which includes a crew of younger meteorologists and various technology that allows you to see storms as they are passing through the area. Huffines often runs a contest called the "Three Degree Guarantee" — if his weather prediction is off by more than three degrees, a viewer gets some cash.

WTOC-CBS
11 The News Place • 234-1111

Lead anchor Doug Weathers is Savannah's most recognizable news personality. He has been with WTOC for three decades and his friendly and affable manner is popular with many locals, especially those who have watched him for years. WTOC regularly wins the 6 PM rating wars and boasts many other longtime on-camera personalities. Meteorologist Pat Prokop has been with WTOC for more than 15 years. More low-key then his WSAV-counterpart, Prokop also has sophisticated weather equipment to help track storms and other weather phenomena.

WVAN-PBS
260 14th St. NW, Atlanta • (800) 222-6006

While getting the more familiar offerings such as *Barney* and *Sesame Street*, this PBS station also runs some very interesting local programming (on Georgia history, B&Bs and such) in cooperation with its Georgia affiliate, Peach State Public Television.

Radio

As was previously mentioned, there are a number of choices on Savannah's airwaves from gospel, jazz and rock to country and classical. Some of the more popular choices, at least among the younger crowd, are the morning talk shows such as the John Boy and Billy show, a nationally syndicated show featuring the antics of these Southern types. If news and serious commentary are more your style, you'll find National Public Radio mixed in among the lot. Savannah State University offers the only local college radio station and provides an interesting mix of jazz, hip-hop and more eclectic stuff if you get tired of the tried-and-tested radio out there.

Adult Contemporary
WAEV 97.3 FM
WYKZ 98.7 FM
WHBZ 99.7 FM
WRHQ 105.3 FM
WJOY 108 FM

Big Band/Swing
WLOW 107.9 FM

College Radio
WHCJ 90.3 FM (Savannah State College)

Country
WCHY 94.1 FM
WJCL 96.5 FM
WCHY 1290 AM

Gospel
WSOK 1230 AM

Hip-Hop
WSGF 103.9 FM

News/Sports/Talk
WBMQ 630 AM
WEAS 900 AM

Oldies
WGCO 98.3 FM

Public Radio
WSVH 91.1 FM

Rock
WIXV 95.5 FM
WZAT 102.1 FM

WXLQ 92.1 FM
WEAS 93.1 FM
WLVH 101.1 FM

Services for the changing needs of an elderly population are in place in Savannah, and they are growing in scope as the demand increases.

Retirement

Savannah's moderate climate, recreational resources and the other charms that make the city attractive to visitors are particularly important to retirees. Savannah is home to a large population of senior citizens — some with families that have been here for generations; others who have chosen this area specifically as their retirement getaway.

Recreational opportunities for the active retiree abound, from the opportunity to play golf virtually year round on a variety of courses to sailing opportunities that were attractive, plentiful and challenging enough to land the city Olympic venue status. Social opportunities are plentiful also, with a variety of organizations tailoring their offerings strictly to older members. Those who are eager to explore new educational horizons have the resources of area universities and their related programs.

Services for the changing needs of an elderly population are in place in Savannah, and they are growing in scope as the demand increases. If you have family members who are likely to need assistance with household chores or daily supervision because of Alzheimer's Disease, programs are in place to help both them and you. Expanded transportation, meal and utility programs have been established to serve the elderly who need additional help.

Senior Citizens Inc.

Think of this nonprofit organization, located at 3025 Bull Street, 236-0363, as a clearinghouse for senior services. It opens its membership rolls at $8 per year to anyone age 55 or older. Social and educational opportunities, as well as discounts provided by various merchants, are the primary benefits available to the younger segment of members. The range of services (some on a fee basis; others free or on sliding scales) runs all the way to home-delivered meals and utility assistance

— whatever it takes to keep even frail and very low-income seniors independent as long as possible.

Senior Citizens handles an annual budget of some $2.4 million, most of it from federal grants, foundation donations and personal bequests. It is also a participating member in the United Way of the Coastal Empire.

The next several listings provide information on Senior Citizens' offerings for active members of the retirement community. We follow those up with Senior Citizens' options that address social service needs.

Club 55
3025 Bull St. • 236-0363

This separate suite within the Senior Citizens complex is designed as a social and educational center for all Senior Citizens members. It includes meeting facilities, rooms for scheduled bridge games and other recreation, exercise facilities that include treadmills and other machines, computers for classes and Internet access, and a gathering place for health screenings, courses and seminars on topics of interest to seniors.

Merchants' Discounts

More than 170 participating merchants and service providers offer discounts to Senior Citizens' members (and many give price reductions to any senior citizen, member or not). Maintaining a current inventory of the very fluid list of participants and the terms of their discount offers has proven to be a pretty overwhelming challenge for the Senior Citizens' staff. Participating merchants are asked to display the Senior Citizens' logo where customers are likely to see it. If a freshly updated list isn't available when you join and if you don't see a logo displayed by a merchant, the organization encourages you to show your membership card and ask if they participate in the program. After all, even if you don't have fixed-income problems, it's nice to pay less if you have the opportunity.

Senior Independent Living Organization

This organization, administered by Senior Citizens, is designed to assist seniors who are not eligible for the programs designed for low-income citizens. It recognizes that such services are needed by a portion of the population that can afford to pay for them, provided they are available at reasonable cost. Through this membership program, older citizens can preserve their independence with low-cost access to delivered meals, housekeeping, transportation and non-emergency home maintenance chores such as starting furnaces or changing filters.

Ruth F. Byck Social Center
64 Jasper St. • 234-6666

The Social Center's adult day-care program provides an option for families facing the hardships of caring for a loved one with Alzheimer's Disease or similar chronic disorders. Residents receive social interaction, exercise and meals while family members are freed to go to work or take a break from constant care. The center is to the rear of the Senior Citizen's complex.

Other Senior Citizens Inc. Services

Other services available to senior citizens in need include Meals on Wheels, which delivers hot lunches on weekdays; a transportation program; a Senior Companion program that offers a stipend to low-income seniors for assisting a frail elderly person they are paired with; social work assessment and advocacy; and the loan of fans and medical equipment. Senior Citizens Inc. programs make heavy use of volunteer labor, and active retirees are well-represented among that corps of volunteers. To inquire about services or volunteer opportunities, call 236-0363.

Other Senior Services

Elderhostel
75 Federal St., Boston, MA 02110
• (617) 426-8056
Armstrong Atlantic State University, 11935 Abercorn St. • 921-5439
Congregation Mickve Israel, 20 E. Gordon St. • 233-1547
Savannah State University, P.O. Box 20523, Savannah, GA 31404 • 356-2253

Elderhostel is a resource everyone 55 or older who travels should become familiar with. It offers noncredit educational opportunities on a wide range of topics (and we do mean wide, from phonics to history to literature). Tuition is moderate, and arrangements are made for you stay near the class site, usually in area motels. The program is generally arranged to allot time for classes, socializing and taking in the various sights around the host location.

Elderhostel is a particularly thriving program in Savannah, where Armstrong Atlantic State University, Savannah State University and Temple Mickve Israel/Jewish Educational Alliance all have course offerings that take particular advantage of the Savannah area setting.

Costs are moderate when you consider prices include motels, meals and, in most cases, local transportation. The offerings we scanned ranged from $350 to $460, with more in the lower end of that range than the higher. Pre-registration is absolutely essential. Local

FYI

Unless otherwise noted, the area code for all phone numbers listed in this guide is 912.

INSIDERS' TIP

State and local regulations give older property owners special exemptions on property taxes. Most, but not all, of the exemptions are keyed to income. If you are interested in purchasing a retirement home in Chatham County, learn more about your property tax status by calling the Tax Assessor's Office at 652-7271.

Photo: Kyle Cason

Many retirees spend their leisure time on the waters around Savannah.

residents can get discounts since they won't need the meals and lodging. They can register through the local addresses, but we really recommend you get the catalog and handle registration through the Massachusetts office. If you call Savannah State, note that the director of that Elderhostel program has other duties, so don't assume you have the wrong number when another office answers.

Courses will vary from quarter to quarter: The ones referenced here are for the first quarter of 1998 and should be a representative sample, although each quarter will differ at least slightly.

Armstrong Atlantic's courses are based in two locations: at the university's Southside Savannah campus and on Tybee Island, Chatham County's beach municipality. You can choose from topics such as the literary heritage of Flannery O'Connor, one of Savannah's most famous writers; the music of native son Johnny Mercer; or "Rebs vs. Yanks," a look at the local Civil War scene. You can

even take a course entitled "Midnight in Savannah," with John Berendt's bestseller as required reading beforehand.

Savannah State University has equally diverse offerings. The university's marsh-front setting comes into play in a course on marine life of the Southeast, and other recent courses include Savannah history, phonics and Gullah culture, which examines the language and African culture retained by a community of Lowcountry slave descendants. Among Savannah State's most popular Elderhostel offerings are its various jazz courses, taught by members of Savannah's thriving community of jazz musicians and scholars.

The courses sponsored by Mickve Israel/Jewish Educational Alliance tend to focus heavily on Jewish culture and history. The Mickve Israel congregation itself, as the oldest Jewish congregation in the South, is the focus of one course. Not all courses are centered on local topics, however: for example,

INSIDERS' TIP

The Chatham-Effingham-Liberty Regional Library offers records and cassettes of print items to those with vision problems and can also arrange to deliver items to homebound patrons. Call 652-3600 for more information.

check out "The Jewish Heritage of the American Musical."

Elderhostel offers a continually changing cycle of courses available both to travelers coming in to the area and local residents.

Retirement Services Office
3rd Infantry Division (Mech.), 368 Hase Rd., Ft. Stewart • 767-3326

We've found that military retirees are well-versed on the benefits they carry into retirement. They probably don't need a reminder that they retain shopping privileges at post exchanges and commissaries and that there are active posts in Savannah for all the various military organizations. But those moving into or passing through the area might be pleased to know the extent of services available in the region, thanks to the major military presence in the region.

Hunter Army Air Field in Savannah is a sub-installation of Fort Stewart, which is about 40 miles southeast of the city. Some 4,300 soldiers are assigned to Hunter, and 16,000 are based at 279,000-acre Fort Stewart, the largest military installation east of the Mississippi. With that many personnel, you've got recreation facilities, and retirees have access to the Morale, Welfare and Recreation programs at these installations. While it is unlikely that many retirees are interested in the concerts staged for young soldiers, they may well want to know about the golf courses, skeet-shooting, movie theaters and other activities and facilities at the two military reservations. Because it is far larger, many of these will be found at Fort Stewart in Hinesville, which is an accessible commute.

On the more serious side of things, Tuttle Army Health Clinic serves Hunter for primary, ambulatory care, and the larger, full-service Wynn Army Community Hospital is at Fort Stewart. The office listed at the head of this entry is largely concerned with such major tasks as straightening out retirement check problems or arranging veteran burials at sea, but personnel there can also provide information on other retiree services.

Hunter's main gate in Savannah is at White Bluff Road and Stephenson Avenue.

Hospital-sponsored Clubs

Each of Savannah's three hospitals offers a special club to senior citizens, focusing not only on healthcare and wellness activities but also on education and social opportunities. Membership is free.

Care65
No. 8 Medical Arts Center, Savannah, GA 31405 • 352-4405

This program of St. Joseph's/Candler Health System provides health seminars, educational programs, medical screenings and visits to members hospitalized at either St. Joseph's Hospital or Candler Hospital, along with a regular newsletter and a holiday party. One of the unexpected annoyances that accompanies retirement is the loss of access to such office conveniences as a copier, and Care65 addresses that by providing free faxing, photocopying, notary services and Internet access. In addition, the group provides member discounts at participating merchants.

Memorial 55 Plus
P.O. Box 23089, Savannah, GA 31403 • 350-7587

This club, sponsored by Memorial Medical Center, offers health fairs and screenings, a member discount program and visits to members hospitalized at MMC. Classes in such areas as arts and crafts, line dancing and bridge are scheduled, along with Senior Net computer classes and Internet access. Seminars are offered on health and retirement issues, healthy aging and safety for the older driver.

Golden Age and Other Senior Centers

Golden Age Centers and Community Centers are daily gathering places that provide active senior citizens with an opportunity to participate in classes and other events. Lunches are served. The centers operated by the City of Savannah are known as Golden Age Centers. Senior Citizens Inc. operates three additional centers in arrangements with the municipalities of Garden City, Port Wentworth and Thunderbolt. Pooler has its own center. All offer very similar programs.

The Golden Age Centers, in alphabetical order, include Cunningham Center, 121 E. 36th Street, 651-6779; Cuyler Center, 812 W. 36th Street, 651-6780; Frazier Center, 805 May Street, 233-4796; Grant Center, 1310 Richard Street, 651-6785; Savannah Gardens Center, 2500 Elgin Street, 651-6775; Stillwell Towers Center, 5100 Waters Avenue, 351-3855; Stubbs Towers Center, 1301 Bee Road, 651-6776; Wimberly Center, 121 W. 37th Street, 651-6778; and Windsor Forest Center, 921-2104.

The three nearby community centers operated by Senior Citizens Inc. include the Garden City Center, 100 Main Street, Garden City, 966-7791; the Port Wentworth Center, 100 Aberfeldy Street, Port Wentworth, 964-5411; and the Thunderbolt Center, 3236 Russell Street, Thunderbolt, 352-4846. The Pooler Center is at 100 W. Collins Street, Pooler, 964-5411.

Savannah is a city of
great religious diversity,
with more than 260
houses of worship.

Worship

You won't have to look very far in Savannah for evidence that you are at least on the fringe of the Bible Belt — simply turn on a radio or television Sunday morning or stroll downtown, where you'll find normally stringently enforced parking regulations abandoned as suburbanites return to the downtown churches.

But don't let the label delude you into thinking you've wandered into a world of one-size-fits-all religion. Savannah is a city of great religious diversity, with more than 260 houses of worship that range from the splendor of a historic cathedral to the simple outreach of humble storefronts. You'll find the major denominations represented, along with other faiths that reflect the growing international community that comes to Savannah via the ports, local colleges or seasonal agricultural needs for the nearby Vidalia onion harvest. You'll find religion here assumes a highly visible position in local life. Elsewhere, it might be unusual for a public meeting to begin with a brief prayer, but the practice still surfaces here from time to time and draws little if any public comment when it does.

Churches and synagogues are also active players in private education in Savannah. Not only is there a kindergarten through grade 12 Catholic school system — certainly not uncommon in any city with a significant Catholic population — but Baptist, Jewish and Pentecostal congregations also sponsor private schools, along with other nondenominational Christian groups. (For information on many of these schools, see our Education and Child Care chapter.)

According to statistics compiled in the University of Georgia's *Georgia County Guide 1996*, a third of Chatham County's population identifies itself with the Baptist faith. That identity covers a lot of ground, however, ranging from churches affiliated with the conservative Southern Baptist Convention to independent Baptist churches to those affiliated with historically African-American branches of the faith. The same survey shows roughly equal numbers of Catholics and United Methodists, each accounting for just more than 8 percent of the population. Smaller percentages are identified as belonging to other denominations or faiths, but the list contains no startling omissions. Local houses of worship include three synagogues (one each for Reform, Conservative and Orthodox Jews) and a mosque.

Unlike several other of the original British colonies, Georgia cannot claim a religious motive for its founding. Instead, economic and social conditions were the driving force behind the settling of this, the 13th of the storied 13 original colonies. Still, religion was a major part of Colonial life from the day Oglethorpe and his original settlers arrived (see our History chapter). The group was largely Anglican in its faith (no surprise there), but its charter provided for religious freedom — for the most part. Catholics were prohibited from settling in the colony in its early days, reflective of Georgia's early role as a military buffer between other English settlements to the north and the Catholic Spanish settlements in Florida.

That proviso about religious freedom got its first major test five months after the colony began. A shipload of mainly Spanish and Portuguese Jews, fleeing religious persecution in Spain, arrived in 1733. Whether the promised religious tolerance in the Georgia colony would have held up under normal circumstances is unclear, but this ship was made welcome —

probably due, in no small part, to its showing up in the midst of a deadly fever epidemic with a doctor on board. Thus, a Jewish community has roots that date back practically to the founding days of the colony. Temple Mickve Israel became the oldest congregation in the state of Georgia and is believed to be the third oldest in the nation (see our Attractions chapter for more on the temple). Methodism, too, has deep historical roots in Savannah. John Wesley preached here in his Anglican days; he went on to become a founding father of the Methodist denomination.

The churches along the downtown Savannah squares house some of the oldest congregations in the country. Some members trace their membership back for generations; others have just moved to town. The buildings themselves are often historic, quite apart from their religious significance, but for the most part the congregations predate the current buildings: The earliest churches were destroyed by the fires that were a constant threat to the city in its earliest centuries.

Savannah's strongest claim to historical religious fame is in African-American history. Savannah is the founding point of the oldest black congregations in the country, and the two churches that sprang from slave roots — First Bryan Baptist Church and First African Baptist Church — are still active and influential participants in the city's spiritual and social life.

Where to Worship?

Finding a spiritual match in an unfamiliar city is an important task that can be time-consuming when you are relocating. If you are vacationing or staying for a short time, however, chances are you are more interested in simply continuing your usual religious observance while away from home. So, how does a spiritually observant traveler go about choosing a congregation to visit? Print media outlets provide several options in Savannah. The *Savannah Morning News* publishes a religion section every Saturday, and you'll find there a collection of religious news items, schedules of special events and advertisements by various churches. *The Herald*, a weekly newspaper, provides detailed coverage of religious news in Savannah's African-American community. The *Morning News* (see our Media chapter) can be found in vending boxes all over town, especially around hotels and motels. You may have to look harder to find *The Herald*: It's in vending boxes in the downtown area, hospital lobbies and major shopping centers, and you can call them at 232-4505 to find out other locations. The *Savannah Jewish News* is a monthly publication serving Savannah's approximately 3,000 Jewish families. It is normally available by subscription only, but there's a good chance you can pick up a current copy at the Jewish Educational Alliance, 5111 Abercorn Street, 355-8111.

New Age interests and other less conventional spiritual paths are harder to track. Your best mainstream media source would be the events columns and ads in *The Georgia Guardian*, a weekly newspaper affiliated with Savannah College of Art and Design. It's available in vending boxes throughout the downtown area and in major shopping areas. You might also check out the event columns of the Savannah edition of *Creative Loafing*, available free at a wide range of locations but especially copious at downtown restaurants and nightclubs.

Other good sources of info are the windows and bulletin boards of shops in the downtown area that sell New Age and non-traditional spiritual products (see our Shopping chapter). This might seem a little hit-or-miss to

www.insiders.com
See this and many other **Insiders' Guide®** destinations online — in their entirety.
Visit us today!

Photo: Kyle Cason

The steeple of St. John's Episcopal Church has towered
over the historic area for generations.

you, but we've discovered that organizers of such less-than-mainstream events are usually extremely diligent about getting flyers posted and word of events circulated.

In Praise of
Those Who Praise

Maybe you are not trying, while traveling, to find a church you believe you would be com-

patible with for a lifetime. Instead, maybe you are more interested in continuing longstanding habits of worship without attention to specific denominational issues. If that's the case, we can heartily suggest the sacred music options available in Savannah's wide range of churches. A visit to a different church often offers a chance to hear the uplifting vocal talents of local choirs, while viewing the architectural grandeur of Savannah's churches.

We asked our musical friends which

INSIDERS' TIP

The Cathedral of St. John the Baptist can comfortably seat 1,000 people. Even so, arrive early to find a seat if you plan on attending Easter services, St. Patrick's Day Mass or Midnight Mass at Christmas.

The twin steeples of the Cathedral of St. John the Baptist mark Savannah's skyline.

churches they felt offered the most outstanding and uplifting sacred music. We had them focus on the geographic areas where visitors are likely to be staying and able to find their way around; that's why you'll note the predominance of downtown churches here. The list that follows is by no means comprehensive. Almost every church has music of some kind, and many play host to visiting singing groups. No doubt we've left some outstanding examples off, but this brief list should give you a starting point.

A full carillon of bells can be heard beginning around 10 AM each Sunday morning, pealing out hymns from atop St. John's Episcopal Church, 1 W. Macon Street, just off Bull Street. The church also has a good organ and choir. The Lutheran Church of the Ascension, 120 Bull Street, has what may be the largest organ in town, along with a fine choir. Wesley Monumental United Methodist Church, 429 Abercorn Street, boasts outstanding organ, choral and even occasional hand-bell performances.

First Baptist Church at 223 Bull Street is known for its organ and choir. Bull Street Baptist Church, at the corner of Bull and Anderson streets, has a wonderful pipe organ and choir. Farther south, another notable choir (accompanied by an electronic organ) sings at the White Bluff United Methodist Church at 11911 White Bluff Road. A performance by the Savannah Community Choir is an event that shouldn't be missed. Consider this group an "all-star team" from Savannah's African-American churches. Their performances are infrequent but well-publicized.

Working Together

Ecumenical services among churches are common during the holiday seasons. Downtown churches, for example, often come together to jointly sponsor Holy Week services at midday. At Christmas one or more churches may stage a living nativity scene, always a popular attraction, and cantatas showcase the best efforts of local choirs. At Easter, a group sunrise service on the beach at Tybee Island greets the day.

Savannah's churches work as well as worship. You'll find them intensely involved in the support of the Inner City Night Shelter, which feeds the homeless and provides shelter, and in other projects addressing the needs of the homeless. Coastal Empire Habitat for Humanity, the local chapter of the international homebuilding project that counts Georgian and former president Jimmy Carter among its carpenters, thrives with help from about 20 different churches. By the fourth quarter of 1997, this group had built 34 homes in the area. To volunteer with Habitat, either through a church or as an individual, call 234-6112.

HAVE FUN

Welcome to our world.

Over 5,000 acres of fun! Exhilarating golf. Championship tennis.
400 homes and villas for rent. First-rate dining.
5 miles of Atlantic Ocean beach. 605-acre Forest Preserve.
Miles of scenic bike paths. Award-winning EcoTour program.
It's all here. It's all for you.

SeaPines®
R E S O R T

Call 1-800 (732-7463) • Hilton Head Island, SC • www.seapines.com

Hilton Head, S.C.

Introduction/History

Something that strikes us when we're on Hilton Head Island — aside from the natural beauty of the place — is the relative newness of what has been built there. This becomes even more evident when the island is compared with the Historic Downtown of Savannah some 35 miles to the southwest, an area where much of what you see dates to the 1800s and early 1900s.

In contrast, most of the structures on Hilton Head are less than 50 years old, the products of two momentous events in the island's history that occurred in the mid-1950s. One was the opening of a set of two bridges connecting the 41-square-mile sea island with the South Carolina mainland. The other was the start of the Sea Pines residential/resort community by a southeast Georgian named Charles Fraser.

"The opening of the bridge had a major impact on development," states Porter M. Thompson in the book *Hilton Head Island Images*. "Suddenly building materials, equipment and people were able to come and go freely — Hilton Head had lost its isolation and a new era had begun."

Sea Pines, in its basic form a residential area built around a golf course, set the tone for the other planned communities that would be created on Hilton Head and spurred the development of the island as a mecca for retirees and vacationers. Back in the early '50s, Hilton Head was home to about 100 families, "little more than a quiet community of farmers and shrimpers," as author Richard Rutt put it in *Hilton Head Island: A Perspective*. Now the island — with its natural assets of marshes, wide creeks, hardwood forests and 12 miles of beach — is the site of 11 planned communities harboring a multitude of stylish homes

and upscale condominiums known locally as villas, 22 beautifully manicured golf courses, nearly 400 tennis courts, 10 marinas, four large hotels, a bevy of villa-style resorts and midsized hotels and motels, 150 restaurants and more than 550 retail stores. Permanent residents now number nearly 29,000, many of them engaged in satisfying the needs of tourists, of whom there were 1.83 million in 1996, according to the island's chamber of commerce.

All this growth has occurred in a manner that places an emphasis on preserving Hilton Head's natural surroundings: live oaks, magnolias, pines, palmettos and other flora. Following ideas originally credited to Fraser, most islanders continue to adhere to the concept that buildings must blend in with the environment and that development be as unobtrusive as possible.

Although Hilton Head's modern era begins in the '50s, the island's recorded history goes back considerably further — to the 1500s, when Spaniards and Frenchmen visited while exploring the area bordering Port Royal Sound, the large bay on Hilton Head's north shore that's one of the world's finest natural harbors. The Spanish and French fought over the sound for almost 50 years, with the Spaniards triumphing but never settling the area. That was left to the British, who in 1717 were responsible for the island's first English settler, John Barnwell.

Englishmen had been in the area well before that, however. In 1663, sea captain William Hilton sailed into the sound and came upon the island. He spotted a headland on the northeastern end and named it after himself. As time went on, the entire island came to be called by the name of this promontory, Hilton Head.

The settlers who came to Hilton Head in the 1700s eventually planted the land in cotton, indigo, sugar cane, rice and other crops. They purchased slaves brought to America from Africa and used them to create large plantations. According to Richard Rutt, there were 24 plantations on the island by 1860, most of them producing cotton. Also by that time, South Carolina was on the verge of seceding from the Union and leading the South into the Civil War, a conflict in which Hilton Head would play an interesting part.

The island was invaded by Union troops on November 7, 1861, seven months after the war began, in an effort to control Port Royal Sound and establish a portion of the blockade of the Confederacy's Atlantic coast. In the Battle of Port Royal, a Union fleet of 15 warships and 31 transports and supply ships exchanged shots with four Confederate gunboats and two forts, one of them on Hilton Head. The Confederate guns were silenced, the forts were evacuated, and Union forces took possession of the island and held it until the end of the war.

The area near the fort on Hilton Head — called Fort Walker by the Southerners and renamed Fort Welles by its Federal conquerors — became a town during the Union occupation, when the population of Hilton Head mushroomed to 40,000. "Enlisted personnel — both soldiers and sailors — constituted the bulk of that population, or, 23-30,000 men," Rutt stated in his book. "The balance of Hilton Head's wartime population consisted primarily of freedmen who sought refuge on the island, civilian dependents, and Yankee tradesmen. The latter opened and operated a variety of

business establishments, ranging from hotels, blacksmith shops, and theatres to photography studios, tattoo parlors and bordellos."

The main street of the town, which was located in what is now Port Royal Plantation, was named Sutler's Row after the merchants who lined it. The military men who paid exorbitant prices for the sutlers' goods called it Robber's Row, the name now borne by one of the plantation's golf courses. Another settlement sprang up in what is now Hilton Head Plantation; it was called Mitchelville and consisted mostly of tents and barracks housing freed slaves who had fled to the island. When the war ended, the military and the sutlers left and, said Rutt, "the shops and houses of Robber's Row and Mitchelville rapidly disappeared from the island, no doubt torn down by freedmen seeking to build homes of their own."

From the end of the Civil War until the middle of the 20th century, Hilton Head was a sleepy sea island largely bypassed and forgotten by the rest of the world. All that began to change in 1950, when Fred Hack, C.C. Stebbins and Lt. Gen. Joseph B. Fraser bought 8,000 acres of pine forest and formed the Hilton Head Company for the purpose of selectively cutting the pines. In 1956, the company's holdings were divided, with Fraser acquiring 4,000 acres on the southern end of the island. A year later Fraser's son Charles, a University of Georgia and Yale Law School graduate in his 20s, bought his family's holdings and another 1,200 acres and started planning and developing Sea Pines.

FYI

Unless otherwise noted, the area code for all phone numbers listed in this guide is 803.

INSIDERS' TIP

The Harbour Town Lighthouse, Hilton Head's most enduring symbol, stands 93 feet tall and is visited by a quarter-million people a year. The observation deck perches 66 feet above the base floor of the lighthouse on Calibogue Sound, and you reach it by climbing 110 steps. Completed in 1970, the lighthouse was the first one built on the Atlantic coast in more than 150 years. Flashing a white light every 2.5 seconds, it's a navigational aid for the sound and the Intracoastal Waterway, even though it's not operated by the U.S. government. (It's run by the company that owns Harbour Town.) The structure is open daily from 8 AM to dusk.

Meanwhile, Hack and O.T. McIntosh, who had purchased 12,000 acres on the northern end of the island in the early '50s, began work on their own developments — Spanish Wells Plantation and Port Royal Plantation. (Sea Pines also used the term "Plantation" in its name in its early years, as have many of the planned communities on the island; it refers to the antebellum plantations once located on the sites of the communities).

"These few men," wrote Porter Thompson in referring to Fraser, Hack, McIntosh and other developers, "began with the idea that large holdings of land could be subdivided into lots and sold for residential purposes. There was a twist to this. Hilton Head is ideally suited by climate and location for resort activity so the communities developed would have to accommodate both resort and residential activities. It is Charles Fraser who is largely credited with first developing the concept that a resort/residential community could be successful, if a few considerations were made. He embodied two excellent and highly compatible interests: the understanding of development and a love of nature and of the natural beauty of the island."

Among the concepts advocated and practiced by Fraser were blending development with the environment, creating green spaces, keeping the density of housing as low as possible, cutting as few trees as necessary and restricting the height of buildings so they were no taller than the tallest surrounding trees.

Under Fraser's direction, Sea Pines became, in the words of the Associated Press, "a big-time leisure landmark, a model for resort playgrounds and planned communities from Virginia to the Philippines." Other developers followed his lead, creating their own

planned communities and, in the process, transforming Hilton Head into the world-renowned resort that it is today.

Getting There

Some people arrive at Hilton Head Island by boat or fly directly onto the island, but if you're like most visitors, you'll be coming by car, either from home in your own vehicle or from the Savannah International Airport in a rental. Whatever the case, here's how to get to the island.

By Car

Getting to Hilton Head by car is fairly simple because there's only one road onto the island, U.S. Highway 278, a four-lane that runs west to east through the South Carolina Lowcountry. Finding U.S. 278 is no big deal, particularly if you're arriving at Savannah International Airport and renting a car for the 40-minute drive to the island (you can find information on flights to Savannah and car rentals in our main Getting Here, Getting Around chapter). U.S. 278 is also easy to get to if you're coming from the south or north on Interstate 95, or if you're arriving from the west via Interstate 16 and I-95.

U.S. 278 intersects I-95 just north of Hardeeville, South Carolina, so once you're on the interstate, all you have to do is watch for the exit for U.S. 278 (Exit 8). Take that exit and head east; it's an 18-mile straight shot to Hilton Head. You'll be on the island in 20 minutes and at the middle of it in about a half-hour. To get to I-95 from Savannah International Airport, take Airways Avenue west for a little more than a mile to the interstate. Get on

INSIDERS' TIP

If you're driving from Savannah to Hilton Head or vice-versa via Alt. S.C. 170 around lunchtime, considering stopping at the Pink Pig restaurant, which is at a bump in the road named Levy, South Carolina. The barbecue pork and Brunswick stew at this small, shockingly pink, cinder-block eatery are terrific, and so is the buffet.

Photo: Kyle Cason

Hilton Head is home to numerous marinas.

I-95 and head north into South Carolina. The U.S. 278 exit is 16.5 miles up the interstate from where you left Airways Avenue.

If you're not renting a car, you can get to Hilton Head from the airport via the Low Country Adventures Ltd. shuttle service. Low County Adventures meets all incoming flights (except the 12:30 AM Delta flight) with either a nine-passenger van or a 21-passenger bus. Fares from the airport to the island are $24 per person one way and $44 round trip. You can arrange to be picked up from the 12:30 AM flight, but you'll need to make a guaranteed reservation and it will cost you $60 for one person or $30 per person for two or more people. You can reach Low Country Adventures at 681-8212 or (800) 845-5582.

If you're visiting Savannah and want to pop over to Hilton Head for the day or spend a night on the island, you can drive there by following the I-95/U.S. 278 route just discussed, or you can go the "back way." If you take the I-95/U.S. 278 route, you'll be on multi-lane highways, and it will take about an hour and five minutes for you to get from Savannah City Hall to the Hilton Head Island Chamber of Commerce building at the middle of the island. (To get to I-95 from City Hall, drive west on Bay Street through three traffic lights to

Martin Luther King Jr. Boulevard, turn left on MLK and head south three traffic lights to the entrance ramp to I-16, then take I-16 west for 8.5 miles to I-95).

The back way is shorter (about 55 minutes from City Hall to the middle of Hilton Head), more scenic and a little more complicated. It involves traveling on two-lane roads. If you want to try it, take Oglethorpe Avenue west to the Eugene Talmadge Memorial Bridge and drive north across the Savannah River into South Carolina. You'll be on U.S. Highway 17 for 5 miles from the South Carolina side of the bridge to the intersection of U.S. 17 and Alternate S.C. Highway 170. Turn right on Alt. S.C. 170 and stay on it for 6 miles until you reach its intersection with S.C. Highway 46 (also labeled for a short distance as S.C. Highway 170). Turn right at the stop sign and drive east on S.C. 46 for 12 miles to U.S. 278. Turn right on U.S. 278 and head east — you'll be on the island in about five minutes. Along your way on S.C. 46 to U.S. 278, you'll pass through piney woods, hardwood swamps and the laid-back, offbeat little town of Bluffton with its Squat & Gobble restaurant, Dog's Breath Saloon and 30 mph speed limit (be sure to observe it). While in Bluffton, you'll come to a four-way stop; turn left to stay on S.C. 46.

By Boat

If you're going to Hilton Head by boat, you can get there via the Intracoastal Waterway, which runs along the west side of the island. There are several public marinas and harbors where you can tie up and enjoy your stay while aboard your vessel. These include Harbour Town Yacht Basin at Sea Pines, 671-2704; Hilton Head Marina at 18 Simmons Road off Marshland Road, 681-7335; Outdoor Resorts Yacht Basin at Intracoastal Waterway Marker 20, 681-3256; Palmetto Bay Marina at 164 Palmetto Bay Road, 785-3910, (800) 448-3875; Shelter Cove Harbour at Shelter Cove, 842-7001; Skull Creek Marina at Hilton Head Plantation, 681-4234; South Beach Marina at Sea Pines, 671-3577; and Windmill Harbour, 681-9235. The maximum length of the slips at these marinas ranges from 35 to 200 feet and the cost per night for docking runs from 50¢ per foot to $1.25 per foot. Call ahead for specific details.

By Airplane

Hilton Head has its own airport on the north end of the island. The Hilton Head Airport is on Beach City Road, which runs north off U.S. 278, the island's main drag. Beach City Road is at Mile Marker 4 on U.S. 278, and the entrance to the airport is about a mile from U.S. 278. There are two fixed-base operators across the runway from the airport terminal that can accommodate private planes. The FBOs are on Gateway Circle off Dillon Road less than a mile north of U.S. 278.

Hilton Head Airport
120 Beach City Rd. • 689-5400

Hilton Head's airport has an up-to-date, spacious terminal that was served in summer 1997 by one commercial carrier, USAir Express, (800) 428-4322. This airline has 10 flights each day to and from Charlotte, North Carolina, plus three more arrivals and two more departures on Saturdays and two more arrivals and three more departures on Sundays.

Five rental-car agencies maintain desks at the airport: Avis Rent A Car, 681-4216, (800) 331-1212; Budget Rent A Car, 689-4040; Hertz Rent A Car, 681-7604, (800) 654-3131; National Car Rental, 681-7368, (800) 227-7368; and Thrifty Car Rental, 689-9990. Taxicab and shuttle services operating from the airport are Diamond Taxi Service, 785-2888; Ferguson Transportation Limo-Van & Taxi, 681-5883; Low Country Taxi & Limousine Service, 681-8294; Low Country Adventures Ltd., 681-8212; and Yellow Taxi Cab Service, 686-6666. Rates to and from the airport are regulated by Beaufort County's taxi ordinance: It's $8 to the Hampton Inn, $10 to the Westin Resort/Port Royal, $12 to the Hyatt Regency/Palmetto Dunes, $14 to Shipyard, $15 to the Holiday Inn Oceanfront, $17 to Sea Pines and $65 to Savannah.

The airport has short- and long-term parking lots: Short-term rates are 50¢ for the first 15 to 30 minutes and 50¢ for each additional half-hour, with a maximum charge of $6 for each 24-hour period; long-term rates are 75¢ for the first hour and 50¢ for each additional half-hour, with a maximum charge of $4.50 for each 24-hour period and a weekly charge of $22.50.

Carolina Air Center Inc.
52 Gateway Cir. • 689-3200

In addition to the usual services you'd expect from a fixed-base operator, Carolina Air Center offers an exercise room with a shower

---

INSIDERS' TIP

A good source of information concerning the island's eating places is *Hilton Head Island Restaurants* magazine, which you should be able to find at rental villas, hotels and motels, shops, grocery stores and other locations, including the Chamber of Commerce building off William Hilton Parkway near Mile Marker 8. This booklet of nearly 150 pages has listings for more than 100 restaurants and reprints of menus. There's also a map to help you locate these eateries.

and a nine-hole putting green. The ramp charge is $5 per night, and fuel service is available 24 hours a day if you call ahead after normal business hours, which run from 6 AM to 10 PM.

Hilton Head Air Service Inc.
38 Gateway Cir. • 681-6386

The ramp charge at this fixed-base operation is $7.50 per night. The facility has on-site car rentals through Budget Rent A Car. Hilton Head Air is open from 6:30 AM to 10 PM and offers 100 LL and Jet A fuel service.

Getting Around

The best way to get around on Hilton Head is by car. Walking isn't much of an option because things are pretty spread out. Bike riding is popular, but if you take to the splendid network of bike trails, be prepared to do some pedaling to far-flung destinations. If you haven't driven your own car or rented one, there are numerous taxi companies and limousine services to help you arrange transportation.

Driving on the Island

Finding your way around Hilton Head is fairly easy, but actually finding the places you're looking for can be a challenge. At first glance that statement might not make much sense, but consider this: Most of what a visitor would be looking for can be found on or very near three main roads (U.S. 278, Pope Avenue and South Forest Beach Drive), but spotting a specific restaurant, shop or motel can be difficult because of town regulations limiting signage and promoting natural beauty. Businesses are not allowed to have signs off the premises, and the signs they do have must conform to strict rules involving size and lighting. That, combined with the emphasis on preserving trees and foliage and having buildings blend in, can make it easy for a traveler to drive right past his intended destination. This is particularly true when it comes to the island's main thoroughfare, U.S. 278, a four-lane, divided highway also known as the William Hilton Parkway — most everything is set back off the road on tree-lined side streets that often resemble driveways.

William Hilton Parkway

Once you cross the Karl S. Bowers and J. Wilton Graves bridges to Hilton Head on U.S. 278, you're on William Hilton Parkway, which runs east for 5 miles to the northern end of the island, then bends south and continues 6 miles to Sea Pines Circle. This 11-mile stretch passes numerous restaurants, motels, shopping centers and other business and the entrances to resort communities such as Hilton Head Plantation, Port Royal, Palmetto Dunes and Shipyard.

To aid motorists, the town has placed mile markers along the parkway, with the lower-numbered markers closer to the bridges and the higher-numbered ones closer to the traffic circle. In many of our individual writeups on businesses on the parkway, we've included a mention of the mile marker nearest the business being discussed.

Sea Pines Circle

When you enter this traffic circle from William Hilton Parkway, you'll encounter exits to the Cross Island Parkway one-quarter of the way around, Greenwood Drive halfway around and Pope Avenue three-quarters of the way around. Greenwood Drive is the main road leading into the Sea Pines resort community. The stretch of the Cross Island Parkway directly west of the circle, also known as Palmetto Bay Road, was widened into a four-lane highway in 1997.

Pope Avenue

Pope Avenue runs east a tad more than a mile from Sea Pines Circle to Coligny Circle. On Pope you'll find a variety of restaurants, stores, shopping plazas, another entrance to Shipyard and the entrance to the public parking lot at Forest Beach.

Coligny Circle

The Coligny traffic circle is practically on Forest Beach, and it routes motorists from Pope Avenue to South Forest Beach Drive (one-quarter of the way around the circle) and North Forest Beach Drive (three-quarters of the way around). North Forest Beach Drive is residential and leads to many of the older vacation homes and permanent residences on the island; short side streets run east to the beach, but access is private and public parking is a no-no.

South Forest Beach Drive

There are several resorts and restaurants along South Forest Beach Drive, which leads to another entrance to Sea Pines. Access to the beach via the side streets is private unless marked otherwise.

Cross Island Parkway

The Cross Island Parkway, a four-lane toll road, was scheduled for completion in mid-January 1998 and is intended to bypass the southern portion of William Hilton Parkway and alleviate traffic congestion on the heavily traveled road. The new, 6-mile thoroughfare stretches from near the intersection of William Hilton Parkway and Spanish Wells Road, at Mile Marker 2 in the northwestern portion of the island, to Sea Pines Circle. Part of the Cross Island Parkway is a 65-foot-high bridge that crosses Broad Creek at Palmetto Bay. The toll for riding the length of the parkway (one way) in a car has been set at $1; it's $1.75 for three-axle trucks and $3.25 for five-axle trucks. Planners say the new road should save motorists from eight to 10 minutes in travel time.

Biking on the Island

Hilton Head has nearly 14 miles of paved public bicycle paths, and there are many more miles of paths within the island's resort communities. The public paths run along William Hilton Parkway from Gumtree Road (just past Mile Marker 2) to Sea Pines Circle for 8.2 miles; along the length of Pope Avenue from Sea Pines Circle to Coligny Circle for 1.1 miles; along North Forest Beach Drive from Coligny Circle to the end of North Forest for 1.3 miles; along South Forest Beach Drive from Coligny Circle to Sea Pines' Ocean Gate for 1.4 miles;

along the Cordillo Parkway from South Forest Beach Drive to Pope Avenue for 1.1 miles; and to the Folly Field Beach Park (see Public Beach Access in this section) from William Hilton Parkway for eight-tenths of a mile. A 3.5-mile path along Gumtree and Squire Pope roads in the northwestern part of the island was under construction as of December 1997.

You can make arrangements to rent a bike through the resort where you're staying or by calling one of the numerous bike rental outlets, including AAA Riding Tigers Bike Rentals, 686-5833; Fish Creek Landing, 785-2021; Hilton Head Bicycle Co., 686-6888; Peddling Pelican Bike Rentals, 785-5470; and South Beach Cycles, 671-2453. Expect to pay $20 to $25 to rent a bike for a week, $15 to $18 for three days, $10 to $12 for a day and $4 to $5 for an hour.

Taxis and Limousines

In addition to the taxicab and limousine companies that serve the Hilton Head Airport (see previous listing), there are several others on the island. Among the taxicab companies are Ambassador Taxi Service, 842-8830; Checker Cab, 842-8294; and XYZ Cab Service, 785-6072. Limousine services include At Your Service Transportation Inc., 837-3783, and Camelot Limousine & Tours, 842-7777.

Taxi rates are not regulated by the City of Hilton Head and vary from company to company and point to point. To find out how much a trip will cost, tell the dispatcher where you are and where you're going and ask what the fee will be. Rates for limousines run from $55 to $65 per hour with a two-hour minimum.

Bus Service

The island is served by the buses of Beaufort County's Lowcountry Regional Transportation Authority, but this public transportation service is mainly a means of getting people from towns on the mainland on and off Hilton Head. There is one bus serving Hilton Head in the morning and one in the afternoon, meaning the LRTA is not a means of conveniently getting around the island throughout the day. However, there is a limited-demand response system through which riders can schedule transportation by calling 757-5782 (a round trip to Bluffton using this system is $5). Plans for improved bus service on the island were being implemented during the latter part of 1997.

Public Beach Access and Parking

The only public parking lots and metered parking spaces on the island are at Hilton Head's public beach access points. As far as parking on the rest of the island goes, there is an abundance of free spaces in the lots of

Photo: Phyl M. Gatlin

You are never too young to love the beaches on Hilton Head.

restaurants, shopping centers, motels and other commercial establishments, much of it shaded by trees, which can be a blessing in the summer months.

Coligny Access Point

The access at Coligny Circle offers about 30 metered spaces and a parking lot with 350 spaces. The meters allow you to park 15 minutes for a quarter, and the maximum amount of time you can obtain per meter-feeding is two hours. Rates when the lot is manned by an attendant — usually on Fridays and weekends — are $4 per day for passenger vehicles and $8 per day for buses, campers and boats. The lot is metered the rest of the time, and rates are 50¢ an hour, $1 for two hours, $1.50 for three hours and $4 until 8 PM.

Driessen Beach Park

Located at the end of Bradley Beach Road, which intersects William Hilton Parkway just past Mile Marker 6, this access has a lot where parking is 50¢ per hour. The lot is about a half-mile from the parkway.

Folly Field Beach Park

This access is on Starfish Drive, which runs off Folly Field Road. Parking here is metered, and the rate is 25¢ for 15 minutes. Folly Field Road also runs into William Hilton Parkway, at Mile Marker 6; it's a little more than a half-mile from the parkway to the access.

Sources of Information

Hilton Head has several visitors centers where you can pick up information that might be helpful to you during you stay.

FYI

Unless otherwise noted, the area code for all phone numbers listed in this guide is 803.

Hilton Head Chamber of Commerce

1 Chamber of Commerce Dr. • 785-3673

The lobby of the chamber building, which is just off William Hilton Parkway near Mile Marker 8, is filled with brochures and other publications dealing with the island's accommodations, restaurants, recreational opportunities and real estate. If you have questions, there are folks at the desk who can provide answers. This information center is open from 8:30 AM to 5:30 PM Monday through Friday.

Hilton Head Chamber of Commerce Welcome Center

100 William Hilton Pkwy. • 785-3673

The Chamber of Commerce staffs a welcome center at this site just past Mile Marker 1 on William Hilton Parkway. Stop here and you'll find displays and brochures involving shopping, dining, lodging, long- and short-term rentals, golf, tennis, fishing and events. There's a large-scale map of the island, plus smaller maps of Hilton Head and the surrounding areas that you can take with you. The center is open from 9 AM to 6 PM daily.

The welcome center shares a building with The Museum of Hilton Head Island, which offers exhibits involving the area's history, native crafts and wildlife. Admission is free, but a $2 donation is suggested. Museum hours are from 10 AM to 5 PM daily, and there's a museum shop featuring books on the Civil War and of local interest.

Hilton Head Welcome Center

1600 Fording Island Rd. • 341-3600, 837-5299, (888) 445-8643

The Hilton Head Welcome Center is primarily a central reservations service specializing in vacation planning and golf and tennis packages. The company also maintains a building on U.S. Highway 278 where you can obtain brochures and information regarding accommodations, shopping, restaurants and other aspects of your visit to the island. This off-island welcome center is at the intersection of U.S. 278 and Fording Island Road on your right just before you reach the bridges leading to Hilton Head. Among the services provided by Hilton Head Welcome Center are arrangement of rentals of accommodations; they can help with everything from short-term visits to those of three to four months in duration. Discounts on accommodations and golf and tennis packages are available. Hours of operation are from 10 AM to 4 PM daily.

Planned Residential Communities

Hilton Head's 11 planned residential communities cover 65 percent of the island. All of the island's golf courses (see subsequent listings) are located within or associated with the communities, as are the four largest hotels and many of Hilton Head's homes, vacation villas, tennis courts and marinas.

These communities are for the most part private, meaning they have gates staffed by security personnel who check the identities of arriving motorists. Some are more private than others: A few admit only residents and their guests; others are accessible to vacationers staying at hotels and villas within the communities and to golfers playing on courses that allow public participation. Sea Pines, which is the site of several restaurants and two shopping areas, allows the public to visit at a charge of $3 per car.

As we've mentioned before, the buildings in these communities are in most cases designed to melt into the landscape — stucco and wood are used extensively as building materials, and painting is in muted colors. The grounds surrounding these structures are often left in as natural a state as possible. In most communities, buildings must be approved by architectural review boards.

This section is comprised of sketches of the island's 11 planned communities, listed in alphabetical order. For each we've provided, when possible, an address and telephone number of a source for additional information — either a sales office, an administrative office or the office of the property owners association.

Hilton Head Plantation

Hilton Head Plantation is the second-largest planned community on the island, covering 4,000 acres on the northern tip of Hilton Head between Port Royal Sound and Skull Creek, which is part of the Intracoastal Waterway. Within the plantation's borders are 4,500 residential lots, 600 of which were undeveloped as of fall 1997; four 18-hole golf courses; 2 miles of beaches; the Whooping Crane Pond and Cypress nature conservancies; the Seabrook Farm garden plots and stables; and tennis courts and swimming pools.

On the Skull Creek side of the plantation are Skull Creek Marina, a deep-water facility with 180 boat slips; the Old Fort Pub restaurant; and Fort Mitchel, a historic site that was a Union gun battery during the Civil War. Two of the golf courses within the plantation, the Country Club of Hilton Head and Oyster Reef, can be played by the public.

Outside the plantation's main gate, which is off William Hilton Parkway near Mile Marker 3, is Main Street, a development of shops and professional offices. The Hilton Head Plantation Property Owners Association is within the plantation at 7 Surrey Lane, and the telephone number there is 681-8800.

Indigo Run

Most of the homesites at this 1,775-acre development on the northern portion of Hilton Head border one of two 18-hole golf courses — The Golf Club at Indigo Run, a members-only layout designed by Jack Nicklaus and his son, Jack Nicklaus II, and opened in 1996; and the Golden Bear Golf Club, which was designed by Nicklaus' company and can be played by the public (see listing in this chapter's Golf section). All property owners at Indigo Run are entitled to join Golden Bear, and membership includes access to Sunningdale Park, which has six tennis courts, an Olympic-size pool, a kiddie pool and a large playground for children. Membership in The Golf Club is open to owners of homesites in The Golf Club community and purchasers of Indigo Run's Berwick Green Club Homes.

As of September 1997, there were 250 homes on the 1,517 acres comprising Indigo Run's private residential community and another 80 in the building or design stages. These residences represent a wide range of styles and construction materials and are valued at $300,000 and up. Fifty of Indigo Run's homesites are in the River Club section along the banks of Broad Creek, and many owners of homes there have backyard boat docks. There are no villas at Indigo Run, and the only rentals allowed are long-term arrangements of a year or more.

Indigo Run is also the site of Indigo Park, a 258-acre retail and commercial center bordering William Hilton Parkway. Started in the mid-1980s by the Hilton Head Co., Indigo Run was acquired in 1991 by the Melrose Co., which continues to develop the community. The Indigo Run sales office is at 100 Indigo Run Drive within the main gate, which is off the parkway near Mile Marker 3. You can reach the sales office by calling 681-3300 or (800) 487-2645

Long Cove Club

The centerpiece of this community is a 6900-yard golf course designed by Pete Dye that's been ranked best in South Carolina and 21st in the nation. Property owners automatically become members of Long Cove Club, entitling them to use the golf course, the elegant 17,000-square-foot clubhouse, the pool, eight tennis courts and docks on Broad Creek that have slips for 100 boats. According to John McKenzie, president of Long Cove Club Realty, some club members live on other parts of Hilton Head but have bought lots at Long Cove just so they can play on the private golf course.

Development of Long Cove began in 1980, and all 570 homesites in the 600-acre community were sold by 1987. Ninety-seven percent of the sites have a view of a lagoon, marsh or the golf course, and about 325 homes have been built, all of them single-family residences. The median price tag for these homes — one- and two-story structures of stucco and cypress — is around $450,000. Privacy is prized here, and there are no short-term rentals. There's a sales office within the community at 44 Long Cove Drive, where the phone number is 842-2442. The entrance to Long Cove is off William Hilton Parkway near Mile Marker 10.

Palmetto Dunes

Spread over 2,000 acres on the eastern side of the island, Palmetto Dunes offers 3 miles of beach bordering the Atlantic Ocean; 5,000 homes and villas, more than 500 of which can be rented by vacationers; three 18-hole golf courses; a world-class tennis facility; an 11-mile lagoon system; and two of the island's "big four" hotels — the 505-room Hyatt Regency Hilton Head Resort and the 323-room Hilton Head Island Hilton Resort (see listings under Accommodations). All three of the golf courses — named for designers Arthur Hills, George Fazio and Robert Trent Jones — are accessible to the public (see listings in this chapter under Golf), as are the 23 clay and two hard courts of the Palmetto Dunes Tennis Center. Homes in Palmetto Dunes range from $250,000 to well over $1 million.

Palmetto Dunes was started in the late 1960s and acquired in 1979 by the Greenwood Development Corporation, which since then has created the Shelter Cove Harbour yacht basin and retail complex and the Leamington community. Shelter Cove — a marina surrounded by shops, restaurants and villas built in the style of a Mediterranean village — opened in 1982 and is directly across William Hilton Parkway from Palmetto Dunes.

INSIDERS' TIP

The man for whom the Coligny traffic circle and the Coligny Plaza shopping center is named was Gaspard de Coligny, who sponsored two exploratory expeditions by French Protestants to the Port Royal Sound area in the mid-1500s.

Leamington, covering 400 acres within Palmetto Dunes, is a private community with security gates that's centered around the Arthur Hills golf course. Development of this area was begun in 1986. You'll find the Palmetto Dunes sales office at the entrance to the community, which is off William Hilton Parkway near Mile Marker 8. The phone number is 842-1111.

Palmetto Hall Plantation

Palmetto Hall is a golf-oriented community covering 775 acres in the northern portion of the island. Most of the 500 homesites border the fairways of the plantation's two 18-hole golf courses — the Arthur Hills and Robert Cupp courses — both of which are open to the public (see listings in this chapter under Golf). Started by Greenwood Development Corporation in late 1990, Palmetto Hall offers its residents a 14,000-square-foot clubhouse and an activities center with pools, tennis courts and a children's playground.

The homes here, all of them single-family residences, reflect the style of the Lowcountry with their verandas, dormers and colorful shutters. Patio homes start at $225,000, and other residences range up to $600,000. Palmetto Hall is also the site of more than 100 acres of nature preserves. The plantation's sales office is at 357 William Hilton Parkway, and the phone number is 689-3333. Palmetto Hall's main gate is on Beach City Road, about a half-mile from the road's intersection with William Hilton Parkway at Mile Marker 4.

Port Royal Plantation

Living on the beach (or having easy access to it) is the main drawing card of this 1,000-acre community in the northeastern corner of the island. There are 2.5 miles of beach stretching along the plantation on the east and southeast, 1.5 miles on the Atlantic Ocean and the rest on Port Royal Sound. The eastern side is the site of the actual Hilton Head, the bluff where English sea captain William Hilton looked out on the sound while exploring the region; it's the spot for which the entire island was eventually named.

Port Royal was one of the island's first planned communities, and the 835 homes within its gates reflect a wide variety of sizes and styles. They range in value from $200,000 to $1.75 million; most are in the $250,000 to $450,000 range, and those on the oceanfront average about $800,000.

Another big attraction at Port Royal is golf. There are three 18-hole courses: Planter's Row, which is outside the gate and is always open to the public, and Barony and Robber's Row, which are within the gate and open to the public on a rotating basis (see listings in this chapter's Golf section). Residents of the plantation can be members at all three courses. Also outside the gate but considered part of Port Royal are the Port Royal Racquet Club, which has grass, composition and hard-surface tennis courts; the 412-room Westin Resort Hilton Head hotel (see listing in this chapter's Accommodations section); and the villas at the Port Royal Village, Ocean Palms and Planter's Quarters developments. The plantation's administrative office is at 10 Coggins Point Road just before the main gate, which is off William Hilton Parkway near Mile Marker 5; the phone number is 681-5114.

Sea Pines

A Hilton Head architect once called Sea Pines the "daddy rabbit" of planned residential/resort communities. It's an apt description of the largest and oldest of the island's major developments — the first community of its kind in the nation.

Sea Pines covers 5,200 acres on the south end of Hilton Head and was started in 1957. It's the site of the island's first golf course, the Ocean Course, one of three courses in the community, all of which can be played by the public (see Golf in this chapter). The most popular of these courses is the Harbour Town Golf Links, which is the site of the island's biggest annual event, the MCI Classic — The Heritage of Golf, a tournament that brings many of the world's best golfers to Hilton Head for four days during April. Also staged that month is the Family Circle Cup, a tournament at Sea Pines Racquet Club that draws the world's top women tennis players. (See this chapter's Annual Events section for more on both events.) The racquet club has 28 courts and offers comprehensive programs of tennis instruction under the direction of former Wimbledon champion Stan Smith.

Sea Pines is the site of Hilton Head's best-known landmark, the maroon and white striped lighthouse at the Harbour Town Yacht Basin. Villas, shops and restaurants ring the basin at Harbour Town; it's one of two marinas in Sea Pines, the other being at South Beach, where you'll also find a New England-style village with shops, restaurants and all sorts of watersports. Both marinas provide access to Calibogue Sound. More shops and eating places are available at the Sea Pines Center.

Within the borders of Sea Pines are a 605-acre nature preserve, 5 miles of beach, the ruins of the Baynard-Stoney Plantation, three swimming pools, the Lawton Stables equestrian center and a beach club that has an open-air grill, an oceanfront bar, a gift shop and picnic tables. The community offers 10,000 square feet of meeting space at the Plantation Club Conference Center and the Harbour Town Clubhouse.

Sea Pines has nearly 3,500 single-family homes, with an average value of $387,000. A total of 430 villas and homes are available for rent by vacationers. To learn more about Sea Pines, visit the reception center at 32 Greenwood Drive or call 785-3333 or (800) SEAPINES. The reception center is right outside the community's main gate, which is on Greenwood Drive just south of the Sea Pines traffic circle.

Shipyard Plantation

Shipyard has a mixture of single-family residences, condominiums, timeshare units and commercial developments within its 834 acres. There are about 250 residences ranging from patio homes valued at $200,000 to larger houses on golf courses that start at $300,000. The plantation, in the southeastern part of the island, is the site of more than 1,400 villas grouped in 20 different villa regimes.

The Shipyard Golf Club consists of 27 holes on three courses open to the public — Brigantine, Clipper and Galleon (see Golf, this chapter). Residents and guests have other forms of recreation available, particularly tennis and the beach. The Van der Meer Shipyard Racquet Club boasts 20 championship courts, and the eastern side of the plantation is on the

FYI

Unless otherwise noted, the area code for all phone numbers listed in this guide is 803.

Atlantic Ocean. Shipyard's ocean side is the site of the 340-room Crowne Plaza Resort hotel (see this chapter's Accommodations section) and a beach club for residents. The plantation is also the home of the Hilton Head Health Institute, a resort for folks seeking to change their lifestyles by learning how to control their weight, reduce stress and become more physically fit.

Ironically, Shipyard has no marina; its name is derived from the cotton plantation that once occupied the site of the community. Administrative offices are at 10 Shipyard Drive, and the phone number is 785-3310. They're just outside the main gate, which is off William Hilton Parkway near Mile Marker 10.

Spanish Wells

Spanish Wells and a development associated with it, Wells East, are about 80 percent built out. There are some 200 single-family homes at this 350-acre community on the western portion of the island; the houses at Spanish Wells are on lots of at least 1 acre. Residences range in value from the low $300,000s to $2 million.

Spanish Wells is the most secluded of the island's communities; it's at the end of Spanish Wells Road, nearly 3 miles from William Hilton Parkway. The private golf club has a nine-hole course and two tennis courts, and a swimming pool is planned. Many of the homes at Spanish Wells are on Calibogue Sound or Broad Creek, and those on Brahms Point, a narrow finger of land at the southwestern reaches of the community, have views of both bodies of water. The community derives its name from the wells from which Spanish explorers drew fresh water while visiting Hilton Head. Also of historical note is the fact that Spanish Wells is the site of Battery Holbrook, a Civil War gun emplacement. To learn more about Spanish Wells, call the property owners' association at 842-4138.

Wexford Plantation

The emphasis is on privacy at Wexford, where rentals are prohibited and admittance is open only to residents, their guests and prospective home buyers. This golf and yachting community covers 525 acres near the middle of the island. All of the 470 lots at Wexford are sold, and 176 homes had been built as of September 1997, most of them two-story, British Colonial-style houses valued from $469,000 to $2 million. Twenty residences were being built during fall 1997.

About a third of the homes are on the plantation's 37.5-acre harbor, which winds through the center of the community and is lock-controlled to keep the water calm and at a minimum of 8 feet deep. The harbor, with slips accommodating yachts up to 75 feet long, provides access to Broad Creek. Most of the other homes are on Wexford's 18-hole golf course, a layout designed by William Byrd and reserved solely for members and their guests. Other amenities take the form of a harborside clubhouse graced with pink Georgian marble and Tiffany glass skylights; a pool with a patio that overlooks the water; six tennis courts, two of them lighted; and a croquet lawn. Sales offices are at 2 Town Center Court and can be reached by calling 686-8800 or (800) 345-2392. Wexford's main entrance is off William Hilton Parkway near Mile Marker 10.

Windmill Harbour

Designed for boaters and other folks who love being around the water, Windmill Harbour covers 172 acres in the northwestern portion of Hilton Head. Unlike the island's other planned communities, Windmill Harbour has no golf course, but it does have a 15.5-acre yacht basin with 261 boat slips. The harbor, the site of the South Carolina Yacht Club, has a lock system that keeps tides and currents to a minimum; the lack of movement of water also inhibits the growth of barnacles on the bottom of boats, allowing their owners to save on maintenance costs. The harbor lies on Calibogue Sound, which is part of the Intracoastal Waterway.

Eighty percent of the homesites at Windmill Harbour have views of the water. Among the 435 residences in existence as of fall 1997 were estates on lots of an acre or more, villas, patio homes and condominiums, all of them reflecting architectural styles seen in the historic district of Charleston and the South Carolina Lowcountry. Prices for condos start at $139,000; homes run from $274,900 to $800,000, with a few topping $2 million.

Residents seeking recreation other than boating can find it at the community's sports center, which provides an Olympic-size lap pool, seven clay tennis courts and extensive workout facilities. The elegant building that serves as headquarters for the yacht club overlooks the harbor and offers a meeting place where residents can dine and attend cookouts, oyster roasts and parties. Although Windmill Harbour is in the main a private community, the yacht basin is open to the boating public, and residents can rent out their dwellings for periods of 60 days or more. Shorterterm rentals are prohibited. The sales office is at 2 Harbour Passage Patio inside the main gate, which is off William Hilton Parkway just after you cross the bridges to the island. You can reach these offices by calling 681-5600 or (800) 733-2625.

Accommodations

When you vacation at Hilton Head, you have the option of staying at hotels or motels, villas or private homes that are being rented out by their owners. The hotels and motels range from modern, well-maintained establishments on the island's main thoroughfares to full-blown resorts situated in or adjacent to Hilton Head's luxurious golf communities. The villas are fully furnished condominiums set in apartment buildings and townhouses, many

INSIDERS' TIP

Unlike many resort areas, Hilton Head is a place where folks on golfing vacations can "stay anywhere, play anywhere." That means you're not locked into playing golf at the courses associated with the resort where you're staying — you can play on any of the public courses, no matter where you're staying.

The MCI Classic — The Heritage of Golf attracts 100,000 spectators to Hilton Head's Harbour Town Golf Links.

of them with pools and locations close to beaches, golf clubs and tennis courts.

There's plenty to choose from — Hilton Head has more than 3,000 hotel and motel rooms, 6,000 villa units and an array of rental homes ranging from oceanfront mansions to laid-back cottages. We've provided a rundown of hotels and motels — places that offer nightly accommodations; for information on villas and private homes, which usually rent for longer-term stays (anywhere from three nights to two weeks), we suggest calling one of the island's numerous central reservations services. Among these are the Condo Hotline, 785-2939, (800)258-5852; Hilton Head Accommodations and Golf Hotline, 686-6662, (800) 444-4772; Hilton Head Central Reservations Center, 785-9050, (800) 845-7018; Hilton Head Island Villa & Hotel Reservations, 842-6212, (800) 845-8602; and Vacations on Hilton Head, 686-3500, (800) BEACH-ME.

In general, rates for accommodations are higher from the end of April through September, although some places raise their prices starting in February and others lower them after Labor Day. Call ahead to see what's available (well ahead if you're planning on staying during the summer, especially on weekends) and ask about special deals — many of the larger establishments have a variety of vacation packages from which to choose. Be aware that some motels and hotels will give you a lower rate if you stay with them early in the week when they might be struggling to fill up their rooms.

Most of the hotels and motels we surveyed don't allow pets and have nonsmoking and handicapped-accessible rooms; we've noted exceptions and have also included a symbol with each entry denoting a price range for the average one-night stay, in-season, for two adults. These prices do not include tax, gratuities and add-on amenities such as room service. Here's the code:

Price Codes

$	$85 or lower
$$	$86 to $125
$$$	$126 to $160
$$$$	$161 to $190
$$$$$	$191 or more

Unless we've indicated otherwise, you'll have to pay to play golf or tennis at the resort where you're staying. Most places have packages or special deals involving these sports, and you should inquire about these if you intend to play. The following properties are listed alphabetically.

Adventure Inn Beach & Golf Club
$$ • 41 S. Forest Beach Dr. • 785-5151, (800) 845-9500

Relax poolside under the graceful branches of the spreading live oak tree, take an early-morning, guided walking tour of the beach or play tennis for free at the Adventure Inn. This oceanfront establishment offers a full slate of activities geared to youngsters from 9 AM to 5 PM Monday through Friday during the summer months. Some of the programs (such as scavenger hunts) are free, and there are fees for others (such as poolside bingo and beach-bag designing).

The tree is a favorite of guests, tennis is complimentary on two courts across South Forest Beach Drive from the Inn, and discounted golf packages for 14 courses on and off the island are offered. Although there is a five-night minimum stay in the majority of the units during summer, daily rentals are available. Some oceanfront efficiency rooms are well-suited for families — each has a queen-size bed, a queen sleeper sofa and a loft with two double beds intended for kids (there's not a lot of head room because of the pitched ceiling).

Fitzgerald's, a restaurant serving dinner seven days a week during summer and every day except Sunday in the off-season, is on the premises. Because the units here are individually owned timeshares, there are no nonsmoking or handicapped-accessible accommodations.

Comfort Inn & Suites
$$ • 2 Tanglewood Dr. • 842-6662, (800) 228-5150

You can walk to the beach in five minutes from the five-story Comfort Inn, but if you'd rather not hoof it, you can hitch a ride on the hotel's beach buggy, which runs continuously from 10 AM to 4 PM. If freshwater activities are more your style, take a dip in the hotel pool, where the surroundings have a Hawaiian flair, or zip down the water slides at the adjacent Water Fun Park, where hotel guests are given a 50 percent discount — it's $7.50 for adults and $5 for children.

The 153-room Comfort Inn, situated on 6 acres graced by three lagoons, sits well back from South Forest Beach Drive a few blocks from the Coligny traffic circle. The hotel began as a Days Inn in 1987, was reborn as a Comfort Inn in the early '90s and was totally renovated in 1996. Guests can partake of deluxe continental breakfasts from 7 to 10 AM in the registration building, which also houses 1,400 square feet of meeting space and Fish Tales, a full-service restaurant with a bar. The hotel accepts pets for a fee of $20.

Crowne Plaza Resort
$$$$$ • 130 Shipyard Dr. • 842-2400, (800) 334-1881

Built in a U-shape on the ocean in Shipyard, the Crowne Plaza opens onto a courtyard with subtropical gardens, extensive green spaces and lagoons crossed by graceful wooden bridges. One bridge is a favorite spot for couples saying their wedding vows, and if you plan to get hitched there, you might consider enlisting the services of Crowne Plaza executive secretary Sue Bennett, a justice of the peace. The large courtyard is also the location of a pool, outdoor hot tub, toddler's pool and Dockers, which serves light fare and drinks.

Amble down to the beach, and you'll pass by the Three Palms snack bar, which specializes in snow cones and hot dogs. Nearby is the hotel's 7,000-square-foot outdoor pavilion, which is popular for meetings, dinners and those weddings we referred to. The Crowne Plaza has 340 rooms, including 25 suites, with views of either the island, the courtyard or the ocean. Portz restaurant offers fine dining in the evening, and you can get brunch and lunch indoors or outdoors at Brellas, which features tables sporting green umbrellas.

The hotel's leisure activities department operates Camp Castaway, a structured and supervised program for children 3 to 12. Among the many activities provided are shell hunts and turtle feedings for the youngest kids, games on the beach and in the pool for those 6 to 8 and bike tours and special tennis and golf instruction for the oldest youngsters. Fees for a full day of fun are $35 per child; children 3 to 5 are restricted to morning sessions, which are $27 per child. Adults seeking opportunities to exercise can find them at the Crowne Plaza's fully equipped fitness center and adjacent indoor pool and at Shipyard's golf courses and tennis courts.

Disney's Hilton Head Island Resort
$$$$$ • 22 Harbourside Ln. • 341-4100, (800) 453-4911

The Disney folks are famous for creating atmosphere, and they've done it again at their Hilton Head Island Resort, where the Live Oak Lodge and 102 villas have the look of Lowcountry hunting and fishing cabins of the 1950s. These are cabins with style, though, rustic but rich with natural-wood accents and first-class reproductions of country-style furniture. There are interesting touches such as pine-log headboards and a reminder or two that you're staying at a Disney property — we found the initials "W.D." carved in one end of a wooden bench in an alcove of a villa, and there were two hearts bearing the names "Mickey" and "Minnie" scratched into the other end.

Accommodations take the form of studios and one-, two- and three-bedroom villas. The villas have whirlpool tubs and full kitchens. The rustic theme is carried throughout the resort, which was built in 1996 and covers wooded Longview Island, a 16-acre tract between Shelter Cove Harbour and Broad Creek: Guests splash and sun at a pool called the Big Dipper Swimming Hole, buy groceries at the Broad Creek Mercantile general store and gather for activities at the Community Hall recreation room. This wouldn't be a Disney place without some characters walking around and entertaining guests, and the resort has 'em — Officer O'Dell the Lowcountry policeman and those two terribly tacky tourists, Bunnie and Skeeter Rotwood.

There's no restaurant on the premises, but there are several at nearby Shelter Cove and there's Royce's Grill, which is near the swimming hole and serves hamburgers, hot dogs and chicken during daylight hours in the summer. Also, there's plenty of marsh but no beach at the resort. However, Disney provides oceanside enjoyment for its guests via its 13,000-square-foot beach house at Palmetto Dunes, a facility that has an Olympic-size pool, a snack bar and children's play area, plus the beach. The beach house is 1.5 miles from the resort, and a shuttle service is provided. The resort also offers the Disney Discovery Club, a special program for children ages 6 to 12 that places emphasis on learning about the environment through activities such as bicycling and crabbing. There's a version of the club for kids 3 to 5, too. Program fees for guests (which are not necessary for use of the beach house) are $25.

Fairfield Inn by Marriott
$ • 9 Marina Side Dr. • 842-4800, (800) TEE-OFF4

Each of the 14 suites at the Fairfield Inn has a nice touch — French doors separating the bedroom from the large sitting room. The other 105 rooms at the three-story motel off U.S. 278 just past Mile Marker 9 have kings and double beds, and there is a pool. A continental breakfast awaits guests in a dining room off the lobby from 6:30 to 9:30 AM at this motel, which is centrally located and near a slew of restaurants and shops.

Four Points Hotel by ITT Sheraton
$$ • 36 S. Forest Beach Dr. • 842-3100, (800) 535-3248

You'll be less than a block from the beach if you stay at this full-service hotel just south of the Coligny traffic circle, and you'll also have access to the pool and poolside activities (including kids' programs) at the nearby Holiday Inn Oceanfront Resort (see listing in this section). The latter is true because the Four Points and Holiday Inn are owned by the same outfit, Servico Management Corp. of Florida. There is also an outdoor pool at each of the Four Points' buildings — the hotel's five-story main building and the three-story villa building.

The Four Points, which was completely remodeled in 1997, has 140 rooms, 72 with kitchenettes and all with small refrigerators. The hotel's restaurant and lounge, Mulligan's Food and Spirits, serves breakfast, lunch and dinner, and offers room service.

Main Street Inn
Hilton Head Island

The Carolina's Only Small Luxury Inn

- *Inviting*
- *Indulgent*
- *Incomparable*

220 Main Street
Hilton Head Island, SC

1-800-471-3001

Hampton Inn
$ • 1 Dillon Rd. • 681-7900,
(800) HAMPTON

If you're not particularly interested in going to the beach, the Hampton Inn might be for you. This two-story, 124-room motel just off U.S. 278 at Mile Marker 5 caters to business travelers, people visiting the island for the golf of it and folks on budgets. And, heck, if you do get a hankering to stick your toes in the ocean, the Atlantic is only a little more than a mile away at the Folly Field Beach access. There's an outdoor pool for those who want to stay close by to do their swimming and a well-equipped exercise room for the fitness-minded. The Hampton offers shuttle service to the Hilton Head Airport upon request, a complimentary continental breakfast from 6 to 10 AM in the sitting room off the lobby and free copies of *USA Today*. Some of the rooms have kitchenettes with microwave ovens and small refrigerators.

FYI
Unless otherwise noted, the area code for all phone numbers listed in this guide is 912.

Harbourside III at Shelter Cove
$$$ • 9 Shelter Cove Ln. • 686-3375,
(800) 542-5535

Harbourside III offers its guests the Mediterranean-style ambiance of Shelter Cove Harbour, which is on U.S. 278 at Mile Marker 8, and free golf and tennis at nearby Palmetto Dunes resort. Harbourside III — a four-story, 39-room, short-term rental property — stands alongside the Harbour, which has slips for 175 boats and is ringed by villas, shops and restaurants. Eating places such as San Miguel's Mexican Cafe, The Little Venice Ristorante Italiano, Scott's Fish Market Restaurant and Bar and Caffe Hilton Head are within easy walking distance and The Mall at Shelter Cove is close by. On Tuesdays from 6:30 to 9:30 PM during the summer, guests can step outside into the midst of HarbourFest, a family-oriented fair featuring live entertainment, fireworks and sales of food and arts and crafts. At the pool, you'll find a hot tub, a shaded sitting area and a gas grill. Harbourside III has one-, two- and three-bedroom units, all furnished in a contemporary beach style. It does not have non-smoking rooms.

Hilton Head Island Hilton Resort
$$$$-$$$$$ • 23 Ocean Ln. • 842-8000,
(800) 845-8001

Hallways open to catch ocean breezes and lagoons winding their way through lush foliage give this beachfront Hilton hotel at Palmetto Dunes a semi-tropical aura. Extra-large rooms open onto equally spacious balconies, each with at least a partial view of the beach and sea. All 323 rooms have kitchenettes and amenities such as ceiling fans in dining areas and separate vanities in bathrooms. The five-story hotel is built in a horseshoe shape that opens onto the beach, and the nooks and crannies of the spacious garden within the horseshoe harbor small courtyards and rambling wooden decks.

The ground-floor Activity Center houses three eating places — the Palmetto Cafe, the Deli Pizza Hut and Mostly Seafood — and the Regatta Lounge, which serves as a sports bar in the afternoons and early evenings and a nightclub after 9 PM Monday through Saturday. Guests can also eat lunch at the Buoy Bar and Grill at the main pool. There's also an adults-only pool for those seeking a quieter atmosphere. For more relaxation, try one of the two oceanfront whirlpool baths or the saunas in the men's and women's locker rooms of the fitness center.

The hotel offers special rates for golf and tennis at the courses and courts at Palmetto Dunes and special activities for children via Vacation Station. This day and evening camp program is for kids ages 4 through 11 and is priced at $35 per child for a full-day session and $30 per child for an evening session. The Hilton has 21,000 square feet of meeting space and a full-scale conference center, and there's a shuttle from the hotel to all the activities Palmetto Dunes and nearby Shelter Cove Harbour have to offer.

Holiday Inn Oceanfront Resort
$$$ • 1 S. Forest Beach Dr. • 785-5126,
(800) 535-3248

Life's just beachy at the Holiday Inn Oceanfront, where the meandering, free-form pool is only steps away from the white sand of the Hilton Head strand. The white-oak furniture and pastel decor of the inn's 201 rooms (all of which open onto interior hallways) carry out the beach motif as do the five-story motel's eating and drinking places — Grouper's & Co. restaurant and the second-floor Parrot's Perch lounge, each with plenty of windows and great views of the ocean; the Island Eatery, which stands on a concrete peninsula jutting into the pool and serves lunch fare from 11 AM to 4 PM; and the poolside Tiki Hut beach bar. The lounge, where the windows will be exchanged for shutters in an attempt to bring the ocean's roar into the room, is open from 5 PM to 1 AM seven days a week and features a dance floor and DJ.

The inn offers numerous recreational activities, some of them free and many intended for the younger set. Among these are the Big Daddy Splash contest, to see who can make the "biggest, craziest and smallest" entries into the pool, relays on the beach and underwater treasure hunts. The inn also has a children's pool and playground and 3,000 square feet of meeting space.

Hyatt Regency Hilton Head Resort
$$$$ • 1 Hyatt Circle • 785-1234, (800) 233-1234

With its 505 rooms and 38,000 square feet of meeting space, this Hyatt is billed as the largest luxury oceanfront resort between Atlantic City, New Jersey, and Palm Beach, Florida. Even so, this 10-story hotel at Palmetto Dunes has the comfortable feel of a place where guests are kicking back and going on vacation. It's not unusual to see youngsters padding through the spacious lobby in their flip-flops on their way to a day at the pool or to take part in the activities provided by Camp Hyatt, a program for kids ages 3 to 12. The camp provides day and evening fun (including nature walks and sand sculpting) at a cost per child of $40 per day or $20 per half-day.

The pool is Olympic-size, and there's also a 1-foot-deep pool for toddlers. Poolside, guests will find the Possum Point restaurant, which serves salads and sandwiches, and the Point Comfort bar, specializing in frozen drinks. For indoor dining, there's The Cafe for breakfast, lunch and dinner, and Hemingway's for dinner and Sunday brunch. Hemingway's

Lounge overlooks the ocean and offers nightly entertainment. If you're in need of snacks, try The Grocery, an offbeat little convenience store on the hotel's lower level. Other shopping opportunities take the form of a large W.H. Smith gift shop and a golf pro shop. If you crave exercise, you can work out in the Hyatt's well-equipped fitness center, play a round of golf at one of five courses within walking or shuttle distance or hit the courts at the Palmetto Dunes Tennis Center.

Main Street Inn
$$$$$ • 2200 Main St. • 681-3001, (800) 342-2282

A couple seeking a spot for a romantic getaway will find it at the elegant Main Street Inn off U.S. 278 between mile markers 3 and 4. The 34 rooms are luxuriously appointed with classic furnishings: wooden armoires handmade on Hilton Head, beds adorned with Italian linens and goose-down pillows and comforters, and baths featuring pedestal sinks and Italian marble floors and shower walls. The Deluxe Queen rooms have fireplaces, and balconies large enough for a wrought-iron table that's a perfect spot for breakfast.

The inn's crowning glories are the four Courtyard King rooms with their bay windows, window seats, whirlpool tubs, glassed-in showers and pine floors fashioned from the 150-year-old beams of a Lowcountry mill. In each King, French doors in the bathroom open onto an intimate courtyard abounding with fig vines, fruit trees and jasmine. Guests staying in rooms on the upper two floors can step outside onto wide verandas complete with rocking chairs. From there, you'll see the Charleston-style gardens of the courtyard and a pool designed for swimming laps; the view beyond is of the lush 15th green and 16th fairway of Hilton Head Plantation's Bear Creek Golf Course and of the forested wetlands of a nature preserve.

Your stay includes European-style buffet breakfasts and afternoon teas served in the dining room-library, the dining room lounge or the courtyard. Much of the fare is prepared by the inn's own baker. If all this isn't relaxing enough, try the massage and aromatherapy at the hotel's second-floor European spa.

Radisson Suite Resort
**$$-$$$ • 12 Park Ln. • 686-5700,
(800) 333-3333**

The only all-suite hotel on the island rambles over a quiet wooded area in the Central Park office complex just off U.S. 278 between mile markers 9 and 10. The centrally located Radisson provides a complimentary shuttle to the beach four times a day and a full-scale continental breakfast in the lobby from 7 to 10 AM. Each of the 156 suites has a balcony and fully-equipped kitchen including a full-size refrigerator, and the King and bi-level Penthouse suites have wood-burning fireplaces (you can buy synthetic logs at the desk or bring your own).

Penthouse suites are designed for entertaining, family gatherings and romantic getaways — each has an enlarged dining area, a sleeper sofa and a loft-type bedroom with its own bathroom. The Radisson offers bell service, and room service is available at discounted prices from adjacent Big Rocco's Italian-American restaurant. If you want refreshments or a light lunch, stop by the poolside Cabana Bar. Golf packages are available, and there's complimentary tennis (plus rent-free rackets and balls) on two lighted tennis courts on the back side of the property, which is also the site of a tree-shaded playground and picnic area.

Red Roof Inn Hilton Head
**$ • 5 Regency Pkwy. • 686-6808,
(800) THE-ROOF**

Take a room at the Red Roof Inn after March 1998, and you'll be staying at a motel that has been thoroughly renovated inside and out. The refurbishing of the 112-room motel just off U.S. 278 at Mile Marker 9 began in September 1997 and was scheduled for completion the following spring. The two-story inn offers rooms with king-size beds and California kings (they're a little smaller than standard kings), along with four spacious suites with kitchenettes. According to General Manager Daryl Dembeck, the emphasis here is on making guests "feel good and giving them value for their dollar." The inn, with a roof that remains brown instead of red because of Hilton Head's stringent building-design regulations, is adjacent to Crabby Nick's restaurant, which serves dinner and late-afternoon lunch.

Shoney's Inn Hilton Head
**$ • 200 Museum St. • 681-3655,
(800) 995-3928**

Located on the rapidly developing north end of the island, Shoney's Inn boasts many of the features you might expect to find at a full-service hotel. Among them are a restaurant serving breakfast, lunch and dinner (a Shoney's, of course); a lounge that's open from 5 to 11 PM Monday through Saturday (appropriately called the Tee Time Lounge, in recognition of the motel's golfing guests and its computerized golfing reservation service); a fitness room; 2,000 square feet of meeting space; same-day, valet laundry and dry cleaning service; and complimentary coffee and *USA Today* newspapers. The 136-room motel, which is on U.S. 278 at Mile Marker 3, was completely renovated in 1996.

South Beach Marina Inn
**$$$ • 232 S. Sea Pines Dr. • 671-6498,
(800) 367-3909**

Were it not for the distinctly Southern foliage and marshlands within view, you might think you're in New England when you stay at the South Beach Marina Inn. This charming, 17-room hotel is part of a small complex of shops and restaurants patterned after a fishing village on Nantucket Island, Massachusetts. The rooms of the inn, a nightly rental property at Sea Pines, reflect the Yankee atmosphere via the highly polished heart-of-pine floors, brass beds and colorful rag rugs.

All of the one- and two-bedroom accommodations have kitchenettes, and most have separate, cozy living rooms that will make you feel as if you've found a second home. Although the inn is deep within Sea Pines, the village and marina offer just about everything a vacationer would need. As Sales Director Cliff Charnes says, you can "literally park your car and not leave," except to play a round of golf on the nearest course, which is a five-minute drive. At your front door is the marina on Braddock's Cove with its varied recreational opportunities for hire — Jet Skiing, boat rentals, charter fishing, parasailing, instruction in windsurfing and sailing lessons. Also near your doorstep are a pool, a dozen tennis courts and 15 miles of paved trails for hiking, bicycling, jogging and in-line skating. You can walk to the beach in three to four minutes, and there are six eating places within the village. All rooms are on the second floor, and there are no nonsmoking or handicapped accommodations. Pets are allowed in some units, and there is a $50 cleanup fee.

Westin Resort Hilton Head
$$$$ • 2 Grasslawn Ave. • 681-4000, (880) WESTIN1

The lobby and circular Gazebo Lounge of the Westin radiate the charm of a classic, turn-of-the-century seaside hotel with their polished wood floors, elaborate chandeliers, area rugs and potted plants. There are even doilies on the armrests of the plush sofas. This feeling of Southern hospitality carries through the hallways and rooms of the five-story oceanfront hotel adjacent to Port Royal. The lounge looks out on the hotel's spacious courtyard, where swans swim in a pond set amid lush foliage. In the cooler months, the lounge and its comfy drawing-room furniture and wood-burning fireplace beckon to guests. When the weather's warm, the courtyard is the place to be — you'll find two pools (a round pool and a lap pool), extensive wooden decks where you can relax in rocking chairs and the Pelican Poolside snack bar. A steel-drum band provides entertainment by the pool during summer afternoons, and you can get a massage at the water's edge if you're so inclined. Close by are an indoor pool with a hydraulic lift for the physically impaired and the Westin Health Club with its aerobics room, sauna, steam room and exercise rooms filled with state-of-the-art strength-training equipment.

Those seeking outdoor recreation can find it at the nearby Port Royal Golf Club, which has three championship courses (see the Golf section of this chapter), or at the Port Royal Racquet Club, which offers grass, clay and hard-surface courts. There's a hotel shuttle to both places. For youngsters ages 4 to 12, Camp Wackatoo provides activities such as Looney Lawn Games and crabbing and shrimping at fees of $50 per child for a full day and $35 for a half-day.

There's fine dining during the evening at Westin's Barony Grill; casual dining and cocktails in the late afternoon and evening at the Playful Pelican, which overlooks the ocean;

and family dining throughout the day at the Carolina Cafe, which features a seafood buffet and 18-foot-long dessert table. The Westin, which has 412 rooms including 30 suites, underwent a renovation that cost $6 million and was completed in April 1997.

Restaurants

The Yellow Pages of the Hilton Head telephone book have more than 25 pages of listings and advertisements for restaurants — make no mistake, there's a lot to choose from here in terms of eateries and cuisine. In this section, we look at 29 of the island's more popular restaurants in an attempt to provide you with selections offering a variety of foods in a variety of atmospheres at a variety of prices.

All the restaurants discussed here serve alcoholic beverages, and most have areas where smoking is allowed; we've noted the exceptions. Many of these eating places either recommend or require that you make reservations, and we've pointed out the ones that do. All take most major credit cards. Listings are in alphabetical order.

Price Code

To give you an idea of the prices at these restaurants, we've provided a dollar-sign code showing what you can expect to pay for a dinner for two minus alcoholic beverages, appetizers, desserts, taxes and tip.

$	**$27 and lower**
$$	**$28 to $33**
$$$	**$34 to $38**
$$$$	**$39 and higher**

Alexander's
$$$ • 76 Queens Folly Rd. • 785-4999

Located on a lagoon at Palmetto Dunes, Alexander's provides casual but dressy dining in three settings — an enclosed porch, a wine bar adorned with a fireplace and a cozy dining room. Established in 1977, the restaurant serves dinner and specializes in seafood, including salmon Oscar and the Island Seafood Collection — a combination of fresh broiled fish, oysters Rockefeller, shrimp scampi, deviled crab Daufuskie and mussels Provençal. If you enjoy wine, you have your choice of 100 different bottles, some hard to find, with 60 of the selections served by the glass. Reservations are suggested.

The Big Bamboo Cafe
$ • Coligny Plaza • 686-3443

According to the legend of The Big Bamboo that appears on the front of the cafe's menu, this restaurant on the ocean side of Coligny Plaza shopping center has been constructed as closely as possible to the configurations of the original Big Bamboo, a bar and grill opened on the Pacific island of Tarawa in 1944 by ex-fighter pilot Jimmy Phipps. From the bamboo of the bar to the thatched palm fronds and camouflage netting of the ceiling to the World War II regalia tacked on the walls, Hilton Head's version of The Big Bamboo reflects the feel of the real thing. . . . If there had been a real thing, that is; for, you see, The Big Bamboo of the Pacific is a figment of restaurant co-owner Scott Takac's imagination, albeit one that he and his associates have brought vividly to life on Hilton Head.

What is real about this 85-seat dining room and bar is the atmosphere of fun that has been created; that and the interesting mix of dishes available — ranging from the meat loaf and roasted turkey dinners (curiously the two biggest sellers) to the barbecue ribs, Greek pasta and black bean burgers. Harder to believe is an item called the "war dog" — a hot dog stuffed with cheddar cheese, wrapped with bacon, dipped in beer batter and fried, then tucked in a toasted roll and smothered with chili, cheeses and onions. Wow! Or as Jimmy Phipps would have put it: "Whew!"

The Big Bamboo — where you can gaze on a mix of authentic memorabilia and reproductions from the '40s while listening to the Big Band music of that era — puts out the welcome mat daily for fighter jocks and other customers seeking dinner; it's closed during January.

The Brick Oven Cafe
$ • 25 Park Plaza, Office Park Rd.
• 686-2233

Gourmet pizzas from the brick oven and "Things To Be Shared" give this restaurant in Park Plaza on Office Park Road an identity all its own. Among the pizzas on the menu are scampi, cordon bleu and mesquite grilled chicken varieties, but you can also build your own. Dining parties are encouraged to share two or three dishes designed for that experience, including sesame-crusted tuna, the oak-roasted portobello mushroom and brick oven brie. The cafe, in existence since December 1996, serves dinner in two areas accommodating a total of 80 people, including the Velvet Room, where live entertainment is provided on Saturday and Sunday nights. The wine list is extensive and offers numerous good values.

Cafe at Wexford
$$$ • Village at Wexford, 1000 William Hilton Pkwy. • 686-5969

The food and atmosphere of a cafe in the French countryside await you at this restaurant in the Village at Wexford near Mile Marker 10 on William Hilton Parkway. Wood floors and lots of brickwork give the 60-seat cafe an intimate aura. The menu offers a wide selection of country French cuisine; among the most popular entrees are the veal sweetbreads, which are sautéed in cream sauce with mushrooms and strips of ham; the roast duckling, which is served with a bing cherry or plum sauce; and the potato-onion crusted fillet of grouper. For an appetizer, try the pâté de foie. The cafe serves lunch and dinner daily and brunch on Saturday and Sunday. Reservations are suggested but not required.

Cafe Europa
$$$ • 160 Lighthouse Rd. • 671-3399

Excellent views of Calibogue Sound are available from just about all of the 140 seats at this restaurant. It's at the boaters' entrance to the Harbour Town Yacht Basin at Sea Pines, meaning the Cafe Europa is a wonderful place to watch a sunset. Linen-covered tables adorned with candles, the awning-covered ceiling and large picture windows give the restaurant an ambiance that's airy and upscale. The

Photo: Kyle Cason

For those not yet old enough for the greens of Hilton head, the beaches are the next best thing.

cuisine is continental with an emphasis on seafood — customer favorites are the baked shrimp Daufuskie; the salmon Southern-style, which comes with stone-ground grits and simmered greens; the Cuban fire-roasted tenderloin of pork, which features a mango barbecue sauce, fried plantains and black beans and rice; and the tournedos au poivre — two filet mignons sautéed with shallots, flambéed with brandy and served in a green peppercorn sauce. Cafe Europa also has outdoor dining in an area at the base of the Harbour Town Lighthouse and overlooking the marina. The cafe serves breakfast, lunch and dinner seven days a week but is closed from November through mid-February. It's completely non-smoking, and reservations are recommended.

Charlie's L'Etoile Verte
$$$$ • 1000 Plantation Ctr. • 785-9277

Ask an islander where to eat on Hilton Head, and the first word out of his or her mouth is liable to be "Charlie's." This busy little bistro

in Plantation Center off William Hilton Parkway near Mile Marker 8 serves lunch and dinner Tuesday through Saturday, specializing in more than a dozen types of fish cooked in many ways. Charlie's is not a French restaurant, despite the name ("L'Etoile Verte" means "green star" in French); this eclectic-looking cafe serves, as its affable owner Charlie Golson puts it, "whatever we feel like cooking," "we" being Golson, his entree chef and his dessert and appetizer chef. The three of them put their heads together and brainstorm during the day, a process that creates a menu that's different each night, written in longhand and copied for distribution to diners.

Among the most popular selections are the chicken salad, Cobb salad, rack of lamb, pompano with mango sauce, and triggerfish in Parmesan crust. Golson grew up in Savannah, apprenticed himself to a French chef for a year in 1970 and eventually moved to Hilton Head to serve as the chef at the now-defunct Hilton Head Inn. He opened Charlie's in 1984 and has been enthralling islanders with his culinary artistry ever since. His 80-seat restaurant is completely nonsmoking.

The Crazy Crab
$$ • 104 William Hilton Pkwy. • 681-5021
$$ • Lighthouse Rd. • 363-2722

The island's two Crazy Crab restaurants serve fresh seafood and steaks in rustic wharfside surroundings offering splendid views of the water. At the Crazy Crab on the William Hilton Parkway near Mile Marker 1, the view is of picturesque Jarvis Creek and its marsh. The other Crazy Crab is among the shops alongside the Harbour Town Yacht Basin in Sea Pines. The menus at both restaurants are the same, with the mainstays being the fried shrimp and the steamed seafood pot, which consists of half a Maine lobster, Alaskan crab legs, mussels, shrimp and oysters. The Crazy Crab at Harbour Town, which has been in business since 1986, is open for lunch and dinner seven days a week. The Crazy Crab on the parkway, which is two years older than its sister establishment, serves dinner on a daily basis.

Damon's, the Place for Ribs
$ • Village at Wexford, 1000 William Hilton Pkwy. • 785-6677

In addition to being "the place for ribs," this restaurant in the Village at Wexford near Mile Marker 10 on William Hilton Parkway is also a place for prime rib, which at Damon's is seared on a red-hot grill and slow-roasted to seal in natural juices. You can also get the prime rib chargrilled, and there are several combinations involving Damon's barbecue ribs (with shrimp, prime rib or chicken). Also on the menu are steaks and a variety of chicken dishes, salads and appetizers, including the crowd-pleasing onion loaf. Damon's, which opened on Hilton Head in 1983 and was recently redecorated in a sports theme, is one of the largest restaurants on the island; it seats 300 people in four dining rooms and has an outdoor deck. The restaurant is open for lunch and dinner seven days a week.

The Gaslight
$$$$ • The Market Place • 785-5814

Serge Prat, formerly of the Rainbow Room in New York City, has prepared classic French cuisine for islanders and visitors to Hilton Head since 1977, when he opened The Gaslight in The Market Place off the Sea Pines traffic circle. Among Prat's specialties are his Beef Wellington, salmon wrapped in puff pastry and Caesar salad. The lobster ravioli is one of several tempting appetizers available at this dressy casual restaurant, which is open for dinner Monday through Saturday and for lunch Monday through Friday. Reservations at The Gaslight, which has two dining rooms seating a total of 120, are preferred but not required.

Hilton Head Brewing Company
$ • 7-C Greenwood Dr. • 785-2739

Billed as South Carolina's first brewpub since Prohibition and the only one on the island, this establishment in Hilton Head Plaza just off the Sea Pines traffic circle always has five handcrafted beers ready for drinking — South Atlantic Pale Ale, Calibogue Amber, Old Duck Dark, Raspberry Wheat and a seasonal brew. Although the pub takes on the atmosphere of a bar late at night, the restaurant offers casual dining for families at lunch and during the evening. Watching the koi, ducks and geese in the pond outside the pub's enclosed porch will keep the kids entertained, and you can feed the fish and fowl from an outdoor deck with food purchased at the restaurant for 25¢ a pop. The menu yields a large variety of choices, including hand-tossed pizzas, chicken wings and penne pasta.

The pub, which opened in December 1994, serves brunch on Saturday and Sunday and has room for about 155 customers, including seats for 60 on the porch. On Wednesday evenings, the staff removes the tables and chairs from the area around the large bar and a DJ presides over Disco Night dancing. On Sundays from Memorial Day to Labor Day, the pub hosts Summerfest, a celebration featuring arts and crafts, a balloon artist, a face painter and a juggler.

Hofbrauhaus
$$ • Pope Avenue Executive Park • 785-3663

This cozy, Bavarian-style restaurant off Pope Avenue offers old standbys of German cuisine such as sauerbraten and wiener

schnitzel, plus a variety of seafood, steaks and fowl, including baked salmon, prime strip sirloin and roast duckling. But if you're in the mood for food from the old country, try the Schlachteplatte, a Bavarian butcher plate consisting of wiener schnitzel, sauerbraten, knockwurst and kassler rippchen, which is smoked pork loin. The Hofbrauhaus, in business since 1973 and featuring an accordion player squeezing out Bavarian music most evenings, serves dinner daily but is closed during the first part of December. Reservations are suggested at the restaurant, which pours up to a dozen different German beers.

Hudson's Seafood House
$$ • 1 Hudson Rd. • 681-2772

The emphasis at Hudson's — a fixture on the Hilton Head restaurant scene since 1967 — is on fresh seafood, much of it caught locally, including shrimp hauled in on the boats you might see tied at the docks just outside. The vessels and Skull Creek can be viewed from the main dining room, one of three at the

335-seat restaurant, which also has an oyster bar. Forty percent of Hudson's business involves shrimp — fried, steamed or broiled — but the steamed oysters, scallops and crab cakes (made with 100 percent lump backfin meat) are also big sellers. As you might expect, the dining rooms at Hudson's have a nautical look, and the tables and bar of the oyster bar are made from shrimp boat doors, the wooden pieces of equipment used in trawling.

The Oyster Factory Dining Room occupies the site of an oyster processing plant built in 1912 and bought by J.B. Hudson in the '20s. The Hudson family added shrimp to the processing operation in the mid-1950s and opened the restaurant with 95 seats in the latter half of the '60s. Brian and Gloria Carmines purchased Hudson's in 1987 and have expanded it since then.

Hudson's serves dinner daily, with lunch available in the oyster bar. Outdoor seating along the docks will be available starting in spring 1998. This area also hosts live entertainment geared to the family on six nights a week from June through August. Among the entertainers is a magician capable of conjuring as many as 150 creations from balloons. Hudson's is off Squire Pope Road about 1.5 miles from Squire Pope's intersection with the William Hilton Parkway between mile markers 1 and 2.

Juleps Restaurant
$$$ • 14 Greenwood Dr. • 842-5857

The name is Southern and so are the surroundings at Juleps, which has the look of the fine old homes of Charleston. The food is continental, says owner/host Sam Cochran, but prepared with Southern ingredients by his chef and wife, Melissa. This combination produces entrees such as Kentucky bourbon ribeye steak, grilled lamb chops and roasted quail, jumbo shrimp stuffed with lump crab meat and Dixie cornmeal flounder. Topping the list of appetizers are the shrimp rolled in crushed pecans and coconut, and oysters rolled in Cajun spices and blackened. While we're on a roll, so to speak, we'll mention that specialty drinks can be ordered from the bar, including — what else? — mint juleps.

This restaurant in the Gallery of Shops near the Sea Pines traffic circle serves dinner seven days a week and is closed during January. Reservations are recommended, and the owners request that diners wear shirts with collars.

La Maisonette
$$$$ • 20 Pope Ave. • 785-6000

You might expect to pay high prices at this elegant, well-established restaurant on Pope Avenue, but the cost of a dinner at La Maisonette is comparable to what is charged at other places on Hilton Head that offer fine dining. La Maisonette — in business since 1976 and owned and operated by Adolph Weinberger since '79 — serves three-course, French continental dinners, each of them priced at $19.95. A dinner consists of an appetizer such as sautéed shrimp, escargot, smoked salmon or a seasonal fruit topped with yogurt; a Caesar salad; and an entree. Among the latter are the rack of lamb baked with dijon and fresh rosemary and glazed with a mint

sauce; flounder stuffed with blue crab meat and topped with a dill sauce; and marinated duckling served with a caramelized fruit sauce. Desserts, priced from $3.50 to $4.50, are extra.

The restaurant has two dining rooms, one designed for private parties. Both are appointed with original art, white linen tablecloths and fine crystal and china. La Maisonette serves dinner Monday through Saturday. Reservations are recommended, and men are asked to wear jackets. Smoking is prohibited.

Old Fort Pub
$$$$ • 65 Skull Creek Dr. • 681-2386

If you're looking for a romantic setting for a meal, end your search at the Old Fort Pub. Set on a bluff along Skull Creek amid a tangle of live oaks, this restaurant offers evening-time diners candlelight, classical music, a rustic Lowcountry atmosphere and spectacular sunsets over the creek and its marsh. There are great views of the water from the first-floor dining room, bar and outdoor deck that get even better as you ascend to the second-floor Sunset Room and the rooftop widow's walk, a wooden deck reached via a cast-iron spiral staircase. Up there in the treetops, you'll find an ideal place for small cocktail parties; it's been the site of marriage proposals and wedding ceremonies.

Old Fort Pub serves Lowcountry cuisine for lunch and dinner seven days a week; reservations are a must in the evenings and should be made three to four days in advance, according to manager Tom Trice. The dinner menu includes dishes such as seared breast of duck, mesquite-smoked filet mignon, grilled filet mignon of tuna, Carolina crab meat cakes and the Skull Creek Medley, which features a crab cake, blackened prawns and grilled fillet of fish. For lunch, try one of the Pub Traditions such as the turkey croissant or the fried oyster sandwich. Wine lovers have a selection of 100 types from which to choose.

While you're at Old Fort Pub, which was built in 1974 in a style inspired by the architecture of the Lowcountry, take time to stroll around the remains of Fort Mitchel, a Civil War gun battery on the site adjacent to the restaurant. Pathways wind through what were once

Hilton Head's Gone Gator

If you get near a body of fresh or brackish water on Hilton Head, which is hard not to do given the preponderance of the island's lakes and lagoons, there's a good chance you will see a creature that looks as though it has crawled right out of *Jurassic Park*. This is the American alligator, the largest reptile on the North American continent and one of the oldest surviving vertebrates on the planet.

Alligators abound on Hilton Head, where developers have provided ready-made homes for them by creating the waterways that decorate the island's communities and golf courses. "If there's a mud puddle in the Lowcountry, there's an alligator in it," says Dean Harrigal, who coordinates the alligator nuisance program in the area. There have been no formal surveys of the alligator population on Hilton Head, but there are probably from 2,000 to 4,000 gators living on the island, says Walt Rhodes, the alligator project supervisor for the South Carolina Department of Natural Resources.

Alligators, which are protected by state and federal law, can grow to a length of 12 feet, but most of the gators removed from Hilton Head under the nuisance program are from 6 to 8 feet long, according to Harrigal. Even so, if left alone, alligators pose little threat to humans, say Rhodes and Harrigal. "Gators are naturally shy of people," says Rhodes. According to the two alligator experts, humans are more of a threat to gators than vice versa.

If the state receives a complaint about a gator on Hilton Head, and the animal is deemed a nuisance because of its behavior or location, the reptile will be removed. Removed, in this case, means destroyed, not relocated. Relocating a gator doesn't work because of the animal's strong homing instinct: Gators have been known to travel

— continued on next page

Photo: Kyle Cason

One of the alligators that abound on Hilton Head Island
suns itself near a pond at an island golf course.

as much as 30 miles to return to their nesting areas, Rhodes and Harrigal say. Fifty to 60 gators are removed from Hilton Head each year because of complaints against them, but the two say that wouldn't be the case if people were more tolerant of the animals, who were here first (present-day gators are direct descendants of a creature that lived in what is now Florida during the Miocene epoch, which occurred 25 million years ago).

People don't like gators for a number of reasons. For one thing, the alligator's appearance is not in its favor. The gator looks like a big lizard, only uglier, and it seems to have a malevolent smile permanently plastered on its bumpy face. "It's not Bambi," says Rhodes. "It's not warm and fuzzy, it's cold and scaly." For another, most people don't know much about alligators and their relatively placid temperament. Folks confuse gators with the crocodiles found on other continents, in particular the 14-foot crocs seen devouring water buffaloes in sensationalized nature flicks. Gators, says Rhodes, "will let you alone if you let them alone, and they'll see you first."

Humans have a tendency to bring out the aggressiveness in gators by feeding them. If a person feeds a gator enough times, the beast's golf ball-sized brain begins to associate the human with food. This is, if you'll pardon the phrase, a recipe for disaster that can be harmful to the human involved and fatal to the gator. It's also against the law; if you're caught feeding an alligator, you can be fined $200 or sentenced to 30 days in jail. There are cases of humans provoking gators into attacking them. Rhodes tells of a golfer who hit his ball near a gator that was sunning itself on a Hilton Head fairway, then smacked the animal with his golf club in the process of recovering the ball. The gator bit the golfer. "The gator did what you would do if someone hit you with a golf club," says Rhodes. There have been reports of people being pursued by gators, but Rhodes says he's handled in excess of 3,000 of the animals and has never been chased.

Rhodes' rules for coexisting with gators: Don't feed them; they find plenty to eat in the form of insects, crustaceans, fish and snakes. Don't tease them. For goodness sake, don't try to pet them. Look at them all you want but do so from afar. "Give the animal the respect it deserves," says Rhodes. "It has as much right to be here as the deer, squirrels and people."

---

the bunkers and moats of a fortification constructed by the Union Army after it captured the island in November 1861.

The restaurant is in Hilton Head Plantation on the northwestern part of the island (see the Planned Residential Communities section of this chapter). To get there, take William Hilton Parkway to Squire Pope Road, which is between mile markers 1 and 2. Turn north on Squire Pope and stay on it until you reach the Hilton Head Plantation gate; the guard there will give you a pass and directions to the restaurant.

The Old Oyster Factory
$$ • 101 Marshland Rd. • 681-6040

With its floor-to-ceiling windows, this multi-level restaurant offers splendid views of beautiful Broad Creek and the adjacent marsh from its 270 seats. Built of pegged timbers on the site of one of Hilton Head's oyster canneries and opened in 1989, the restaurant serves steaks and seafood, including oysters from surrounding waters prepared six or seven different ways. The shrimp offered by The Old Oyster Factory comes from nearby Calibogue Sound, provided by Capt. Woody Collins and brought to the restaurant's dock aboard his boat. Shrimp is part of one of the restaurant's big sellers, the seafood medley, which also consists of scallops, oysters, grouper and mahi mahi. Another popular dish is the salmon en croûte (in pastry), but you'll have to ask your server about it — it's not on the menu. The Old Oyster Factory is open for dinner daily and provides live entertainment on the dock from May through September.

Primo!
$$$ • Orleans Plaza, New Orleans Rd. • 785-2343

You gotta love a place with the confidence to place an exclamation point after its name. This restaurant on New Orleans Road has earned the right to do so by serving top-quality homemade pasta and chargrilled seafood to islanders and visitors since 1984. Among the favorites of long-time customers are the grilled grouper, the double-cut veal chop and the angel hair al fresca — delicate pasta topped with a mixture of artichoke hearts, mushrooms, shrimp, scallops and chives and sautéed with white wine, olive oil, scallions and boursin cheese. Primo! has seating for 90 to 100 in two dining rooms that are elegant in their simplicity, and space for 18 to 20 in its trattoria-style bar. The restaurant serves dinner and is closed on Sunday; reservations are accepted but not required.

The Quarterdeck
$$ • 149 Lighthouse Rd. • 671-2222

When it comes to Hilton Head, we can't think of a better location for a restaurant than that occupied by The Quarterdeck. From the picture windows of the second-floor dining room and bar of this establishment at Harbour Town in Sea Pines, you can watch sailboats ply the waters of Calibogue Sound against a backdrop of Daufuskie Island or observe golfers finishing up their rounds on Harbour Town Golf Links' renowned 18th hole. There's also a ground-floor deck by the sound and a patio overlooking the Harbour Town Yacht Basin, all of this adjacent to the marina's famed lighthouse.

The Quarterdeck serves American fare and seafood, with the restaurant's signature items being coconut fried shrimp, Lowcountry seafood stew and steamed seafood platters. Orders from a raw bar are available outside and in the downstairs lounge, which features live entertainment seven days a week. In the afternoons, the patio is the site of live performances of reggae music. You can get breakfast, lunch and dinner on a daily basis at The Quarterdeck, which opened in 1975.

Reilly's
$ • 7-D Greenwood Dr. • 842-4414
$ • Port Royal Plaza, Mathews Dr. • 681-4153

The easygoing atmosphere of the Reilly's in Hilton Head Plaza on Greenwood Drive is what you'd expect from a restaurant that has a deck called the "Bar-muda Triangle" and a sign outside the door that counts down the days remaining until St. Patrick's Day. Reilly's menu, adorned with shamrocks and leprechauns, lists a wide variety of offerings including several variations of Blarney Burgers and Super Sandwiches. If you're in the mood for a dinner, flip to the Meat & Potatoes section, where you'll find steaks and a couple of dishes

Photo: Phyl M. Gatlin

Hilton Head is heaven on earth for the golfer.

suited to Gaelic tastes — the corned beef and cabbage and the cottage pie, which is ground chuck seasoned with mushrooms and onions and topped with peas, homemade mashed potatoes and cheddar cheese.

Reilly's takes credit for organizing the island's first St. Patrick's Day parade, a celebration started in 1983, the year after the restaurant opened in the Gallery of Shops. In 1995 the restaurant moved to its existing location in Hilton Head Plaza just south of the Sea Pines traffic circle. Reilly's serves lunch and dinner daily and offers a champagne and eggs brunch on Saturdays and Sundays. The menu and atmosphere are the same at the Reilly's at Port Royal Plaza on Mathews Drive, but there's no deck.

Rendez-vous Cafe
$$ • The Gallery of Shops • 785-5070

Operated by chef Serge Prat, who also owns another favorite of islanders, The Gaslight Restaurant, this cafe off Greenwood Drive just south of the Sea Pines traffic circle offers the atmosphere of a French bistro and cuisine from the provinces of France. The bouillabaisse, pâté, escargot, oyster provençale and Cassoulet de Castelnaudary — casserole of duck, lamb, sausage and beans — will have you proclaiming "Vive la France!" The Rendez-vous, which also features a wine bar, was opened in 1996 and serves lunch and dinner seven days a week.

Santa Fe Cafe
$$$ • 700 Plantation Ctr. • 785-3838

Owner and chef Jim Buckingham spent his younger days in the Southwest, and he brings his appreciation for that region to his cooking. The upscale Southwestern cuisine of his Santa Fe Cafe is spicy food based on many types of chiles, resulting in dishes such as grilled pork tenderloin with smoked habañero barbecue sauce, black beans and sweet potato fries; herb-roasted free range chicken with jalapeño corn bread stuffing and red chile mashed potatoes; and grouper with chipotle (smoked chile) Parmesan au gratin.

After several years of operating a limited chain of Mexican restaurants, Buckingham decided to concentrate his efforts on one establishment and in 1993 opened this cafe off William Hilton Parkway near Mile Marker 8. The stylishly Southwestern Santa Fe serves dinner seven nights a week and lunch on Monday through Friday, and reservations are accepted.

Spartina Grill
$$$ • 70 Marshland Rd. • 689-2433

Managing partner/chef Richard Vaughan calls the food served at the Spartina Grill cross-cultural, meaning "everything from Greek to Jamaican." You might also think of the atmosphere of the Spartina in the same way: It's located in a one-time Mexican restaurant whose decor now has a Mediterranean flair. We get a relaxed feeling just driving up to the Spartina, with its white stucco exterior and red-tile roof resting under the oaks in a secluded spot on Marshland Road.

Among the entrees served here are the Chopstix Chicken, consisting of tempura-fried boneless pieces of chicken breast; the Phoenix duck, which is stir-fried duckling with straw mushrooms, water chestnuts, snow peas and carrot threads, all in a wonton basket; and the Pork Loin Imbroglio, in which the meat is pan-seared and served with wild mushroom ravioli and three-herb pesto. Leading off the list of appetizers is "pazza," a combination of pasta and pizza. The Spartina has a wine room for private parties of up to eight and a bar featuring martinis and cigars. Dinner is available every day but Monday. A champagne oyster roast is held every Sunday with the oysters roasted Lowcountry style on the hood of an old Chevy truck. Reservations are suggested.

Steamers Seafood Company
$ • 28 Coligny Plaza • 785-2070

Steamers specializes in fresh fish, shrimp, lobster tails and certified Angus beef, all cooked over a hardwood-burning grill. For shellfish lovers, there's a platter consisting of steamed oysters, clams, mussels, shrimp, crawfish, stone crab and snow crab. At Steamers, you can eat outside on the decks beside the Coligny Plaza shopping center lagoon or inside in the fish-camp atmosphere of the dining room or raw bar. Buckets are recessed in the middle of the tables of these two rooms, and that's where you toss your oyster shells, shrimp tails and other scraps; each table also has a roll of paper towels for cleaning up your hands and face. Barn and dock wood on the walls and bars composed of wood and corrugated tin complete the pier-side look.

Steamers, which serves lunch and dinner daily, offers 50 traditional and unique appetizers and 200 beers from around the world. Among the appetizers are Oysters Rockabilly, Oysters Benedict Arnold, The Black Shrimp of the Family and Louisiana Mud Bugs. Reservations are accepted for parties of four or more wishing to eat in the dining room at this fun-loving restaurant. It's been in business on Hilton Head since 1991.

Stellini Italian Restaurant
$$$ • 15 Pope Avenue Executive Park • 785-7006

This "little star" of an Italian restaurant shines forth from a wooded nook off Pope Avenue. Owner Joe Pesce and his partners have created the comfortable look of the Little Italy section of New York and New Jersey at Stellini, which serves dinner Monday through Saturday. Especially inviting is the 40-seat Carolina Room, a porch with views of the surrounding forest. The restaurant also has a main dining room for 50.

The menu provides an extensive selection of northern Italian fare, including chicken pancetta — a chicken breast sautéed in a light cream sauce with pancetta bacon and broccoli over angel hair pasta; veal sorrento — medallions of veal sautéed in white wine topped with eggplant and melted mozzarella cheese in marinara sauce over angel hair; and zuppa di pesce — clams, shrimp, scallops, mussels, calamari and grouper in marinara over linguine. One item you won't find on the menu is a special that's offered often: the veal chop stuffed with prosciutto and mozzarella. Pesce suggests making reservations to dine at Stellini, which opened in 1988. The restaurant is closed on Sunday and during the first three weeks in January.

Stripes: An American Grill
$$$$ • 114 Office Park Rd. • 686-4747

Co-owner and chef Steve Hancotte describes the food served at his restaurant near the Sea Pines traffic circle as "American regional." By that, Hancotte means that in creating his dishes he takes advantage of all the United States has to offer in the way of cuisine. Some examples of his red, white and blue artistry: jumbo lump shrimp tossed with diced bacon, shiitake mushrooms and toasted pine nuts served on a homemade spinach capellini; charbroiled Angus beef Delmonico served with roasted garlic mashed potatoes and toasted onion and horseradish custard; and Louisiana catfish filet, pan-fried in Cajun spices and served with Smithfield ham on a black pepper cream.

Stripes, which opened in 1991, has seating for 72 in a casual atmosphere featuring caned chairs. The full bar offers a long wine list that's constantly changing and growing. The menu at Stripes also changes, with the list of dishes being revised on a seasonal basis. The restaurant is open for dinner seven days a week and is closed during the first two weeks of December. Reservations are recommended.

The Tapas Restaurant
$$$ • 11 Northridge Plaza • 681-8590

Ever wanted to try something a companion is eating but felt self-conscious taking it from him or her? When you dine at The Tapas, such behavior is not only acceptable, it's expected. Tapas is Spanish for "little bits," and the small dishes served at this cozy, elegant bistro in Northridge Plaza off William Hilton Parkway between mile markers 4 and 5 are perfect for sharing. Say you're dining with four other people and each of you orders three different selections from the restaurant's menu of about 40 items; that means you get a taste of 12 different dishes. Each item is served on an individual plate, and diners are provided with sharing plates.

Among the dishes you might try are the Veal Anthony (tenderloin of veal sautéed in garlic butter, cream sherry and mushrooms), escargot spinnochi (snails sautéed with garlic, spinach, bacon cream sauce, topped with Parmesan cheese and baked) and shrimp Parthenon (shrimp sautéed with feta cheese, oregano and tomato bisque and served in a phylo shell). While you're at The Tapas, be sure to look up — at a ceiling with a multitude of hanging wicker baskets. The 56-seat restaurant is open for dinner Monday through

Saturday, and reservations are suggested. Smoking is not allowed.

Truffles Cafe
$$ • 71 Lighthouse Rd. • 671-6136

Islander Price Beall has owned and operated this casually elegant restaurant in Sea Pines Center since its opening in 1983. With seating for 150, Truffles is larger than the typical cafe but retains the atmosphere of a bistro. The food is American in style, with specialties like chicken pot pie made with white wine sauce and chicken New Orleans — a chicken breast served over pasta, tossed in a spicy cream sauce. Other favorites of regular customers are the ribs, grilled fish, pasta dishes and Monterey and Cajun salads, both of which feature grilled chicken. Lunch and dinner are served daily.

Two Eleven Park Wine Bar & Bistro
$$$ • 211 Park Plaza • 686-5212

Two Eleven Park owner Bill Cubbage refers to the fare offered at his restaurant as "Southern fusion," meaning it combines the cuisine of many cultures with that of Dixie. Many of the exotic sounding entrees — the grilled filet of eggplant, the cedar planked salmon and the grilled quail, for example — are accompanied by down-home side dishes such as mashed potatoes, whipped sweet potatoes and/or collard greens. The smothered shrimp is served with country ham, black-eyed peas and Vidalia onions over creamy grits.

These intriguing combinations are purveyed in an equally intriguing atmosphere — it's another combination: the New York and California bistro scenes. A local hangout of major proportions since it opened in 1994, Two Eleven Park serves dinner and is closed on Sunday. The wine list includes 150 selections, 75 of them served by the glass. Two Eleven Park is near the cinemas of Park Plaza shopping center, which is off Greenwood Drive near the Sea Pines traffic circle. Reservations are not required but are accepted.

Villella l'Osteria del Sole
$$$ • 841 William Hilton Pkwy. • 341-5111

Owner and chef Gennaro Villella says he endeavors to make each meal at his Italian restaurant in South Island Square an experience in fine dining. He does this, he says, by cooking with "emotion" and "passion" and striving for simplicity. "To be simple is difficult because you need the best ingredients," says Villella. With that in mind, he prepares his dishes with organically grown vegetables, little butter and no cream. Among his offerings are the sautéed red snapper with braised artichoke hearts and wild capers, the breast of duck tenderloin and the scallop salad. Villella opened his Mediterranean-style restaurant, near Mile Marker 9 on the William Hilton Parkway, in the summer of 1997. Dinner is served daily, and lunch is available Monday through Friday.

Nightlife

Hilton Head is a resort that caters to families who are on the go throughout the day and to golfers with early-morning tee times, so it's not exactly a hotbed of nightlife activity. There are, however, nightspots at several hotels and motels, including the Regatta Lounge at the Hilton, Signals at the Crowne Plaza, the Playful Pelican at the Westin, the Parrot's Perch at the Holiday Inn, Hemingway's Lounge at the Hyatt Regency, Mulligan's at the Four Points and the Tee Time Lounge at Shoney's Inn (see the Accommodations section of this chapter). Some of Hilton Head's restaurants also have lounges where you can hang out and catch live entertainment.

There are three movie theaters on the island — Main Street Cinemas in the Main Street retail/office complex off William Hilton Parkway at Mile Marker 3, Northridge Cinemas at 435 William Hilton Parkway at Mile Marker 5, and Park Plaza Cinemas in the Park Plaza Shopping Center off Greenwood Drive. Main Street has three screens, Northridge has 10 and Park Plaza has five.

If you've spent your day knocking a tennis ball around, pedaling a few miles on bicycle paths and frolicking in the surf, and you still haven't pooped out, you might consider these other nighttime entertainment options:

Coconuts Comedy Club
15 Heritage Plaza • 686-6887

Coconuts brings to its stage up-and-coming comedians who tour nationally, many of whom have appeared on HBO and late-night network TV. Included in those ranks are comics such as Dennis Regan, Jerry Farber and Ronnie Bullard. Admission is $10 per person, and showtimes are at 9:30 PM Wednesday through Friday and 10 PM on Saturday, with a second show Friday at midnight. The Thursday night performance is designated nonsmoking. Coconuts has a full bar and a light snack menu. It's in the Heritage Plaza shopping center, which is on the north side of Pope Avenue near the Coligny traffic circle.

Monkey Business
25 Park Plaza • 686-3545

This upscale dance club in the Park Plaza shopping center off Greenwood Drive features music for a variety of ages and tastes and a state-of-the-art lighting system. A DJ cranks out the sound on Tuesdays through Saturdays, with live entertainment provided on Sundays and Mondays by local bands and some nationally known groups such as Drivin' and Cryin' and the Swinging Medallions. On Tuesdays, there's country music until 10 PM, when the DJ starts taking requests. Wednesdays are flashback nights featuring beach and shag music and oldies. Females are admitted free on Thursdays, and there are dance parties on Fridays and Saturdays, with an older crowd taking up the floor early in the evening and the younger set moving in as the clock approaches midnight. There's a $3 cover charge for non-locals Tuesdays through Saturdays (locals get in free), and admission is $5 or $10 on Sundays and Mondays, depending on the band that's playing.

The lighting system uses lasers and roboscans, flashing a multitude of shapes and colors on the dance floor and walls of the club, which is done up in a midnight black, hot pink and electric blue color scheme and decked out with fake bananas and photographs of playful chimpanzees. Monkey Business has a full bar and seating for 450.

The Lodge
Hilton Head Plaza • 842-8966

The island's only cigar bar has an interior resembling a hunting lodge. You can satisfy your competitive instincts at four billiards tables, the shuffleboard table and the pinball machines, or you can relax in front of one of the two fireplaces with a drink from the full bar or a cigar from The Lodge's large stock of smokes. In addition to wine by the glass, single malts, ales, cognacs and bourbons, the bar serves a specialty drink, the chocolate martini. This establishment in Hilton Head Plaza off Greenwood Drive near the Sea Pines traffic circle is open from 10 AM to 2 AM daily, with hours extended to 3 AM on Wednesdays and Fridays.

Shopping

The shopping is plentiful on Hilton Head, which has stores of every description located in large shopping centers, in strip centers and along the island's out-of-the-way streets and byways. To get you started, we've provided rundowns on a few of the bigger shopping areas and pointed out some of the stores you can find there. Knock yourself out.

Shopping Centers

Coligny Plaza
124 N. Forest Beach Dr. • 842-6050

Coligny Plaza, the island's oldest and largest shopping center, rambles over nearly 9 acres at the Coligny traffic circle on the south end of the island. Sixty retail stores and restaurants — some of them tucked into nooks and crannies along the center's covered walkways — offer a wide range of goods and dining experiences.

The Plaza mixes conventional businesses such as a Servistar auto parts and hardware store, a Piggly Wiggly supermarket and Nash Discount Drugs with specialty shops. Among the latter are Black Market Minerals, a rock and stone store; Chili Chompers, where things hot and spicy are sold; The Hammock Company; Jamaican Me Crazy, a clothing store that's Caribbean in character; the Mole Hole, which handles unique gifts and accessories for the home; the Island Fudge Shop, where sweets are made before your eyes; and The Magic Puppet & Toys Too.

More than a dozen eating places offer everything from fine dining at the Alligator Grille to the seafood at Steamers Seafood Company (see listing in Restaurants) to the sandwiches at Grinders Express, Coligny Deli and The Earle of Sandwich.

The shopping center was called Circle Square when it was started by J. Norris Richardson and his wife, Lois, in 1956. Consisting in its earliest form of the Forest Beach Market grocery store, a laundromat, a real estate office and a beauty shop, the center has been expanded four times since the mid-'50s and was given its existing name in 1965. Members of the Richardson clan continue to operate the center, which is composed mostly of family-owned businesses.

On summertime evenings, Coligny Plaza stages puppet shows and other family-oriented entertainment in the piazza off N. Forest Beach Drive. The shopping center also hosts special events during the year, including an Irish festival held in conjunction with the island's St. Patrick's Day parade; the Chocolate Fair, a springtime celebration featuring desserts concocted by local chefs; a Halloween festival, during which shop owners open their doors to trick-or-treaters; and appearances by the Easter Bunny and Santa Claus, who arrives at the shopping center via fire truck.

Shoppes on the Parkway Factory Outlets
890 William Hilton Pkwy. • 686-6233

Discover discounts ranging from 20 to 70 percent at many of the 25 stores offering brand-name merchandise at this shopping center near the parkway's Mile Marker 10. The majority of the Shoppes on the Parkway sell clothing, with Anne Klein, Bogner, Carole Little, Dress Barn, Ellen Tracy, harve benard, Jones New York, Royal Robbins and Van Heusen among the manufacturers represented. The Hilton Head Shirt Company and Islandwear stores offer sportswear and other goods that sport the name of the island, and the He-Ro Group outlet specializes in designer evening wear.

Golfers will find items for on and off the course at Players World of Golf, and folks with a sweet tooth might want to duck into The Gourmet Alligator food store to check out the cookies, chocolates, ice creams, truffles and gift baskets. The shopping center's two eating places, The Island Restaurant and Gruby's New York Deli, serve breakfast, lunch and dinner.

The Mall at Shelter Cove
24 Shelter Cove Ln. • 686-3090

Hilton Head's only enclosed shopping mall accommodates 55 stores in a tropical setting featuring potted palm trees and other plants. Anchoring the northern end of the mall is a department store you might not expect to find on a Southern sea island — Saks Fifth Avenue, which opened in March 1997. At the southern end of the shopping center is the other anchor, Belk, and scattered in between are several stores offering high-quality wearing apparel including Ann Taylor, Banana Republic, Mondi, Polo Ralph Lauren, Talbots, The Gap, The White House and Victoria's Secret.

Shoppers seeking to pamper themselves should find products to their liking at Bath & Body Works and Crabtree & Evelyn. The mall has spacious corridors and a large center court that's the site of special events, arts and crafts shows and prolonged visits by Santa Claus and the Easter Bunny. On the fringes of the center area is a food court with lots of seating and three vendors — Chick-Fil-A, Sbarro and Ice Creams & Coffee Beans. The mall, which opened in 1988, is off William Hilton Parkway near Mile Marker 9.

Village at Wexford
1000 William Hilton Pkwy. • 842-2240

If you're looking for variety, you'll find it at the Village at Wexford, where the majority of the 35 stores and eating places are locally owned. This retail and office complex sits on 9 wooded acres off the parkway near Mile Marker 10 and houses in its quaint-looking, stucco buildings the Island Christmas shop, a Hilton Head Surf Shop, Creative Kitchens, an Audubon Nature Store, Golf Classics & Collectibles and Smith Galleries, which deals in artwork and jewelry. Several stores offer women's apparel, including Bitsy's, The Honey Vine, Carousel and Porcupine, and Island Child specializes in clothing and shoes for youngsters. The restaurants at the Village at Wexford range from those offering fast food to those devoted to casual and fine dining; at one end of the spectrum are Wendy's and Subway, with Damon's, Antonio's Italian Cuisine and the Cafe at Wexford (see this chapter's Restaurants section) at the other.

Bookstores

Authors Bookstore
Village at Wexford, 1000 William Hilton Pkwy. • 686-5020

Authors Bookstore caters to browsers — partitions separate shelves of books grouped by subject matter, and each area contains chairs where customers can plop down and leaf through their selections. You can also sit and read at one of the tables in the store's spacious cafe, which serves breakfast, lunch and desserts and coffee-type drinks in the evenings. The cafe seats 45 and is open seven days a week. Authors sells all types of books and specializes in bestsellers, books involving golf and tennis and those of regional interest.

Port Royal Bookstore
95 Mathews Dr. • 689-9996

Owner John Stern refers to his small but well-stocked bookstore in Port Royal Plaza as being old-fashioned — one where you can sit in a comfortable chair and read a book or have the staff special-order a hard-to-find volume. Stern constantly peruses catalogs in an effort to maintain an extensive inventory of books covering a wide range of topics including "The War of Northern Aggression," which is what some Southerners still call the Civil War.

Speaking of that conflict, Stern also sells handpainted pewter miniatures of Civil War soldiers, both North and South. They make unique gifts, as do the first editions and unusual fore-edge books in the store's rare book department. The edges of the latter type of books are decorated with intricate paintings concealed by gold leaf. The store rents bestsellers by the day or week, a service designed with vacationers in mind. While you're at the store, take a gander at Stern's collection of miniature lead soldiers, which is displayed near the front of the shop.

The Island Bookseller
71 Lighthouse Rd. • 671-3773

Although Joni and Jon Minier's bookstore at Sea Pines Center covers only 1,400 square feet, it offers a full range of fiction and nonfiction categories and includes a comprehensive collection of children's books. Another section of the store is devoted to volumes featuring the Lowcountry, and the Miniers do their utmost to promote local authors.

During the summer months, The Island Bookseller keeps on hand a hefty stock of what Jon Minier calls "beach reads" — paperbacks for the side of the pool or the sands near the ocean's edge. This store, which has been in business in Sea Pines since 1983, does a lot of special-ordering of books and also carries greeting cards, journals, calendars, puzzles and games.

Golf

Hilton Head is heaven on earth for golfers. There are 22 courses on the island, many of them world-class and all of them dripping with Lowcountry charm. Seventeen are open to the public, and information on these follow. (For a more comprehensive look at Hilton Head golf courses, pick up a copy of *The Insiders' Guide® to Golf in the Carolinas*.)

The courses we've described have amenities such as pro shops, practice greens and driving ranges. Many of these courses do not allow walking, but we've pointed out which ones do and to what extent. The greens fees listed include carts, and we've provided a range of rates, with the higher fee reflecting the charge during the most popular playing times (generally spring and fall) and the lower fee reflecting the charge for the slower months (winter).

The rates included are for players not staying at the resorts associated with the courses. You can make arrangements to play these courses by calling directly, through the resort where you're staying or via central golf reservation services such as Central Tee Time Center, 681-6681, (800) 767-5423; Sea to Tee Reservations, 842-5759, (800) HOLE-IN-1; or Tee-Times Enterprises, (203) 355-5539, (800) 562-5532. That said, let's tee it up and take a swing at golfing on Hilton Head Island at . . .

Country Club of Hilton Head
70 Skull Creek Dr. • 681-4653

Many of the greens on this par 72, 6543-yard course at Hilton Head Plantation run near the Intracoastal Waterway, and the 12th is right on it. Designed by Rees Jones and built in 1985, the course has two holes longer than 575 yards, including the uphill, par 5, 579-yard 18th. Greens and fairways are bermudagrass. Greens fees range from $52 to $79.

Golden Bear Golf Club
72 Golden Bear Way • 689-2200

What a great name for a golf course! Interestingly enough, the chief architect of this Jack Nicklaus design was not the Golden Bear himself but Bruce Borland. Players of this 6643-yard layout at Indigo Run will find a real challenge in the 11th hole — it runs 446 yards and features a long dogleg to the left and water on the left side of the green. This par 72 course has fairways and greens of bermudagrass set among lagoons and stands of pine and hardwoods. Among the amenities are a bar and grill. You'll spend from $56 to $82 in greens fees to play this course.

Oyster Reef Golf Club
155 High Bluff Rd. • 681-7717

The 6th hole at Oyster Reef — a par 3, 192-yarder — overlooks Port Royal Sound, giving golfers a fine view of that majestic body of water on the northern side of Hilton Head. The par 72 layout, which is the work of Rees Jones, covers 6440 yards at Hilton Head Plantation. Greens and fairways are of bermudagrass, and there are nine ponds and 66 bunkers for players to contend with. At the end of a round, players can relax at the club's bar and restaurant. Greens fees run from $43 to $90.

Palmetto Dunes Golf Courses
1 Trent Jones Ln. • 785-1138

Palmetto Dunes offers golfers three 18-hole courses from which to choose, each of them named for their heavy-hitting designers — Arthur Hills, George Fazio and Robert Trent Jones. You can cover them on foot if you want to: Unrestricted walking is allowed at all times of the day. Rates on the Fazio and Jones

courses run from $52.50 to $80 and on the Hills Course from $75 to $110.

Arthur Hills Course

This heavily wooded par 72 was reconditioned during the mid-'90s, with all the greens being rebuilt. Among the most interesting holes is the 12th, a par 4 that's bordered by water along one side. The course measures 6122 yards.

George Fazio Course

The Fazio Course covers 6239 yards and is characterized by rolling fairways and lots of long par 4s — there are only two par 5s and three par 3s. You'll have to shoot 70 to make par on this layout, which ends with a hole where two bunkers provide a significant challenge.

Robert Trent Jones Course

If you like playing by the water, you'll enjoy this 6148-yard course, which provides a winding lagoon system tied into 11 holes and a great view of the ocean from No. 10. Other hallmarks of this par 72 are open fairways and large greens.

Palmetto Hall Plantation
108 Fort Howell Dr. • 689-4100

Palmetto Hall offers golfers the opportunity to enjoy a Lowcountry-style clubhouse and 18-hole courses designed by Arthur Hills and Robert Cupp. The 14,000-square-foot clubhouse is a repository of historic artifacts (both Lowcountry- and golfing-related), antiques and paintings and features a grill room with the aura of a gentlemen's club. Greens fees for the par 72 courses range from $58 to $81.

Arthur Hills Course

The signature hole here is No. 18, a 434-yarder with water running up the left side of the fairway. It's a challenging par 4. Another hole featuring plenty of water is the 5th, but the water on this beauty is on the right side. The hole runs 490 yards and is a par 5. This 6582-yard course was opened in 1991.

Robert Cupp Course

Unrestricted walking is allowed on this

6522-yard course, which was unveiled two years after the Arthur Hills layout. Vistas of marshlands and forests of oak and pine are features of this par 72 course, along with its straight lines and sharp angles.

Port Royal Golf Club
10A Grasslawn Ave. • 686-8801

This golf club at the Port Royal resort community has three 18-hole courses — Barony, Planters Row and Robbers Row — plus a bar and restaurant. Walking is allowed on occasion during the winter, but be sure to ask before you set out on foot. Greens fees run from $57 to $91.

Barony Course

The long drivers will take a back seat to the shot makers on this 6038-yard course, which has many small greens. The Barony, which was designed by George Cobb, presents players with a test of skill at No. 12 — a par 4, 428-yard hole with water on both sides of the fairway.

Planters Row Course

Walter Byrd is the designer responsible for Planters Row, where golfers finish on a par 5, 480-yard hole featuring woods and water. If that's not enough of a challenge, consider No. 12, a narrow, 424-yard hole where you've got to cross water to get to the green. The course measures 6009 yards, and par is 72.

Robbers Row Course

Robbers Row represents a team effort by designers George Cobb and Pete Dye. The course was built in 1967 and reconfigured recently by Dye, who added several water hazards. This par 72 course runs 6188 yards.

Shipyard Golf Club
45 Shipyard Dr. • 689-5600

Shipyard offers three nine-hole courses appropriately named for three types of sailing vessels — Galleon, Clipper and Brigantine. There is water involved on 25 of the 27 holes, which have bermudagrass fairways and greens. There's a bar and restaurant on the premises, and walking is allowed after 5 PM during summer. Greens fees are from $44 to $89.

Galleon Course

This George Cobb-designed, par 36 course is best-known for No. 2, a par 5 with an elevated green fronted by water and with bunkers all around. Total yardage for the course is 3035.

Clipper Course

The 3132-yard Clipper has a tough 9th hole with lots of bunkers. Water comes into play on all the holes except No. 6, which is a par 4, 427-yarder. George Cobb also designed this course, which carries a par 36.

Brigantine Course

The work of designer Willard Byrd, the Brigantine is a 2959-yard, par 36 surrounded by private homes and rental condominiums that blend in with the natural environment. You'll be challenged by No. 6, a long par 4, and No. 9. This last hole is a par 5 that runs 523 yards and has water on one side of the fairway.

Sea Pines Resort

Sea Pines is the home of three of the island's most popular golf courses, including the Harbour Town Golf Links, which is the site of Hilton Head's No. 1 sporting event, the MCI Classic — the Heritage of Golf.

Harbour Town Golf Links
11 Lighthouse Ln. • 363-4485

The signature hole at Harbour Town is the one you've seen countless times on television — the windswept 18th, a par 4 on Calibogue Sound where shots to the green often end up among the fiddler crabs in the adjacent marsh. Consistently ranked among the world's top courses, this one was designed by Pete Dye and Jack Nicklaus and has some outstanding par 3s. The yardage at this par 71 course totals 6119. Greens fees range from $126 to $140.

Ocean Course
100 N. Sea Pines Dr. • 363-4475

The 15th hole on this oldest and newest of island courses offers a terrific view of the ocean. It's the oldest because it was designed by George Cobb in 1962 and the newest because it was remodeled by Mark McCumber in 1995. Greens fees for this par 72, 6213-yard layout run from $82 to $94.50.

Sea Marsh Course
100 N. Sea Pines Dr. • 363-4475

You'll encounter wide fairways and lots of lagoons, trees and marshes when you play this par 72 course, which was also designed by George Cobb. It was remodeled in 1990 by Clyde Johnston, and it measures 6129 yards. Expect to pay from $72 to $84 in greens fees at Sea Marsh.

Annual Events

The island's two biggest annual events involve spectator sports, and both occur in spring.

Family Circle Cup
Sea Pines Racquet Club, 5 Lighthouse Ln. • 363-3500, (800) 677-2293

The majority of the world's top-ranked women tennis players compete in this nine-day tournament at Sea Pines Racquet Club. In 1997, Martina Hingis defeated Monica Seles in the finals, and the list of recent champions of the event reads like a women's tennis who's who: Arantxa Sanchez Vicario, Steffi Graf, Gabriela Sabatini, Martina Navratilova, Chris Evert and Tracy Austin. A total of 82,000 spectators attended Family Circle Cup matches in 1997, when $926,250 in prize money was awarded, and 56 singles players and 32 doubles teams took part. The event, originally held in 1973, was the first women's tourney to be broadcast on network television and the first to offer $100,000 in prize money.

The tournament is staged from the last Saturday in March through the first Sunday in April on as many as five clay courts at the racquet club, where the center-court stadium holds 8,200-plus spectators. A variety of ticket packages are available, with admission for individual sessions ranging from the low $20s to the mid-$40s. Parking is in lots within Sea Pines, and you can take shuttle buses to the racquet club.

MCI Classic — The Heritage of Golf
Harbour Town Golf Links, 11 Lighthouse Ln. • 671-2448, (800) 234-1107

The MCI Classic brings 120 invited players and 100,000 spectators to famed Harbour Town Golf Links in Sea Pines during four days

in April. In 1997 the golfers competed for a total of $1.5 million in prize money and the right to wear the red and green Tartan plaid jacket awarded to the winner of this prestigious tournament. Nick Price captured the jacket and the winner's share of $270,000 in '97 by shooting a 15-under-par 269 over 72 holes of play. Price joined a list of champions that includes Jack Nicklaus, Greg Norman, Davis Love III, Hale Irwin, Tom Watson and Arnold Palmer, who won the tournament in its inaugural year of 1969 when it was known as the Heritage Classic.

Attending the MCI Classic — which some longtime residents of the Savannah-Hilton Head area still call The Heritage — involves more than watching a golf tournament. The event is usually held during the third week in April, when the weather is generally lovely and nature is putting on a springtime show; it's a terrific time to get outdoors, amble around the verdant Harbour Town course, visit the shops and restaurants at the Harbour Town Yacht Basin near the first tee and 18th green, gawk at the high-priced boats docked in the marina and observe the hordes of spectators doing all of the above. Sometime during their day at the course, those attending are invariably drawn to the 18th hole, which overlooks Calibogue Sound and has the Harbour Town Lighthouse as part of its backdrop, to see how the players finish up and deal with the wind blowing off the water.

During the three days leading up to the tournament, which starts on Thursday and ends on Sunday, there are two pro-am events, a challenge in which several members of the PGA tour play a select group of Harbour Town's holes, and a youth clinic at which two stars from the tour give youngsters 18 and younger free golf lessons. At 4 PM on the Tuesday before Thursday's first round of play, the MCI Classic presents opening ceremonies focusing on golf's Scottish heritage and the game's long history in South Carolina (the South Carolina Golf Club of Charleston was founded in 1786 and is reputed to be the oldest membership golf club in America). The defending champion, tournament board members clad in plaid and bagpipers from The Citadel military college parade along the yacht basin to the 18th green, where the champ gets the tourney under way by smacking a ball into Calibogue Sound as a Civil War-era cannon is fired. The opening ceremonies and youth clinic are free and open to the public; there's a $30 fee for watching the other pre-tournament events, with admission included in the cost of purchasing a tournament practice-round badge.

A season badge, which is good for admission to the tournament grounds for the entire week of MCI Classic events, is $85 through February 2, 1998, and $95 thereafter. A clubhouse badge — which gives you access for the entire week to the grounds, the clubhouse and the Heritage Pavilion, a corporate hospitality tent being introduced in 1998 — costs $130. As stated earlier, practice-round badges are $30 and enable you to attend all the events leading up to the four-day tournament. Also, there are patron plans available for large groups of spectators; for details on these, contact the MCI Classic staff at the phone numbers listed for this entry. Parking for the MCI Classic is in lots within Sea Pines, and spectators are shuttled by bus to Harbour Town.

Arts

Hilton Head has for years radiated a vibrant cultural presence. Some 20 community groups — ranging from the Hilton Head Art League to the Barbershop Harmony Society to the Hilton Head Orchestra — foster and promote an appreciation of the visual and performing arts. Recently the community created a new artistic resource, The Self Family Arts Center, which has become the cultural hub of the island.

The Self Family Arts Center
14 Shelter Cove Ln. • 842-ARTS

A big-city facility on a resort island, this $10 million visual and performing arts center offers productions staged by The Hilton Head Playhouse theater company, performances by musicians and dancers, art shows, education programs and community service programs.

The center opened in March 1996 on 4.4 acres at Shelter Cove donated by the James C. Self family of Greenwood, South Carolina, owners of the Greenwood Development Corporation of Hilton Head. The result of the Self family gift and a fund-raising effort involving numerous corporations and the community, the center grew out of an idea hatched in 1985 by a group of local arts organizations. The group was incorporated as the Cultural Council of Hilton Head Island and was joined in its efforts by The Hilton Head Playhouse, which has produced more than 200 dramas, comedies and musicals since its first performance in 1977.

The Self Center's 350-seat Elizabeth Wallace Theatre each year hosts up to six productions by The Hilton Head Playhouse. Among the presentations for the 1997-98 season are the classic comedy *The Importance of Being Earnest*, the award-winning drama *A Shayna Maidel* and the musical *I Do! I Do!* The theater complex has dressing and costume rooms and a green room. A rehearsal hall has seating for 150.

The center also presents a performing arts series featuring local talent and regional and national touring companies. Six to eight art shows are exhibited annually in the center's 2,300-square-foot Walter Greer Gallery, which has 12-foot-high ceilings and flexible lighting for showcasing paintings, sculpture and other displays. Through its education program, the center co-sponsors residencies by professional artists in area schools and provides a School of Visual and Performing Arts for people of all ages. The center also offers services and assistance to artists and art groups from throughout the island, providing a home for organizations such as the Hilton Head Dance Theatre.

A full-season ticket package for The Hilton Head Playhouse productions was $110 for 1997-98, and general admission for most presentations in the center's performing arts series is $10 to $15. The Walter Greer Gallery is open from 10 AM to 4 PM Monday through Saturday.

This small island 18 miles east of Savannah on the Atlantic Ocean is known for its laid-back attitude, fierce sense of identity and unwavering pride.

Tybee Island

History/Overview

They call it Tybee-itis.

Ask any Islander about their bouts with this ailment and most will say it sets in the minute they cross Lazaretto Creek Bridge and Tybee Island is in the rearview mirror. Some describe it as a longing — a need to get back to their island home where they find relief from the hurry-up of city life. Others are less circumspect. "It is the fear of crossing Lazaretto Creek Bridge," one resident explained. "We only go into Savannah when we need to and then we are in a hurry to get back."

Regardless of the explanation, it is vintage Tybee. This small island 18 miles east of Savannah on the Atlantic Ocean is known for its laid-back attitude, fierce sense of identity and unwavering pride. It is a place where million-dollar beach homes are a block or two away from cinder-block houses. Where each May, the 4,000 or so residents march through town squirting each other with water guns in an annual rite of spring known as the Beach Bum Parade. And every fall, after the last tourist has packed up and driven over Lazaretto Creek Bridge, a sign goes up at the local market announcing, "It's Tybee Time Again."

While other beach communities succumb to high-rises, slick resorts and gated communities with lawns pristine enough to putt on, Tybee stubbornly resists. Look around downtown during summer and you will see a Ferris wheel and souvenir shops hawking seashells and bargain T-shirts for less than $10. The only golf you'll find is the miniature kind, complete with dinosaurs and waterfalls. Meanwhile over at City Hall, council members busily guard ordinances restricting the height of buildings and giving older residents tax breaks so they don't get pushed out by outsiders with fatter wallets.

It is a place where folksy eccentricity is celebrated and many things have been practiced. Things like gambling, which took place in back rooms throughout Tybee until being exposed and cleared out in the early 1960s. A decade or so later, nearly every bar in town was shut down for staying open too late on Saturday night. Seems people were having too good a time to remember that selling beer on Sundays was illegal. That's the thing about Tybee islanders — they just sorta do their own thing.

"Once you cross Lazaretto Creek Bridge into Tybee you get a laid-back attitude. Not a don't-care attitude but a laid-back one," said Walter Parker, who has served as Tybee's mayor four times and has lived there most of his life. "When you leave Tybee, you can't wait to get back."

Tybee's past is as colorful as its present. It served a role in several wars and has been home to Lt. Col. George C. Marshall (creator of the Marshall Plan) and to a quarantine station for people with infectious ailments. In the early 1800s, scientists believed the marshes in and around the island held harmful vapors or miasma that rose from the marsh vegetation and were carried by the wind into Savannah. However, it was also widely theorized that the vapors were counteracted by the healing properties of sea air. That was a notion that eventually played a role in Tybee's foray into tourism in the late 1880s.

Native Americans were the first Tybee islanders. They settled this small island (2½ miles long and two-thirds-of-a-mile wide) and also are generally credited with giving the island its name, which means salt, though there are other competing theories. Next came the Spanish in the 1500s, followed 200 years later by Georgia's founder, Gen. James Edward Oglethorpe.

Because of its location at the mouth of the Savannah River, Tybee was important strategically. Soon after his arrival, Oglethorpe ordered the construction of a lighthouse, which was completed in 1736. During the War of 1812, the lighthouse (see Things to Do in this chapter) was used to warn Savannah of possible attack by the British, but this never occurred. A fortress known as a "Martello Tower," designed with round walls that hopefully would deflect cannonballs, was also built on Tybee Island in 1815 to help guard the Savannah River from attack. It was one of only a few in North America.

On the western end of the island, a quarantine station was set up to house sick passengers coming in off ships. This is how Lazaretto Creek Bridge got its name. Lazaretto is an Italian word for an institution or hospital for those with contagious diseases. "They kept them in quarantine there for four months," said James Mack Adams, associate editor for the *Tybee News*, who also writes a history column about Tybee for the *Savannah Morning News*. "If they got sick and died, they buried them right there."

In 1829, construction began on Fort Pulaski (see Things to Do, below). Located just down the road from Tybee, the fort was made of 25 million bricks and had walls 7½ feet thick. Robert E. Lee was one of the engineers who planned and supervised construction. During the Civil War, Union forces attacked the fort using a new weapon called "rifled cannon." It took only 30 hours of bombardment for the fort to fall into Union hands. The attack had such devastating effects on the brick fort that after the surrender, all forts like Pulaski were considered obsolete.

Following the war, Tybee turned its attention toward tourism. Before 1885, the only way to get to the island from Savannah was a two-hour boat ride through the narrow and dangerously swift Savannah River. This all changed two years later when a locomotive made its maiden trip to the island, and the era of the railroad began. That same year Tybee was officially incorporated as Ocean City. A year later it was changed to Tybee, only to be changed in 1929 to Savannah Beach. It wasn't until many decades, in the early '70s, that it became Tybee again. In fact, many Savannahians still refer to it as Savannah Beach.

Daytrippers, as they were known, would come on the train, rent bathing suits from a local hotel and spend the day at the beach. Some would arrive later in the day to dance to Big Band music supplied by outfits playing at one of the islands biggest attractions — the Tybrisa Pier. When the Tybee Road opened in 1923, the stream of people coming to the island continued to grow. In a column that ran in the local newspaper in 1931, E.B. Izlar, reflected about the "good old days" on Tybee. "The decline of mosquitoes, of picnickers, of bars and of yardage in women's bathing suits constitute the most radical changes in reviewing the past thirty years on Tybee Island," the column stated. "Today, Mr. Izlar declares that mosquitoes, except in the dense wooded places are rare, and he bears out his statement by remarking that he has only seen three this season. . . ."

Reminiscing on the bathing suits of the early years, Mr. Izlar lamented the time when suits were sold for $2.50 to $4 a dozen (except, of course, when special suits for women were as high as $12 a dozen) in the days when women "wrapped up" to cover everything. As for bars, Mr. Izlar said that though

FYI

Unless otherwise noted, the area code for all phone numbers listed in this guide is 912.

INSIDERS' TIP

You might notice in your wanderings around town that many of the souvenir and other stores on Tybee are called "Chu's." This is after T.S. Chu, a Chinese immigrant who came to Tybee in the early part of the 1900s and eventually became Tybee's leading merchant. His family still owns several stores on Tybee and in Savannah.

they abounded in bygone days, there was little disorder — only friendly fights. "There was not even need for a jail in those days. . ."

While the islanders focused on tourism, the U.S. War Department began construction of Fort Screven on the north end of the island. The fort was made up of seven gun batteries that ended up being fired only for practice, not for war. During World War I, part of the Eighth Infantry Regiment was assigned to Fort Screven. One of its commanders was Lt. Col. George C. Marshall, who after leaving Tybee became a five-star general and served as Secretary of State, Secretary of Defense and author of the Marshall Plan for rebuilding western Europe after World War II.

In the meantime, Savannahians were beginning to build houses at the beach for the summer months. The ocean breezes would give them relief from the sweltering summer heat. Many of these magnificent old beach homes can still be found on the island today. Current resident Walter Parker recalls how empty the island was in those days. "I can remember in the winter you could go for several blocks before you saw a light on," said Parker. "No one lived here year round."

Eventually, that began to change and

Photo: Phil M. Gatlin

Re-enactors stage a cannon firing at Fort Pulaski National Monument.

Tybee's year-round population slowly grew. However, several factors — from beach erosion to pollution from local industries to the closing of Fort Screven — resulted in several years of decline on the island beginning in the 1940s. Residents cultivated the outlaw attitude during this era by engaging in backroom gambling and illegal drinking, which got the attention of the news media. It also helped fuel the island's reputation in some circles as Georgia's unruly stepchild. Eventually, local and state law enforcement agencies cracked down to curb Tybee's wanton ways. The pollution, gambling and other sins were eventually cleaned up, and Tybee once again became a popular tourist spot.

Since 1980 or so, the island's year-round population has been on the rise to its current level of around 4,000. Today, locals who have called Tybee home for generations, live amongst a thriving community of artists and writers, most of whom migrated during the '80s. There are also many retirees whose hometowns are places far away from Tybee. Every socio-economic group is represented, from the poor to the very wealthy. Come by in May during the Big Kahuna Beach Party, which is held every year following the Beach Bum Parade, and you will see all these people together doing one of the things Tybee islanders do best — having a good time. For them, it sure beats Tybee-itis.

"I think Tybee is an easy place to live," said Parker. "I think it has more than its share of characters. . . . But it has a small community feeling and most want it to stay that way."

Getting There, Getting Around

Tybee is about 18 miles outside Savannah. There is only one road to get you there — U.S. Highway 80. You can reach it from the Historic Downtown by heading east on Bay Street. In less than a mile, it will run into President Street, then President Street Extension. After about 3 miles it merges with U.S. 80 East. From Midtown, hop on Victory Drive and head east, it eventually turns into U.S. 80 East. (How many miles it takes depends on where you enter Victory Drive. However, it shouldn't be more than 5.)

After entering Tybee, U.S. 80 turns into Butler Avenue, the community's main drag that will take you past hotels, beach houses and the small downtown area. You will know U.S. 80 has become Butler Avenue after going around a fairly sharp curve. You can't miss it. Follow Butler a mile or so farther into downtown, and you will be deposited in a city parking lot next to the pier.

Most places you need to go on Tybee should be accessible from this main strip. Near the beginning of Butler Avenue, streets running east and west are numbered, starting with First Street at the northern end of the city and ending with 19th Street at the southern end. These are crossed by north and south running streets that are named and numbered, starting with Butler Avenue closest to the beach and ending with Sixth Avenue.

If you are going to spend the day at the beach on Tybee, you will have to pay for parking. The streets closest to the beach are metered, with costs ranging from 50¢ to $1 an hour. The city operates three parking lots, at the end of 16th and 14th streets and at North Beach — all are accessible from Butler Avenue. It costs $5 all day to park in one of these lots. Parking is patrolled every day year round from 8 AM until midnight. Like the Savannah authorities, the parking enforcers are very generous when doling out tickets and are fairly vigilant. So if you don't want a $6 expired meter

---

INSIDERS' TIP

Geologically speaking, Tybee is very young — only about 1,000 years old. Savannah's other islands including Wilmington and Skidaway are more than 40,000 years old.

ticket, don't leave your meter expired. It usually isn't any trouble finding parking on Tybee, except for a few very busy weekends. Even then, if you drive around long enough, you will almost certainly get a spot.

Accommodations

Affordable hotel rooms, sprawling beach houses and oceanview condos are some of the choices you will find when searching for accommodations on Tybee Island. Tybee is known as a family beach, so a lot of what is available is geared toward those lugging not only beach chairs but high chairs as well. Regardless of where you land, more likely than not you will be within comfortable walking distance to the beach.

Tybee's season runs typically from the middle of April through the middle of September. After that, the streets become less crowded and rates go down. Stay during the peak season, especially on weekends, and the rates are going to be higher. A few weekends, including July 4, are especially busy.

While we list some Realtors who can help land you in a beach house and condo, some owners handle property rental on their own. Most simply post a "For Rent" sign in the front yard — when you're in town, pick one of these places that you like and jot down the number for future reference. Some private owners also put listings in the *Savannah Morning News* (see our Media chapter for more information), so check there as well. Our listings begin with hotels and motels, we throw in one bed and breakfast, then move on to rentals.

Hotels and Motels

There are only a handful of hotels and motels to choose from on the island. Most are chains with names you will recognize and offer standard, sometimes modest accommodations. The ones we list have nonsmoking and handicapped-accessible rooms and come

with ample free parking. Although Tybee is outside Savannah, it shares area code 912.

Price Code

Our price code is designed to make it easier for you to gauge the cost of staying at one of Tybee's hotels. The dollar sign indicates the average cost for a one-night stay for two adults during peak season, typically mid-April through mid-September.

$	$50 and less
$$	$51 to $100
$$$	$101 to $150
$$$$	$151 and more

Best Western Dunes Inn
$$ • 1409 Butler Ave. • 786-4591, (800) 528-1234

The Best Western Dunes Inn is across the street from the beach and a block or so away from Tybee's small shopping district, where you can find everything from a new swimsuit to suntan lotion. This motel offers spacious rooms comfortably furnished with two double beds or one king bed. Some have balconies overlooking the pool, and a few kitchenettes are also available. Complimentary coffee is served every morning.

Days Inn
$$ • 1402 Butler Ave. • 786-4576

Another economical choice, the Days Inn is within walking distance to Tybee's downtown and is one of the newest motels on the island. It is on the beach side of Butler Avenue — Tybee's main thoroughfare. The motel offers a pool, movie rentals and free continental breakfast each morning. The rooms are fresh, with bright-colored bedspreads and white walls. Although just a short stroll to the beach, none of the rooms have ocean views.

INSIDERS' TIP

Like to collect seashells? According to expert seashell hunters, Tybee's North Beach provides the best bounty.

Savannah Beach Econo Lodge
$$ • 404 Butler Ave. • 786-4535, (800) 424-4777

The Econo Lodge recently underwent a renovation resulting in attractive and neatly styled rooms in light pastel colors. Located on the ocean, there is a pool, sun deck and cabana along with Spanky's Restaurant, one of the most popular hangouts for the young and bikini-clad. Come during summer or spring break and watch the college students gathered at the bar, on the deck or at the volleyball net, sipping Margaritas and trying to get a tan. The hotel juts onto the beach sideways — for the best view, request a room on the second floor on the end closest to the ocean. King, queen and double beds are available, and all rooms have balconies. Fax and copy service are also available.

Howard Johnson Admiral's Inn
$$ • 1501 Butler Ave. • 786-0700, (800) 446-4656

A nice, two-story hotel, Admiral's Inn has 41 spacious rooms, a swimming pool and is across the street from the ocean. The standard room comes with two queen beds, but if you need a little more space, deluxe king rooms with sitting areas are available. For those coming to Tybee after tying the knot, there is also a bridal suite. Many groups choose the Admiral's Inn when staying on Tybee, including senior citizens from across the country participating in the nationwide educational Elderhostel program. Part of the instruction is given in the hotel's meeting room, which holds up to 75 people.

Computer, phone/fax and copy service are available for those unfortunate souls who have to work while at the beach. The hotel is within comfortable walking distance to downtown Tybee and is adjacent to Cap'n Chris' Restaurant, where you can get breakfast, lunch and dinner at reasonable prices. Seafood and Southern fare like fried chicken and Key lime pie are among the menu selections.

Ocean Plaza Beach Resort
$$ • 15th St. and Ocean Front • 786-7664, (800) 215-6370

This is Tybee's largest hotel, with 240 rooms and suites and two swimming pools. It is also one of the few properties that offers a view of the ocean. Head out your door, walk through a parking lot and within a few steps you are on the sand. Located on the southern end of the island, there are actually three buildings at Ocean Plaza, including two four-story structures facing the ocean. The rooms are spacious and decorated in bright pastel colors. All oceanfront rooms have balconies overlooking the Atlantic.

Many room options are available including a single room with a king bed, one-room suites with queen beds and two-room suites with one king and one double bed. Kitchenettes are also available. Regardless of the room type, all come with a choice of poolside or oceanview location. Rollaway beds can be rented for $10, and cribs cost $5. The Ocean Plaza offers free HBO .

Bed and Breakfasts

Hunter House
$$$ • 1701 Butler Ave. • 786-7515

When John Hunter purchased a beach house on the southern end of Butler Avenue with hopes of converting it into a bed and breakfast, he had his work cut out for him. It was 1988, and the 14-unit apartment house he bought was nicknamed "Animal House." Since then, Hunter has successfully converted the three-story, 1910 beach house into a four-room bed and breakfast, and one of Tybee's finer restaurants is also on the premises (see subsequent listing).

All rooms include queen beds, private baths and entrances and range in size from a single to a large, four-room suite complete with living room and small kitchenette. In one smaller room, you will find bright pink walls, a white wicker settee and matching headboard, while another includes a four-poster queen bed with a massive fireplace in the living area. There is a wonderful wraparound porch perfect for relaxing and taking in the ocean breezes. It's a good place to enjoy your continental breakfast, which includes coffee, cereal and other goodies. Hunter describes his establishment as having "Southern Charm With a Beach Atmosphere." Prices are very competitive at Hunter House, so if you like the feel of a bed and breakfast, it may be worth a call.

Rentals

Tybee Beach Rentals, Inc.
Solomon Properties, 211 Butler Ave.
• 786-8805, (800) 755-8562

Solomon Properties is a local company of Realtors with several private condos and homes for rent. Their offices are on the right after you round the bend (U.S. 80/Butler Avenue) heading toward downtown Tybee. Like all the rental agencies listed here, inside the offices are lists of properties, pictures, rates and other valuable information. Some of the rentals available when we stopped in included new, three-story condos with ocean views renting for $1,400 a week during the summer season; a five-bedroom, three-bath house for $1,000 a week; and a three-story townhome just off the beach for $1,000 a week. Many rentals are available on a nightly basis.

Tybee Island Realty
1016 First St. • 786-7070, (800) 379-2298

Husband and wife team John and Judy

O'Neill own this real estate company, which also deals with several private rentals. You can stop in at the offices, located on your right a mile or so after crossing Lazaretto Creek Bridge into town, and pick up one of their rental brochures. Again, these give all the information you need: pictures of available properties, price ranges and lists of amenities. When we stopped by, they had many listings — everything from oceanfront condos for $1,175 per week to beachfront homes that sleep 14 for $2,000 a week. Many rentals were also available nightly.

Tybee Island Rentals, Inc.
U.S. Hwy. 80 and Second Ave. • 786-4034, (800) 476-0807

Beach homes, condos and cottages of all shapes and sizes can be rented from Tybee Island Rentals. Check out the varied selection at their offices, located about 2 miles past the bridge into Tybee. Whether you are looking for a romantic getaway for two or to bring the whole family for a week at the beach, you should be able to find something that suits your needs. Choices include everything from a five-bedroom, six-bath home overlooking the ocean for $2,200 a week to a one-bedroom efficiency for $375.

Tybee Real Estate

Like the Historic Downtown in Savannah, Tybee has been one of the most popular places to buy real estate in the last few years. Prices have been on the rise and in many cases have jumped significantly — up to 50 percent in some cases. The small-town atmosphere, along with its proximity to Savannah, has made this island community attractive as a year-round residence for many.

This interest has led to some development

INSIDERS' TIP

The Tybee Island Historical Society has launched a fund-raising drive to help restore Tybee Lighthouse. Over the years, crumbling mortar, cracked bricks and rusting windows, among other dangers, have crept in, creating safety hazards at the 154-foot navigation aid. It's still safe to tour, but if repairs aren't made, the lighthouse is in danger of closing its doors to the thousands of tourists who visit it each year. Cost of the entire restoration of the lighthouse structure will be around $1 million.

and a few growing pains. After a large hotel went up on the beach, a movement was started to restrict the height of all development on Tybee to avoid a resort full of high-rises. Many residents want to keep the beach community what it is — a small town by the sea.

It is hard to draw distinct neighborhoods on Tybee. In some neighborhoods, you might find older beach houses next door to modest, one-story homes. A few doors down there could be two or three new homes or a set of two or three new townhouses. Near Fort Screven or North Beach, you will find a few new housing developments that can offer large two- and sometimes three-story homes with ocean views and wraparound porches on fairly large lots. A few streets away there could be a modest home needing quite a lot of work. It's worth noting that streets often don't follow a particular pattern on Tybee; many are dirt roads that zig, zag and in some cases just stop.

Tybee's older beach homes are usually found along Butler Avenue, the city's main thoroughfare, which goes to the southern end of the island. Here the streets follow a grid pattern with the numbered streets increasing the closer you get to downtown. Again, in many blocks, there is a smattering of new homes followed by several older ones. During the last few years, many older homes have been torn down to make room for condos, townhomes and the like.

Single-family homes on the island range from around $100,000 for an older two- or three-bedroom home up to more than $500,000 for a large home with an ocean view. All new homes must be built several feet off the ground to prevent flooding.

The realty companies listed above are ready to assist you with inquiries concerning the Tybee Island real estate scene. Call for more details.

Restaurants

Most of the restaurants on Tybee are very reasonable. You and a friend shouldn't have any problem eating comfortably without breaking the bank. Your check shouldn't come to much more than $20 or $30; most of the time it will be considerably less.

Price Code

Each listing contains a pricing code representing the amount two adults can expect to pay for a standard meal, not including alcoholic beverages, appetizers, tax or tip. Of course, what you pay can vary widely, so use this as a general guide. Unless otherwise noted, all these establishments take major credit cards.

$	$10 or less
$$	$11 to $20
$$$	$21 to $30
$$$$	$31 or more

The Breakfast Club
$$ • 1500 Butler Ave. • 786-5984

If you want to get a table at The Breakfast Club without waiting in line, you may have to get up a little early, especially during the summer months. Lines start forming outside this very popular eatery about 7 AM on weekends. During the week, sleep in much past 8:30 AM, and you will most likely find yourself waiting outside with a handful of other people. Regardless, it is worth the wait. As the line (which moves fast) attests, this diner on the southern end of the island near downtown is one of Tybee's best.

For more than 20 years, members of the Farrow family have been serving up breakfast specialties like chorizo con huevos (flour tortillas, sausage, sharp cheese, salsa and sour cream) and pecan waffles. For $8.95 you can get the surf and turf omelet, complete with fresh rib eye and local shrimp with garlic butter. While omelets are a menu favorite, you will also find many other choices from grits to burgers. Chef Jodee Sadowsky, who purchased the diner from his mother, Helen Farrow, was named one of North America's 101 best cooks in *Cooking Across America*. You can often catch locals sitting in the booths or at the counter at this casual hometown diner, talking about the latest happenings on their island home.

Hitting the Beach with "Crawfish" Crawford

There is good news for swimmers diving into the ocean off Tybee, according to John "Crawfish" Crawford, a University of Georgia educator and expert on Tybee and its marine life. The 30 to 40 species of sharks lurking in the waters offshore probably aren't that hungry.

Close-up

"We have well-fed sharks here," said Crawford. "The water is full of plenty of food which they would rather eat instead of fooling with something the size of a human being."

Words to live by. Although shark attacks are so rare they are nearly unheard of on Tybee, Crawford says to reduce your risk even further by avoiding swimming during twilight hours when sharks typically feed. Also, don't use a flutter kick — to a shark it could sound like a wounded fish.

Besides sharks, beachgoers might encounter an abundance of other marine life on Tybee, according to Crawford. Some of the more common things you might come across during your day at the beach include:

• Sandpipers — These tiny, fleet-footed birds seen running up and down the beach are born and nest in the Arctic tundra. They fly all the way to Tybee just to engage in a little 50-yard beach dash for food.

• Ghost Crabs — Look near the dune line, and you might see whitish-colored crabs scurrying then disappearing into a hole. Besides spending their time digging their hole homes, these crabs serve as beach garbage collectors, picking up parts of dead fish and others things cluttering their front yards.

• Jellyfish — Several different species of jellyfish live in our waters. The cannonball variety has a brown rim around the edge, and you can't be stung by them. The sea nettle, which comes out typically in the late summer and has long wispy tentacles, is responsible for the most stings off Tybee. If you get stung, putting meat tenderizer on the sting helps ease the pain, according to Crawford.

— continued on next page

Photo: Phyl M. Gatlin

Tybee Island offers picture-perfect landscapes, but its waters are filled with surprises — from ghost shrimp to jellyfish.

• Ghost Shrimp — If you run across tiny holes just above the low tide line, you most likely have encountered a ghost shrimp. These tiny shrimp live in a network of burrows that twist and turn in the sand and are only ¾-inch in diameter. Those little brown things you see near the entrance of the hole are their fecal pellets.

• Sand dollars — These small disks are actually live animals. Many people mistakenly take them home while they are still alive, Crawford said. If you find a sand dollar on the beach and it is a greenish color on top and reddish on the bottom, it is still alive, so leave it on the beach. A white color indicates that the sand dollar has died.

• Sting rays — If you happen to see a sting ray while swimming in the surf don't panic — they aren't aggressive and won't bother you a bit. If you happen to be unfortunate enough to step on a sting ray, however, they do consider this an attack and will sting. To avoid such a confrontation, shuffle your feet back and forth while walking in the surf. This gives them enough time to realize you are coming and head in a different direction.

• Sea turtle nests — Sea turtles regularly nest on Tybee Island. The city's public works department patrols the beaches for the nests to mark them with wire so people don't run over them. If you do run across a nest, don't disturb it.

The Crab Shack
$$ • 40 Estill Hammock Rd. • 786-9857

Going to the Crab Shack is as much about atmosphere as it is about great seafood. Located in Chimney Creek, a hamlet off U.S. 80 just past the Lazaretto Creek Bridge (you can't miss the signs), the Crab Shack's motto is, "Where the Elite Eat in Their Bare Feet." What started as a small, rustic restaurant on the marsh has grown into a tourist and local favorite. While munching on giant plates of seafood delicacies like Georgia blue crab, snow crab, golden crab, Alaskan king crab, shrimp and oysters, you can sit out on the huge porch overlooking the marsh. Oak trees decorated with white lights give The Crab Shack a casual, relaxed, fun flair. If you want to try a local specialty, try the Lowcountry boil, which includes boiled shrimp, corn, potatoes and sausage. As for drinks, the frozen Margarita is a good choice along with the piña coladas and daiquiris.

The North Beach Grill
$$$ • 41-A Meddin Dr. • 786-9003

The North Beach Grill is one of those places you have to go looking for but are glad once you find it. Located steps from the sand on Tybee's North Beach, it specializes in long, relaxing dinners with a Car-ibbean flair. If you are in a hurry, you might want to try someplace else. Sit out on the patio or inside the small, inviting dining room to enjoy the many menu choices — there are 11 appetizers and 11 entrees. You will find things like plantain, jerk chicken, jerk salmon, crab cakes, flounder and much more to pick from.

Hunter House
$$$$ • 1701 Butler Ave. • 786-7515

Hunter House is known as one of Tybee's more formal fine dining establishments. Housed in a 1910 beach house at the southern tip of the city's main thoroughfare, it features three intimate dining rooms that seat only a few people at a time. Wooden walls line the entryway, and each room is decorated in simple and sophisticated decor. Owner John Hunter says he likes the small size of his restaurant and would rather concentrate on serving 40 quality meals instead of 60 or more mediocre ones. Chef Espy is well-known for his delicious creations and nightly specials. These include tomato, basil and cognac seafood bisque with shrimp, scallops and lump crabmeat; rack of lamb roasted Provençal; and fresh fillet of pompano with an orange butter sauce. Because of the restaurant's small size and popularity, reservations are recommended.

Photo: Kyle Cason

Sea oats flourish on Tybee Island.

Things to Do

Tired of the beach? Nursing a sunburn? Here are some other things to check out while whiling away the hours on Tybee. For more ideas, check out the Tybee Island Visitors Center located 2 miles past the Lazaretto Creek Bridge in a shopping center on your right. The center is open from 9 AM to 5 PM seven days a week, or you can reach them by calling 786-5444 or (800) 868-2322.

Bull River Marina
8005 Old Tybee Rd., U.S. 80 E. toward Tybee • 898-9222

See bottle-nosed dolphins on a 90-minute narrated nature cruise down Bull River. The marina also offers parasailing and Jet Ski rentals. Prices for nature cruises range from $10 to $14; times and fees vary.

The Tybee Arts Association
P.O. Box 2344, Tybee Island, GA 31328 • 786-5920

This nonprofit group is dedicated to developing and promoting arts throughout the area. Besides operating the Lighthouse Gal-

lery near Tybee Lighthouse, the organization holds exhibits and gives art classes for adults and children. Adult classes can include pottery, stained glass and painting, while children's classes include wearable art, make-your-own-puppet, sand and beach art, painting and drawing, among others. Weekly classes are $60; times vary.

Tybee Island Marine Science Center
14th Street Parking Lot • 786-5917

Learn about Tybee's marine life at the Tybee Island Marine Science Center. Located just steps from the sand in the 14th Street Parking Lot, the center has aquariums with species indigenous to the area such as starfish and jellyfish. There is a small library, a touch tank and displays featuring such things as sharks and shells — always favorites with the kids. One of the more popular programs the center offers are beach walks. Folks are invited to stroll the beach to learn about the things that inhabit it. The center staff also throws a seine net into the ocean to see what they might catch. The center is open Monday through Saturday from 9 AM to 4 PM and from

Photo: Phyl M. Gatlin

The Cockspur Lighthouse is one of Chatham County's two beacons.

1 to 4 PM on Sunday. There is no admission charge.

Tybee Museum
30 Meddin Dr. • 786-4077

Besides learning about Tybee's history, visitors to the Tybee Museum get to walk around one of the few remaining structures at the former Fort Screven. Inside Battery Garland, one of the original seven-gun batteries built at the fort, you can learn about hundreds of years of Tybee lore — from the arrival of Native Americans to Tybee's role in the Civil War to the beginning of tourism on the island. From April 1 to Labor Day, the museum is open 10 AM to 6 PM every day but Tuesday. After Labor Day, it is open from noon to 4 PM on weekdays (except Tuesdays), and from 10 AM to 4 PM on weekends. Admission is $3 for adults, $2 for seniors and children ages 6 to 14; children younger than 6 get in free. The fee includes admission to the Tybee Island Lighthouse just across the street (see subsequent listing).

Tybee Pier and Pavilion
16th St.

The $2.5-million wooden pier was unveiled in time for the 1996 Summer Olympics. It was built in almost the exact location of the Tybrisa, Tybee's former pier and pavilion that was known for its Big Band concerts before it burned several years ago. Wander out to the end of the pier, and you will see anglers casting into the ocean to see what they might catch. You can rent fishing poles and bait on the pier, and you can pick up a snack too. The pier's pavilion, a large wooden platform you cross before heading out over the ocean, is also a popular spot for concerts. While in town, check the *Tybee News*, the local newspaper distributed throughout the community, to see if a concert is taking place while you are here. Concerts are often free.

Tybee Island Lighthouse
30 Meddin Dr. • 786-5801

Throughout history there have actually been four, not just one, Tybee Island Lighthouses. The original was completed in 1736, but it sat too close to the shore and was washed away during a storm. Hurricanes, fires and even an attack by Union forces during the Civil War led to partial or complete destruction of two other stations. In 1866, the fourth Tybee Lighthouse was authorized and was a combination of old and new. It used the lower 65 feet of the 1773 Tybee Light as the base, then 94 more feet were stacked on top. The light, a first-order Fresnel lens, was displayed for the first time October 1, 1867, and it has been there ever since. It is one of only two of the 15 original light stations built in Georgia that is still functioning.

Learn about the history of the lighthouse and take a 154-foot climb to the top for a wonderful view of the area. From April 1 to Labor Day the lighthouse is open 10 AM to 6 PM every day except Tuesdays. After Labor Day, it is open from noon to 4 PM on weekdays (except Tuesdays). During weekends after Labor Day and before April, it is open from 10 AM to 4 PM. Cost is $3 for adults, $2 for seniors and children 6 to 14; children younger than 6 get in free. The price includes admission to the Tybee Museum (see previous listing).

Fort Pulaski National Monument
U.S. 80 E. • 786-5787

Explore a 19th-century fort from top to bottom at Fort Pulaski. Located about 15 miles outside Savannah on the way to Tybee, the fort is remarkably preserved and gives a fascinating glimpse into coastal warfare. The fort was completed in 1847 and considered the ultimate defense system of its day. Audio stations provide information on the pivotal role the fort played in the Civil War and how it changed defense strategy worldwide after an attack by Union forces. The 5,600-acre monument also provides picnic areas, a boat launch ramp and nature trails, along with panoramic views of the Atlantic Ocean and scenic salt marshes. The fort is open during spring, summer and fall from 8:30 AM to 6:45 PM daily. Winter hours are 8:30 AM to 5:15 PM. Cost is $2.

Lazaretto Creek Marina
U.S. 80 E., just across Lazaretto Creek Bridge • 786-5848, (800) 242-0166

Dolphin tours, fishing, diving and sunset cruises are offered at Lazaretto Creek Marina. Rates for dolphin tours are $5 to $12; offshore fishing ranges from $250 to $850, depending on the length of the trip.

Index of Advertisers

Index

Jones, Wimberly 3
Judy Nease Realty 233
Juicy Lucy's Flamingo Cafe 65
Juleps Restaurant 300
Juliette Gordon Low Center 108

K

Kehoe House, The 43
Keller's Flea Market 102
Kelly, Emma 80, 136
Kevin Barry's Irish Pub 80
Kids Day 154
Kidstuff 169
King George II 1
King-Tisdell Cottage 121, 183
Kirkin' O' the Tartan 157
Kitchen Kaboodle 101
Konter Realty 232

L

L. Scott Stell Community Park 192
La Maisonette 300
La Quinta Inn 57
Lady and Sons 65
Lady Astor 11
Lady Chablis 83, 130, 138
Lafayette, Marquis de 6
Lafayette Square 113
Lake Mayer 170
Lake Mayer Community Park 189, 192, 194
Landings, The 16
Larry's Restaurant 74
Laurel Hill Wildlife Drive 193
Law Lecture Series 163
Lazaretto Creek Marina 169, 327
Leamington 285
LeConte, Louis 219
LeConte-Woodmanston Plantation 219
Leigh, Jack 136
Leile, George 120
Liberty Boys 3, 133
Liberty County 215
LIFESTAR 249
Lightship Restaurant 203
Lightship Tavern 70
Lincoln, Abraham 8
Lion's Den 51
Lion's Head Inn 44, 113
Little House 99
Little St. Simons 220
Lodge, The 307
Long Cove Club 284
Long Point 228
Love's Seafood Restaurant 77
Lovezzola's Pizza Restaurant 77
Low, Andrew 114
Low Country Adventures 25, 32, 277, 278
Low Country Taxi & Limousine Service 278
Low, Juliette Gordon 108
Lowcountry Boil 75
Lowcountry Regional Transportation
        Authority 280
Lucas Theatre 116

Lucas Theatre for the Arts Inc. 116
Lutheran Church of the Ascension 108, 271

M

M.D.'s Lounge 70, 80
Mack's 5 and 10 Cent Store 96
Madison Square 110
Magazines 256
Magic Puppet & Toys Too 307
Magnet Academy 237
Magnolia Carriage Company 119
Main Street 283
Main Street Cinemas 306
Main Street Inn 293
Malbone, Edward Green 114
Mall at Shelter Cove 308
Malls 88
Malone's Food and Spirits 80
Manor House, The 44
March to the Sea 8, 216
Marinas 196
Marketplace Restaurant 56
Marshall, Lt. Col. George C. 317
Martin Luther King Jr. Observance Day
        Activities 149
Mary Calder Golf Club 202
Mary's Seafood and Steakhouse 74
Massie Heritage Interpretation Center 113, 238
Masterworks Series 178
MCI Classic — The Heritage of Golf 311, 312
McIntosh, Col. John 217
McIntosh, O.T. 276
McMillan Inn 44
Meals on Wheels 262
Media 255
Media Play 94
Medway River 217
Memorial 55 Plus 264
Memorial Day at Old Fort Jackson 158
Memorial Day School 240
Memorial Medical Center 19, 249, 264
Memorial Stadium 189
Memorial WellNet 251
Mercer, Gen. Hugh 111
Mercer House 111, 130, 135
Mercer, Johnny 132, 177, 263
Merry Times 91
Mickve Israel 2
Midnight in the Garden of Good and
        Evil 83, 129, 185
Midnight Newsletter 134
Midnight Star Pottery 99, 171
Midpoint 229
Midtown 18
Midway 218
Midway Cemetery 219
Midway Congregational Church 219
Midway Corporate Express 24
Midway Museum 219
Midway Society 218
Mighty Eighth Air Force Heritage Museum 125
Miss Judy Charters 199
Mistletoe Cottage 221
Mitchelville 274

Going Somewhere?

Insiders' Publishing Inc. presents 48 current and upcoming titles to popular destinations all over the country (including the titles below) — and we're planning on adding many more. To order a title, go to your local bookstore or call (800) 582-2665 and we'll direct you to one.

Adirondacks	Minneapolis/St. Paul, MN
Atlanta, GA	Mississippi
Bermuda	Myrtle Beach, SC
Boca Raton and the Palm Beaches, FL	Nashville, TN
Boulder, CO, and Rocky Mountain National Park	New Hampshire
Bradenton/Sarasota, FL	North Carolina's Central Coast and New Bern
Branson, MO, and the Ozark Mountains	North Carolina's Mountains
California's Wine Country	Outer Banks of North Carolina
Cape Cod, Nantucket and Martha's Vineyard, MA	The Pocono Mountains
Charleston, SC	Relocation
Cincinnati, OH	Richmond, VA
Civil War Sites in the Eastern Theater	Salt Lake City
Colorado's Mountains	Santa Fe
Denver, CO	Savannah
Florida Keys and Key West	Southwestern Utah
Florida's Great Northwest	Tampa/St. Petersburg, FL
Golf in the Carolinas	Tuscon
Indianapolis, IN	Virginia's Blue Ridge
The Lake Superior Region	Virginia's Chesapeake Bay
Las Vegas	Washington, D.C.
Lexington, KY	Wichita, KS
Louisville, KY	Williamsburg, VA
Madison, WI	Wilmington, NC
Maine's Mid-Coast	Yellowstone

THE INSIDERS'® GUIDE

Insiders' Publishing Inc. • P.O. Box 2057 • Manteo, NC 27954
Phone (919) 473-6100 • Fax (919) 473-5869 • INTERNET address: *http://www.insiders.com*